HOW TO AUDITION
FOR THE MUSICAL THEATRE
A STEP-BY-STEP GUIDE
TO EFFECTIVE PREPARATION

Donald Oliver

DRAMA BOOK PUBLISHERS
NEW YORK

No practitioner of the arts can survive without a
nurturing environment. I am blessed with a large, warm,
wise, loving, and unshakably supportive family. It is
to all of them that I dedicate this book; but most
especially to Rosalind Oliver, my aunt, and to the
memory of Bernard Oliver, my beloved uncle.

First Edition

10 9 8 7 6 5 4 3 2 1

Library of Congress Cataloging-in-Publication Data

Oliver, Donald.
    How to audition for the musical theatre.

    1. Singing—Auditions. 2. Music—Performance.
I. Title.
MT892.04 1985   782.81'071   85-20529
ISBN 0-89676-080-4

Manufactured in the United States of America

ACKNOWLEDGEMENTS

Both as a professional and personal colleague, director Bill Gile played an important role in my developing many of the ideas in this book. So I take this opportunity to thank him, not only for all the times he hired me as an audition accompanist, which allowed these theories to develop, but also for his advice and opinions as this manuscript took shape. I was also fortunate to have received guidance early on from the extraordinary pianist and composer Sande Campbell - her comments and recommendations have been freely incorporated in the text and I am in her debt.

I am also deeply appreciative of those people who took the time to share their helpful ideas and audition stories: Jeanie Breall, Mary Jo Catlett, Morton DaCosta, Jeffrey Dunn, Rob Fisher, Jerry Herman, Sheldon Harnick, John Kander, James Kirkwood, Jack Lee, Edward Strauss, and Peter Wandel.

It was one thing to gather all these ideas; it was quite another to write them down in an organized fashion. And so I was lucky to have received the editorial help of Phillipa Keil and Judith Holmes.

One last thank-you goes to David Spencer for his keen comments on the final manuscript. This book has benefited from his acute observations and suggestions.

CONTENTS

PREPARATION - Part 2: The Mechanics

PREPARATION - Part 3: Performing

APPENDICES

THE EXPLANATION DEPARTMENT

This is a manual on how to prepare for a musical audition - and how to present yourself and your talent in the best possible light at an audition.

Over the course of the last ten years I have played the piano for literally thousands of auditions. It has always amazed me how many talented people make similar mistakes while auditioning, diminishing their chances of being seriously considered, while some performers with less natural ability make the absolute most of their potential - and get the jobs.

From all this I have come to the somewhat less-than-earth-shattering conclusion that if you have your act together, it *is* possible to weight auditions in your favor by minimizing the risks.

This book will lay out the proper guidelines. Although geared primarily for people new to the business, it should be helpful to performers at any stage of their career. If an actor or actress is just starting out, following the advice herein can make him or her seem to be a seasoned professional at their very first audition. Those experienced at auditioning will find much useful information, especially if they are constantly auditioning and not getting jobs. As you will see, there's usually a reason for that, and the solution to the problem can be found between these covers.

The assumption with how-to books is that once read and absorbed, mastery of the subject discussed and imminent success are inevitable. Look closely at the title of this book; it is not called *How to Get Cast in a Show*. I couldn't make that kind of promise.

But there *is* a methodical way of approaching an audition - and subsequently building a career. The methods proposed in the following pages come from experience. Most are founded on some very simple principles that can be put to use immediately - at your next audition.

There are four things that should be brought to your attention before we begin.

First: In order to prevent the awkwardness caused by trying to avoid sexist terminology - see earlier in this chapter - I will employ the standard masculine usage throughout the text. Unless specifically indicated, all remarks and advice are meant for both men and women.

Second: In discussing the audition techniques in the pages that follow, I mention for the purposes of illustration many specific songs. They are discussed here *based only on their relative appropriateness as audition material*. They have not been selected with regard to their inherent merits - or demerits - as songs, or with regard to their suitability in their original dramatic contexts. And at no time is it my intention to show disrespect to the songs' creators.

Third: All the stories in this book are true. Honestly. I couldn't've made up the shenanigans you'll read about. If you recognize an error of your own in one of these stories, don't waste time whipping yourself - just pay attention to how to correct your mistakes. Quoting an oft-used line, anyone claiming resemblance to those described should be ashamed to admit it.

Fourth: This book focuses exclusively on the musical audition. Certain subjects I merely touch on are covered in great detail in two books that should be staples in every performer's library: *Audition* by Michael Shurtleff (New York: Bantam Books, 1980) and *On Singing Onstage* by David Craig (New York: Schirmer Books, a division of Macmillan Publishing Co., 1978). Use my book as an adjunct to these. They should be required reading for everyone in the business, whether aspiring or accomplished.

There is one word that encapsulates everything that follows –

– a word there is no substitute for

– a word that if taken to heart will make a huge difference in your career

– That magic word is *preparation*.

This book will show you how to prepare effectively for almost any kind of musical audition you will ever encounter. The basics are the same, whether you are auditioning for a college show, a lodge pageant, an end-of-season summer-camp production, or the latest $5 million Broadway extravaganza.

Read this book carefully.

Prepare.

Break a Leg.

ALL ABOUT AUDITIONS

Can you remember the moment you first decided to pursue a career in the musical theatre? Was it when you had a solo in a school show and heard the audience applaud you for the first time? Was it when your favorite relative heard you sing or saw you dance and said you were every bit as good as anyone already on the New York Stage? Or did you get bitten when you saw a certain movie or live show - perhaps a touring company - and afterwards, exhilarated, you proclaimed to all who would listen, "That's what I want to do!"

Well, congratulations! You have picked a field that is simultaneously demanding, competitive, frustrating, and glamorous. Always remember that show business is a *business,* filled with myths and misconceptions, legends and lore. Within this most changeable and unreliable of professions there is only one constant: an unbelievably high rate of unemployment - over 80 percent at any given time. Almost all struggling performers are forced to work at decidedly unglamorous jobs in order to support themselves while waiting for opportunities to display their craft in public.

So before I go into the actual step-by-step discussion on how to prepare your audition material, it's important to explore some of the realities of the industry, answer some questions, and clue you in as to what tools-of-the-trade you'll need to begin.

Since you have this idea that you'd like to sing and dance on Broadway someday, you'll have to let those people who can make your dream come true know you're alive and kicking. You'll have to attend auditions.

An audition is an event at which performers desirous of being part of a production demonstrate their talent to the people who will make casting decisions. If the membership of Actors' Equity were polled, it would most likely be found that a full 95 percent of them really don't like auditioning. Nor do the people who must evaluate auditions much like the process. But it's interesting to note that as of yet no one has found a more effective system for viewing and evaluating talent.

The process of auditioning has many drawbacks. For one, actors are performing without costumes, makeup, or proper lighting - hardly optimal circumstances.

And, for two, most are nervous.

With good reason. An audition is the show-business version of a job interview. In a very short amount of time, actors have to perform a mini-commercial, and the product they are hawking is *themselves.* One young man was so nervous at his audition that, as he was singing the song "Oklahoma!," he spelled it, "O - K - L - M - N ..."

A lot of people don't realize that an audition can represent the first of several appearances before the people doing the hiring. Casting their show is a serious enterprise for the creative team, so they reserve the right to have you audition for them on more than one occasion. These return visits are termed "callbacks."

The excitement of being called back for a second, or a third hearing doesn't make actors any less nervous than they were the first time. The pressure increases as the stakes become higher.

The fallibility of the whole audition process produces many unfortunate situations. There are marvelously talented performers who are capable and inventive in a rehearsal or performance situation, but who just don't audition well; and the reverse - performers who audition brilliantly but don't live up to their potential when cast.

But *everyone* - including any star you can name - has had to audition at one time or another in his career.

Barbra Streisand auditioned for Eddie Blum of the Rodgers and Hammerstein casting office when *The Sound of Music* was on Broadway. She sang for three hours, hoping to take over the featured role of Liesl - who sings "Sixteen Going on Seventeen". Afterwards, she was given much encouragement by Mr. Blum but was told she wasn't right for anything in *The Sound of Music*. The lucky one here was Mr. Blum, who was the recipient of a free, private, three-hour Barbra Streisand concert.

Even a performer as gifted as John Travolta had to learn the basics of auditioning. While performing in an Off-Broadway production of *Rain*, a nonmusical play, he was asked to audition for the prestigious Goodspeed Opera House in Connecticut. According to witnesses, he apparently hadn't been previously coached in the *mechanics* of a musical audition. Not being prepared to sing with a live pianist, he brought a cassette recorder with him - his musical accompaniment was on tape - and when he sang, he was not quite in sync with the recording. Extremely nervous, he made a bad showing, and couldn't convince the producer of his potential worth. Now at that time, he was merely one of many performers who auditioned for Goodspeed and didn't make it. But he didn't let it discourage him; he kept at it and learned what he didn't know. Soon thereafter he landed important roles in the Broadway shows *Grease* and *Over Here!*, which led directly to his exciting television and movie career.

It should be clear that it takes guts to audition, at any stage in your career. Here are three more stories that tell about star performers with guts; coincidentally, each story has to do with Jerry Herman's musicals. Remember as you read - at the time these incidents took place, none of the three shows mentioned were the celebrated, wildly successful, award-winning musicals we now know them to be.

Carol Channing has been a star since 1949 when she played Lorelei Lee in *Gentlemen Prefer Blondes* and introduced the song "Diamonds Are A Girl's Best Friend." In 1963 she had to audition for *Hello, Dolly!* Why? Because the role of Dolly would be a departure for her from Lorelei Lee and the other kinds of roles she had been associated with. She was neither offended nor afraid - she knew what she had to offer, and she understood that the production team needed to be convinced she had the particular quality they were looking for. She went on to win the 1964 Tony Award for Best Actress in a Musical. Just for the record, her competition that year was none other than Barbra Streisand in *Funny Girl*; Beatrice Lillie in *High Spirits*; and Inga Swenson in *110 in the Shade*.

In 1965 when the musical *Mame* was looking for its leading lady, Angela Lansbury had already been nominated for three Academy Awards. Every major female star at that time was either considered for or approached to play Mame. Everyone from Judy Garland to Ethel Merman to Mary Martin. Everyone but Angela Lansbury. Ms. Lansbury, who had starred in the musical *Anyone Can Whistle* on Broadway the year before, came to New York on her own and

auditioned. But on the day of her audition the only one
of *Mame*'s creators she impressed was its composer-
lyricist, Jerry Herman. Afterwards, without the knowledge
of the producers or director, Mr. Herman secretly taught
her "If He Walked Into My Life," the stunning song from
the score, and arranged for a second audition at which he
played the piano, accompanying her. We all know now about
Ms. Lansbury's subsequent triumph in the show, but at the
time it was very brave on her part to go along with the
second audition, because it could've gone the other way.
She too, as did Ms. Channing, won a Tony Award, beating
out Gwen Verdon in *Sweet Charity*, Julie Harris in
Skyscraper, and Barbara Harris in *On A Clear Day You Can
See Forever.*

La Cage aux Folles was a show for which auditions
were mandatory especially for stars. The requirements for
the leading roles were so unique that the previous work of
any actor wasn't enough to show the creators exactly what
they needed for their leads. George Hearn was a much
respected, hard-working, versatile actor with an off-stage
reputation as an accomplished lothario, who, prior to
1983 never even *fantasized* about dressing in women's
clothing. But he wanted to play the role of Albin in *La
Cage*, and with absolutely no guarantees that it would turn
out positively, he had the courage to agree to have Ted
Azar - *La Cage*'s very talented hair and makeup designer -
help him get completely done up in female attire for his
audition. In drag, Mr. Hearn marched onto the stage, sang
"My Heart Belongs To Daddy," and the part was his. He
showed the production team that he had the theatrical guts
they needed for *La Cage*. When he accepted *his* Tony Award,
he pointed to it and said, "What some people won't do..."

THE CASTING TEAM

For a moment, let's look at things from the point of
view of those casting the show.

- 8 -

The creative team has to see and seriously consider sometimes up to 100 people a day for several days in a row. They have to remember who was good, who was not, who should be seen again for the current production, and who may be useful at some later time - all through this process comparing the relative abilities of everyone who auditions.

In a conversation with me composer John Kander (*Cabaret, Chicago, The Rink*) underscored the fact that the people judging an audition really do want you to be good when you step out in front of them because they have to cast all the roles in their show - except, sometimes, the star parts - from the people who audition. Jerry Herman said, "We're really nice guys who want to hire everybody. It's painful to see talented people walk by and not be able to use them." In their minds, the casting team usually has a pretty good idea of what they are looking for, and they long for you to be it. They can relax only when someone appears who is perfect for their needs.

Director Morton DaCosta (*Auntie Mame, The Music Man*) told me that at auditions he suffers as much as the people who are auditioning. Having first been an actor - most directors and choreographers started out as performers - he has firsthand knowledge of what people go through.

Because of the stakes, the members of the creative team are often just as nervous and apprehensive as you are. Mr. Kander remembers an incident during the casting of his show *The Happy Time* when someone auditioning had an unusually large nose. The late Gower Champion, who directed and choreographed the show, was well known for his kindness and consideration during his auditions. Mr. Champion and the authors felt so sorry for this particular performer that, although pressed for time, they allowed a complete song to be sung and were overly solicitous afterward. In an ill-fated attempt at graciousness, Mr.

Champion jumped out of his seat in the theatre and rushed up onto the stage where he said, "Thank you, that was very *nose*."

Actors often gripe that "the same people get hired over and over, and newcomers don't have a chance." That is not true by design. All directors and writers are excited by the possibility of discovering fresh talent at an audition. There is a certain kind of thrill that comes when an actor or actress unknown to the production team displays the talent and the vitality necessary for the show.

Please believe that finding and developing new performers is sort of an unofficial mission of everyone connected with the theatre. Like Dracula's, the theatre's only hope of survival is through continually replenishing the supplies of fresh blood.

THE INTERACTIVE ELEMENTS OF AN AUDITION

There are many complex factors that come into play during an audition. You are judged by an infinite number of combinations of the following elements:

1. YOUR "LOOK"

In other words, how close you come to the author's or director's *physical* concept of the role. If they're set on a blonde and you're a brunette, you probably have very little chance of changing their minds. However, and here's where the interactive nature of the audition process shows itself, your strengths in any of the other areas talked about later *can* make a difference.

Try to get an accurate gauge of what "type" you are. Are you the "handsome, strong, leading man" or "beautiful leading lady" type? Or does your face and figure suggest a "character" type? Do you look your age? Younger? Older? Can you vary your look to expand your suitable age range?

You must come up with HONEST answers to the above questions and, at the same time, be ruthless about any positive changes you may be able to affect in your appearance. For example, if you are overweight and perceive yourself as the leading man or leading lady type, you'd be well advised to shed the extra poundage immediately. Think about it: How frequently do you see an obviously chubby hero or heroine in the theatre or films? Not often. And even then, how often is the lead's chubbiness not an integral part of the story?

2. YOUR VOICE

This category has to do with the quality of your vocal instrument and your range. If you are a lyric soprano and the score doesn't call for that, you could have the most magnificent voice ever heard by human ears and still not get a callback.

It is imperative that women develop a "chest voice" as well as a "head voice" - with proper training, both techniques can be used without hurting your throat. Remember: the more versatile you are, the greater are your chances of getting cast.

This may come as a surprise, but you don't have to be an extraordinary singer to get cast in a musical. If you are strong in most of the other areas mentioned in this section, your voice might be "good enough" for the purposes of the show. As will be discussed at length later, you must carefully select songs to sing that show off your voice - whatever your ability - to maximum advantage.

3. YOUR ACTING ABILITY

More on this later in the book. (See Interpretation: Acting the Song.) In brief, having a glorious voice is not enough. You must have something going on behind your eyes. You can't just *sing* your song; you must *act* it as well.

4. YOUR DANCE ABILITY

All actors are counseled to be as well equipped with the tools of their trade as possible. To this end, I strongly suggest that everyone who wants to be a professional performer in the musical theatre should enroll in some kind of dance class, whether it be ballet, jazz, or tap. Dance training gives people an awareness of and confidence in their bodies, in the way they move, and in the way they look to others. One-line parts in shows - such as "Telegram for you, Sir" - are almost always given to dancers rather than to singers simply because dancers are more certain to look graceful crossing the stage. Dance classes are relatively inexpensive - they cost a lot less than vocal coaching - and, at least in New York City, there are so many different classes taking place each day it's easy to find one at a convenient time.

True, to land a lead in a show you don't have to be as proficient a dancer as a chorus gypsy; but if you are called upon to execute a few dance steps as part of a song routine, you won't look graceful without training.

Remember: You can never be too talented - or too skilled. You must be as versatile as possible. The competition is too stiff.

5. YOUR CHOICE OF MATERIAL

A large section of this book is devoted to helping you choose the right material to audition with. Briefly, just as the proper choice of a song can perk up the ears of the listeners and make them react favorably to your talent, the wrong choice can adversely affect your "castability." The casting team writes down what songs you sing and later, when the inevitable discussion takes place as to whether or not you should be given a callback, you are often remembered chiefly by what song you sang.

6. YOUR APPEARANCE

Although being in show business grants people the right to a certain amount of flamboyance, you should *always* come to an audition dressed as neatly as possible. For men, a jacket and tie is the safest way to go except during hot weather when a clean sport shirt will do adequately. For women, the best outfit is a skirt or dress that is flattering, feminine, and comfortable - no pants, please, unless you look absolutely smashing in them. A little glamour couldn't hurt, but avoid overdressing; don't wear hats or excessive jewelry. Be well groomed with a sensible, as in not-too-trendy, haircut. I realize there are other clothing choices for both men and women that would serve nicely. I am talking about safe, all-purpose dressing.

And now a few words about footwear, ladies first. Please wear attractive shoes which help you move gracefully. Platform shoes are cumbersome and ungainly. Bedroom slippers, no matter how comfortable, are best left under the bed. Buy one good pair of fashionable shoes in a neutral color

which would go with many different outfits and only
wear them as your "audition shoes." As for the men,
although I've seen sneakers and boots look both
stylish and flattering they may not be appropriate
for all occasions. You cannot go wrong if you follow
my cautious, conservative, middle-of-the-road
approach to your appearance. Don't forget what you
were told in school: "Neatness counts."

There is one other factor to consider: If you
have specific knowledge of the show for which you are
auditioning, you may want to choose your clothes by
taking into account the age and style of the
character for which you will be considered. You do
not have to show up in costume – George Hearn was
asked to dress in drag for his *La Cage aux Folles*
audition – but if you are young and the role calls
for a more mature performer, dressing appropriately
can help you be seen in the right context.
Similarly, if you are auditioning for a production of
Fiddler on the Roof, looking vaguely "peasanty" is
better than showing up in smart, tailored clothing.

7. YOUR CREDITS AND EXPERIENCE

This is based, of course, on what appears on
your resume. As I mentioned earlier, people are
always looking for fresh talent, so an extensive list
of credits is not de rigueur if you are right for a
particular role. (See Appendix D for more specific
advice about the look and content of your resume.)

8. YOUR PERSONALITY

This is arguably the most important variable.
And it brings up the single most valuable piece of
advice – given to me by a Broadway director – I can
give you about auditioning:

*You must make the director want to work with you
in the first thirty seconds of your audition.*

For example Liliane Montevecchi's role in *Nine*
was originally intended for a man, but the lady's
personality so dazzled Tommy Tune, the director-
choreographer, and Maury Yeston, the composer-
lyricist, that at the audition they reconceived the
part. Mr. Yeston then wrote the song "Follies
Bergeres" specifically for her and she went on to win
a Tony Award. Similarly, Ben Vereen's Tony
Award-winning part in *Pippin* was originally intended
for a much older man.

The lesson to be drawn from this is that if you
display a knockout package consisting of charm, a
sense of humor, a sense of security, and a great
measure of talent, the people sitting behind the desk
in that audition room are going to notice you. And
even if there is no place for you in that particular
show, you *will* be remembered for future projects.

Now to confuse matters further, sometimes getting
cast has very little to do with any of the above, as
exemplified in this amusing story:

James Kirkwood, now the Pulitzer Prize-winning
coauthor of *A Chorus Line*, began his career as an actor
and nightclub performer. During his stint on the then
popular television soap opera *Valiant Lady* he was informed
that he was to audition for Tallulah Bankhead, who was set
to star in *Welcome, Darlings*, a summer stock package being
created and tailored for her. This show was to include
some of the same material from Ms. Bankhead's disastrous
edition of the *Ziegfeld Follies*, which closed during its
pre-Broadway tryout a few months prior. Mr. Kirkwood was
to meet Tallulah at her town house because she did not
want to go to a theatre.

He was extremely nervous when he arrived at her home in the East Sixties in Manhattan. She was still getting dressed upstairs, and he could hear her yelling at one of her dogs, "Delores, stop that! Get out of there, Delores!"

Finally, she came down the stairs, picking at her eyelashes. "Hello, darling. I just got up and I always get this garbage in my eyes when I wake up. Do *you* have all of that crap in your eyes when you wake up?" Nonplussed, he answered, "Yes, of course I do."

Peering at him she said, "James Kirkwood, right? I've seen you on the soap opera. I like you very much; I like your acting. Somebody told me you were a nightclub comic too. What kind of material do you do? Do you have anything you can audition for me now?"

"Actually," he said, dreading the idea of doing his nightclub-styled satire for an audience of one in a living room in the middle of the afternoon, "I have a takeoff on the *Reader's Digest* - "

Tallulah interrupted, "When I was in the *Follies*, I had a number and I came down the stairs..." She proceeded to sing and act out the entire song.

"Now darling, tell me, what kind of comedy do you do? I don't want a vulgar comedian like David Burns. I want somebody young and clean and you look right but I *have* to know what kind of stuff you do."

Once again, he tried, "Well, I have this takeoff on the *Reader's Digest* - "

"When I was in London," Tallulah started, and launched into another lengthy story.

The rest of the afternoon was the same: Mr. Kirkwood never got to do his prepared piece, he just listened to Tallulah.

At last, she sat down next to him on the sofa and said, "Well darling, I just think you're perfect. You're funny, you're witty, I love what you do, and you look right. I'm going to have an entirely young cast, and I think you've got the part."

Suddenly she swung her legs up onto his lap, pulled the bottoms of her pants up and said, "Have you ever seen more beautiful ankles than these, darling?"

If an experience like this ever comes your way, Great! But don't count on it happening more than once in your lifetime.

AUDITION ANNOUNCEMENTS: THE TRADE PAPERS

You can find out about auditions from notices that are posted in the weekly trade publications. *Variety* and *Backstage* are the two most widely read papers.

In New York City, *Variety* is usually published on Wednesdays and *Backstage* on Thursdays. Read these papers thoroughly, for they contain a wealth of information useful to anyone in the industry. *Backstage* has many more casting notices than *Variety*, and *Variety* has more general news of who's-doing-what in the various media - films, television, recordings, as well as legitimate theatre.

What follows are some actual casting announcements culled from recent editions of these "trades":

Broadway

Chorus Line" (M). Equity us auditions for possible cements being held Thursday male dancers who sing very t 10 a.m. and femme dancers ing very well at 2 p.m., at the rt Theatre (...) West ... St., use stage door entrance).

NON-EQ. DT "WHOREHOUSE"

4/16 from 2-4 & 6-8 PM at Neil's New Yorker DT, Mountain Lakes, NJ.

Auditions for a non-Equity production of "The Best Little Whorehouse in Texas" will be held at Neil's New Yorker Dinner Theatre, Route 46, Mountain Lakes, NJ on Mon. April 16 from 2-4 PM & 6-8 PM. From Port Authority, take Lakeland Bus from platform 405 to The Boulevard in Mountain Lakes. (50 minute ride). All roles open. If needed call (20.) 001-0700 for information . . . ADVT.

Stock

PITTSBURGH

Civic Light Opera. Equity principal interviews being held next Tuesday (6) and Wednesday (7) from 9:30 a.m. to 1 p.m. and from 2-5:30 p.m., at the Actors Equity Audition Center (... West ... St., N.Y.).

Off-Broadway

"And I Still Believe In Love" (M). Mini contract. Available parts: male, early 30s, baritone, handsome, struggling actor with tremendous promise and talent, lonely, driven, romantic; femme, early 30s, soprano, attractive, stylish corporate executive on the way up, been around, cynical, but still hopeful; male, early to mid-20s, baritone, tall, strong mid-western farm boy, very handsome in superb physical condition, non-macho masculine, sensitive, aggressive; femme, late 30s, early 40s, alto-mezzo, superb singer with exquisite face and figure. Successful cabaret singer, strong, vulnerable, very feminine and loving; male, early 20s, WASP upper-class collegiate type, handsome, in excellent physical condition, introspective, brooding, very masculine but sexually ambivalent; femme, black, early 20s, mezzo with good belt, social worker, alive and loving, stunningly beautiful, very innocent; male, late 20s-early 30s, tenor, bright, witty, cabaret pianist (playing skills helpful but not mandatory), strong comedic skills, handsome, charming, ready for anything; male, character actor, strong baritone and dancer to play 10 different roles, must be able to age from 25-65. Equity interviews being held Wednesday (29) and Thursday (1) from 9:30 a.m. to 1 p.m. and from 2-5:30 p.m., at the Actors Equity Audition Center (165 West 46th St., N.Y.). Non-Equity actors and actresses should send photos and resumes to BBS Productions, c/o Kojak (3 ½ West 5th St., N.Y. 10019).

Out Of Town
LOS ANGELES
"La Cage aux Folles" (M). Equity auditions being held Friday (2): femme singers at 10 a.m., early 20s, good-looking, legit soprano with ballet training to sing in chorus and understudy role of "Anne;" femme, late 30s or older, legit soprano and belt, to sing in chorus and understudy "Jacqueline;" male singers at 2 p.m.: early-late 20s, handsome, legit baritone, to sing in chorus and understudy "Jean-Michel;" mature character man, good-looking, comedic flair, to sing in chorus and understudy "Albin," all at the Actors Equity Audition Center (165 West 46th St., N.Y.). Prepare 16 bars of Broadway sound, no pop, rock, soul, blues or gospel. May be asked to read and/or move and/or dance after you sing. No one who has already auditioned should re-audition.

Two of the blurbs contain cast breakdowns for the shows, which are prepared by the casting director along with the creative team. It indicates the ideal types of performers needed. Remember the discussion earlier of your type? Here's where you need to know it, so you can tell if anything in the breakdown sounds like a possible role for you. If so, follow the instructions in the announcement *to the letter.*

The breakdown notwithstanding, if the call is for a new show, it may be worth your while to attempt to get an audition even if you do not visualize yourself in one of the parts described. There's still a little leeway because, as I mentioned earlier, the show can change if the creative team gets excited about a particular performer. If it is an old show, or a current show seeking replacements – as in the above announcement for *La Cage aux Folles* – they'll stay fairly close to what was done in the past or to the types they are using now, even to the point of hiring clones.

Unfair as it may seem, often the only way you can get an audition scheduled for a major Broadway production is through a reputable show-business agent. That's merely a fact of life, in the You-Can't-Fight-City-Hall Department. If you don't have an agent now, you will get one in time. In the meantime, there are plenty of auditions listed in the trade papers that you can attend at every stage of your career. See Appendix E for more information regarding agents and your career development.

NOW TO BEGIN...

I'm sure you have discerned from the foregoing that show business is tough, challenging, confusing, contradictory, intimidating – and more than a little discouraging. It's no secret that anyone who pursues a career in "The Biz" is in for a rough ride.

So think back to the beginning of this chapter and try to remember the exciting moment when you first decided to go into the business. Hold on to that moment and keep it somewhere in your memory. Feel lucky that you know what you want to do with your life and are in a position to pursue it. As Oscar Hammerstein wrote in the song "Happy Talk" from *South Pacific*:

You got to have a dream –
If you don't have a dream
How you gonna have a dream come true?

If you want a career in show business badly enough, you'll do whatever is necessary to make it happen. And the first step is learning how to master an audition.

PREPARATION PART - 1: SELECTING

WHERE TO FIND AN ACCOMPANIST

One of the first things you will have to do is work with a pianist to help you find, prepare, and rehearse your material.

So where _do_ you find an accompanist? Easy.

Anywhere.

Anyone who plays the piano is a potential accompanist. Yes, there is an art of sorts to accompanying; but for now, anyone will do - a friend, neighbor, voice teacher, or a relative are all good people to begin with. If they can't or won't play for you, ask if they know someone - you will undoubtedly find someone to work with through a recommendation.

Accompanists advertise in the trade papers and also post their business cards up on the bulletin boards at the rehearsal studios in New York City. Pick a few at random, call them up, and talk over the phone. Ask the price and where the sessions are held - in their home or in a studio. Find one you like talking to and arrange a session. No one can promise that the first time will work out for everyone, but if you don't like the person, find another quickly via the same means. At least now you'll have some basis for comparison.

As your credits grow and you get more accomplished, you will meet new people and thus be exposed to new musicians. Eventually, you'll be able to recognize the difference between good and bad pianists, and you will establish a rapport with certain musicians with whom you prefer to work.

But for starters, find anyone who seems suitable, and begin preparing.

YOUR AUDITION REPERTOIRE

You have to have something to do at an audition to show off your talent. Everyone is at the very least expected to have prepared two songs: a "ballad" and an "up-tune."

At it's simplest, a ballad should show your emotional range and the way you phrase a lyric - your sensitivity to the words and thoughts.

An up-tune should show your sense of rhythm and how exciting you are as a performer. As a by-product, it can show how enjoyable you would be to have in the cast. There are always so many problems attached to putting on a show that no one wants to work with people perceived as boring or unpleasant. So find a zingy up-number that shows off your sense of humor and sense of fun. Try to dazzle them.

The best kind of audition number in either category is a humorous one. The worst kind of number in either category is a song of self-pity. The latter type makes the listener uncomfortable, whereas the former allows the listener to sit back and relax. There is no rule anywhere that says you can't *entertain* at an audition. If you are able to unselfconsciously entertain the people casting a show, you may find yourself in the cast as a result.

In tandem, the ballad and the up-tune provide a needed contrast for the listeners. And the two should be as different as possible in order to show the broadest range of your abilities. Find songs with which you connect emotionally and for which you are right agewise.

Emotional Considerations: Although your first choice for any song should of course be one you can sing believably without too much strain, you do not have to "agree" with all the lyrics of a song. If you have chosen an interesting song but the lyrics don't espouse your personal beliefs, you can still use it. Be someone else for those few minutes. Create a character to sing the song. Act.

Chronological Considerations: Anyone under the age of about forty, should not sing "Send In The Clowns" from *A Little Night Music* or "I'm Still Here" from *Follies* or "Before The Parade Passes By" from *Hello, Dolly!*. It is disorienting to see someone young, with no obvious backlog of experience, sing songs whose words were written to reflect the experiences of a mature person. The reverse is also true with songs like "I Feel Pretty" from *West Side Story* and "Tomorrow" from *Annie*. As you search for the songs to fill your portfolio, you will find there are dozens of candidates to choose from that will fit your age, range, and personality. Don't fret about not singing the few that don't.

BUILDING A SONG PORTFOLIO

Okay, ready for this one? I *know* that just two songs aren't enough. You must prepare more than two. If you spark interest from the director or one of the writers, they may need to see you show values other than the ones demonstrated in your ballad or up-tune, so it is advisable to prepare several different types of songs and to have them in performance- shape at all times. You should build a song portfolio. This will be a whole collection of songs you will use as audition material. In this portfolio you should have at least one of each of the following types of songs:

1. Ballad

2. Up-tune

3. Comedy song

4. Contemporary (rock) song

5. Patter song

6. Standard torch song - only for women

At almost every audition I have ever played, someone sitting behind the decision-table has asked to hear a song from each of these categories. Too many times, performers have only two songs prepared - sometimes only one - and when asked for additional material, instead of saying "No, I haven't prepared anything else," they try to improvise something with the pianist. Instead of impressing the production team with their versatility, they generally make a mess of their audition. It's better to be prepared.

Good comedy songs are notoriously difficult to find. The same songs tend to be used over and over. The works of Noel Coward, Howard Dietz, E.Y. Harburg, Lorenz Hart, and Cole Porter - to mention just a few of the immortals - are chock full of great, little-known, sure-fire comic material. Finding these songs takes a lot of digging, but they are there to be found.

HOW TO AUDITION FOR THE MUSICAL THEATRE

At a recent audition, all the actors were asked to prepare a comedy song. One young man entered the room and said, "I don't have a comedy song so I'll just sing 'Being Alive' very fast and see if it's funny."

It wasn't.

Here's a dangerous idea that can work: Take a standard song that everyone knows and is sick of and rewrite the lyrics a la some of Allan Sherman's material. Be careful - your rewrite must be very clever and you must never do it in front of the original writers.

As for the contemporary number, please pick one with a pretty, singable melody. Although the theme song from the motion picture *Shaft* may have won the Academy Award as best song of its year, it hardly has a catchy lyric. Turn instead to something soft-rock, such as songs by Neil Diamond, Dan Fogelberg, Billy Joel, Melissa Manchester, Randy Newman, Paul Simon, or Stevie Wonder.

A "patter song" is one that has a complicated, wordy lyric. There's at least one in every Gilbert and Sullivan operetta - and any of them will suffice. Cole Porter, Noel Coward, and Lorenz Hart each wrote many of them. Another recent example would be "Another Hundred People" from *Company* - although, as I will discuss later, you would be wise to avoid Stephen Sondheim's songs.

Torch songs: Prime examples would be "The Man That Got Away", from the movie *A Star Is Born* by Harold Arlen and Ira Gershwin; "The Man I Love" by the Gershwin brothers - George and Ira - ; and "Bill", from *Show Boat*, by Jerome Kern and P.G. Wodehouse. Linda Ronstadt recorded 24 suitable torch/ballads for her albums "What's New" and "Lush Life." Check your Judy Garland and Barbra Streisand records for some choice, little-known ones.

You may want to add a Country-Western song to the above list. Although it is rarely called for, it couldn't hurt to have one ready.

Steel yourself - here's another zinger:

You should also have a back-up song ready for each of the categories.

Why?

Because what if the person just ahead of you - and this happens all the time! - sings the same song you were planning to do. Now don't say, "But that happened to me and I know I sang the song a hundred times better than the one who did it before me." That may indeed be true, but please understand the point of view of the people listening. They don't want to be bored by hearing the identical song twice in a row. That's why you have - and should use - your back-up song.

I once played the auditions for a touring company of *The Wiz*. Eighteen people in a row - I counted - sang either "God Bless The Child" or "Be A Lion" and not one person brought another song to even offer a choice. It drove the director and the choreographer mad - because after a short while the actors lost their individuality, and it was difficult afterwards to remember accurately who sang better than who.

If you have talent, your alternate choice will show it off just as well as your first choice. After all, didn't you choose both on the basis of their ability to do just that?

People are always uncertain about how long their songs should be. The quick answer: probably no more than two minutes for each song. The people auditioning you make an immediate judgment based on your look as soon as you enter the room. They are also extremely practised listeners and can tell rather quickly whether or not you have the requisite vocal ability; some musical directors boast that they know within the first eight bars of a song. So doing a long song with many choruses is rather an imposition, no matter how good you are. You can make a clear case for your talent in a very short time. If your song goes on for too long, there is a great possibility that you will be cut off midstream. I promise you you'll feel terrible if this happens.

Remember the expression, leave them wanting more? If you doubt the wisdom of this, take a look at the W.C. Fields movie *The Old Fashioned Way*. In it, Fields is forced to hear Cleopatra Pepperday - an untalented, wealthy woman - audition for him. He wants her money to put on a creaky melodrama in her town. She wants to be in the show, so in her living room he listens to her sing "The Seashell Song." At the end of the first chorus, Fields politely rises from his seat, applauds, and starts to heartily congratulate her as if it were the end of the song, only to have her launch into the next verse. This continues a few more times. Mr. Fields' hilarious facial expressions and antics are representative of what the casting team goes through when you sing long songs.

Use two minutes as your guide. If your song takes considerably longer than that to make its point, *choose another song.*

WHAT NOT TO SING

The opinions that follow are admittedly debatable, but they do come from experience. Sometimes I feel that singers resist the advice in this section merely because it means they have to do some homework - once I have eliminated 99 percent of the songs they know as potential audition material, they are left with a lot of hard work in front of them, finding and selecting what are considered to be better choices.

There are certain kinds of songs that don't do for you the wonders you think they will if you sing them. Heading this category is anything extremely well-known. The people auditioning you more often than not are quite well versed in the standard show-music repertoire and can generally sing along with any of the familiar songs from most shows. They like those songs. They may even *love* some of those songs. But hearing them in an audition situation is, frankly, boring. The purpose of an audition is to make the director pay close attention to you and give you serious consideration. Well, one way to accomplish this from your point of view is to sing something the director doesn't know by heart.

One woman protested, "But I thought people like to hear familiar songs?" Yes, they do, but not at an audition. You must perk them up - in a sense, *force* them to listen closely. You cannot accomplish that if you lull them with the familiarity of your material.

However, there seems to be an exception to this rule. I recently played auditions for a Country-Western show and it was greatly appreciated when someone came in with a Country-Western standard rather than an obscure song in the genre. The difference in quality between the Nashville hits and the misses is significant, so if you are auditioning for that kind of show and you can't find a dynamite unknown song, don't look too hard. Stick with a well-known one that has a great, singable melody and actable lyrics.

Don't sing songs closely associated with a particular singer - "signature" songs. If, for example, you sing "Over The Rainbow," the listeners will unconsciously and involuntarily compare you with Judy Garland - no matter how good you are, you can't make people forget the original rendition. You want *your* talent evaluated and, hopefully, appreciated. You don't want your valuable audition time spent standing in someone else's shadow.

I'll never forget the young man who sang the Barbra Streisand slowed-down version of "Happy Days Are Here Again," complete with Streisand-like arm gestures. He was genuinely surprised and a little miffed when, after he sang, the director suggested the man sing something on his own and not flagrantly copy someone else's style.

At one audition a few years ago, a young lady sang "Nothing" from *A Chorus Line*. After the song, the director took her aside and explained that because she did a song that was from a show currently running on Broadway,

it was very difficult to evaluate her particular gifts.
He went on to say that the song wasn't a particularly good
choice because the exquisite performance by the original
actress, Priscilla Lopez, was so ingrained in his memory
and in the memories of the others looking at this girl
that they couldn't get a clear sense of what she could
really do. He advised her to prepare another song and
come to the callback. Tears began to well up in her
eyes. She said, "My mother told me I do this song *better*
than Priscilla Lopez."

In Appendix A you will find a long list of the songs
that are, at the time of this writing, considered to be
the most overdone audition songs, and should therefore be
avoided. In 1985. Obviously, as tastes and times change,
so will this list. Be on your guard. When in doubt, ask
questions.

Try to put yourself in your listener's place when you
select your material. Remember that depending on the time
of your audition, they either have a long day ahead of or
behind them. Taking this into consideration, stay away
from songs that are spiritually or morally uplifting -
"You'll Never Walk Alone"; relentlessly cheerful - "On A
Wonderful Day Like Today"; or so cloyingly sweet as to
send the listeners instantly into a diabetic coma - of
which there are numerous examples, many written by my
idols, the Messrs. Rodgers and Hammerstein. Also be aware
that songs of self-aggrandizement provoke perverse
thoughts in the listener. Examples:

"I'm The Greatest Star" - *According to whom?*

"You're Gonna Hear From Me" - *Not if I have anything
to say about it!*

"I've Gotta Be Me" - *But why?*

"Nothing Can Stop Me Now" - *Oh, yeah? I can!*

It's usually not a great idea to sing original songs
- either written by yourself, your pianist, or by your
friends - at auditions. These songs are not always as
good as you think they are. Being fair about this,
obscure show songs are often obscure for very good reasons
as well. But if you've made a poor choice, and the song
you're performing makes the mice pull out earplugs, and
someone in the room asks, *"Where* did you find *that* song":
you're much better off being able to say "It was cut from
Via Galactica" rather than saying that it was written by a
friend. There are exceptions to this, of course, just as
there are exceptions to all the points in this book. But
bear in mind that directors have rejected many a performer
because of a bad song choice. Why risk it?

Unless it is specifically requested in advance, do
not sing songs written by the composer or authors you are
auditioning for. The same goes for songs from shows with
which the director, choreographer, or musical director
were closely associated. This point was strongly echoed
by everyone I spoke to while preparing this book. If you
think they will be flattered by your choices you are
right, but there are other factors that will probably work
against you.

Most - if not all - composers and lyricists have very
definite ideas about how their songs should be performed.
So they will be busy *comparing* during your audition,
rather than watching and listening.

And if you think they will be impressed with your
"different," "novel," or "definitive" rendition of their
material, you may be correct - but not under these
circumstances. You are there to show off yourself and
your talent to best advantage. You don't want to waste
your precious few minutes of audition time distracting
your listeners. If they are for any reason whatsoever
displeased with your performance of their material, you

will have wasted all your preparation and may as well kiss that job good-bye.

The same advice holds for when you audition for an established show - either as a replacement in a production that's running or for a new production anywhere. Unless you're asked, don't sing from that particular show.

A WORD ON SONDHEIM...

Stephen Sondheim, one of the theatre's true geniuses, has written the music and lyrics for many brilliant, melodic, witty, singable, and highly actable songs. His material is challenging, complex, and rewarding to perform - not only because he understands the capabilities and limitations of voices, but also because he has a thorough knowledge of the theatre and the possibilities for songs within the framework of a show. Mr. Sondheim conceives his songs as complete one-act plays, with a beginning, a middle, and an end. Many of his songs can stand alone, outside the context of the show, and would therefore seem to make very good audition pieces.

Now for the bad news.

Most people think it inadvisable to sing Mr. Sondheim's songs at auditions.

Quite frankly, his songs are so good they can magnify any flaws in your voice or technique. Remember that the purpose of the audition is to show off yourself at your *best*. And if you are nervous, or have had a particularly busy day prior to the audition, or are not thoroughly warmed up, his songs will not serve you well.

Also, the same rule about the people who audition you knowing the songs too well applies doubly here. There are so many songs to pick and choose from that will be better for you during an audition situation than any of Mr. Sondheim's - save his splendid material for your club act.

Don't kill yourself at an audition. I feel like I'm divulging a well-kept secret when I tell you it's not necessary to perform a difficult or tricky song to be noticed. That type of number usually contains many pitfalls and traps that you could easily fall into if you are edgy. For a time the song "What Are You Doing The Rest Of Your Life?" was a popular audition number. It's a stunning song, but it has a melodic line composed of small, chromatic intervals that are hard to sing accurately in the best of circumstances. Over the years many good singers have inadvertently gone off-pitch singing that song. The moral is: Sing something simple. Sing a song that won't work against you if you're nervous.

WHERE TO FIND SONGS

I can't print a list of the songs I feel would be appropriate for auditions. As you will see, there are so many possibilities that I would be severely limiting you by even listing a hundred or so. What I can do is tell you where *you* can find good material. It's not that difficult to do - it just takes time. And considerable research. But trust me, the results will pay off a thousand-fold over the years.

Too many performers know very little about the musical theatre. I can't think of any other occupation where its practitioners are not required to have even a minimal knowledge of their field. Can you imagine a doctor, lawyer, architect, or engineer doing his work without thoroughly knowing the history and craft of his chosen profession, and instead operating on "feelings," "gut instincts," and "natural abilities"?

When I was growing up and developing my interest in theatre, I read Stanley Green's wonderful book *The World*

of Musical Comedy cover to cover. Many times. It's still
an excellent book, still in print (New York: Da Capo
Press, fourth edition, 1984), and I still refer to it from
time to time. If you seek this book out and read it, it
will give you, in a highly entertaining way, an overview
of where the musical theatre of today has come from.
Ditto another, more recent book, Lehman Engel's *The
American Musical Theatre* (New York: Collier Books, a
division of Macmillan Publishing Co., 1975).

In addition, I believe that every aspiring performer
should have a basic knowledge of and familiarity with the
songs in all the major musicals that have been performed
on Broadway. You can call this part of your training,
Doing Your Homework.

The minimum list of shows you should know includes
the following:

> The five mega-hit shows by Rodgers and
> Hammerstein -
> > *Oklahoma!, Carousel, South Pacific, The
> > King and I,* and *The Sound of Music*;
>
> Lerner and Loewe's *Brigadoon, My Fair
> Lady,* and *Camelot*;
>
> Jerry Herman's *Hello, Dolly!, Mame*
> and *La Cage aux Folles*;
>
> Stephen Sondheim's *Company, Follies,
> A Little Night Music,* and *Sweeney Todd*;
>
> Along with the following - *A Chorus Line,
> Annie Get Your Gun, Bells are Ringing,
> Cabaret, Damn Yankees, Fiddler on the Roof,
> Finian's Rainbow, Funny Girl, Guys and
> Dolls, Gypsy, Kismet, Kiss Me, Kate,*

*Man of la Mancha, The Fantasticks, The
Music Man, The Pajama Game,* and *West Side
Story.*

This is by no means an exhaustive list, but if at the
very least you know these shows, you will have a pretty
solid grounding in what a good theatre song is, so when
you select your songs you will have a strong basis for
comparison. As a by-product you will have a large list of
songs *not* to sing - ever - at an audition.

Why?

Because the songs in all the above shows are much too
well known - go back to "What Not To Sing" for the
explanation. But many's the time a director has said to a
singer something like, "Do you have anything similar to
'It Only Takes a Moment' from *Hello, Dolly!*" - and the
singer has sheepishly admitted not knowing "It Only Takes
a Moment." Knowing these shows gives you not only a
background in your chosen field, but also a common
vocabulary with your peers.

Also - the roster of musicals performed in summer
stock and dinner theatres across the country is largely
culled from the above list, augmented by whatever fairly
recent shows have just become available. When those
theatres put out audition announcements in the trades,
they only list the names of the shows, not full cast
breakdowns. If you know the shows, you automatically know
which roles are right for you.

Okay, now that you have taken the time to do the
above, where do you find those "obscure" songs that
promise to work miracles for you?

The answer is coming in just a moment.

Be aware of this: There have been well over 1,000
musicals performed on and off Broadway since the beginning
of this century. Each show contains, on an average, 12 to

14 songs. Doing some simple multiplication in round numbers, we're now in the range of about 12,000 songs. Add to this number several hundred film musicals with about 5 or 6 songs in each movie and our total is now well over 13,500. To this total we can, if we wish, add songs that were written strictly for the pop market - or Tin Pan Alley as it was called in an earlier age - and the numbers skyrocket.

I do hear your immediate protests: "Most of those songs aren't that good, or they're not useable for our purposes. After all, your total includes opening choruses and other discountable material."

Fine, I say. Throw out three-fourths of them and we still have a staggering number to select from.

So, if there are so many, why do people pick the same few over and over? Because, admittedly, many - if not most - of the songs I am alluding to are out-of-print, unpublished, or similarly not available for perusal, therefore leaving the readily available standard repertoire to choose from. Which is what most people do.

We happen to be living in a lucky era right now. For finding songs, that is. There have been revues upon revues in the last few years, presenting well-known and not-so-well-known songs by both major and - pardon the easy categorizing - minor theatre composers. If you didn't see any of them, perhaps you know someone who was in one who may have the music and could recommend some songs.

Also, Ben Bagley's Painted Smiles record company* has by now issued more than forty albums devoted to the undeservedly lesser-known songs of nearly every famous Broadway songwriter. The records, which are widely available in many record stores - and by mail, directly from the company - are a treasure-trove of great audition material.

*See Appendix G for addresses and telephone numbers.

There is also a company called Music Masters*, which at the time of this writing has issued over sixty albums containing both previously out-of-print recordings and never-before-issued-on-record material by show and movie composers and lyricists. Their Music of Broadway series alone - eighteen discs full of fabulous songs - will provide you with dozens of choices for audition songs.

You should also check out early Frank Sinatra, Dean Martin, or Peggy Lee albums. These singers had great songwriters penning their material, and you just may find a not-too-well known song to your liking among them. Obviously there are many more singers to add to the three mentioned - look through and listen to the records in your parents' collection.

So, now you've found a song you like and you don't have any sheet music. What do you do?

First, you call whichever local store sells sheet music to see if, by chance, they have it - most stores in small neighborhoods have very small selections, though. Check with your musical friends. Look in the piano bench in your parents' home. Ask your piano-playing aunt who, if she had the song, would be delighted to give it to you. I asked her.

If you've still yielded no results, don't be discouraged. The great search is on! Your next step is to call a store like Colony* in New York City, which maintains one of the largest collections - for sale, of course - of in-print sheet music. See if the song is still available. Aside from individual song sheets, the song may be published in one of the hundreds of published collections - including so-called Fake Books, which provide lead vocal lines and chord symbols for about 1,000 songs per book; as well as specialized volumes like Great Songs of the 1960's. Several decades worth of these last were issued.

*See Appendix G for addresses and telephone numbers.

HOW TO AUDITION FOR THE MUSICAL THEATRE

If you have no luck at Colony, or a similar store, call the Music Exchange*, also in New York City, which sells its extensive collection of out-of-print music.

If you are still coming a cropper, go to the Library and Museum of the Performing Arts at Lincoln Center. On the first floor, in the music division, there exists a large and unusual collection of out-of-print sheet music, which can be photocopied on the premises for fifteen cents a page. There is an index of songs by title only, so be sure you know the correct title.

If you still haven't found the song through any of the aforementioned sources and if the sales help at the stores or the librarians can't recommend anywhere else to try, you can surely get a pianist to write out the music - at least a lead sheet - taking it off the record on which you found it.

The above suggestions certainly do not represent the only places to find songs. I offer them merely as a starting point, and I hope my thoughts will inspire and trigger some clever ones of your own. Undoubtedly the pianist with whom you work will have some ideas for you.

No, it's not easy, but doing all that listening and research can only help you in the long run. After all, you are immersing yourself in the worlds of theatre and music - could there be more pleasurable homework?

*See Appendix G for addresses and telephone numbers.

PREPARATION - PART 2: THE MECHANICS

HOW TO PREPARE YOUR MUSIC

Here's the only irrefutable rule of auditioning:

If you are auditioning for a musical, you must always bring your own music.

I can't stress this strongly enough. Once upon a time I accompanied someone on his audition for the original cast of *Barnum*. There were about thirty-five guys seated in the first few rows of the Edison Theatre, where the auditions were being held. The first man was called. He stepped onto the stage, conferred with the pianist, then went over to center stage and sang "Happy Birthday."

"You didn't bring any music with you?" asked Joe Layton, the director.

"No," replied the actor.

The second guy was called, and surprisingly the exact same process was repeated.

Mr. Layton stood up and said, "How many of you don't have your own music?"

More than half of those present raised their hands.

So Mr. Layton had to make his choices after hearing about twenty actors in a row sing "Happy Birthday."

Okay. Let's keep things in perspective. That's not such a terrible anecdote. The world didn't come to an end. Mr. Layton didn't run out of the Edison Theatre screaming and immediately quit the business. *Barnum* wasn't cancelled or postponed until those auditioning could get their act together.

And as far as I was concerned, this story had a happy ending: My friend - who did *not* sing "Happy Birthday" but, rather, sang an obscure song we prepared and rehearsed - was chosen for the show and played in it throughout its New York run.

But I would bet a substantial sum of money that had all the auditionees prepared songs, a slightly different group of them would have made telephone calls to their families saying they were cast in a show.

More perspective now.

The above occurrence was a rarity. Most people who audition for musicals know they should prepare a song and bring the music. Although the number of unenlightened performers makes the previous case noteworthy, it was not an isolated happening. I have sat at the piano during many other auditions at which at least one person came up to the piano stating, "I didn't know I had to bring music."

Always carry music with you, especially if you're not sure.

But if you come to an audition and don't have music, *don't ever sing a cappella.* It is extraordinarily difficult to stay on pitch without the aid of a musical instrument and it is extremely awkward-sounding. There has never been a reason good enough to warrant it. If your music is for whatever reason unavailable, it is best to attempt to reschedule your audition to a time when you can bring the music. If you insist on singing a cappella, the only thing you will accomplish is writing off the audition. You might as well have stayed home.

On the other side of the coin, there is are astounding number of talented performers who come to auditions smartly dressed, every hair in place, in all visible ways charming and gracious - the very model of perfection. And, yes, they even have music with them. But the music they hand to the pianist is distressingly illegible. The only thing I can attribute this to is perhaps an unconscious feeling on the actor's part that his music is no more than a necessary evil. Since many actors do not read music I would further assume they really can't tell if their music is truly playable or not.

Accompanists often wonder why, with the inexpensive cost and relative availability of duplicating services, so much music carried to auditions is in large books, or if a single copy, in an advanced state of deterioration. Some people are even aware of their music's condition. They apologize, saying, "I know I should get another copy of this song - I'm sorry it's in such bad shape." Or they offer an excuse, such as, "I didn't have time to tape the music together."

Enough complaining - here comes the advice.

First and foremost, your music must be legible. If it isn't, you cannot expect anyone to be able to play it.

Next, keep in mind two facts about the pianist provided by the production company:

HOW TO AUDITION FOR THE MUSICAL THEATRE

1. He already *has* his job; don't make him audition.

2. The pianist – all rumors to the contrary – is there to work for you; and he will, if provided the basic professional courtesies. Like having your music properly prepared.

TRANSPOSITION

If you are singing a song that has been published, and you have the sheet music, and you do it in the published key, you are indeed fortunate. If you aren't so lucky, you will have to have your music specially prepared or doctored – transposed – to make it functional.

Songs that are published are usually issued in a key deemed either by the composer or someone at the publisher's office to be the easiest for a mass audience to deal with – even if it is different from the key the song was originally written or performed in. For example, in the show *Funny Girl*, Barbra Streisand sang the song "People" in the key of A-flat. The sheet music was transposed up to the key of B-flat, even though that put the song out of the range of a lot of singers. This was done because B-flat is considered to be an easier key than A-flat for amateur pianists. So if you've ever sung along comfortably with a recording, then purchased the sheet music and couldn't reach the high notes when it was played on the piano, now you know why.

Every song can either be transposed up or down. With your accompanist or vocal coach try several different keys until you find the one that sounds and feels comfortable for your voice.

Many times people have walked over to the piano at an audition, handed their music to a pianist they were seeing for the first time and said, "Can you play this in a key I can sing it in?" What does the singer expect - that the pianist is Marvo the Magnificent Mind Reader? How could the pianist possibly know the singer's voice and which key would be suitable? Equally bad are those who say, for example, "Play 'As Time Goes By' in D-flat." I do agree that any pianist worth his salt should know any standard song like "As Time Goes By" and should be able to play it off the top of his head in most keys - but why leave anything to chance? Bring a copy of the music that has been prepared in advance - *in your key* - so the pianist can be comfortable playing for you, thus giving you the support you need and deserve.

If your music is to be transposed, it is advisable to have it fully written out in your key. However, this can be expensive, depending on the arrangement and number of pages; so it is permissible and quite common - but mind you, not as good as having the music fully written out - to have the transposed chords written over the measures. Keep the original chords visible - don't scratch them out or use White-Out - and have the transposed chords written in a different-color ink, usually red. That makes it easier for pianists to follow and play from.

Please remember that in preparing to sing music that must be transposed, writing the new chords over the measures is the barest minimum you should have done. As I said before, never come in with the music in the original key and say, "Play it in E-flat." It only takes ten to fifteen minutes at the most for a musician to write in the proper chords. Don't ever say there wasn't time to have it done.

Also - do not under any circumstances present music on which *two* sets of transposed chords are visible. Since it is for your own personal use and not for sale, the original music can be copied as many times as you like, and you can have each copy transposed once to a different key.

HOW TO AUDITION FOR THE MUSICAL THEATRE

PROFESSIONAL COPYING

There are professional copyists who do beautiful work
hand-copying music in ink. It may be worth it to you to
have your music meticulously prepared, especially if the
music is transposed, or if you are using a complicated or
special arrangement. Some copyists put their business
cards, with their phone numbers, on the bulletin boards at
the audition studios, and some advertise in the trades; so
if you don't have any personal references - ask your
friends first - contact one, and if he's unknown to you,
ask to see samples of his work before you give your song
to be worked on.

Standard minimum fees for this kind of work -
according to Local 802 of the American Federation of
Musicians in New York - run $7.39 per page, which includes
the vocal line, the piano part, and the lyrics. If the
music is to be transposed, it will cost an additional 50
percent per page, bringing the total to exactly $11.08 per
page. These prices are current as of February 1985.
Unions being what they are, the prices will eventually go
up. Also, fees vary slightly with the union locals across
the country. I quote prices here merely to give you an
approximate idea of the cost.

If your music is hand-copied, the lyrics and the
melody line *must* be fully written out on the music.
So-called charts - a sheet of music divided into the
number of bars in the song with only the chord changes
indicated - may be sufficient for jazz musicians and your
own accompanist, but they are almost useless for anyone
else. It takes the same ten to fifteen minutes at the
most to write down the lyrics on a chart. Why it is not
done universally is beyond me. There is one major reason
for having both the lyrics and the melody on the music
page: If you forget the words or go off-pitch for any
reason, the pianist can come to your rescue.

THE CARE AND FEEDING OF YOUR MUSIC

Most of the pianos we pianists find to play on in audition rooms are, to put it nicely, not in the best of shape. Often there are several keys broken, and rarely are they in perfect tune.

Another almost standard feature of those instruments is the lack of a proper stand for sheet music. Which is why a lot of the highly original ways people have of putting their music together simply don't work. It may be the piano's fault and not the actor's, but whatever the reason, it's mighty hard to play well for somebody when the music won't stay upright, or when it falls off the stand onto the keys, the pianist's lap, or onto the floor. And it *does* fall - with amazing regularity.

Sheet music you purchase from stores is printed on fairly sturdy paper - sturdier, anyway, than stationery or conventional bond paper. If you are going to use a photocopy of your music at an audition, it is better to have it copied onto a heavyweight stock - your music will stay in acceptable shape a lot longer. Remember, the music isn't staying at home, lying on your piano. It is being transported constantly, shoved in your dance bag or briefcase, and touched and played by many different hands. Regular paper wasn't designed to take that kind of abuse. Some neighborhood copy centers routinely have what is sometimes referred to as card-stock on hand. Otherwise, you can take your music to one of several places that service the music industry. The names, addresses, and phone numbers of a few of these places are listed in Appendix G, at the back of this book. The cost of photocopying onto this kind of paper usually runs around forty to fifty cents a page.

Please do not, for any reason whatsoever, fold your music in half. It just won't stay put even on a good music stand if it has been folded. Keep it flat.

HOW TO AUDITION FOR THE MUSICAL THEATRE

Some people - especially some voice teachers - advocate placing each page of music between sheets of transparent plastic in a loose-leaf notebook. Certainly this presents a neat appearance, but there are several problems. The book is simply too cumbersome and heavy to carry around. The plastic covers tend to reflect light. Because it is impossible to control the light source in an audition room, your music may be hard to read from. In addition, the plastic pages are hard to grasp. Pianists often inadvertently turn two pages at a time. Or the plastic sticks to the binder rings and the pages can't be turned at all.

Individual copies of your songs are a much better solution.

Keep your audition songs in one place. Get a strong folder or envelope to store them in - it should be sturdy enough to travel with. Do not put extraneous music in this portfolio, and do not remove any of the songs from the portfolio lest they not be there when you need them.

To be on the safe side, you should have a spare copy of your music tucked away at home. What if you lose your bag? What if you leave your music on the piano at the audition and can't remember later where it is? My personal collection of music grew significantly in this manner. Consider this a word to the wise. Or is it "a stitch in time?"

So now that you have your music copies, the pages must be attached.

Never staple your music together. It is impossible to play from.

Always tape your music. There are a lot of reasons why you shouldn't leave your sheet music unattached; I mentioned earlier about pages falling to the floor - so all I'll add here is that I wish I had a dollar for every person who handed me their sheets of unattached music with a page missing, usually the last. "Oh, gosh, I'm sorry," they say, "I must have left that page at home." An all-too-obviously avoidable situation. (See Appendix C for directions on the most effective way of taping your music together.)

The first time playing through any piece of music there is one problem for every pianist: Page turns. If your music is not the standard store-bought version, make sure it is printed on only one side of the page and accordion-folded as described in Appendix C. This way, the music can be opened up flat and there will be no page turns to worry about. Four to five pages across will fit on most pianos. If your music is longer than five pages, your song is too long.

INTERPRETATION: ACTING THE SONG

This book will not go into the techniques of vocal production. That subject could fill a volume of its own. So what this part covers is not how to sing a song, but rather a very brief discussion of how to perform a song.

In the words of theatrical agent Jeffrey Dunn, "Singing is acting on pitch." (See Appendix E for an interview with Mr. Dunn.)

To elaborate, it's not enough to merely learn the words and the notes. You must completely understand what the song is saying and figure out how to project its meaning.

Take a look at the structure of the song. Is there a "verse" - a section which precedes the main melody? Verses are written to set up the song's subject matter. Often the main body of a song - the chorus - is written in general terms - a bid for wide-spread appeal. But the verse makes the song specific to a certain situation and can delineate a character. While verses are important lyrically, they are usually very simple and unmemorable musically. An almost singular exception to this is the haunting verse to Jerome Kern and Oscar Hammerstein's "All The Things You Are." But because of the general rule, verses are almost always performed "freely," that is, not in tempo, with maximum attention given to the words. Underneath this, the pianist usually plays a minimal accompaniment, following the singer's lead.

So now that you know the song's structure, continue your analysis by clearly defining the character who is singing the song. Ask yourself, What is he or she trying to accomplish by singing? What is the subtext? Subtext is the thoughts *behind* the words - sometimes very different from what is actually being sung.

After you answer these questions for yourself, speak the lyric out loud as if it were a monologue. Do this a few times. Rephrase the song in your own words. Then sing it again to the music - but this time sing the lyric as simply as if you were speaking it.

To continue your analysis of the song, find the natural phrases of the lyric and see how they rise or fall with the music. If you train yourself to think of the song as a series of phrases, rather than as a sequence of individual words, your performance will be more natural. I always advise people to sing the *lyric*, and not to be concerned with making pretty sounds at the expense of the meaning or intent of the song.

Never distort the English language as you sing. Good songwriters are extremely careful to accent the correct syllables. If the song you have chosen seems to force the language in places, you can usually bend the words back into their natural sound and compensate for the unevenness when you perform. Look for the rhymes and make sure you rhyme them properly as you sing.

A question I get asked a lot is, "Where should I
breathe?" There is a simple, all-purpose, all-inclusive
answer to that: Always breathe with the lyric. Breathe
when there is a pause in the thought. Look for
punctuation marks, chiefly the commas and the periods.
You can always take a breath wherever there is a period
and, depending on the speed of the music, usually where
there is a comma. And if you sometimes have to take a big
breath and make it last a long time, it is probably
unavoidable. The result of all this intellectualization
of the breathing process is that your interpretation
sounds intelligent.

Following my earlier suggestions about listening to
recordings, try to listen to more than one singer perform
your song. It's not always possible, especially with
obscure songs, but you'll be amazed at the different ways
a song can be interpreted. As an exercise, listen to
Stephen Sondheim's magnificent song "Send In The Clowns,"
from *A Little Night Music*, as performed by Glynis Johns on
the original Broadway cast recording; by Jean Simmons on
the original London cast recording; by Elizabeth Taylor on
the movie soundtrack; and in the pop field, by Frank
Sinatra and Judy Collins. Each sings the same song in
fairly similar arrangements, but there are worlds of
difference in the nuances these very talented performers
find in the identical material, without distorting the
song's meaning.

It would be wonderful if you could move and sing at
the same time. Standing like a statue won't do. Find
some movement that is natural, loose, and appropriate for
the song you're singing. If you have a tendency towards
stiffness - as in, "He is so wooden, if you light a match
to him, he'll go up in flames" - get a friend who directs
and/or choreographs to help devise some easy and effective
movement for you. It could make all the difference.

Some of the music put in front of me at the piano has
been heavily annotated with acting suggestions, such as

"Open up here," "Think of all people in this situation,"
"Look serious," and "Arms up." Although gestures can be
expressive and effective, don't overdo them. They must be
derived naturally. Nor while singing should you ever
illustrate the various words or images in the song with
your hands, as if performing for the hearing-impaired.
Try to think in terms of the complete thought or the
intent. If there is a particular word that conjures up a
strong image, use it to your advantage but first
understand what mood and effect the *entire* song is going
after.

Singing is a form of communication. Think of a song
as a sung monologue - acting while singing is not as
difficult as it may seem if you aren't tense and up-tight
about it. If you understand what it is you want to
communicate, that's more than half the battle.

WORKING WITH A VOCAL COACH

Don't confuse a vocal coach with a singing teacher. A singing teacher can help you with the actual production of sound and with breathing and support, and can also give lots of other technical advice. If you have vocal problems, or merely need advice on how to sing better, go to a singing teacher rather than a coach.

The vocal coach is used for other services, mainly for guiding you in putting over the song to maximum effectiveness. At some point you will have to work with one to rehearse your material. Often, but not always, your accompanist is also a vocal coach. Since anyone who plays the piano can call himself a vocal coach, there are several things to keep in mind so as to get the most for your money.

You should work with a coach who is also a pianist.

Your coach must be able to help you determine whether the music needs to be transposed and must have the skill to actually play the transposition. Then he should be able to prepare your music so that anyone else can play it easily - at the very least your vocal coach should be able to accurately write the new chords in on your music. Be aware that some music you purchase may have inaccurate chords printed - your pianist should be able to spot and correct the errors, so that when it is transposed, the chords are correct.

As I said before - and it bears repeating - it only takes ten to fifteen minutes at the most to write new chords on an existing song, so there's never any reason to say that there wasn't time to get the song transposed. Lots of people use this excuse!

Know the key you are performing in. It makes you sound smart and knowledgeable to be able to say, "I do this song in the key of C and the music is in the correct key" or, "I'm doing this in E-flat, and the transposed chords are written in red ink" - instead of having to say, "I don't know what key I do this in. Isn't it on the music?" You don't even have to know what C or E-flat means. The pianist at the audition will know and you both will be more secure.

Another true story: At one audition an actor gave me his music and, without saying a word, headed for the center of the room. I called him back. "What kind of introduction would you like?" I asked. "I don't know," he said, "what kinds of introductions are there?"

The real answer to that question is there are many different kinds. From simple bell tones to arpeggiated chords to full four- or eight-measure piano solos. With your vocal coach, pick a simple, functional intro that will help you establish both the key and the mood for the beginning of the song. And get it written down so that any person playing your music will play the same thing. A common complaint I hear from singers is, "I had no idea *what* the pianist was playing for an intro. I couldn't

find my first note." This is easily avoidable if the
introduction is notated.

Not only the introduction, but the ending, as well as
cuts or repeats should be clearly marked and indicated.
Ditto for any tempo and dynamic markings. Some pianists
charge extra for this service; some will charge according
to their regular hourly rate. Remember that once the music
is done properly, it is yours forever; so if the cost
factor is amortized over the time you spend using the
music, you'll find that it costs very little to have it
prepared correctly.

Ask your coach to show you what has been done to the
music so that you can explain it to others. When I work
with singers, I tell them specifically what to say
regarding all of the above points, then we rehearse them.
And don't accept a line from your accompanist like, "Don't
worry, I'll always play for you." One day he won't be
available and you'll be stuck. There's no reason in the
world you shouldn't know everything about your music.

Your coach should allow you to make a cassette tape
of the accompaniments to your songs so that you can
practice on your own. Don't ever work with someone who
refuses to do this. You must practice your songs often,
expecially during long periods between auditions. If you
have a tape, you can always keep your material freshly
prepared and keep yourself in shape to sing without
spending extra money for coaching every time there's an
audition.

Because of time restrictions at many auditions, you
may be asked to sing only sixteen bars of a song. Plan
for this by picking the sixteen bars of your favorite
audition song that make a complete statement lyrically and
musically. If the top notes of your range are strong, you
may want to select the part of the piece that contains the
highest notes. Rehearse the sixteen-bar section complete
with a *short* introduction, and an ending as if it were

an entire song. And mark the music so it is clear where
the starting place and the finish are for the abbreviated
version.

PREPARATION - PART 3: PERFORMING

WHEN TO BRING YOUR OWN PIANIST

Because of monetary considerations the answer to this one depends to a great extent on how much the job means to you. Now I know that most people who try out for a job hope to get it as a result of the audition. So if this book is all about minimizing the risks and maximizing your effectiveness, my advice would be that if you are auditioning for a featured role as opposed to a chorus job in a Broadway show or with a national touring company you should *always* bring your own pianist and find some way of working it out financially.

But I have to clarify that last statement a bit. The pianist you bring must be one with whom you have worked and who knows your material. I have seen more than one person come in to an audition with a pianist in tow and declare, "I just found out about this and only had enough time to call the pianist to get here in time. We haven't worked through the songs yet." As far as I am concerned, that is a waste of money. The hired pianist winds up playing the music while seeing it for the first time, and usually ends up transposing at sight, the same as the staff pianist would. So there is no advantage for the performer.

Yes, I too have heard of auditions where the staff pianist was not up to snuff and word - and panic - spreads among the hopefuls. This is the only case in which there is the slightest excuse for the situation in the previous paragraph; and this does not occur often. Most of the audition pianists, especially in New York, are skilled, talented, patient people who truly want you to look good.

I am aware that most people simply can't afford to spend the money to bring their own pianist every time they audition; which makes it inexcusable not to have one's music in perfect condition so that it can be played easily by anyone at any time. But if you are auditioning with difficult or special material that has many changes of rhythm and tempo that demand perfect synchronization between the music and the voice, you must not expect any pianist, no matter how facile he is, to be able to give you the support that someone who knows the piece and has rehearsed it with you can.

I once played piano for the auditions of an Off-Broadway musical and in walked a woman none of us in the room knew, but whom we were all looking forward to seeing. This was a woman whose work was known to us and who stood a better-than-average chance of getting the part she was up for based on her proven talent.

She brought in a song that she had sung in a flop musical on Broadway some years before. The song was unknown to me. The music was in manuscript, in smeared pencil, with no lyrics anywhere on the pages. A few tempo indications were barely decipherable, and there were several sets of chords above each measure - a sign that she had performed this piece in several different keys.

But she had no idea which key was the most current, or even which key she wished to sing it in that day. She was used to having her own pianist, who knew all her music, come with her to auditions; so she wasn't able to communicate anything to me before having to sing. "Just follow me," she said impatiently. I did - and badly. I couldn't read the music, and because there were no lyrics, I couldn't be sure we were ever in the same place at the same time. It was truly my most frustrating experience ever at the piano.

She compounded the felony by being exceedingly rude to me in front of the director and choreographer, degrading me and my abilities because I was unable to play her music properly. Needless to say, she brought nothing else with her to sing - "My pianist has all my music" - and the outcome was also unsurprising: She not only didn't get the part; her behavior negated any chance of a callback.

But what should she have done under those circumstances?

She actually had several choices - all better than the one she picked. She could have tried to postpone or change her audition to a time when her own pianist would have been available. Or she could have found someone else with whom she could have worked beforehand to play for her. Or she could have found something simpler to sing. She also could have phoned me to suggest working with her the night before - she could have gotten my number from her agent or from the casting director of the show. She is a talented lady and has worked, to great acclaim, since that unfortunate afternoon; so she must've gotten it all together at some point afterwards.

AT THE AUDITION:

DO'S AND DON'T'S - HINTS AND SECRETS

A lovely and talented singer-actress I have worked with confided to me she conquered her panic over auditioning by thinking of each audition as a performance. She said that if she adds up all the auditions she does in a year, it amounts to quite a lot of performing time. So in a way, she has psyched herself to the point where she actually looks forward to auditioning.

Did you ever hear the famous Noel Coward story? It seems there was a woman who showed up at the casting call for every show Mr. Coward did - musicals, straight plays, and revues. She always appeared well dressed, but her singing left lots to be desired. After many years Mr. Coward, in deference to her tenacity rather than her talent, stepped up to the edge of the stage and said, "I'm very happy to tell you that at last we have a part for you." "Oh, no, Mr. Coward," she said, "I don't take parts. I just audition," and she grandly swept out.

WHEN TO BRING YOUR OWN PIANIST

No matter how prepared you are physically or emotionally, auditioning is a nervewracking business for most people. And nerves have to be the cause of some of the awkward actions actors engage in. Hence, another list of do's and don't's, with accompanying explanations:

1. Take the same advice your mother gave you before a long car trip: Use the rest room before you are called in to perform. 'Nuff said.

2. No matter how unimportant the job may seem at the time, *always* take auditions seriously. Always do your best. You never know what's going to happen in the future. Some people have long memories, and some have short. Assume that the people you audition for fall into the former category.

3. No matter what else you've had to do before the audition, pull yourself together somewhere outside of the place where the auditions are being held. Always remember that you are in a spotlight from the moment you are seen by any member of the production team of the show. If you walk into the room, or even the audition area dishevelled and "spacey," it will be difficult later on to erase that first impression.

4. Auditions are notoriously off-schedule. You will most likely have to wait for some period of time before you are called. Instead of sitting there worrying, there are several things you can do to pass the time: Go over the songs you plan to sing, read a book, do a crossword puzzle - anything to help relieve the anxiety. Often you will know some of the others whose scheduled audition times are just before or just after yours, so you can spend a pleasant few minutes chatting with old friends or making new ones.

5. There's an important question you should ask the
person who checks you in and that is, "For whom will
I be auditioning?" By asking this, you will know how
many people you will be facing – the number can vary
from one person to as many as a dozen or so – and
which members of the production team will be
present. You are well within your rights to know
this information. The roster of people will change
with every audition. For musicals, there will most
often be a director, a choreographer, a musical
director – who either will conduct the orchestra or
play the piano during performances – and a producer,
more than likely several. When you audition for a
new show in New York, you can expect the writers to
be present. In some cases there will be assistants,
friends, wives, husbands, and even lovers of the
various aforementioned participants.

6. If you arrive later than your appointed time, it
is usually unnecessary to offer any kind of excuse
for your lateness. Everyone is aware of the
unpredictability of public transportation and the
unreliability of taxicabs in city traffic. It's not
uncommon for actors to be seen in an order different
from the planned schedule. If many people are
auditioned in a day, the director and his cohorts are
usually not aware that you *are* late until you tell
them. I don't mean to condone lateness, but if you
find yourself unavoidably late, just be composed when
you enter the room and say nothing. If you are
asked, take the advice Michael Shurtleff gives in his
book *Audition*, which is to lie, saying "I was
detained at another audition" rather than offering
such excuses as "I had to take my ferret to the vet
this morning and it threw me off schedule all day."
(See Appendix B for more advice regarding excuses.)

7. Leave your disappointments and anxieties outside
the audition area. At the chorus auditions for the
original production of *The Music Man*, one fellow

came in and sang his sixteen bars. As with everybody else, the director, Morton DaCosta, didn't have time to say anything but "Thank you very much." The actor walked down to the footlights and said, "That's easy for *you* to say, you son-of-a-bitch!" and harangued Mr. DaCosta for several minutes until he was dragged off the stage. Obviously the actor was frustrated by several failed auditions. You must, to the best of your ability, leave all of that behind and forget the ogres who are out front. Your attitude must "read" success, not failure.

8. When you enter the audition room you need only have your photo and resume, which are attached, and your music with you. Try not to come in with all your personal belongings – if you have a coat, a dance bag, a purse, or a spare pair of shoes, you immediately convey a bag-lady image. It is usually possible to leave your things in the waiting area and ask one of the other people auditioning to keep an eye on them while you are inside. If you must bring your bags and coat in with you, place them right beside the door so they can be grabbed quickly on your way out – it makes for the swiftest and most graceful exit. Do not under any circumstances place your things on the same table the director uses. Don't laugh, people have done that! If the audition is on a stage, leave your things at the edge of the proscenium arch, and, if possible, out of sight of the audience.

9. When you are ushered into your performing area, your name will be announced and, if you have not brought your own pianist, you should proceed directly to the piano. Sometimes you will be introduced to the people observing the audition, sometimes not. If you are not personally introduced, don't ask "Who are you?" of anyone. If you didn't ask outside, you can question the pianist about who is who.

10. Don't try to engage the director or writers in "ice-breaker" conversation. Excessive chatting is almost always counter-productive. Although you're trying to be charming and friendly - and attempting to ease your own nerves before you sing - it rarely comes off quite that smoothly. It can seem intrusive and, in truth, just slows things down. I know it sounds harsh, but the rule "Don't speak unless you're spoken to" seems to be a good one to follow.

And for heaven's sake, don't offer any sob stories to the production staff. One woman *always* comes in with a story on the order of "I really have to do this show because my son is going to college in the fall and I need the tuition." I'm sure her reasons are true. But nobody will hire her out of sympathy. Her remarks have always provoked the opposite reaction - I heard the comments made after she left the room. They were not full of warmth and compassion. It's much better to let your talent do the talking.

11. Do figure out what you are going to sing *before* you enter the audition room. You'll be a lot calmer if you have that planned ahead of time. It happens fairly frequently that the director asks what you brought, and after you rattle off the list, he may ask you to sing something other than what would have been your first choice. If the decision is yours, sing your most exciting song first; sing the song you would do if you were only going to sing one number. In addition, have your music - and your picture and resume - ready and in your hands before entering the room; don't search through your bags while everyone waits.

Make sure that you are familiar and comfortable with whatever music you bring with you to the audition. If you don't have with you the music for a song you performed only once ten years ago and whose

words you don't really remember all that well, you
won't be tempted to use it if you're asked to sing an
extra song.

12. If the audition is in a room, rather than a
theatre, pick a spot to sing from that is near - but
not right next to - the piano and that is also a
comfortable distance away from the people watching.
That distance is important and allows those observing
to approximate the way you would look onstage. Since
you will want to move a bit while you sing, as
opposed to standing like a statue, do so laterally -
sideways. Do not creep forward toward the casting
team. Moving toward those auditioning you can
intimidate and make them uncomfortable.

13. If you are in a theatre, this next point is not
a concern, but in a studio you have to be aware of
where you look while you sing. Most people advise
you not to look directly at the people auditioning
you so as not to challenge them with the lyrics to
the song. You should focus on a spot just over their
heads. But pick at least one phrase that can be sung
right to one of the members of the casting team. The
phrase should be informational in content - not
something that either challenges or requires an
answer from the listener.

14. Don't use props while you audition. Even
depending on a chair to be present can cause problems
in some audition rooms, and also takes time to set
up. It is very important for the director to see how
you use your body when you sing, so sitting in a
chair somewhat defeats the purpose. Don't depend on
the piano to lean on or refer to. What if your
audition is on a stage and the piano is in the pit?
It's better to stay as self-contained as possible.
And as flexible as possible.

Speaking of props, there was a young man who came to auditions carrying his rather large teddy bear. He never let go of the bear and even held it close to him when he sang. He probably carried it for the same reason children hold security blankets. But the bear was never referred to in the guy's song. Once, the director was grouping people by type and this young man was one of ten lined up - only to the director's surprise there were eleven faces in the row.

15. If the director suddenly asks you to perform your song in a manner different from the way you are used to, don't fight him or resist. Make an honest attempt to follow the instructions, even if you think you look or sound foolish. The director is obviously trying to see how adaptable you are and how speedily you can absorb new ideas. You will get extra brownie points if you show you are willing to go out on a limb.

16. Don't ask the question "Do you want me to sing two songs?" either before or after you do your first one. Everyone in the room assumes you have brought more than one, so the best procedure is to pause after your first song and wait for some response. Either you will be asked to sing something else or you will be told something like "Thank you, that song showed us everything we needed to hear," in which case you should politely make preparations to leave the room. Don't put them on the spot. The remark that sounds like a brush-off may not be. Most trained listeners can tell after the first sixteen bars how well you sing, and one song may indeed be sufficient for them to determine whether or not you fit in with the specific needs of the show.

SINGING THE RIGHT KIND OF SONG

If you've done your homework, as I outlined earlier, you now have a potent - and full - song portfolio. How do you know which songs to sing for which audition?

If possible, and it usually is, find out what kind of show it is you are auditioning for. Is it contemporary? Rock? Traditional? Old-fashioned? Country-Western? A revival? Each would have very different types of music and therefore different requirements for singers.

Under ideal conditions, pick a song that is in the right period and style as the show. Don't make yourself crazy trying to match the score exactly. All I want to bring to your attention is that if you are auditioning for a traditional Broadway musical, it won't do you much good to sing a song written by the Rolling Stones. Or if you are auditioning for a Country-Western show, it is inappropriate to sing a Victor Herbert aria.

If your song portfolio consists of a number of different songs from several styles and periods, you won't ever be in the uncomfortable position of having to learn a new song overnight because you have just gotten an audition for which you don't have anything suitable.

Jerry Herman cautions: "Don't learn a new song for each audition. The best auditions I have listened to are by people who have been doing the same material for years and years. There's nothing that can replace the comfort of a song that you have been singing and feel secure with. So many people who came to the *La Cage aux Folles* auditions prepared something French or something they thought had a French sound, not realizing that we just wanted to hear their voices. Don't underestimate the imaginations of the people who are sitting out there in the dark. They really only need to hear what sounds best on you."

Lyricist Sheldon Harnick (*Fiorello!, She Loves Me, Fiddler on the Roof*) remembers an audition for one of his shows at which the stage manager came out and announced the next performer, someone with an African name. Out walked a tall, majestic-looking young black man carrying a Conga drum. He was wearing what appeared to be colorful African ceremonial robes, which made him look like a tribal chief. He strode to center stage, put the drum in front of him, and struck it several times with the palm of his hand. Mr. Harnick and his cohorts were primed for some wild, stirring, primitive chant. Instead, in a high nasal tenor, the actor launched into "On The Street Where You Live," a capella, except for an occasional blow to the drum. The effect was so ludicrously incongruous that those watching the audition could only laugh - it was impossible for them to evaluate the performer's talent. P.S. The man wasn't trying to be funny!

HOW TO TALK TO THE PIANIST

AND WHAT TO SAY

If you are not bringing your own accompanist, the staff pianist provided by the production is - usually - your only friend in the audition room. Since, as I said earlier, he is there to serve you, there are things you must do to give him the greatest possible chance to play your music with as much assurance as your own pianist would. But remember, no pianist can be expected to be a mind reader and correctly guess at your interpretation.

Thus, the first rule: Take your time at the piano. Even if the audition is running behind, you will be allowed a few moments to explain the routine, tempo, and feeling of your song to the pianist.

I am assuming at this point that your music is legible and transposed, and that the introduction and the ending, as well as any tempo and dynamic markings, are clearly indicated. If this is the case, you will not need more than about twenty seconds to point out some of the tricky spots.

It is imperative that you give the pianist a clear idea of the tempo. Do this by softly singing a few measures of the song to him at the speed you wish to perform it.

In brief, here are the four things to tell a pianist:

1. The key

2. Where to start

3. Where to stop

4. How fast to play.

Also, don't treat the pianist like a human extension of the piano. Remember the old barroom sign, "Please don't shoot the piano player - he's doing the best he can?" The audition pianists really do try to support you properly. Considering the horrendous state of most of the music they must play from, they do a yeoman's work in accompanying sometimes up to a hundred people a day. After you are done, it is courteous to say "Thank you." Take it from me, it is noticed by everyone in the room.

WHAT TO DO IF YOU FORGET THE LYRICS

In two words: Keep calm. It happens more often than anyone realizes. Maybe in one out of every ten auditions. It is not the end of the world. Naturally no one would ever wish for it to happen, but if it does, your aplomb in dealing with it can turn what seems like a disaster into quite a victory for you.

Once again, don't try to make excuses. They are not necessary and almost always make you look bad.

People most often forget lyrics when they aren't fully concentrating on what they are doing. Don't let your mind wander, no matter how many times you have performed that particular song. Keep it fresh.

But if you should suddenly go blank and can't remember what word comes next, you can simply turn to the

pianist, who will throw you the lyric so you can
continue. If the lyrics are not on the music, that truly
is a disaster, and you should immediately go back to the
section entitled "How to Prepare Your Music" and memorize
it.

Even singing la-la-la is all right until you remember
the words - if it is a short lapse. Listen to Judy
Garland singing "You Go To My Head" on her live Judy at
Carnegie Hall album. Yes, *Judy Garland* forgot the
lyrics. A big star. At Carnegie Hall, yet. And
preserved forever on a best-selling phonograph record.
But she handled it with her marvelous sense of humor.
Brilliantly.

You can, as Judy did, sing *anything* over the notes.
If you think quickly on your feet and are entertaining
enough, you'll get away with it.

THE OPEN CALL

The first professional audition most people encounter will probably be an "open call" - commonly referred to as a "cattle call." At this time you will be one of hundreds competing for just a mere handful of whatever chorus positions are available.

Open call means just that - it is open to anyone who wishes to be seen and considered. You probably will have to stand on a long line in order to put your name at the end of a lengthy list of contenders. Sometimes, before even getting a chance to sing, people are "typed out" - that is, only those who have the right look for the show are asked to stay. A frustrating situation, but don't let it discourage you. Keep going to these kinds of auditions. Eventually you will be allowed to show your stuff.

Because of the sheer numbers of people who show up to be auditioned at an open call, you will rarely be permitted to sing an entire song. Instead, you will usually be asked to sing sixteen bars of any song with which you are familiar and comfortable. An accompanist is almost always provided.

Follow the instructions precisely! Don't ask the accompanist to do more than sixteen bars, even if the song is very fast or very short. He is bound by the same time constraints you are, and must carry out the wishes of the production staff. If you are requested to sing a ballad, don't do an up-tune, and vice versa. Of course, you should be able to perform the whole song all the way through if you are asked - but *only* if you are asked!

Don't be put off if you have to sing in front of the others auditioning. Because of time considerations, it is sometimes more expedient to keep everyone in the audition room while one by one you are called upon to perform. This often happens in professional dance calls. It is an uncomfortable situation, but remember that everyone feels the same way and the production staff is aware of it. But the performers who appear the most fearless and who do the best under the peer pressure will have an edge over the competition.

Although - as you know by now only too well - I have gone through great pains to convince you to perform little-known material, in the open-call situation it is not vitally important to knock yourself out finding an obscure song. You may sing something well-known. What matters here is to make the best impression as quickly as possible. Sing something that shows off your vocal prowess. If you look right and sound right, you will stand out.

SUMMER STOCK

If you are auditioning for a part in a summer stock production, it is essential that you familiarize yourself with the show - or shows, if you are auditioning for the whole season of productions the theatre is doing. You should find out what the roles in the shows require in terms of age, look, and type, as well as what songs those characters sing.

Along with your standard audition material, you should prepare the songs sung by the characters for which you may be considered. In the current economic situation, most summer stock theatres or dinner theatres are struggling financially; so it is folly on your part to audition for the role of, say, Lois Lane in *Kiss Me, Kate* if you are a soprano. The theatres simply do not have the money to transpose the standard orchestrations, let alone have the songs rescored, no matter how much they want you in their production.

You should have prepared not only the actual show songs, but also at least one song that is *similar* to the real songs. When you get to the audition, ask the person who checks off your name when you arrive if those hearing the auditions are asking for songs from the show or if they are asking for other material. This way you can be mentally prepared and you won't have to ask once you are in the room. If the person outside doesn't know, ask the pianist what others have been doing. If you've taken my advice, you'll be ready either way - and in an especially good position if you sing a song of your choosing, which interests the production team, and then are asked to sing from the show. If you have readied the song beforehand, you could secure yourself the part in those few minutes. If you fumble, the last impression you leave will not be the best.

Most summer stock theatres and dinner theatres do fairly standardfare presentations, so the libretti and scores - as well as recordings - are widely available in libraries and theatre book stores.

Once again, there's no substitute for preparation. You'll have an edge over those unprepared.

AT THE CALLBACK

Final casting decisions are never made in the first round of auditions. During that time, the people doing the casting are making special note of anyone who could possibly fill the roles in the show. These actors are given a callback - which is just another chance to audition on a different day. Most often the callback is scheduled within a week of the first audition. However, there have been cases of callbacks being scheduled months later. If you have been selected for a return visit, it means that you are under serious consideration.

There are certain accepted practices for callbacks:

1. Wear the same clothes you wore to the first audition. You were called back because your talent and your appearance were liked sufficiently to warrant a second look. If you dress or fashion your hair differently you may look entirely wrong to the production team and thus do yourself a disservice.

2. The same goes for songs. Bring the same two songs you sang the first time. But it is imperative

that you bring additional material. Once again, your song portfolio can come in handy at the callback – the director may want to see you display colors other than the ones you showed previously.

It is permissible at this juncture to ask if you should sing a different song or do the one you sang the last time. Since, as I mentioned earlier, the casting people wrote down what you did at the first audition, they will welcome being given the option.

If it is *your* choice, my previous advice holds: Sing the flashiest, most exciting song in your repertoire. Since you don't know if they will want a second number – *and don't ask!* – do as your first number the one you would pick if you were told you would only sing one song.

Once again, if when you are in the room you are suddenly asked to do a certain type of song you have not prepared, for heaven's sake don't attempt to fumble through something you may only half-know. Don't ever try to perform when you are not ready. If you do, the last impression you leave with the production team will be one of sloppiness. If you have a parcel of songs to choose from and are still asked to do something else, it is not bad form to say, "I'm sorry, I don't have anything like that under my belt. If you'd like, I could work up that kind of song and come in again." Most often, you will not have to learn anything new, although you may be asked to return for a second callback. If you do get a special request, try to get from the director – or whoever is doing the asking – as specific an assignment as possible, so that when you return, you will be doing precisely what they thought they wanted.

A TOUCH OF THE OUTRAGEOUS

I tremble a bit to include this topic for fear of its consequences. Throwing caution to the winds, I dutifully mention that some performers have gotten some mileage out of their auditions by being slightly outrageous.

On a recent *Tonight Show* on television, director-choreographer Tommy Tune (*Nine, My One and Only*) described to guest-hostess Joan Rivers how he auditioned in his performing days: While he sang the song "M-O-T-H-E-R" - "M is for the million things she gave me..." - he twisted his tall, lanky body to form the letters M--O--T--H--E--R. Ms. Rivers asked Mr. Tune if he would hire a person who came in to audition and did that same routine. Mr. Tune said yes, because it would show him that the actor had some imagination and a sense of humor.

Two of the most quoted stories in recent memory involve Mary Jo Catlett. Now well known for her appearances on Raid commercials and for her role as Pearl on television's *Diff'rent Strokes*, Ms. Catlett had, by the time the first incident described below took place, already been on Broadway in *Hello, Dolly!* among other shows.

She, like many other performers, had a fear of auditioning - translation: fear of rejection - and it took her some time to conquer it. When she did, she too treated the audition as if she were performing a part in a play. Then it became great fun for her, and she went to just about any lengths to get a part - especially if she knew in advance something about the show.

In 1971, at the time her appointment was scheduled by the casting director for the Broadway musical *Different Times* - no relation to the similarly named television show - Ms. Catlett was asked to prepare a song and sing it as if hung over. After due consideration, she picked a song that would suggest the opposite of how one would feel in that condition: "I Feel Pretty" from *West Side Story*. In the audition room she put three chairs together, laid down on them on her back, and sang. After the first quatrain, she rolled over and fell flat on the floor and continued singing, face down. She got the part.

Another story involving Ms. Catlett falls into the Chutzpah Department. For the Broadway revival of *The Pajama Game* which was to be directed by the show's original director, George Abbott, she auditioned for the part of the executive secretary, Mabel, and didn't hear anything after her audition. Through the grapevine she found out that the producers were on the brink of hiring someone else but weren't enthusiastic about their choice. She got a call to go back and audition again as if she had never been there before. It was suggested that she wear a blonde wig - she is a brunette - and sing a different song; because if she did, in theory, Mr. Abbott would never know she was the same woman he wasn't interested in earlier. She took the suggestion and got the job, although she's convinced she didn't fool the ever-wise Mr. Abbott. P.S. She didn't have to wear the wig in the show.

A TOUCH OF THE OUTRAGEOUS

The funniest audition I ever witnessed was for *Trixie True, Teen Detective*. The director asked everyone to bring a comedy number. Almost half of the men brought the song "Floozies" from *The Grass Harp* - an amusing song, but not really comic. One man, tall, rugged, and very masculine in a natural, self-assured way, had us all in stitches when he sang "I Enjoy Being a Girl" from *Flower Drum Song*.

It's a fine line, but if you can find a way to make yourself stand out by doing something extraordinarily different, try it. A word of caution: First try it out on several of your more staid friends before you gamble at an audition. If you're at all in doubt as to the true humor of your plan, stick to something safe.

AFTER THE AUDITION

So now you've been conscientious, done all the preparation, and worked your tail off. You've also just done an audition and you feel, well, strange. Perhaps a little let down. It's natural. Perhaps your thoughts fall into one of the following categories:

1. I was terrible - they're never going to hire me.

2. I have no idea how it went.

3. I was terrific - I'm sure I'm going to get cast.

4. I was terrific - they didn't seem the least bit interested.

Within reason, you should be able to tell how well you sang and/or danced and how comfortable you felt as a performer, but that's about all. You cannot accurately measure the reactions of the production team. Even if they talked and ate sandwiches during your audition - which is rude on their part, but it's done - you shouldn't take that as a certain sign of a negative attitude towards you.

If you think you weren't at your best, try to figure out why so that you can correct the problems next time. Most importantly, if you think you gave a great audition but still didn't get cast, don't start to think you are terrible or untalented.

There are many variables out of your control in an audition situation, which include the specific requirements of the show and the particular preferences of the creative team. You can't - and therefore shouldn't try to - second-guess what is on their minds as they listen to you. And if you have heard any "inside" information from other actors, you should only listen with one ear: Your actor colleagues constantly exchange misinformation and are not necessarily reliable sources.

Another factor most people are unaware of is that when shows currently running are looking for replacements, actors who fit the costumes and don't require transpositions can save a lot of money for the company. If you're the wrong size or vocal range, you're probably out of luck regardless of your talent and preparation.

Unfortunately, it is simply not possible for you to get feedback on how your audition went. If you thought you did everything right and got cut early, or didn't get at least a callback, you probably will never know why. The only thing you should ever be concerned with is taking charge of your own presentation and demonstrating your talent in the most satisfactory way possible. Don't blame the world for not recognizing your true genius; the place to look is within yourself. Whatever you may be doing wrong *can* be corrected.

But once in a great while, one of the members of the production team may just have it in for you, and your audition, no matter how good, may be doomed before you start, as happened at the following audition:

HOW TO AUDITION FOR THE MUSICAL THEATRE

Several years ago in New York City all the people awaiting their turn to sing - about twenty - were invited to sit on little chairs on the stage to watch the other auditions. In the group was the girl friend of one of the producers. She had been flown in from Los Angeles by her producer-friend to try out, and was tastefully and becomingly attired in a black sheath with a strand of pearls around her neck. When her name was announced, she gave her music to the staff pianist and in a soprano voice sang "And This Is My Beloved." Beautifully. A nasty little voice from out front said, "Miss, you know that's not the right kind of song for our show. Do you have anything to *belt*?" Composed, she turned to the pianist and said, "I'll do 'Johnny One- Note' - start in D then move up to E-flat." And she told him at which point to modulate. She blew the roof off the theatre. She was so terrific, in fact, that afterwards, everyone on stage spontaneously applauded her. Up from the audience came the man who had spoken earlier - the director. On the stage, in front of everyone, he said, "Miss, I know you're from the Coast but first of all, your choice of material is terrible. You must never wear a black velvet sheath, and pearls are outclassed. Now tell me, *what have you done before?*" Summoning up all the dignity she could muster after that gratuitous humiliation, she said, "Well, in the beginning, I created heaven and earth."

Whatever your particular experience may be, always remember the words of the late Lehman Engel: "Rejection at an audition is not the conclusion of anything, only the end of a single exploration."

Keep plugging.

Try new things.

Keep auditioning.

You'll get there. Talent will out.

APPENDICES

APPENDIX A

A PARTIAL LIST OF THE MOST OVERDONE AUDITION SONGS

If you are using any song on this list, please immediately find substitutes. If you are saying now "But I use that song and I always get jobs with it," I'm truly happy to be proved wrong in your case - but you are an anomaly.

Anyway, this list is more or less current as of this writing. Songs seem to go in and out of vogue - one month everyone will be doing the same song, and the next month, just as suddenly, no one will bring it in. Use this list as a general guide to songs that have been used the most in the last few years.

Any song from *Jacques Brel*
All I Need is the Girl (*Gypsy*)
All the Things You Are (*Very Warm for May*)
Almost Like Being in Love (*Brigadoon*)
And This is My Beloved (*Kismet*)
Anyone Can Whistle (*Anyone Can Whistle*)
Art is Calling for Me (*The Enchantress*)
A Wonderful Guy (*South Pacific*)
Be a Lion (*The Wiz*)

Being Alive (*Company*)
Cabaret (*Cabaret*)
Corner of the Sky (*Pippin*)
Don't Tell Mama (*Cabaret*)
Everybody Says Don't (*Anyone Can Whistle*)
Everything's Coming Up Roses (*Gypsy*)
Feelin' Good (*The Roar of the Greasepaint...*)
Glitter and Be Gay (*Candide*)
God Bless the Child
Her Face (*Carnival*)
Hit Me with a Hot Note (*Sophisticated Ladies*)
I Can Cook Too (*On The Town*)
Ice Cream (*She Loves Me*)
If I Loved You (*Carousel*)
I Got Rhythm (*Girl Crazy*)
I'll Build a Stairway to Paradise (*George White's
    Scandals*)
I'll Never Fall in Love Again (*Promises,
    Promises*)
I Met a Girl (*Bells are Ringing*)
I Wish I Were in Love Again (*Babes in Arms*)
Joey, Joey, Joey (*The Most Happy Fella*)
Johnny One-Note (*Babes in Arms*)
Luck Be a Lady (*Guys and Dolls*)
Maria (*West Side Story*)
Maybe This Time (*Cabaret* - the movie)
Metaphor (*The Fantasticks*)
Mama, a Rainbow (*Minnie's Boys*)
Nobody Does it Like Me (*Seesaw*)
Nothing (*A Chorus Line*)
Once Upon a Time (*All American*)
On the Other Side of the Tracks (*Little Me*)
On the Street Where You Live (*My Fair Lady*)
People (*Funny Girl*)
Promises, Promises (*Promises, Promises*)
Real Live Girl (*Little Me*)
She Loves Me (*She Loves Me*)
Soliloquy (*Carousel*)
Stranger in Paradise (*Kismet*)
The Impossible Dream (*Man of la Mancha*)

The Joker (*The Roar of the Greasepaint...*)
They Call the Wind Maria (*Paint Your Wagon*)
They Were You (*The Fantasticks*)
Tomorrow (*Annie*)
Tonight at Eight (*She Loves Me*)
Try Me (*She Loves Me*)
Wait Till You See Her (*By Jupiter*)
What I Did For Love (*A Chorus Line*)
Where Am I Going? (*Sweet Charity*)
Why Can't I Walk Away? (*Maggie Flynn*)

It's also a good idea to avoid brand-new hit songs.
Even before *Cats* opened on Broadway too many singers
performed "Memory" at auditions, each one thinking that he
would be the only one to be doing it at that point in
time. Play it safer with little-known, older material.
There's tons of it to choose from!

APPENDIX B

EXCUSES, EXCUSES

All of you who think you are being original when you offer an explanation as to why you are not at your best at an audition, please think again. Every possible excuse has been offered too many times. And they are all incredibly self-defeating. I'd be filthy rich if I had a dollar for every time the following have been said:

I have a cold.

I have just recovered from a cold.

I feel a cold coming on.

I didn't have any music to sing so I just stopped at the Colony and bought this song. How does it go?

I just found out about the audition this morning, so I couldn't prepare adequately.

My pianist has my music.

I'm in the process of moving - or, I have just moved
- so my music isn't in good shape.

I just learned this song yesterday.

I learned this song from the record, but I never
heard the accompaniment before.

It's too early to sing - my voice isn't warmed up.
(Said at every audition before noon.)

Please note that a once-popular excuse is not heard
much anymore: "My dog chewed up my music." I don't know
whether the disappearance of this excuse means that more
actors have cats than have dogs or that maybe there are
just better-trained canines around.

APPENDIX C

TAPING YOUR MUSIC

Now I realize that it may sound incredibly picky, but there is a right way and a wrong way to tape music together. Since it is just as easy to tape it either way, please try the method I describe.

Let's assume you have a four-page song with music printed on only one side of each sheet. Take pages 1 and 2 and lay them flat on a table facing you, with page 2 to the right of page 1. The first trick here is to leave a small hairline space between the pages. This is to allow for the thickness of the tape when you fold the pages – the result is that the music folds flat and opens flat. Put tape down the front of the music only. Use three pieces of tape rather than one long one. This is done so that if one piece splits down the center, the other two are still there hanging in.

To attach page 3 requires a second trick. You put page 3 to the right of page 2, leaving the hairline space between the pages; but this time you attach the tape from the *back* side of the music only. This is so that when you fold the music, the sticky part of the tape is always on the *inside* of the fold.

Now as for page 4, place it to the right of page 3, leaving the space between the pages, and put the tape, once again, on the front.

You fold the music by leaving page 1 facing you on the front, with the other pages arranged in an accordion fold. Page 4 will face you on the back. Voila, you're done.

If the song has five pages, follow the instructions for page 3. If any of this sounds confusing, it'll all make lots of sense when you try your first one.

APPENDIX D

YOUR PHOTO AND RESUME

Until that pie-in-the-sky day arrives when you achieve stardom, you will need to have current pictures and up-to-date resumes ready to give to anyone who may cast you in anything. So, as promised earlier, here are a few observations on that ubiquitous duo.

Note to newcomers: The trade papers are full of ads for photographers and for resume-typing services. If you don't have one that is personally recommended, shop around, compare prices and the quality of the work. Then, if you have to, draw straws and pick one.

First and foremost, your picture and resume should be attached. There's nothing that looks more unprofessional than carrying them around unattached. Spend a few minutes at home pasting the resumes to the backs of the photographs, using rubber cement.

Don't present a packet of reviews and clippings at an audition. The people evaluating the auditions don't have time to read them - neither when you are in the room nor later on. Nor are they the least bit interested in doing so. All the great things that have been said about you in print will do no earthly good if you make a poor showing in person.

Keep your resume to one page. If you have so many credits that it takes more than one page to list them all, just put the more important ones down. Or make up two separate resumes, each geared to different types of work – i.e., one that lists all your theatrical credits, and another that lists all your commercials and your industrial shows.

Don't make the resume too cluttered. You want your experience to be immediately comprehensible. In this regard, always list your more important credits first. Use this order as a guideline for your musical resume:

1. Broadway productions

2. National tours

3. Stock, regional, and dinner theatre productions.

4. College productions

5. Film and television shows

Be factual. I remember one particular actor who listed he had worked for a particular director. Unfortunately for the actor, he was auditioning that day for the director named – and the director was certain he had never worked with that actor. My point is: *Don't fabricate credits.* If you're worried that your resume looks unimpressive, don't worry. If you're talented, your credits will grow quickly enough.

Never put any unnecessary information on the resume. At an audition I played at some years ago an actress presented her resume, and after her less-than-impressive audition it was immediately consigned to the trash basket. I retrieved it, kept it, and still have it in my files because it was so bizarre. On it was written: "My most exciting experience was natural childbirth. However, it's hardly marketable."

As for your photo, make sure it is recent and that it looks like you. You always want a flattering photograph, but it is important that your picture resembles the person standing in front of those casting the show. After you leave the room, your photo is all they have to remember you by. The picture *must* call to mind the actor the casting people just saw.

A surprising number of women have had composite photo resumes done containing pictures of themselves in the nude. This is certainly an attention-getting device and it does work. The resumes do stand out from the others and are often kept by the male members of the production team. They are also frequently tacked up on office walls. But the ladies are *never* seriously considered for roles. Unless, maybe, for *Oh, Calcutta!*

You should always carry a few photos and resumes around with you wherever you go. You may be asked for an extra at an audition or you may run into someone else there – another director, or perhaps a casting agent – who could have a use for one. It doesn't weigh that much to take a handful with you. And the one time you don't have an extra is the time you'll be asked for one.

APPENDIX E

TO AGENT OR NOT TO AGENT

And Other Questions Answered

Of primary concern to all new performers is the acquisition of an Equity card - tangible evidence that one is a member of Actors' Equity, the union to which all theatre performers must belong in order to appear in any of the nation's legitimate theatres. Non-Equity performers are not usually auditioned for Broadway shows, although some may be depending on the specific needs of the show. But there's no guarantee.

Another major concern is how to go about getting an agent interested in you. To discuss these topics, and answer a lot of other related questions, here's an edited version of an interview I conducted with Jeffrey Dunn, an agent in the Musical Theatre department of the Fifi Oscard agency.

JEFFREY DUNN: If you've just arrived in town, I don't think the best idea is to get your Equity card immediately. Unless you're interested in being a chorus person for the rest of your life, you're better off getting roles under your belt in good non-Equity stock companies. If you're talented, it's quite possible you can get some really good parts that you wouldn't get in an Equity company for years. It's also a way to start making contacts and connections. Quite frequently the directors at those theatres do move into better things. The second-assistant stage manager of this year's dinner-theatre production could be directing a Broadway show in five years.

QUESTION: Where does someone find out about these theatres?

JD: There's a book published called the *Non-Equity Performer's SUMMER THEATRE GUIDE from an Actor's Viewpoint* by John Allen (see Appendix G for information on ordering.) From interviews with people who have worked in them, the book discusses all the stock theatres: What the pay scale is like; what the living conditions are; whether people enjoy working there, etc. It's important to know this ahead of time, because when you're talking about non-Equity you're not covered by any rulings except public health, and that sometimes comes into play at some of these theatres.

Q: So for how long should a performer continue to do non-Equity work before he gets his Equity card?

JD: Remember that once you get your card, you can never act in a professional non-Equity production again without Equity's express permission. I know many young actors who, having finished a successful season of stock - doing nine musicals in nine weeks - think, "Now I'm ready! I want my Equity card!" They somehow get it within about a year and never get another Equity job again. Many promising careers grind to a halt as a result of getting the card. I see people all the time who come to me with resumes with one Equity credit and the rest is all nonunion, and not recent nonunion work at that, and I can't do a lot with them because they're competing with everybody who has ever been in a Broadway show or national tour. I think you should always be functioning on the level where you're competitive. And those who attend non-Equity open calls for Broadway shows and are not getting the jobs think, "All I need is to get my card and then I'll work." Do they really think that if they go to the same calls and compete with the Equity people they're going to get cast? That the letters A.E.A. next to their names will make them sound better? It won't. If you need an Equity card, you'll get it - and I've rarely seen somebody not get it when he was ready. But I've seen many people who got it when they weren't.

Q: When should performers get an agent?

JD: Again, when they're ready. An agent tends to work in the more important venues, the ones that are going to be income-producing or career-building. An agent is not going to be that interested in booking you for a summer in New Hampshire - making minimum doing interesting shows every week - or putting you in an Off-Off-Broadway musical, unless it seems to have the potential to move somewhere. There are many people who come to me who are very talented, but whom I don't think I can do a lot with yet because they are just so green. They don't have the experience. I'm reluctant to take on somebody that I can't get seen. Even with people who've been on Broadway - assuming that their agents have good reputations and good credibility - if casting directors don't know the actor's work it is sometimes difficult to get them seen for every project - or even for the ones they're right for. Be sure when you go after an agent that you have something to offer him other than just your talent. You have to have credentials that you were able to get on your own. Start looking as soon as you feel your talent is at a level when you can utilize an agent, but don't expect to be a signed client until agents are going to be able to keep you busy working. An agent is happiest when his clients are working.

HOW TO AUDITION FOR THE MUSICAL THEATRE

It's never a bad thing at any point in your career to send a picture and resume to an agent with a note saying, "I'm not represented right now. Perhaps if you're interested, we can talk." Don't be crestfallen if they won't see you initially. And then if they'll meet with you but won't do anything for you, just keep in touch with them; let them know when you're doing things, and gradually if they see that your career seems to be moving, they will jump on the bandwagon quickly. They'd be foolish not to. But when you first get to town, it's just important to work, because work begets work.

Q: Obviously, if an actor is working, he's also being seen and exposed to others in the business.

JD: Also, the people you meet and work with form a network where you exchange information. Although not always 100 percent reliable, it's a start in learning which director is good and which isn't; which agent is good, which isn't; whom you can trust, whom you can't; don't work at this theatre, and so on. From working, people know you. Even if they just see your name in a program, it's better than not. Your name should get to be familiar to people. But you shouldn't work in stuff that's not good. It's very possible to take mediocre material and make it wonderful, as many Tony Award winners who've been in mediocre musicals would bear out. But don't be involved in something that you would be embarrassed to invite people to. As important as it is to keep working, it's also important to keep an eye on the long term - that you're looking to build a career. Certainly, don't invite an agent to a show if you're the only good thing in it; don't make them spend an evening seeing a rotten show for your terrific five minutes. Better to drop them a note and say, "I'm doing this show and I think I'm very good in it, however, I don't think the rest of it is that good. If you're really interested in seeing me, come between 9:30 and 10:00, that's when I do my stuff." It's unlikely that the agent will come, but the fact that you had that much faith in your work and

were considerate of the agent at the same time will not go
unnoticed.

Q: Do agents scour the town going to showcases and the
like looking for new talent?

JD: As with any group of people, you can't generalize. I
do go out a lot to cover people for the areas I work in.
However, one of the areas I work in is musicals, so I
don't miss an important musical project anywhere.

Q: Do you approach people you like in shows to see if
they're represented?

JD: Yes, definitely. If they say they're not
represented, then I give them my card and tell them to
call. And do you want to hear something amazing? Quite
frequently they don't. Maybe they're afraid to call or
they wonder if I really meant it. I don't give out my
card if I don't want to hear from them, even at the risk
of hurting somebody's feelings, which I hate to do, but I
really won't lead people on. If you do good work and
people see it, and they think that you have a big career,
they're going to go up and talk to you afterwards. I
think most agents would.

Q: Okay, you're an actor, and an agent has asked to see
you. Should you sign with the agent?

JD: With some agents, the minute they meet you they want
to sign you. You have to find the right agent. Signing
with an agent is like a marriage. It's a relationship.
You have to have good communication. I don't think that
can happen in a fifteen-minute meeting; it can only happen
in time. And it takes two for it to work well. For the
agent, he needs to be sure that he can get you seen, that
he can keep you busy. And you have to find out whether
you're going to be submitted for things that you're right
for and for the kinds of things you want to be doing. You
can have a somewhat successful career without being signed

with an agent. There are several people who have had
Broadway careers but who, for one reason or another, are
unsigned. Getting signed means finding an agent who knows
what you do, likes what you do, and knows what to do with
it. And that doesn't always happen. However, when you
get to a certain point, you've got to have an agent or a
manager, at least to do your contract negotiating.

Q: Any more general advice?

JD: You have to have the confidence in your own talent
and your own ability - to know you're going to hit it, but
to keep working on it and nurturing it like any growing
thing. And the patience to put up with everything you
have to put up with until that time comes without going
crazy. You have to find things that you can do to keep
yourself from getting nuts.

Q: Like what?

JD: Like getting together with actors and spending an
evening reading a play. Going to the Lincoln Center
Library every two weeks and taking out albums of two
musicals you never heard before. Getting together with a
friend who plays the piano - and maybe even with a bunch
of friends - and just singing through music. Going to the
movie musicals that play the revival houses. Buying
standing room for a Broadway show that you've seen already
and seeing what has happened to it six months later, or
seeing how the replacements are doing. I learned a great
deal when I would go to see shows many times and see
replacements and see how many different ways there are to
approach a character. To see every single lady play Dolly
was very instructive. There's no one way. When I sold
orange drinks at the Shubert Theatre when *Promises,
Promises* was playing, I saw over a long period of time
what happened to the performances. Jerry Orbach was able
to keep his performance absolutely fresh every night;
other people were not quite as good at it. To see where
the laughs came with different houses. To keep learning

and growing is so important. That's what you do in between jobs. Just because nobody's paying you to work doesn't mean you stop working. Go to dance classes. Do those auditions. Try to keep yourself happy. Because if you're depressed and go into an audition depressed, it's going to show. Nobody wants to hire anyone who's desperate.

At the end of *The Count of Monte Cristo* by Alexandre Dumas is a wonderful quote, which reads:

> The Count just told us that all human wisdom was contained in these two words: wait and hope.

Show business is a lot like that.

APPENDIX F

ADVICE TO THE PERSONAL ACCOMPANIST

Please remember that you are there as an accompanist. You are not auditioning - or rather, you *shouldn't* be auditioning at the same time as the person who brought you.

This may sound strange, but *sensational piano playing at an audition is distracting. The attention and focus must be placed squarely on the singer.* Keep your accompaniments simple, straightforward, and supportive and you will be doing your job well.

If the audition atmosphere is relaxed enough to permit some dialogue between the singer and the director, it is customary for the singer to introduce you; otherwise, you usually remain nameless. It comes with the territory.

However, if you hear that a piano job is available on the show, it is permissible to let your interest be known by giving your resume to the stage manager, or whoever is checking people in at the audition. If they are interested, they will get in touch and arrange for you to audition for the proper people.

APPENDIX G

HELPFUL NAMES AND ADDRESSES

The first - and best - place to look for names and addresses of book, record, and sheet-music stores is in your local Yellow Pages under the headings "Book Dlrs.," "Records-Phonograph-Retail," and "Sheet Music," respectively. Music copyists can either be found through your city's local chapter of the musician's union - American Federation of Musicians, or A.F. of M. - or through the music department of a university. Pianists can be located through the latter as well. Remember that the musician's union cannot recommend a certain music copyist over another, but they can provide you with a list of those available in your area.

In cities with a substantial theatrical industry, such as New York, Los Angeles, and London, there are a number of related businesses prepared to serve the trade knowledgeably. What follows is a workable but incomplete listing of some of the larger, more established firms that you could contact for assistance by phone, by mail, or, if it is a retail store, in person.

MUSIC PREPARATION - NEW YORK CITY

Associated Music - Copy Service
231 West 54 Street
New York, NY 10019
(212) 265-2400
Duplicating and copyist services provided, as well as
music supplies (paper, etc.).

ABC Music Reproduction Service
1633 Broadway
New York, NY 10036
(212) 583-9334
Services include music reproduction.

Chelsea Music Service
1841 Broadway
New York, NY 10023
(212) 541-8656
Copyists and music reproduction service provided.

Ideal Reproduction Company
1697 Broadway
New York, NY 10019
(212) 581-7355
Copyists and music reproduction service provided.

King Brand Music Papers
1595 Broadway
New York, NY 10036
(212) 246-0488
Provides music reproduction service, as well as music
paper and supplies.

Music Preparation International
1697 Broadway
New York, NY 10019
(212) 586-2140
Provides copyists and music reproduction service.

MUSIC PREPARATION - LOS ANGELES

Alpheus Music Corporation
1433 North Cole Place
Hollywood, CA 90028
(213) 466-1371
Provides music reproduction service, as well as music
paper and supplies.

Bob Bornstein
c/o Paramount Pictures Music Library
5555 Melrose Avenue
Hollywood, CA 90038
(213) 468-5000
Provides copyist services.

Judy Green Music
1634 Cahuenga Boulevard
Hollywood, CA 90028
(213) 466-2491
Provides music reproduction services, as well as
music paper and supplies.

Bill Hughes
1251 Vine Street
Los Angeles, CA 90038
(213) 462-8390
Provides copyist and music reproduction services.

Joann Kane
14110 Valley Vista
Sherman Oaks, CA 91423
(213) 906-1325
Provides copyist services.

Pacific Music Papers
1305 North Highland Avenue
Hollywood, CA 90028
(213) 462-7257
Provides music reproduction services, as well as
music paper and supplies.

SHEET MUSIC - NEW YORK CITY

Colony Music
1619 Broadway
New York, NY 10019
(212) 265-2050
They stock a large selection of current in-print
sheet music and occasionally have some out-of-print
oddities. They also have a huge selection of
phonograph records, both in-print and out-of-print.

Music Exchange
1619 Broadway
New York, NY 10019
(212) 245-8860
They stock a large selection of out-of-print sheet
music.

BOOK STORES - NEW YORK CITY

Earlier in this book I mentioned the importance of
becoming familiar with the standard repertory of the music
theatre. Many musicals have had their scripts published
and are therefore available to read and study. First, try
your local library. Then, try the following book stores -
again, an incomplete list:

Actor's Heritage
262 West 44 Street
New York, NY 10036
(212) 944-7490

Applause Theatre Books
211 West 71 Street
New York, NY 10023
(212) 496-7511

Coliseum Books
1771 Broadway
New York, NY 10019
(212) 757-8381

Drama Book Shop
723 Seventh Avenue
New York, NY 10019
(212) 944-0595

Theatre Arts Bookstore
405 West 42 Street
New York, NY 10036
(212) 564-0402

Theatrebooks
1576 Broadway
New York, NY 10036
(212) 757-2834

BOOKSTORES - LOS ANGELES

Larry Edmunds Bookshop
6658 Hollywood Boulevard
Hollywood, CA 90028
(213) 463-3273

Samuel French
7623 Sunset Boulevard
Los Angeles, CA 90046
(213) 876-0570

The book *Non-Equity Performer's SUMMER THEATRE GUIDE from an Actor's Viewpoint*, by John Allen, can be found in most of the above book stores or can be ordered directly from Mr. Allen at P.O. Box 2129, New York, NY 10185.

PHONOGRAPH RECORDS

Music Masters
25 West 43 Street
New York, NY   10036
(212) 840-1958

Painted Smiles Record Company
116 Nassau Street
Room 516
New York, NY   10038
(212) 964-3140

Note: Both the above companies sell their records
directly through the mail. Write or phone for catalogs.

LAGNIAPPE

MY FAVORITE AUDITION STORY

Once upon a time a pretty young woman approached the piano and gave me her music. It was the vocally demanding coloratura aria "Glitter and Be Gay" from *Candide*, by Leonard Bernstein and Richard Wilbur. A six- minute number containing many passages that push the abilities of even the most accomplished sopranos to their limits, it builds to a vocally demanding high E-flat - the fourth note from the end.

Incredulously, I asked her, "Are you planning to sing the whole song?"

"Yes," she replied, "why, can't you play it?"

"Of course I can," I said.

She was halfway to the stage when she hurriedly came back to me and said, "I forgot to tell you - when we get to the ending, transpose it down a third."

ABOUT THE AUTHOR

Donald Oliver is an author and composer. He has compiled
and edited the acclaimed collection of George S. Kaufman's
writings entitled *By George*, and *The Greatest Revue
Sketches*, a collection of fifty-seven short comic playlets
culled from Broadway's most famous revues. He began
writing musical comedies when he was in the eighth grade
and later collaborated on several original musicals, which
were produced at Tulane University. After graduation, he
returned to his native New York, became a member of Lehman
Engel's BMI workshop, and landed his first professional
stint as an audition pianist for the Broadway show *Molly*,
with Kaye Ballard. During the day, he taught music to
children at the Dalton School, and at night found time to
become artistic director of the Octagon Theatre Company
for which he coproduced well-received revivals of a number
of musicals, including *Drat! The Cat!*, *Zorba*, and
Knickerbocker Holiday. He was back on Broadway with the
Marilyn Chambers show *Le Bellybutton* and then became the
music coordinator for the Alpha Team project of The
American Dance Machine. Two of the happiest summers of
his life were spent playing the piano for the tours of
Gypsy, which starred Angela Lansbury. He was musical
director for an intimate revue presented at Lincoln Center
called *2* and conducted the music for the cast album of
that show. Three original children's musicals for which
he composed the music and coauthored the scripts have been
published by Chappell Music and are frequently performed
throughout the United States. Having studied at the
Manhattan School of Music, he continues to compose and has
written the scores for the musicals *Murder at the Vanities*
(book by James Kirkwood, lyrics by David Spencer) and *The
Case of the Dead Flamingo Dancer* (book and lyrics by Dan
Butler).

Understanding Second Language Learning Difficulties

Madeline E. Ehrman

SAGE Publications
International Educational and Professional Publisher
Thousand Oaks London New Delhi

For information address:

SAGE Publications, Inc.
2455 Teller Road
Thousand Oaks, California 91320
E-mail: order@sagepub.com

SAGE Publications Ltd.
6 Bonhill Street
London EC2A 4PU
United Kingdom

SAGE Publications India Pvt. Ltd.
M-32 Market
Greater Kailash I
New Delhi 110 048 India

Printed in the United States of America

Library of Congress Cataloging-in-Publication Data

Ehrman, Madeline Elizabeth.
    Understanding second language learning difficulties/author
Madeline E. Ehrman.
        p. cm.
    Includes bibliographical references and index.
    ISBN 0-7619-0190-6 (cloth: acid-free paper).—ISBN 0-7619-0191-4
(pbk.: acid-free paper)
    1. Second language acquisition.   2. Language and languages—Study
and teaching (Continuing education)   3. Learning disabilities.
4. Learning, Psychology of.   I. Title.
P118.2.E37   1996   96-9999
418—dc20

This book is printed on acid-free paper.

96 97 98 99 00 10 9 8 7 6 5 4 3 2 1

Production Editor: Michèle Lingre
Typesetter: Marion S. Warren
Cover Designer: Candice Harman

Contents

LIST OF BOXES

LIST OF FIGURES

LIST OF TABLES

Preface

Why I Wrote This Book

For the past 25 years, I have worked with adult foreign language learners at the Foreign Service Institute (FSI) in a variety of capacities: language training supervisor (leader of a team of teachers), department chair for the FSI Department of Asian and African Languages, curriculum and training specialist, and now as director of the FSI School of Language Studies Center for Research, Evaluation and Development. Under my leadership, my unit has recently begun to accept referrals of students in over 60 languages who are having learning difficulties.

In the course of all this work, I have come to realize that students are often referred when the teachers and supervisors are not able to look beyond the "presenting problem," for example, emotional outbursts or learning blocks, to find an underlying cause or set of causes. Often, the section is focused on its own methodology and view of the teaching process. Many times, my role is to listen to the student and then help the language section do the same. I then try to help both student and teachers see that there are many ways to reach the learning goal.

Many of the difficulties ultimately stem from mismatches of student learning styles or patterns of abilities and the section's teaching methodology. By the time the students reach me, however, the situation has usually become quite complex, with strong feelings on the part of student and teachers. The causes of the difficulties frequently are multiple, involving cognition, personalities, and feelings. I undertake to sort them out and then work with the student and the teachers.

Purpose

This book is intended to make available some of the insights, techniques, and skills I have developed to understand what is going on with adult students who are having difficulties with learning. My premise is that what appears on the surface is often not the real source of the learner's difficulty.

In writing this book and working with the cases in it, I will attempt to help the reader look at learner difficulties in a similar way to those that have worked for me and seek similar kinds of solution. A unifying theme is that teaching and other interventions should be student driven, not methodology driven. This means that it is important to understand students in all their diversity as well as learn to understand the methodologies by which we teach.

Who Can Use the Book

This work is usable by a range of people involved in the learning process: classroom teachers, teacher trainers, program administrators, consultants who may be called in to help, and students themselves, who may find material in this book that is useful to them in working with their own difficulties. It is, however, designed for use primarily by classroom teachers, so *you* ordinarily refers to teachers unless otherwise specified.

Because the material is aimed at classroom teachers primarily, it does not emphasize use of diagnostic instruments restricted to professionals or go deeply into such technical subjects as learning disabilities. Instead, it is intended to help teachers and others to distinguish between what they can deal with alone and what they need more help with—for example, further consultation or even referral of the student. Principles are illustrated throughout by case material.

Most of the material in the book can apply to subjects other than second language acquisition. After all, styles, personality, and feelings have an effect on most of the things we do, learning not least. Although the cases are drawn from the world of second- and foreign language learning, much of the discussion is relevant to other subjects and skills. I urge the reader to go through the material that follows from the point of view of appropriate adaptation by teachers and teacher trainers in other disciplines.

What the Book Is About

The emphasis is on diagnosis, in that this is the foundation on which effective interventions are designed. However, I include a number of suggestions throughout on addressing the difficulties that emerge from the diagnostic process.

My focus is on learning styles, affective factors, and learning strategies, because I have found that these have permitted me to diagnose the bulk of the learning difficulties I have encountered without getting into highly technical knowledge areas. (Chapter 11 addresses some situations that may be beyond the diagnostic tools I offer.)

The language learners discussed herein are all either late teenagers or adults. Most have reached the stage of "formal operations" (Piaget, 1967), in which they can handle abstract concepts. People usually reach this stage at adolescence.

Many of the students described here are learning foreign languages, and some are working on second languages, particularly English as a second language (ESL). For the most part, the issues with which the teacher must deal are the same, but when they are different, they are noted.

The book is addressed primarily to classroom teachers. Many suggestions and case descriptions are given as if each teacher can go into the needs of each student in depth. For some of you, this will be true. For others, however—for example the high school teacher with a student load of 150 students a day—such detailed treatment may be much less realistic.

For the latter, I hope you will take away some ideas that can be used for many of your students and will gain some help in working with 3 to 5 of your most difficult students, for whom a more in-depth treatment may be appropriate.

Multiple Theories and Models in the Book

Human beings are complex. No two are alike. Psychologists have devoted lifetimes to finding ways to describe some of the systematic differences among us and have come up with many different systems. All the systems are valuable, but they are not all equally applicable to a given person or situation at a given time. For student A, theory X may provide just the right information, whereas for A's classmate B, theory Y may be more explanatory today. In both cases, the alternate theory adds useful information that helps illuminate the dominant theory; in this case we can say that, for instance, in the case of student A, theory X is in the foreground, and theory Y is in the background, and vice versa for student B. In a few weeks, it may be theory Y that better helps us understand what is going on with student A and is thus in the foreground, whereas theory X, though still useful, is now in the background.

Because of this kind of complexity both between individuals at one time and between times for one individual, this book will present multiple theories and models of learning in Chapters 4, 5, and 6 and will adduce several of those models in each of the cases in Chapters 7 through 12. If you find the number of models confusing, choose one or two and keep your focus on them throughout the book. I recommend in particular, field independence-field sensitivity (Chapter 5), the psychological type model, and tolerance of ambiguity (Chapter 6).

Methodology

A variety of methodologies are described in this book. Students come from classes where a variety of approaches are used, some very current, and others more dated. It is not my intention to advocate or attack any methodology; instead, I aim to indicate that every approach matches some learners better than others. When a student is having difficulty, it is important to look at the match or mismatch between the prevailing methodology and the student.

Cases

Most of the cases represent real people or composites of actual individuals, but they all are real people who are typical of the students we meet. Names have been changed, as have important identifying details, to protect the privacy of those on whom cases are based. Biographical details are minimized to make the cases as universally applicable as possible.

Acknowledgments

This book represents the contributions of a multitude of colleagues and friends. High on the list is the Foreign Service Institute, its staff and students, from whom I have learned so much. My colleagues in Research Evaluation and Development have worked with me on much of the research that led to this book and with students who provided some of the cases, as well as providing much encouragement and useful critique. They are Lucinda Hart-Gonzalez, Christina Hoffman, Frederick Jackson, Anjum Khilji, Joselyn Pegues, Lydie Stefanopoulos, and Bob Wilson. Other FSI colleagues have also joined with us in thinking about languages and referred students whose difficulties are reflected in the cases; my work with these colleagues has helped shape my thinking about how languages are learned. Among them are Neire Johnson, Marsha Kaplan, Mary Kim, Beatrice Litt, Masako Nanto, James North, David Red, Maureen Riley, Gerd Ritchie, Sigrun Rockmaker, Joseph White, as well as the many other training supervisors and language instructors with whom I have worked as colleague, supervisor, trainer, or consultant. Former colleague Ann Welden, now with the United States Information Agency, has had an

The content of this book does not represent official policy of the U.S. Department of State; the opinions and observations are my own. Myers-Briggs Type Indicator® and MBTI® are registered trademarks of Consulting Psychologists Press, Inc., Palo Alto, California.

influence she will recognize in a number of places in this book, not least because of our sharing an atypical learning style.

I have worked with students in programs under my supervision, as research participants, as workshop members, and as clients in individual consultations. They have taught me at least as much about learning as I have imparted to them.

Rebecca Oxford of the University of Alabama—co-author and good friend—took a special role in this book: Its genesis was a conversation about the case material that each of us had and how it could be used. Rebecca has provided unfailing encouragement throughout the project and, just as valuable, insightful critique that made the book much better. A number of my ideas have been affected by the work we have done together over the past 10 years.

Mary Lee Scott (Brigham Young University) and Robert Sternberg (Yale University) provided encouragement and valuable critique, both much appreciated. The book benefited a great deal from Frederick Jackson's careful reading and his discussions with me about a number of points in it. Kara VanHooser Dodge, M.S., CCC-SLP, speech language pathologist, contributed very helpful comments on the sections treating learning disabilities.

Much of my thinking bears the influence of Earl Stevick, now retired from FSI. Earl began to inspire me to pursue my interest in the psychology of learning 20 years ago, and his sensible, humane approach continues to inform my work.

My work with Sage Publications has been greatly facilitated by editor Alex Schwartz and editorial assistant Nancy Hale. Alex had the intuition to guess that I might have "something for Sage" when I was enthusiastically inspecting the Sage display at a convention with a day-old outline of this book in my pocket, and he has been the source of good advice and much-appreciated encouragement ever since. Nancy has distinguished herself by her dependability and her excellent "people skills" that enhanced the review process.

Finally, without my mate, Bill Dodge, master of household logistics, gourmet cook, source of unfailing common sense, and on-the-spot drafts-man (Figure 6.4), this book would have been much longer in the making. Bill's willing efforts—from trips to copy shop and post office through grocery shopping and cooking to cat care—made it possible for me to devote my time away from the office to this project. To him I dedicate this book.

Introduction

What Is This Book For?

In this chapter, you meet a student, John, who is having difficulty. John will appear from time to time in later chapters as well, along with a number of other individuals who provide illustrative case material. In addition, the chapter introduces the importance of staying open to new information and revising interpretations to understand students.

Throughout the book, a recurring theme is that interpretations of our students' behavior are hypothetical, and our interviews, interventions, and analyses may support the hypotheses we make about the students, but they are seldom conclusive. Because this book is meant to be useful to a variety of people, there is a section suggesting some ways to use it.

1.1 Introducing *John*

John is a highly successful senior executive with considerable experience in taking over and solving problem situations. He was appointed to a responsible position that required substantial language proficiency in speaking and reading. John began his language study with a great deal of self-confidence and motivation. He says he has never encountered a problem for which he could not find a practical solution. After 6 weeks of language training, using a mix of communicative and more structured training to help prepare him for this position, he found out that his proposed assignment had been canceled. Despite the fact that his training has been difficult for him, he wishes to continue studying the language to go to another position in which the language is spoken, so he has remained in class.

After 8 weeks of language learning, John is still not making very good progress, and his classmates have begun to complain that he is holding them back. John himself has started to express concern that he will not achieve the level of language he needs for his professional purposes. You, as his teacher for the last month, are experiencing increasing frustration with his learning.

1.2 The Purpose of This Book

As John's teacher or training supervisor, you want to help him. Furthermore, John is not the only student who seems to be having difficulties in your classes, and no two students seem to be having the same difficulties. How can you better reach all of your students?

The first step is to *understand* as clearly as possible what is going on with John (and the other learners who are having difficulties). Only after you understand can you decide on what is the most effective thing to do for each student. When you decide on a course of action, of course, you will want to evaluate the success of the action: If it works, you will do it some more; if it does not work, you need to take another look and make some changes.

There are four basic steps in this process:

1. *Observation:* Observe and gather data.
2. *Hypothesis formation:* Make hypotheses—guesses about what you think is going on.
3. *Hypothesis testing:* Decide what to do based on your hypotheses and try it out.
4. *Evaluation:* Evaluate the success of your intervention:
   a. If it works: keep doing it;
   b. If it doesn't work, revise your action plan or even your working hypothesis.

This volume focuses on the first two steps. I will make reference to different kinds of action and to evaluation of your interventions throughout, but these will receive less emphasis because I cannot be in your classroom with you. Only you will have all the facts you need to make the right decision for each individual. This book is meant to give you some tools for observing and making guesses about what is happening, so you can make informed decisions, but they will have to be *your* decisions. As you read further—especially Chapters 4, 5, and 6, about learning styles and personality dispositions—the uncertainty about solutions to the problems posed by the learning difficulties may make some of you a little uncomfortable, whereas others may appreciate the freedom to make their own decisions.

What *won't* the book do for you? It will not give you *the answer* to your students' problems. It won't provide a "magic language pill." There are no prescriptions in this book, just a number of ideas to try out.

What *will* this volume do for you? I hope it will increase your awareness of learner variables and provide you with tools to understand what is happening in your classrooms. These tools then can serve as the base for designing more effective interventions with students having difficulties.

The following quote from Schön (1983) describes the process of "reflection-in-action" that this book is promoting. Although you are encouraged to become familiar with established categories, such as learning styles, and to make hypotheses to test, the hope is that you will achieve the kind of expert comfort with these processes that will permit you to combine your reflection and your implementation as described in the following:

> When someone reflects-in-action, he becomes a researcher in the practice context. He is not dependent on the categories of established theory and technique, but constructs a new theory of the unique case. His inquiry is not limited to a deliberation about means which depends on a prior agreement about ends. He does not keep means and ends separate, but defines them interactively as he frames a problematic situation. He does not separate thinking from doing, ratiocinating his way to a decision which he must later convert into action. Because his experimenting is a kind of action, implementation is built into his inquiry. (p. 68)

1.3 Using This Book

Sequence of Reading. Just as people learn in different ways, so people use a reference in different ways. This book is written with the assumption that you are reading it from beginning to end. You do not, however, need to read it sequentially. Some of you may want to read it straight through. This is a good way to become very familiar with everything in it. Others may choose to use it to address a specific problem. For you, chapter headings, the index of cases, and the topic index will be good starting points. Some of you may find one of the topics of special interest; you may wish either to skim the Contents or to flip casually through and see what catches your eye. If you want some of the background material you may have missed in a nonsequential approach, you can always go back to it, using cross-references, the Contents, and the topic index.

The Cases. You will probably get the most out of the cases if you think about them and try to answer the questions provided with some of them before you read the discussion. This is a way for you to have a kind of dialogue with the book as you use it. (If you wish to discuss cases with me in a more interactive way, you can write to me care of the publisher.)

Cases are presented in a variety of ways: Some of them are in the first person, some are excerpts from interviews, some are taken from a teacher's or counselor's case notes, and some are descriptions. This apparent inconsistency is deliberate: You will gather data in multiple formats; in this book, you get a little practice in using your diagnostic skills in similar formats.

Use for Training. Some of you may have teacher training responsibilities. Many of the cases in this book have served me well in my teacher development work. The cases—and the material they illustrate—may be helpful to you in the same way. I suggest that you permit trainees to talk about the cases in small groups before you process the material with them. If you provide only the case material and the questions first, the trainees will have the opportunity to try out their own ideas before they get such answers or hints as may be included in the discussion.

Use by Students. Some of your students may find this book helpful. They will probably enjoy figuring out what kinds of learner they and their classmates are. That kind of diagnosis can be the basis for work with them to help them seek some of their own solutions. They might also benefit from discussions of some of the case material, both as a means to help them understand themselves better (and try some self-prescription) and as a means to work more effectively with their classmates.

1.4 More About John

In the course of class activities and after a short interview with John, you get the following information:

John has never learned a foreign language before. As a child, he had some problems with stuttering and received considerable training and attention from specialists for it. Today, his speech shows no sign of a stutter.

The first 2 weeks of training, John was in a class where students had a variety of language learning abilities. From the start, it was apparent that he had considerable trouble with listening comprehension and pronunciation and was trailing his classmates. Following the second week, for logistic reasons he was moved into a class with two students younger than he. His new classmates take a more leisurely approach to their study than his previous class. John was upset by the change and wanted to remain with his previous classmates. He believed that he should be in class along with the "best and brightest" students, as well as people in more senior positions, so he could be stimulated and challenged as well as associate with those closer in occupation.

When the curriculum follows the textbook closely, John works steadily and systematically. He readily performs the drills and exercises that fill the text. When asked to participate in more free-form activities such as storytelling or roleplays, John grumbles and stumbles.

John asked to be returned to his original class and was counseled that he would do better in a class that moved ahead at a less pressured pace, so that he could get a solid base in the language on which to build as he continued to progress. He went along with this advice and continues to work in the slower-moving class, but he socializes actively during the breaks and outside class with his previous classmates. He thinks his current classmates are overly laid back and do not take their language learning seriously.

What are your guesses about what is going on with John?
What is your evidence for the guesses?
What are the assets you see in John that you can use to work with him?
What are his weak areas?
What more would you like to know about him?

This set of questions will serve you well as you read the case material in the rest of the book and as you work with your students.

1.5 Multiple Hypotheses: A Beginning

John may seem fairly typical of some of your adult students. He certainly seems to be motivated to succeed, and he is persistent. He is not an experienced language learner—one of the things you may want to know is when he last was in a classroom as a student. He certainly does not seem to have the learning strategies more experienced learners usually develop. He may also be having some difficulty adjusting to the role of student, in which he perceives the power balance as in the teacher's favor. This may be especially hard for him, because, as a senior executive, he is used to being in charge. His behavior out of class suggests that his self-perception as effective and competent is involved in some way. It must be very difficult for someone who describes himself as never having failed to solve a problem to run up against something he cannot conquer by force of effort and will.

John has a fairly clear preference for certain kinds of learning activity. These preferences are strong enough that they can probably be called a *learning style*. He is sufficiently uncomfortable with certain other kinds of activities that they may interfere with his ability to learn.

So just a little information is already providing some hypotheses about John. All of them have some probable validity, and as you, the teacher, investigate further, you will need to keep all of them in mind.

The following are areas of further investigation for John's teacher and are presented more systematically by category. Included in the categories are the corresponding chapters in which they are addressed:

Background: Age, previous learning experience, previous life experience, and more are looked at in Chapter 8.

Feelings: Motivation, self-efficacy, anxiety, feelings about the role as a student, and so forth are addressed in Chapter 7.

Learning strategies: How does the student go about the learning task, planning, evaluating self, building associations and other "deep" processing strategies, maximizing assets, and so forth? Learning strategies are referenced in Chapters 2 and 3. Strategies will also come up in Chapters 4 through 8.

Learning style: What preference does the student have for certain ways of learning and discomfort with, or interference from, other ways? Chapters 4 through 6 treat this topic fairly intensively.

1.6 The Rest of the Book

Chapters 2 and 3 address techniques for data collection available to any teacher: observation and interviewing. These are important techniques for getting answers to questions such as those that were asked above about John. I discuss these first because good data are the foundation of accurate diagnosis. (If you are eager to get to the diagnostic categories, you can skim these two chapters and move on to Chapter 4, of course.)

Surveys and questionnaires are not addressed until Chapter 9 for two reasons: (a) because I hope to enable you to operate independently of instrumentation (tests and surveys) or at least to be able to use paper-and-pencil instruments with appropriate skepticism, and (b) so that practice activities using multiple assessment instruments selected from those described in earlier chapters can be combined in cases that illustrate the use of such instruments together.

Chapters 4 through 8 address various categories of influence on learning: learning styles, feelings, biographic background data, and learning strategies. They are organized in roughly the order of value I have found in my work with students: That is, I have found that the most frequent cause of learning difficulty is mismatch of learning style and teaching style.

Chapters 4, 5, and 6 address the kinds of preferences—sometimes rigidities—that tend to affect the choices that are made in learning (and teaching) techniques and the degree of openness students have toward new material. Chapter 4 treats common cognitive styles: sequential random, concrete-abstract, deductive-inductive, and the "left-right hemisphere" metaphor that is widely used in the language learning literature. Chapter 5 is devoted to the field independence construct, which I have rendered as two parallel scales and used to generate a typology that informs the content of the following chapters. In Chapter 6, I offer a model of learning that uses personality dispositions as the foundation for learning styles and learning strategy choices.

Each of these three chapters (4-6) also describes instruments that are used to assess the learning style dimensions discussed in the chapters. I strongly recommend that you also read the portions of Chapter 9 on general principles of using data from surveys, tests, and questionnaires and work with the cases in that chapter before using these instruments.

Chapter 7 is about the feelings students bring to their learning. Feelings pervade every aspect of learning and teaching. We will look at motivation, self-efficacy, and some of the negative feelings that can interfere with learning. I also say a little about the teacher's feelings, because they also have an effect on the interaction between teacher and student.

Chapter 8 adds biographical background information to the mix. Learning strategies and study skills are also addressed in this chapter. Learning strategies are introduced after learning styles, because learning styles frequently are the basis for choice of specific learning techniques: Some learning strategies are much more comfortable for individuals with one style than for those with another.

Up to this point, the sources of information have been mostly available to any teacher. In Chapter 9, I treat principles of using the questionnaires and diagnostic tests that some of you may have access to and provide some suggestions on how to use such data. Discussions of aptitude, achievement, and proficiency testing are also to be found in this chapter. A number of cases illustrate use of survey information.

Chapter 10 provides an opportunity to practice with more complex cases, in which multiple hypotheses are needed, things are not always what they seem to be, and the context plays a role.

Few of you will be able to help in all the cases you encounter. Chapter 11 addresses some situations in which you will probably need some outside assistance, including learning disabilities, psychological disorders, and extreme affective reactions.

Chapter 12, on the other hand, suggests some things you *can* do for yourself, ranging from helping students with certain kinds of learning strategies to managing your own feelings and expectations of yourself.

John is only the first of many cases to come. To help you track the many personalities you will meet, there is an index of cases at the end of the book.

1.7 Practice

In preparation for reading the rest of this book, think of one or two students whose needs you have had particular difficulty meeting. Make a few initial hypotheses about what is going on with them. As you read further, keep them in mind.

Direct Data Collection

Observation

This chapter begins a pair of chapters that address direct data collection. To make and test hypotheses, it is important to know what is actually going on. Among the most common ways to do this are observation, which can be done with or without a student's knowledge, and interviewing, which brings the student in as a direct collaborator. (Data gathering by surveys and tests is treated in Chapter 9.)

The key to successful observation is managing your attention. This chapter addresses how to decide what to look at. *Sensitizing concepts* are the categories that determine what we look for and what we notice (selective attention). These frames of reference are the filters that may affect what is noticed. This chapter provides some guidelines for understanding your frame of reference and establishing your sensitizing concepts.

2.1 Collecting Information

This chapter begins a set of chapters that address all the different ways to get information about your students— observation (this chapter), interviews (Chapter 3), and formal instrumentation such as question-naires and psychological tests (Chapter 9)— have drawbacks, and all have certain advantages. Your best information will come from multiple sources.

You will probably find that one or another source is especially com-fortable for you to use, or you may develop a level of special skill in one or more. As you gain confidence in one or more tools, you may explore and practice use of others. For instance, I am finding the subscale scores of the Modern Language Aptitude Test (see Chapter 9) increasingly helpful as I use them to generate and test hypotheses, along with other questionnaires, interviews, and observation. This is a relatively new element in my repertoire of diagnostic tools.

Another point of variation in use of multiple sources of information is that the key to understanding a given student is likely to come from a source that is different from the previous case. So, for instance, something a student said in an interview may be just what you need to pull together all the other data about him or her. Or a score on a subscale of a questionnaire may be precisely the right clue to solve the puzzle of the student's behavior, interview data, and other test scores. When this happened to me not too long ago, it provided the crucial factor in building the model of tolerance of ambiguity that is described in Chapter 6.

2.2 Signs of Trouble: *Sandy*

Sandy is one of two students in trouble in her language class. You and another teacher both work with her in class and outside of class in specially arranged help sessions. You have been increasingly con-cerned about Sandy. When she first started class, she made average progress and seemed to be fairly comfortable with the learning process, though she appeared somewhat tense. Over the past weeks, however, you can hardly miss the tears and angry outbursts, especially in that some of them are directed at you. Sandy is now talking about how she hates this city and wants to be anywhere else. Her performance is deteriorating far below what you think she is capable of doing.

How do you know there is trouble to be dealt with? Sometimes a student will come and ask for help directly, but more often than not, you notice something in the student's behavior indicating a difficulty of which the student may be unaware. What you notice may be as blatant as Sandy's emotional outbursts or as subtle as avoidance behavior when a certain kind of topic or grammatical construction comes up. You may see overuse or underuse of certain learning strategies (learning techniques) or patterns of failure, such as inappropriate use of new vocabulary that seems to represent unthinking translation from the student's native language.

Sometimes the content of what you hear may give you a cue that something is wrong: For instance, an immigrant in an ESL (English as a Second Language) class may suddenly begin to express bitterness about the United States that you had not heard before. In such a case, something is probably going on in the student's life outside your classroom. On the other hand, one of your working hypotheses could also be that the ESL class in some way is representing an assault on the student's self-esteem. A common way to deal with hurt and angry feelings is "displacement," in which the anger is expressed at someone or something else other than the real target, if the real target is very important to one. It is possible that you and the ESL class are too important to the student for whatever reason (this will differ from person to person) for him or her to attack directly. (You will find more discussion of this kind of defense mechanism in Chapter 7.)

2.3 Doing Observation

Countless teacher trainers, anthropologists, and program evaluators have written innumerable books on the subject of observation skills. Some of the references cited in this chapter and at the end provide you much more detail on this subject. The following is an overview designed to help you understand individuals such as Sandy, John (Chapter 1), and other students you will meet in this book.

You may be asking, "Why do I have to know all this methodological stuff, anyway?" Much of the time, you can probably do without it. As you read on in this chapter and the next, however, you may find that you are already doing a lot of what is described, so that what you may pick up are tips and tricks that will help you do even better. Also, if you gain at least a passing familiarity with the approaches described below, they may be available to you when you need them, and the habits of thinking involved may eventually become automatic. Finally, the most important reason for paying some attention to how you collect information is that your information will be more accurate and trustworthy, so your interventions will work better and will therefore repay the time invested.

You may also say, "I have 100 students to look after. I can't do this!" Indeed you cannot—not for all 100. You do not need to do everything I describe for all your students: Careful data collection is needed primarily for your very few most challenging students, but some of the techniques can be used for less detailed, informal observation as well.

2.3.1 About the Nature of the Observation Process

The concepts in the paragraphs that follow are presented in the context of observation. Most of them, however, apply well to interviewing and to interpreting questionnaires.

Selective Attention. Human observation is limited by the fact that it is impossible to take in everything, so attention must be selective. We tend to pay attention to what is important to us. If we have just bought a car or are planning to buy one, we are likely to notice the cars that others drive. On the other hand, we may not notice what a student is wearing today because clothing is not currently of interest to us. This fact can cause trouble if we miss important data. We can also put it to use, by using it as a way to make sure important things get noticed. A useful notion is the *sensitizing concept* (Patton, 1980, p. 137). This term refers to large ranges of observation, not necessarily specific behaviors. For instance, a sensitizing concept useful to a teacher trying to understand a student having difficulty might be social interaction patterns; another might be kinds of errors made (e.g., syntactic, semantic, pronunciation, discourse, etc.). As questions, these could be, "How does Jeff interact with others, for example, classmates, friends, teachers, native speakers of the target language?" or, "In what domain does Jane have difficulty with speaking the new language?" This would be different from, "What are Jane's mistakes?" which would focus only on a specific behavior. We may be particularly aware of learning strategies or age or learning style, for example. At different times for each of us, different categories of information may come into the foreground and constitute the current sensitizing concepts.

What's Important? Sensitizing concepts help determine what is important. Only a short period of intent observation, in which one tries to track every word, body movement, social interaction, and so forth will be enough to show the novice that there is too much to take in. All of us need some way to separate the useful from the trivial. Major areas of observation such as those framed by sensitizing concepts help us limit what we make ourselves responsible for. So do our working hypotheses; indeed, working hypotheses help us select which sensitizing concepts to use for an intentional observation. For example, for Sandy, we might want to look at evidence for the effects of class events on her feelings. We would probably be watching for information on the effectiveness of John's study strategies, and so on. Needless to say, we can be alert to more than one sensitizing concept area at once.

Objectivity. The literature on doing fieldwork or observation for program evaluation addresses the difference between observation as a participant in the action versus observation from outside. This concept is important because it may impact how deeply you can understand the student. People using this book will play different organizational roles that will affect how much it is appropriate for them to participate in the teaching-learning process. The most participatory observer is the student; if you are a student using this book, you will have innumerable opportunities to observe yourself, and you will be the closest of all to what your experiences mean to you. If you are a teacher, you will participate in the process more than trainers, administrators, or consultants and will have access to more data than they do. (Direct participation or closeness to the process is, of course, both an advantage because of the richness of the data and also a drawback because the job of discriminating the important from the trivial is much more complex.)

Effects of Observation on Observed Behavior. In any form, the act of observation (or of other forms of data gathering) will itself have an effect on the teaching and learning process. In the physical sciences, this phenomenon is called the "observer's paradox"; that is, the act of measurement changes what is being measured. This is certainly true in the kinds of information collection you need to do to form and test hypotheses. Nonparticipant observers, especially those without an ongoing relationship with students, may bring about so much self-consciousness that behavior of both students and teachers changes from the usual, especially at first. (Once they get used to you—or a tape recorder—they may revert to more usual behavior over time.) On the other hand, if you have an ongoing relationship with students, you may be able to do a considerable amount of observation as you undertake other activities without seriously disrupting routine behavior. However, you can be almost certain that if you are paying attention to certain categories of behavior, your own behavior will probably change in subtle ways, and your students will take heed of this, with concomitant effects on their behavior (they are likely to notice and react subliminally). Knowing that this will happen—it is inevitable—the trick is not to prevent it but to keep an eye on these effects and take them into account when you make interpretations.

Your Frame of Reference. In a related vein, what you know and how you think about things can be both unhelpful and helpful. Your previous experience and your interpretations of it can get in the way of your perceptions; they may not let you even notice something important, let alone interpret it in a new way that makes sense of your problem. This is a danger that is best handled by questioning your assumptions as much as you can. Getting an outside skeptic to serve as a constructive critic can be very helpful, even if not always comfortable.

On the other hand, what you know can also be a major asset. The more you know, the more possibilities you have to make associations— "Oh say, that reminds me of when . . ." Agatha Christie's detective character Miss Marple is an elderly woman who solved mysteries by associating the behavior of the characters she met in the course of the story with that of the varied people she knew in her home village over her long lifetime. She is a good example of someone who made maximum use of her experience to make the associations that helped her solve homicide cases. It worked for her; something similar can help you.

Similarly, you probably have an operating framework that you use to interpret what you experience. This is a kind of theory of how things work. Courses in psychology and organizational behavior widely cite the psychologist Kurt Lewin, who said that there is nothing so practical as a good theory. This is because a theory provides the basis for the hypotheses we test daily to make sense of our lives; it gives us a frame of reference. Observations benefit from a good theory because it provides a starting point and a way to check if we are on track. For example, Miss Marple operated on a theory that there are finite categories of human nature, and that most of them will show up in ordinary village life. To be maximally effective, of course, she also had to stay open to the possibility that there were some kinds of people who were outside her experience and add those patterns to her repertoire when she met up with them. That is, she had to be able to change her theory. You will find yourself doing this too, when too many of the hypotheses your theory generates do not hold up.

2.3.2 Taking Notes and Keeping Records

Why Keep a Record? In addition to selective attention, effect of observation on what is observed and personal frame of reference as described above, there is one other important threat to the integrity of your data. That is the fallibility of human memory. Countless experiments in psychology show how important material is lost or revised in memory over time. One important way to minimize such effects is to make a record of your observations. (The same applies to interviews, which can be seen as a special form of observation.)

When to Take Notes. Circumstances such as the relationship between you and the student and the amount of other activity going on affect when you make your notes. Your own personal style may also play a role here. When possible, I prefer to take notes on the spot. Others are less comfortable with this. It is frequently inappropriate to take notes—they may be intrusive for students, teachers, interviewees. If I am participating myself, I may not have time to do more than jot down a word or two to remind me of something I want to remember. When I do make notes on the spot, especially when interviewing, I bring up the subject at the beginning, saying that I take notes as we talk to help my memory and asking for their permission, which is usually—but not always—granted. When I take notes during an interview, I try to take down almost everything so the interviewee will not need to wonder why anything was selected as especially important and become more self-conscious.

In most cases, you will make your records after the opportunity for observation is over. Even if you make notes at the same time as an observation or interview, it is a good idea to review, refine, and fill them in. Do this as soon as possible, while your memory is fresh.

What Should Be Included in Your Notes? Here is where your sensitizing concepts (see 2.3.1. above), the hypotheses you are testing, and your goals play a vital role. You cannot take down everything, so these will help you select. It is also important to make note of anomalies and unexpected events. For example, if the student is usually talkative but goes silent suddenly, what took place just before that? If you are trying to cope with a very heavy teaching load, try to get at least the main points, even if you do not have time for much detail.

Fact Versus Interpretation. Your notes should be as concrete as possible. Patton (1980) provides examples of inappropriate and appropriate levels of description. One of his examples is adapted as follows:

(a) The student was quite uneasy waiting for the placement interview.

This is contrasted with the following:

(b) At first the student sat very stiffly on the chair. She picked up a magazine and let the pages flutter through her fingers very quickly without looking at any of the pages. She set the magazine down, looked at her watch, pulled her skirt down, and picked up the magazine again. This time she didn't look at the magazine [and so on.]. (p. 161)

Statement *a* differs from statement *b* in important ways. First, *a* is vague and general. Even more important, it represents an *interpretation* of the data. Statement *b* simply provides data.

Ordinarily, you will not need this level of detail, which is characteristic of careful ethnography. At a more everyday level, you might use a statement such as, "At first she sat stiffly, handled a variety of objects briefly, pulled her skirt down . . ." This statement is still a series of observations. Indeed, the amount of specificity in statement *b* could get in the way of your seeing patterns of behavior. The point of this example is to show the difference between inference and observation, and it is important that you be able to distinguish between the two. You will often need to back up your inferences with observations and facts; if you have the facts, you can change your inferences when they do not work.

Although some interpretation is inherent in the selection of what to report in statement *b*, the level of interpretation is far, far less than in statement *a*. Interpretative terms also may imply a frame of reference or value system not shared by others who could interpret the data differently. If I say, "He's a good student," you could interpret this as meaning he gets good grades on tests. Someone else might hear that the student is enthusiastic about learning my subject, or that he is compliant and cooperates well with me. Any of these descriptions is better than "good student."

Records. Keep backup copies! If your records are handwritten or typed, make photocopies. If you use a computer, keep copies on floppy disks, in hard copy (printouts), and even on multiple computers. For extra thoroughness and ease in retrieval, you can make a face sheet for each file that gives such information as the student's name, class, biographic information, areas of difficulty, and main findings of interest. Again, if you work under pressure, select the most important material—you do not have to get everything.

2.3.3 What To Look for and Record: A Starter List

Some of the following categories can provide you with sensitizing concepts that will help organize your observations:

1. *The physical setting:* We often take this for granted, but it may have an effect on what's going on with a student. A fairly common case in point is noise level. Some students may find noise distracting; others may find it facilitating. Older students may have hearing loss. What looks like a cognitive difficulty may be just that they can't hear what's being said.

2. *The social setting:* How does the student relate socially? Is he or she a member of a stigmatized group? Who talks to whom? Is the student in the communication flow? Does he or she study with others? Do your students form groups by gender, ethnic group, occupation?

3. *Roles:* What role does the student play in helping make decisions about the way learning goes? How is this role determined—student's own choice, your choice, or institutional structure? How does the student interact in general with peers, with authority?

4. *Activities:* What are the activities to which the student must react? In language class, these might include drilling, structured practice, guided conversation, language experience activities, or work with authentic materials. These provide a good opportunity to notice learning strategies the student uses. (I will say more about learning strategies in Chapter 8.)

5. *What happens in informal settings:* There is likely to be very great richness in the data during breaks, at parties, or on field trips. The downside is that there is a lot more to sort out. The positive side is that you have a chance to observe the choices the student makes for him-or herself about what to do and what to say and to whom. The observations about John's desire to interact with more senior students came from what his teacher saw him do during breaks. These observations provided the basis for an inference about some effects on his self-esteem in his language class.

Specific Observation Foci

As you work with each student and develop your own methods, you will change and add to the following list of what to observe in class and in interviews. This list is intended to give you a start.

Student Behavior

— What did the student do or say? What was going on when it happened?
— What words does the student often use? Do these words (and speech mannerisms) also show up when she or he is speaking his or her native language?
— Are there any telling nonverbal behaviors? For instance, when a student is corrected, what do you see him or her do? What happens when another student is speaking?
— How does the student go about performing learning tasks? For instance, is the student slow, deliberate, and careful, or are tasks done hastily? What happens if I ask students to close their books? What kinds of notes does the student take, and when?

Teacher Behavior

— What was I doing when it happened?
— How did I react to it?
— What was the effect of my reaction?

Teacher Assumptions

— Are my beliefs about how people learn (languages especially) interfering with my ability to see what is going on?
— Is there another way to interpret what is happening other than the one I am using? (A *yes* answer might open the way to seeing things that have suffered from selective inattention.)

Indirect Cues

— What can I see in the environment or in the things that express information about the student? For instance, the kinds of native language recreational reading materials the student brings to class may suggest something interesting.
— What's *not* happening that might otherwise be expected? (This is something similar to the admonitions of drawing instructors to look at the white spaces as part of the structure of a visual image.) A simple example might be that an apparently motivated student is not doing the homework.

Introspection and use of your intuition is an important source of information. The guesses you make about a student without being entirely sure where they came from are usually based on subliminal observation and information synthesis. So you can use yourself as a source of observational data about the student, as well as observing your own behavior. The following are some starter questions that may trigger some intuitions for you? (Go with the things that flash into your mind.)

— What's different about this student from what I'm used to? What surprises me about him or her?
— How do I feel when I'm with the student? How do I feel when the student does *X* or says *Y*? What does it remind me of in my experience?
— If I were this student, how would I react?

2.4 Making Initial Hypotheses and Testing Them

Let's return to Sandy, who has started having such a hard time. Make some initial guesses about what may be going on with her. Using the categories above in Section 2.3.3, list some of the things you would look for when you next observe Sandy. What would you want to ask her?

Keep these three lists (your initial hypotheses about what is going on with her, what you would like to observe, and what you would like to find out in an interview with her). We shall return to Sandy from time to time.

2.5 Practice

The following are some exercises you can use to begin sharpening your observation skills (1-3 are adapted from Patton, 1980, p. 139).

1. Write a description of a setting or a short event. Have another person read it. Ask if the other person can visualize it. What more would the other person like to know about it?

2. Write a description of a setting or a short event and ask someone else to write about the same thing. Exchange descriptions. What did you notice or describe that the other person did not? What did they notice or describe that you did not?

3. Return to the paired descriptions in exercise 2 or write new ones with a partner. How many interpretive adjectives did each of you use (see Section 2.3.2 on description and will interpretation, above)? Try rewriting your description so it has only facts, no interpretation.

4. Briefly describe how you think people learn, especially how they learn languages. Compare notes with someone else, preferably someone you know thinks differently from you. What assumptions are you making that may interfere with your clarity of understanding of what you experience with your students?

5. Ask someone whom you believe to be a skilled observer to visit your class or observe you in some other activity. Ask for their feedback (in writing, if possible, so you can review it more than once and to avoid overburdening your memory). How do they handle the distinction between fact and inference? What kinds of things did they choose as their "sensitizing concepts?" What aspect of what they told you seemed in accord with your experience of yourself? What was incongruent? What surprised you? What will you do with the surprising material?

2.6 More Information and Activities

Ruth Wajnryb (1992) has compiled a set of classroom-focused obser-vation tasks addressing a range of highly relevant topics: the learner, the language used in the classroom, how learning takes place, lesson material, teaching strategies, classroom management, and materials. For further practice in observation skills, use this excellent book. Parrott (1993) in his book of activities also includes observational tasks, though this is not that work's main focus. If you are especially interested in the nature of the interactions in your classroom, refer to Malamah-Thomas (1987) which is made up of a variety of tasks, many of them centered on sharpening observations.

Additional tasks are provided in Allright (1988). This book is heavily oriented toward teacher training in general and toward classroom research of rather formal sort. Very detailed classroom observation models are provided in Allright and Bailey. They are intended more for teacher development and classroom-based research than for solving individual learning problems, but they may provide ideas that you can use as you do your detective work. To put the kinds of observation of yourself and your students into a wider context, refer to the material on reflective teaching in Richards and Nunan's (1990).

Direct Data Collection

Interviewing Students

This is the second of two chapters on data collection, and it addresses techniques for interviewing students, both formally and informally. (General principles of gathering information through surveys will be treated in Chapter 9, together with cases that illustrate use of multiple tests and questionnaires described in intervening chapters.) A key to getting good information is to listen well, both because you hear what is being said (and sometimes what is not being said directly) and because good listening encourages your interlocutor to keep giving you more information. This chapter, therefore, treats not only what to ask and listen for but also how to listen to it and let the student know you understand what you have heard. Most of the techniques in this chapter can be used for 5-minute interactions in the corridor as well as for more formal hour-long counseling sessions.

3.1 About Interviewing

Here is more detail from one of Sandy's teachers:

I am very concerned about Sandy. She seems quite depressed and distressed. The day before yesterday she came in and banged her fist on the table and then started to cry. She cried for nearly 2 hours and said she hates this language. I spent most of the time trying to calm her. Yesterday she was also tense and made some very sharp comments to me that I thought were rude. During one of our teaching activities—vocabulary practice—she burst out crying when there was a mention of parents and also remarked that marriage was a depressing issue.

Last week, when there was an unexpected change in the class schedule, she lost her temper and was very uncooperative during our special (remedial) class. However, every time she is upset, she says it is her "own stuff" that has "messed her up." I am reluctant to interact with her on any level. I don't even say "how are you?" any more, so she won't erupt. If she does not want to do anything, I just skip it. It is hard to have an agenda for the class since it has become hard to predict how she is going to react. The times when I try to explain something, she frowns, kicks her feet around, and says that if she wants an explanation, she will ask for one. I keep urging her to listen to the tapes, but she doesn't do it.

The above passage contains some observations of Sandy's behavior. The description is relatively free of interpretive words, though there are some (where are they?). It is not perfect—this is not a research document but rather the kind of statement an observant and caring teacher might make.

What are your hypotheses about what is going on with Sandy now that you have a little more information? If you were going to interview her later today, what are some of the things you would want to find out from her? How do you think you would begin the interview to put Sandy at ease? (In answering questions such as this, I suggest that you put yourself in the role you are most likely to play in your real life, such as teacher, teacher trainer, outside consultant, administrator, etc.)

3.1.1 Why Interview?

There is a great deal to be learned by careful observation. As we have seen, however, it is unwise to assume interpretations of the observed behavior. Interpersonal training teaches fledgling counselors and trainers to check out the meaning of behavior by asking questions such as, "When you banged your fist on the table, I felt startled and wondered if you were angry." This kind of question might seem silly—a third person might say, "Of course she was angry!" On the other hand, you might hear directly from the fist-banger, "I saw a bug and was startled. I'm afraid of insects, so I hit it." Knowing what is on a person's mind allows us to take an appropriate course of action ourselves.

Checking out, for example, what someone is thinking is a form of interviewing. You probably do short interviews all the time to check things out, to find out what happened when homework was not done. You probably do such interviews very well (but you still might pick up some ideas from this chapter). When you are working with a student having difficulties, though, you may decide that you want to do a more extended form of interviewing. The interview may last anywhere from 5 minutes to a couple of hours, depending on the complexity of the content, the rapport you and the interviewee build, and the available time.

3.1.2 What Do We Want to Learn From Interviewing?

Certainly, an important goal for an interview is to test our own hypotheses that we have made about a student. To put together a complete picture of what is going on with the student, though, it is vital to learn how the world looks to him or her, without reference to our guesses. To understand what is going on with Sandy when she has an outburst, it would be helpful to hear from her how *she* interpreted the event that triggered it.

> In order to capture participants "in their own terms" one must learn their categories for rendering explicable and coherent the flux of raw reality. That, indeed, is the first principle of qualitative analysis. (Lofland, 1971, quoted in Patton, 1989, p. 28)
>
> Direct quotations are a basic source of raw data in qualitative measurement, revealing respondents' level of emotion, the ways in which they have organized their world, their thoughts about what is happening, their experiences, and their basic perceptions. (Patton, 1980, p. 28)

An interview is a *negotiation of meaning* between you and the interviewee. Each of you comes from a different world, both in your backgrounds and in your immediate roles. As the interviewer, it is your responsibility to enter the world of the interviewee as much as he or she will let you. Part of the art of interviewing is to make it easy for the other person to "let you in" to his or her world—this is the role of building rapport. Indeed, one of the reasons for doing an interview is to build rapport that might not come from the other data collection techniques.

3.1.3 Interview Types

In his classic work on qualitative research, Patton (1980) lists three interview types:

1. The informal conversational interview
2. The general interview guide approach (semi-structured)
3. The standardized open-ended interview (structured) (p. 197)

You will probably do much of your interviewing in the first format, perhaps some in the second. You will probably do relatively little structured, standardized interviewing unless you are participating in a formal research or evaluation project or you have responsibilities for student placement.

Informal Conversational Interviewing. Interviews of the first sort are often spontaneous (or look that way); the interviewee may not even be aware that an interview is taking place. When I was a supervisor of language training programs, many of my most effective formative evaluation sessions took place in the hallway, with both of us leaning against the wall and carrying on an informal conversation. I often had sought the student out, but the interaction looked spontaneous, and I began with either a small point of business or a general, "How's it going?" Listening skills and the student's desire to unburden himself or herself permitted the interaction to move into substance. You can use informal conversations outside of class as opportunities for this kind of data gathering. The trick to such an interview is to maintain a conversational relationship and at the same time get information you want.

General Interview Guide Approach. When a student is in difficulty, and I am asked to work with him or her, it is more usual that I will have a more formal interview. Likewise, a classroom teacher or a supervisor can request a meeting. In this case, I would be more likely to use a semistructured interview, in which there are issues that I intend to address with the interviewee, though they may not come up in any particular order. For most interviews, there is a common set of topics I cover, and in addition there are usually specific topics related to the student's difficulties. (You will find more about interview content below, in Section 3.4.) The relationship can be largely conversational within the issues of your interview guide, but because the topic has been preset and the roles are specified (interviewer and interviewee), there may be somewhat less spontaneity, and you may have to work harder to build rapport. (In the informal interview, rapport is frequently an existing condition that enables the conversation to continue.) An interview guide need not be written down—it can be a mental list in your head.

Techniques for Successful Interviewing. There are a number of important features to this process of building rapport and getting the information you want. Your introduction of yourself and your purpose, your listening skills—including your ability to listen without preconception or evaluation— and your cognitive skills of finding threads of meaning worth following up—are among these.

3.2 Some Elements of Interviewing Technique

In this section, I describe basics of interviewing—getting started and using active listening to establish rapport and elicit information.

3.2.1 Introducing the Interview

Your introduction of yourself and the consultation process is critical to working effectively with your "client." Errors and missteps can be repaired, but it takes time and effort; it is much better if you can get the interview and its concomitant rapport-building off to a good start. On the other hand, this does not mean that there is only one way to do it—as in so many other forms of human relations, each of us has a personal style that can serve us well if we use it judiciously and flexibly.

How you introduce yourself and the interview depends on your role with respect to the student. If you are the student's teacher, you will probably find it easier to engage in informal interviewing than will people in other roles. You and the student will probably have so much shared context that you can move fairly directly into the topic of interest to you without a great deal of preamble. For instance, you might lead into an inquiry about the student's background with something similar to, "Say, I was curious about your experience with other languages."

In a more formal interview situation, if you and the student do not know each other, you will need to introduce yourself and let the student know why you are asking for the interview. (If the student has asked for the interview, you have a golden lead-in: "I'd like to be of assistance. Please tell me why you are here.") I sometimes use this moment as an opportunity to establish my credentials—and by this I mean only something as simple as, "I was a language training supervisor for many years and am familiar with the kind of program you're in now," not a recitation of my academic qualifications and publication record. (If a student asks for more information about that kind of thing, I give the briefest possible answer.)

Depending on how the student comes across, I may engage in a little small talk, but even the small talk is aimed at getting at the purposes of the interview. Questions such as "How long have you been in this city/program?" are naturals for ESL; for foreign language learners, I may ask about the anticipated overseas assignment or where the interviewee has been. Some students make it clear that they would like to get down to business, and with them I do so more quickly. Some are so chatty that the interview begins seamlessly from the small talk phase.

If I previously collected information in questionnaires, I may walk through the instruments and the scores with the student before the interview, or I may do an open-ended interview before we look at the questionnaires together. Again, this depends on the purpose of the interview and the interaction style of the interviewee and may be decided on the spot. If I am working with a written interview guide, I usually give a copy to the interviewee. This helps both of us make sure that the relevant topics get addressed.

It is very important to address confidentiality. For research and counseling purposes, I assure students that nothing will leave my office and my records without their permission. When doing interviewing for organizational purposes, I ask interviewees for permission to attribute or quote them in my reporting.

3.2.2 Asking Questions

Because you have some things you want to find out, you will need to guide the interview. This means that you will need to ask questions from time to time.

Yes-No Questions Versus Open-Ended Questions. Ideally, your questions should be as open-ended as possible, to give plenty of space to the interviewee to tell you what is on his or her mind. It often seems natural to ask questions that are answered by yes or no, such as, "Did it help when your teacher started introducing the lesson differently?" The trouble with this kind of question is that it can be answered by the laconic with a monosyllabic "yes" or "no." Even worse, it may close off possibilities which you might not have thought of.

You might be surprised at the answer to the same question phrased more open-endedly: "What was the effect of the change in the way your teacher introduced the lesson?" In fact, the answer to this or another equally open question might be the key that unlocks the puzzle of what is going on with the student. If you had not given the student the chance to tell you something you did not expect, you might still be scratching your head.

Yes-no questions have another drawback regarding the relationship you want to establish with the interviewee. A series of questions of this sort begins to sound and feel similar to an interrogation. It makes it "my" interview, instead of "our" interview. The latter feeling is more likely to encourage the interviewee to provide a lot of information for you to work with.

Questions With Presuppositions. A more subtle pitfall that affects even experienced interviewers is the apparently open-ended question that implicitly prestructures the answer. For instance, "How satisfied are you with the computer-assisted learning portion of the program?" has already set up the lines along which the question is to be answered. A more open-ended version is "What's your opinion of the computer-assisted learning portion?" Another example is, "What are you doing to study that you did not do before?" This presupposes that the interviewee is doing something differently. One possibility of a less loaded question is "How are you studying now?"

Multiple Questions. At the grocery store, two-for-one is a good deal. In an interview, it is costly. An example is, "What do you think of the teachers and curriculum in this program?" The interviewee may have trouble deciding which to answer first. If he or she begins with one, the other may be forgotten. At best, there will be some unnecessary tension when the interviewee tries to keep both of the implicit questions in mind. You may have intended to give a preview of where the interview is going to go. Better ways to do this are to provide a set of topics to be addressed in writing, or to do it orally. For instance, you might begin with, "As we look at what is going on with you, we will want to touch on the curriculum, the teachers, the methodology, the language lab, and your homework. Let's start with the curriculum." Even better would be to list the main categories, then ask an even more open-ended question such as, "How are things going for you in this program?"

Breaking the Rules. There will be times when it will be appropriate to use both yes-no questions and questions with implicit presuppositions. They will be relatively rare, however, and they should contribute to the flow of the interview. In most cases, when you are tempted to use a yes-no question or a question with a presupposition, there will be an open-ended alternative that is at least as good and usually better.

Air Time. Interviewing is similar to language teaching, in a way. A really effective interviewer talks much less than the interviewee, just as an effective teacher ordinarily gives most of the "air time" to the students. If you catch yourself talking a lot, you are probably missing out on a lot of information you would be getting if you talked less. Ideally, you should ask questions to keep the interview going in directions you want it to go, provide encouragement ("uh huh," "I see," and so on), and use active listening paraphrases to make sure that you are understanding what the interviewee is trying to tell you. Once in a while, sharing a little of your own experience can help the interviewee stay open to you, but this should be done sparingly. Ideally, you should be talking less than a third of the time.

3.2.3 Staying Open

The fewer preconceptions you have when you begin an interview, the more effective the interview will be. We have seen that you may enter an interview with some working hypotheses. It is vital that you be prepared to see your guesses about the person "shot down in flames" by something they say. Usually, it is the opening to an even more interesting discovery, when you find that you have to reassess the evidence and your interpretation of it because of something your student tells you that you did not expect. If you can see this kind of situation as a challenge, not a defeat, you can keep the information coming and make something valuable of it.

We have seen that some questions imply preconceptions about what the answer will be (see Section 3.2.2 above). It is useful to stay on guard against questions that close off options or possibilities of new information.

The concept of neutrality is also an important one. It is vital when interviewing to take a nonjudgmental stance. This leaves the student free to really tell you what is on his or her mind. Patton (1980) puts it very well when he says *"Rapport is a stance vis-à-vis the person being interviewed. Neutrality is a stance vis-à-vis the content of what that person says"* (p. 231, emphasis in the original). The following list of things to avoid represents common ways of compromising neutrality.

The following are some of the main saboteurs not only of good active listening but of effective interviewing. Most of them are things we say every day in ordinary conversation, often with the best intentions.

> *Giving advice:* Your interlocutor may ask, "What do you think?" You can usually avoid answering this until after the speaker has had a chance to work things out for himself or herself. Sometimes the other person does not really want your opinions; the real question is often, "Do you approve of me?"

> *Arguing:* The best way to manage showing whether you approve of the speaker is to keep *all* your responses nonjudgmental, even when you strongly disagree. If you really stay in the other person's world, this is easier than it sounds. Reflection of what someone says does not mean you agree with it, only that you heard it.

Sympathizing: Saying such things as "You poor thing" or "How terrible it was that they did that" is not listening. They are expressions of your opinion and come from your world. They also imply that your "clients" need your sympathy and approval more than they need you to help them work out their own thoughts, feelings, or solutions. Empathy is, "I understand you." Sympathy is, "I feel sorry for you." Most of us would prefer the former.

Praise: Nothing turns a neutral listening interaction into a judgment faster than praise. Avoid the temptation to say, "You really handled that stressful situation well." Again, it is your world, not the speaker's. Affirmation can be an important tool to reinforce behavior that is helpful to the student, but use it carefully.

3.3 Active Listening Skills

Beginning interviewers—counselors, qualitative researchers, evaluators, and the like—are often preoccupied with such issues as where to sit, what to call the interviewee, how to introduce themselves, and so on. Matters of specific technique such as how to introduce yourself are far less important than how you listen. Listening is probably the single most important aspect of interviewing: It is more important than planning, asking specific questions, or other details that can loom large to the inexperienced. If the interviewee thinks you really want to hear what he or she has to say, you are likely to hear it.

You have probably heard of active listening. It is part of the training for telephone hot line listeners, for trainers, and for many teachers. Active listening techniques are at the base of programs for parent or teacher effectiveness. Couples are often taught how to listen to each other.

You may ask, "Why do we need training in listening—isn't it something we all do all the time?" The answer is that a lot of material reaches our ears, but we frequently do not hear it. When I conduct training in active listening skills, I tell participants that what they are learning to do is actually *highly unnatural* for people from U.S. culture (and many others). This means that they are likely to find it difficult, will make a lot of mistakes, and may not succeed in early attempts to use the new skill. It is enormously difficult for inexperienced listeners to avoid giving advice or countering with something from their own experience. On the other hand, countless people have learned to listen. My trainees can learn, and so can you.

Active listening is best practiced with another person who will provide feedback on your listening skills. In this book, I offer some guidelines on active listening, but to really develop the skill, you will need to practice, practice, practice. Be patient with yourself. This is truly a skill that is not built in a day or even many days.

Your body language is the starting point. In active listening training, the first exercise is sometimes to listen to someone else speak for several minutes without saying anything at all. When the people who were being listened to are debriefed about the experience, they inevitably talk about the importance of eye contact, facial expression, and a posture that is both relaxed and yet expressive of alert interest (usually this means leaning forward some, but not so much as to crowd the speaker). Even without a word having been said, the speakers will say that they felt that the listener was "with" them.

In conversation, we use "encouragers" such as "uh huh" or "is that so" or "mmm" to let our interlocutor know we are still part of the interaction. In active listening, these are also used, together with such phrases as, "tell me about it," or "tell me more," or "I'm listening, go ahead." These are part of the repertoire of a good listener.

Active listening, on the other hand, consists of reflecting back to the speaker what was just said. (For this reason, active listening is sometimes called *reflective listening*.) In its simplest form, active listening is a paraphrase, putting what was heard into different words. For example, you may hear, "I really had a bad day today." A typical but not reflective response is something such as, "You think you had a bad one? Let me tell you about *my* day!" Somewhat better, but not really on target, is, "I'm sorry to hear that." At least the second response stays in the first speaker's world, unlike the first example, which pulled the first speaker into the second speaker's world. A much better response is something such as, "You had a rough one, huh?" This picks up and reflects both the cognitive content (bad day) and some of the feeling (I am exhausted) and also leaves an opening for the first speaker to tell more.

Effective active listening, whether for data collection or for counseling, reflects feelings as well as content. Respectful, nonjudgmental reflection of feelings—without becoming invasive—makes interlocutors more willing to talk with you. You get valuable information about what is important to your interviewee; you may also get cues about things the interviewee is not telling you, often things he or she is not aware of at a conscious level. The emphasis on content or feelings (or both more or less equally) will depend on the circumstances and the needs of the interviewee. If the interviewee is very upset or feeling something else strongly, begin with a focus on feelings. After a time, this will enable the interview to move on to content.

3.3.1 Active Listening Response Types

The following is a listing adapted from Rogers (1979) of some of the common responses available to an active listener.

1. *Mirroring:* Giving back the exact words. This can be used with considerable effect when you do not know what else to say, if not overused. Take the following, for instance:

> **Student.** When the teacher laughed at my mistake, I felt really humiliated and worthless.
> **Listener.** You really felt humiliated.

2. *Paraphrasing:* Restating what you heard in new words. This is at the heart of active listening. It is more than just saying what you heard in different words, though. You actually reflect the words ("You felt put down."), the content ("The teacher laughed at you."), and the feelings ("It really hurt!"). The feelings are usually the most important part. Sometimes, the feeling behind a remark may not be obvious. In this case, you can try reflecting the feeling that you think is there. For instance, "I really had a lot of studying to do: reading a passage, reviewing my vocabulary, and starting a new lesson. I hardly had time to listen to any tapes." The content is, "You had a lot to do and couldn't get to everything you wanted to do." You can see if you catch the feeling by trying something such as, "You're really feeling a lot of pressure!" The nice thing about this kind of listening is that the other person will usually correct you if you got it wrong, "Oh, no, I'm really feeling good about what I got done!" Then you can reflect again to show you got it this time, "You have a feeling of accomplishment."

3. *Clarifying:* Making sure that you (and the speaker) are on the right track. This can be done with a question. For example, the student might say, "I just am no good at grammar." A clarifying response using a question might be something such as, "No good? How so—learning rules, using it, or what?" An even better response, because it is more open ended, is "No good?" This is a clear invitation to say more, and you will usually get more.

4. *Summarizing:* Pulls together a number of statements, to show the idea or feeling underlying all of them. For example, your student might say, "I started late and everyone was ahead of me, and then I could never feel I caught up. My language aptitude isn't very high anyway, and it's really bad when I can't understand the words my classmates use. I don't think I'll ever master the grammar, either." You can summarize with something such as, "It's been really difficult for you since the beginning, and it doesn't seem to be getting better."

5. *Refocusing:* Sometimes a student may avoid talking about what is really important to him or her by going off into what seems to be small talk. For instance, "I had a great weekend. I went sailing, and then we had friends to dinner. And there was some really good television, too." What you really want to know is how the student is using homework time. You could say something such as "It sounds terrific [and a little more about the weekend]. But your study routine—what's been happening there?" Avoid being dictatorial, but keep your interview on track.

6. *Silence:* Sometimes just keeping quiet is the best response. If a speaker is really caught up in what he or she is saying, you can stay silent (or give only minimal encouragers such as, "uh huh") for quite a long time. Often, at the beginning of an interaction, a period of silence is very helpful for finding out what in general the speaker wants to say.

Active listening is very difficult to do for long periods of time. It takes intense concentration, the ability to listen for both content and feelings and decide at every point which is more important, the capacity to follow loose threads and bring them back to the point of what the person is trying to say, and choice of the right words to catch exactly what your interlocutor is trying to say. You also need to be monitoring the speaker's responses to your paraphrases to make sure you are on track.

If there is expression of intense emotion, you may have to manage the anxiety this may arouse in you. You should be clear with yourself that you do not have to be a counseling professional. If the emotions are too intense or there are personal issues that are beyond your ability to deal with, you do not have to take them on. If you think the interaction may go beyond your professional competence, take steps to redirect the interview, empathically. You can change direction by a new question, or you may find it is appropriate to state "up front" that you do not think you can be helpful in a given area but that there are some places where you hope to be able to help. There is more in Chapter 11 about staying within your area of competence and comfort.

Active listening is made more difficult in that the speaker may not be entirely clear about his or her own feelings or thoughts until they are processed through an active listening interaction. The work is very hard, but the payoff is very high in good information.

3.3.2 Standing and Understanding

Interviewing (as with other listening activities) is not only receptive. You will sometimes need to make statements that in fact come from your world, but are in the service of the other person's process or in the service of a common or larger task or goal. Curran (1978) calls this "standing" in contrast to "understanding," which is what we have been talking about up to now. (Another term he uses is "overstanding," which implies being overbearing, putting the other person on the defensive in some way.) Standing may consist of information, feedback, or a directive.

The usual format for standing in a listening relationship is the "sandwich." In this case, the bread is the active listening responses; the "meat" is the information, feedback, and so forth. The format is understanding, then standing, then understanding again, often about the person's reaction to the information in the standing portion. An example is the following:

> **Interviewer.** You really like Ms. Jones; she seems to meet your needs very well. Unfortunately, this will be her last year here; she's moving in June. But I do see that part of what has made her such a successful teacher for you is that she gives you lots of time to give answers, instead of jumping right in.
>
> **Interviewee.** That's really bad news about Ms. Jones! I wish she weren't leaving.

Interviewer. You're disappointed about her leaving.

The "meat" in this example is the sentence that begins with "Unfortunately." The second part of the sandwich "bread" comes twice: once is when the information is followed immediately by a response that is back in the speaker's world ("But I do see . . ."); the second time is when the interviewee expresses dismay, and the interviewer stays nondefensively with the interviewee's feelings.

Shifting to a new topic or question is a way of standing. It does not necessarily need to be done in a sandwich, but it should be done with some sort of reasonably smooth transition, which usually acknowledges what the interviewee has been saying.

3.4 What to Ask About and What to Listen For

3.4.1 Basic Question Topics

Michael Patton lists the following basic question types. Most of what you want to learn is probably provided for in one of these question categories:

> *Experience-behavior questions:* These are about what someone has done or does. Examples might be, "If I were in the classroom, what would I see you doing?" "Tell me about how you studied last night."
>
> *Opinion-value questions:* Such questions ask for what a person thinks about a topic. They are in contrast to how the person feels (see the following). They are phrased in forms such as, "What is your opinion about . . .?" "What do you believe on the subject of . . .?" or even "What do you think of . . .?"
>
> *Feeling questions:* These questions are directed toward the interlocutor's emotional response, as opposed to his or her opinion. An opinion question is oriented to the head; a feeling question is oriented toward the heart or the gut. Some examples include, "How did you feel when . . .?" or "What was that like for you?" If you want to find out what someone thinks, avoid asking, "How do you feel about that?" to avoid confusion about your intentions.
>
> *Knowledge questions:* This kind of question focuses on factual information that a person knows, such as the textbooks in the course, the names of the person's classmates, the rules of the classroom. Patton

(1980) points out that the facts are only part of the answer to such questions; the other piece is the student's perspective on his or her world.

Sensory questions: These questions have to do with the physical experience of the interviewee, what he or she actually saw, heard, felt, for example. They take the form of "What did your teacher actually say?" or "What do you see when you go into the classroom?"

Background-demographic questions: Questions of this sort "help the interviewer locate the respondent in relation to other people. Age, education, occupation, residence/mobility questions, and the like are standard background questions" (Patton, 1980, p. 209).

3.4.2 Sample Interview Guide

You will probably find that it is best to put together your own list of questions. Just to give you a start, however, the following are some questions I would probably make sure were in my interview with a student having difficulties. Each of these questions will, of course, be followed up, depending on what the student tells you. They need not be asked in this order; again, circumstances and student responses will determine when they are addressed.

1. Tell me about what is going on now with you.
2. What about your learning in the past?
3. What seems to be working well for you now?
4. What does not seem to be working so well?
5. What would you like to change?
6. Describe how you go about studying X.
7. What catches your interest? What do you do for fun and relaxation?

3.4.3 Things to Listen For

When a student is responding to one of these very general opener questions or one of the follow-up questions, I listen for information in these categories:

1. *Language learning strategies:* How does the student go about performing the learning task? I listen especially for signs that the student is working hard but not smart. Signs that a student is not working "smart"

are too much brute force memorizing, very long study hours, lack of planning and evaluation of own study, surface learning without making connections and associations, or low risk taking. I also listen for indications that there is a mismatch between the student's preferred learning strategies and the expectations of the program: For instance, a student may learn largely by reading, but the teacher assumes that he or she is using audiotapes. Learning strategies, they are often good cues to where difficulties may be. There is more on learning strategies in Chapter 8.

2. *Learning styles:* What are the student's preferences for going about the business of learning? Common style dimensions are visual-auditory-kinesthetic, sequential-random, field independent-field sensitive, concrete-abstract. Preferred learning strategies are realizations of learning styles and often provide indirect information about them. Some students are self-aware and may tell you something such as "I have to see it on the blackboard" or "I hate it when I don't learn the fundamentals first before I try to speak." I will discuss learning styles in detail in Chapters 4, 5, and 6.

3. *Motivation:* Why is the student learning the language and how much does he or she want to be doing so? Motivation may be extrinsic (it is a requirement for my program) or intrinsic (this is really exciting and fun!). Motivation is likely to be affected by what happens in the classroom—a statement such as Sandy's, "I was really eager to learn this language, but after 6 weeks, I'm fed up!" raises a lot of further questions. Sandy's motivation dropped drastically, and this was part of what was so disturbing to her teachers.

4. *Anxiety and other feelings:* John has talked about how put down he feels by being put in a class with people who are junior to him and moving more slowly than his previous class. He is anxious not only about his success but about his standing in his own eyes and those of others. The things that make students put energy into defending their self-esteem instead of into learning come up in interviews.

5. *Skills and assets:* As you listen to what students have studied before, their occupational interests, how they use their spare time, and what they are interested in, you may find out about some skills that can be tapped in their learning. At the very least, you can draw on their interests and areas of knowledge to make metaphors that will enhance your communication with the student. For instance, with a student who likes mechanical things, I may talk about language in terms of components to be manipulated; with one who likes sports, I might talk of rules of play.

6. *Evidence of learning disability or dyslexia:* Stories of trouble with learning to read or with spelling can alert you to the possibility of cognitive processing difficulties. When a student has unusual difficulty with short-term memory, I wonder about learning disabilities. Similarly, unusual rigidity in learning style may indicate a learning disability. Most students who are undiagnosed (and some who have diagnoses) are sensitive about this issue, so follow-up questions and probing must be handled carefully.

7. *Nonverbal behavior:* Subtle cues such as averting the eyes, beginning to move one's feet, little grimaces, pulling back in the chair, and so on indicate something is going on. I sometimes check into it: "I noticed that you frowned a little just then—what was that about?" A lot of fidgeting may also indicate a kinesthetic learner.

3.5 Recording Interviews

Much of what is written in Chapter 2 (2.3.2) applies to keeping records of interviews. There are three main ways to make records of interviews: taping, recall, and note taking (Merriam, 1988), which are described below.

The best from the point of view of richness is a tape recording of the interview (audiotape or, even better, videotape). There are sometimes logistic difficulties with taping, and it can be intrusive. Even more of a drawback is that transcription of tapes is extremely labor-intensive and expensive. Most researchers simply cannot afford to capture all the data in a tape.

The least desirable approach is to make notes from memory. Sometimes this is unavoidable because of logistics again, or because the interviewee rejects on-the-spot note taking or taping. In this case, it is important to put down notes as quickly as possible to avoid forgetting or distorting the information.

The middle ground is to take notes while interviewing. This is the approach I usually use. I either take notes myself, or sometimes I am fortunate enough to have a colleague present to take notes while I interview. I ask permission first, explaining that I am easing the burden on my memory and trying to make sure that what I get is accurate. Permission is almost always granted. The note taking is often itself a form of "listening" or at least of "attending." When I confirm with the student what I have heard to ensure that my notes will be accurate, it is a form of paraphrase. I cannot always get verbatim quotes, but I try to do so for statements I deem important. I usually try to indicate my question or other stimulus, as well as the response.

If I make comments or interpretations in my notes, I indicate that this is what they are, so they are separate from the actual content of the interview.

3.6 Part of an Interview With *Kelly*

Kelly is taking intensive language training. It is currently her "full-time job" to learn this language. There are 5 hours of classroom time plus an hour of directed self-study in the language laboratory, and students are expected to put in more time at home to prepare for classes. Kelly has only been in class for about a month but is running into trouble. This portion of the interview begins after the preliminaries have been gone through. The interviewer has a little information about Kelly from a biographical data questionnaire that was filled out at the beginning of the class.

(The selection begins after a few minutes of introductions, preamble, and getting acquainted.)

Interviewer. What's going on for you now?

Kelly. I'm having problems with listening. I did badly on a dictation quiz, and I'm falling behind in other areas—I can't keep up with the vocabulary, and my grammar is bad. I don't think I'm putting in enough time.

Interviewer. You feel as if you're constantly playing catch-up, and you don't think you're giving it enough time. [Kelly nods.] How much time do you give it?

Kelly. I was doing 2 or 3 hours a day, and that included the lab time during the day. I guess that would be an hour of lab time and a couple of hours at night. Now I'm giving it 5 hours a day, and that's working better.

Interviewer. So you're feeling less concerned that you aren't spending enough time?

Kelly. Yes, but I still get blocked in listening. This happened before when I learned another language. In the past, I think it was linked to a reluctance to listen to the tapes for the course.

Interviewer. Hmmm. Sounds like you really dislike listening tasks.

Kelly. Yeah, I do, but I have tried to use the tapes for dictation practice. This didn't work very well, so now I review words, which I read aloud, and then I listen to the tapes. I repeat after the tape and try to pick up the general meaning of what I hear. On the second listening, I practice pronunciation. I go through slowly to connect the sound and written form and meaning. It's like doing grammar drills—I look at the pattern then the meaning.

Interviewer. So you like to get control of the form, then think about what it means.

Kelly. Yes, most of the time. I really like studying reading—the foreign alphabet is really interesting to learn. What's really hard is comprehension in class, especially if I haven't seen it in writing or on the blackboard. I just get lost. It goes too fast, and I can't keep up with it.

Interviewer. You can manage the reading and enjoy it, but in-class comprehension just gets out of control.

Kelly. Yes, I just never know what to expect in class when I have to listen.

3.6.2 Questions About the Interview

The following are some points to consider about the previous interview.

What do you notice about the listening process (what is going on between the interviewer and Kelly)?

What do you think is going on with Kelly?

What comments would you make about her learning strategies?

What is your current guess about her beliefs about learning?

Where do you think this interview will go next?

What is your working hypothesis about what is happening with Kelly?

What would you want to pursue further if you were the interviewer?

3.7 The Relationship Between Observation and Interviews

Observation and interviewing complement each other. Observation suffers from unpredictable influence by the act of observation and the fact that it is limited to external behaviors. Interpretation must be inferential. Interviewing, on the other hand, is a way to explore the interpretation of observational data. It in turn suffers in that interviewees are limited to reporting their perceptions, which may be subject to distortion due to anxiety, outside pressures, biases, or limited perspective, for example. Observations can be used to check out interview data.

3.8 More About Direct Data Collection

When you try to work out what is going on with a student who is having learning difficulties, you are undertaking *research*. Observation and interviewing are classic research methods. As with any other form of research, it must be done carefully so the results are valid. The following is a summary of principles for this kind of qualitative inquiry that is compact and usable as a reference (Patton, 1980):

> The mandates of field research include being careful to be descriptive in taking field notes; gathering a variety of information from different perspectives; cross-validating emergent patterns by gathering data from multiple sources and by gathering different kinds of data—observations, interviews, and documentation; . . . *representing participants in their own terms*; reporting on the observer's own experience, location, and feelings; and clearly separating description from interpretation as one puts together a comprehensive, holistic, and sufficiently detailed picture of what has been observed to allow the reader . . . to enter into the situation. (p. 192, italics added)

Chapters 2 and 3 have addressed two ways of gathering information about your students that you can do informally and unobtrusively. There are other ways to collect data, including having students try a task and describe aloud to you what they are doing and why ("think-aloud" procedures) and having them keep language learning diaries that could be considered written forms of think-aloud procedures. A variant on diaries is dialogue journals, in which students write about aspects of their learning and exchange with either another student or with teachers, thus engaging in a kind of correspondence that offers them feedback. All of these methods have proved useful to students and teachers; their main drawback is that they add "overhead" to the classroom in the form of more instructions and time required.

Even more commonly used are surveys, questionnaires, and tests. These are addressed in Chapters 4 through 9, especially Chapter 9. I have postponed the discussion of these "instruments" until Chapter 9 to provide you with concepts that you can use to interpret the results of your observations and interviews—or student think-alouds or diaries. If you can use the various concepts and models to interpret directly gathered data, you can be less dependent on surveys (which should always be used with some skepticism in any case). You will also be able to interpret surveys and questionnaires in a more informed way, in that the concepts treated in Chapters 4 through 8 underlie almost all of the survey instruments.

From the material you have about John, Sandy, and Kelly, take a guess about how each of these students learns. What is your evidence?

3.9 Practice

Listening

1. Eavesdrop on a couple of people having a conversation. Are they really listening to each other? How do you know? If not, what is happening instead? Try rephrasing (to yourself) some of the responses you hear, to make them closer to the kinds of response that indicate that someone is really listening.

2. In an informal conversation, try listening without speaking for a while. Give every signal you think is appropriate, but do not use words. How long can you go and have the other person remain comfortable that you are "with" him or her?

3. During a conversation on a topic in which you do not have strong feelings, try responding for a short time only with paraphrases or

open-ended questions to what you hear, without interjecting what you think or feel. Do this often.

4. Practice paraphrasing. Try to pick up feelings as well as content and words. You will need to be alert for signals that you have gone deeper than the other person wants you to go (i.e., may be treading on sensitive ground); in that case, back off.

Interviewing

1. Find an experienced interviewer and watch him or her. Perhaps you could offer to take notes for the interviewer. Take note for yourself of how the interviewer manages the relationship, the kinds of questions asked, listening skills, when the interviewer "stands" and when he or she "understands." If you can, ask questions afterwards and discuss what your model did.

2. Get friends and family to serve as interviewees. Decide on something you want to know about them that you do not already know. Design a set of starter questions and try interviewing them. Ask them for feedback about how it felt to be interviewed. Did they feel that they had a chance to say what they wanted to say? You can let them choose the subject in some instances; at other times you might ask them to talk about some of their learning experiences.

3. Try interviewing some students. Either do it on videotape or get a colleague to observe. Go over the tape (with a colleague, if possible) or the observer's notes afterwards to get feedback. Ask the students the same questions you asked your friends and family in Exercise 2. See if the observer has comments on the same issues.

4. While you are getting feedback, treat it as another interview opportunity. Practice the same skills.

3.10 More Information

Many of these references have been around for a relatively long period of time. They are still used because they are good and still valid. Newer works offer many of the same principles.

Patton's (1980) *Qualitative Evaluation Methods* is a superb source of information about both observation and interviewing techniques and principles. If you want to go into more depth on these subjects, this is the place to go. Other books addressing qualitative data collection refer regularly to this work.

A good and less dense reference covering similar material is Merriam (1988). For more information about active listening, consult Rogers (1979) *Understanding People*. This book, especially Chapter 3, provides a good basic outline of the process with specifics on how to go about it. A more philosophical but still very practical introduction to active listening is to be found in Curran (1978), especially Chapters 3 and 6.

General information on such techniques and diaries and think-alouds can be found in Tarone and Yule (1989). More detail on these techniques is also available in Cohen and Hosenfeld (1981) and Bailey (1983).

Cognitive
Learning Styles

Chapters 4 through 6 introduce ways to look at how students learn differently. Chapter 4 treats some common approaches to understanding differences in cognitive processing, Chapter 5 focuses on the field independence construct, and Chapter 6 explores learning differences that are based largely on personality factors.

After a discussion of the meaning of learning styles, this chapter describes several commonly used models that affect student receptivity to various teaching methods and activities, beginning with sensory channel input preferences (auditory, kinesthetic, visual). Next come the sequential-random, concrete-abstract, and deductive and inductive dimensions and the commonly used metaphor of left- and right-hemisphere processing. Each section ends with a description of relevant assessment instruments.

4.1 Indications of Learning Styles

In Chapter 1, we learned the following about John:

When the curriculum follows the textbook closely, John works steadily and systematically. He readily performs the drills and exercises that fill the text. When asked to participate in more free-form activities such as storytelling or roleplays, John grumbles and stumbles.

In Chapter 3, one of Sandy's teachers said the following:

The times when I try to explain something, she frowns, kicks her feet around, and says that if she wants an explanation, she will ask for one. I keep urging her to listen to the tapes, but she doesn't do it.

In addition, on a questionnaire about preferred classroom activities, Sandy also responded with "nearly indispensable" to an item that is phrased: "Classroom exercises use my hands (drawing, pointing, construction, etc.)."

Kelly tells us a lot about her learning style in her interview from Chapter 3.

Kelly. I have tried to use the tapes for dictation practice. This didn't work very well, so now I review words, which I read aloud, and then I listen to the tapes. I repeat after the tape and try to pick up the general meaning of what I hear. On the second listening, I practice pronunciation. I go through slowly to connect the sound and written form and meaning. It's like doing grammar drills—I look at the pattern then the meaning.

Interviewer. So you like to get control of the form, then think about what it means.

Kelly. Yes, most of the time. I really like studying reading—the foreign alphabet is really interesting to learn. What's really hard is comprehension in class, especially if I haven't seen it in writing or on the blackboard. I just get lost. It goes too fast, and I can't keep up with it.

Interviewer. You can manage the reading and enjoy it, but in-class comprehension just gets out of control.

Kelly. Yes, I just never know what to expect in class when I have to listen.

Learning styles are broad preferences for going about the business of learning. They are general characteristics, rather than specific behaviors. They are made concrete ("realized") by specific learning strategies. A few students know a lot about how they learn, and they may tell you something such as, "I'm a very visual learner," or "I prefer to learn the rule first, then look at examples, before I use it." For most students, however, we discover their learning styles by making inferences from their descriptions or our observations of their preferred ways of going about the learning task, that is, from their preferred learning strategies. (Keep in mind that an inference—about learning style as much as about any other learner characteristic—is a hypothesis, and so it must be tested continually.)

The description of John suggests that he prefers to learn things one step at a time and in a clearly established order and that in relatively uncontrolled situations he is uncomfortable taking risks involved in using language he does not feel he has mastered. We can make a hypothesis about John that he will much prefer a program with a clear and detailed syllabus and that sticks quite closely to lesson plans that build up control of each piece of language in an orderly way.

Sandy shows strong indications that she likes to learn kinesthetically, that is, by moving around and using her hands. She kicks her feet around under emotional pressure, and she strongly endorses classroom activities in which she uses her hands.

Kelly tells us that she is probably similar to John in that she prefers to control the form of a linguistic item before she deals with what it means. In fact, the short segment of interview above suggests that control in general is very important to Kelly, and when she thinks she has lost control—and rather tight control at that—she loses confidence in her ability to cope with the language.

The interview fragment with Kelly shows how hypothesis testing can work. The interviewer started off with a hypothesis that Kelly might have a low preference for auditory learning. As the interview went on, this seemed a less fruitful hypothesis than one about Kelly's need for firm mastery and tight control of target language material, and this is where the exploration was beginning to go in the interview.

4.2 About Learning Styles

Learning style mismatches are at the root of many learning difficulties. For this reason, this chapter and the next two will discuss learning styles and a model of learning based on learning styles in considerable detail.

Are auditory intake preference and need for control and firm mastery both learning styles of the same order? To the degree that learning styles are "preferences" or "needs," they are much the same kind of thing, even though the former represents a more limited domain than the latter, which is not just a learning preference but a personality disposition. Both have a direct effect on the learning strategies, classroom activities, and other choices a learner makes. When there is a mismatch between the learner's style on any of the dimensions that we will look at in this chapter and the curriculum and teaching style of the course, there will be effects on the efficiency and effectiveness of the learning.

Because they operate in a similar way for purposes of diagnosing learning difficulties, learning styles and personality dispositions will be addressed together as "learning styles," except when a distinction between them is appropriate.

4.2.1 What Is Meant by Learning Style

Learning styles are described above as preferences, which is meant to suggest that one or another style of a learning style dimension is as good as the others. To make the meaning of preference clear, I often ask participants in workshops to do a simple exercise such as crossing their arms or writing their names.

Cross Your Arms. For instance, try crossing your arms. Which arm is on top, the left or the right? If you are in a group, how many people have the right arm on top? The left on top? Which way is better? Needless to say, the last question is silly. Neither way is better under ordinary circumstances. So which arm you put on top is a preference. It is something that is your choice.

Handwriting. An even better example is the handwriting exercise. Write your name on a piece of scratch paper. Then write your name with the other hand. Think back to the first time you wrote your name just then. What was it like? (Most people answer something such as "I didn't have to think about it, it was fast, it looks good, it was comfortable and easy," and so on). Now think about the second time: What was that like? (Most people answer something such as "It was slow, difficult, I had to concentrate, it looks messy, I was anxious, it was awkward," and so on. Once in a while someone says "challenging" or "fun.")

I then point out that learning style variables are similar to our hands. Just as we have a preferred hand for writing and doing most other things—a dominant hand—so we have a preference for how to learn on any of the many learning style scales. For example, if we prefer to learn sequentially, it will come relatively automatically, whereas learning randomly with no set agenda from outside will be slow, awkward, and very tiring until we get practiced at it, and the product will probably not be as mature.

I also point out that no one voluntarily uses only one hand all the time. Just as we use the dominant hand for many tasks, we also need the nondominant hand for other tasks and to support the work of the dominant hand. We are quite literally crippled without both hands. Similarly, a person who prefers to learn inductively (discovering rules from the data) most of the time sometimes needs—or even wants—to learn deductively (learn rules first, then apply them), depending on material to be learned, time available, or other circumstances.

4.2.2 Variability in Styles

As we have seen in the hand metaphor, very few people operate only in one style all the time. We vary, going back and forth most of the time. In fact, although most learning style models are bipolar (i.e., they have two clearly established end points), they really represent a continuum of behavior. That is, one is seldom always sequential, for example, or always random, even for the same kind of activity. Instead, one more or less acts in a way represented by a point on an imaginary line between the two poles. The diagrams in Figure 4.1 show several of the infinite variations on the XY learning style scale.

The diagrams in Figure 4.1 show that a learning style designation need not "put people into boxes." A person of the first sort (1), with a clear

1. Preference for X

X _____ Y
****** *** * *   **   *   *

2. Preference for Y

X _____ Y
* * *   *   *   ******   *   ****   *

3. Strong Preference for Y

X _____ Y
        *   *   **   ***************

4. Rigid Preference for Y

X _____ Y
                      *   ********

5. Generally In the Middle, Tilt to X Under Pressure?

X _____ Y
  *   *   ****   ********   *****   **

6. In the Middle, Very Slight Preference for X

X _____ Y
  *   *   ***   ***** **   **   *

NOTE: Each * indicates an act that takes place over a given period of time.

Figure 4.1. Some of the Almost Infinite Variations on a Given Bipolar Learning Style Dimension

preference for X, uses X most of the time, some of the time is more or less in the middle, and rarely is all the way over in Y. Person 2 has a less pronounced preference for Y (a "weaker" style Y, we could say): He or she is less exclusively Y, more often near the middle though "Y-ishly" so, and more often than Person 1 on the X side of the continuum. The third person has a very strong preference for Y, even more strong than the first person's preference for X. Person 3 is seldom on the X side of the midpoint, and his or her activities never go all the way to real X behavior. The fourth person has a rigid Y style, with behavior that never varies from Y.

The preferences shown in the last two examples are in the middle of the XY continuum. Most people, even those in the middle of a continuum, have some slight preference for one or the other; a few are truly "ambidextrous," but not many. This is shown in these last two cases. Person 5 is more or less in the middle most of the time, but when not in the middle, he or she is more often on the X side than the Y side. The sixth person, on the other hand, is nearly evenly split, but the frequency of X-type acts is very slightly higher than that of Y-type acts, so we can guess that when the pressure is on, this person will act in a more X-like manner.

All of these examples suggest that there is an interaction between style and situation. This is usually the case. Just as situations determine which hand to use (write with one hand, grip jars to open with the other), so they also have considerable influence on choice of learning strategies associated with one learning style or another.

For example, when I learn a new computer program such as a spreadsheet or a database manager, I usually prefer to jump right in and try it out on a real application, without doing the step-by-step tutorial or taking a class. Instead, I read just enough in the documentation to get me into the program and open an application, then try it out with something I need the program for, using the help screens and sometimes the manuals when I get stuck or have an unanswered question. This approach is very characteristic of what is meant by a "random" learning style. On the other hand, sometimes I need to learn something very fast, or I want to be sure I do not miss any details. Then I may read through the manual, trying things as they are described, or I may do part of the on-line tutorial, though that would not be my usual choice.

In short, then, classification into styles such as inductive-deductive, auditory-visual-kinesthetic, or extravert-introvert are convenient oversimplifications for those of us who teach, train teachers, do research, design programs, and build models. Because this oversimplification is so convenient, I will continue to use the learning style models in this book as if they were classifications but will ask you to keep Figure 4.1 in mind as you read.

4.2.3 How Rigid Are Learning Styles?

Another way to describe preferences is as "comfort zones." For most of us, a preference is just that—something we find more comfortable but can do another way if circumstances require it. Thus, most people who prefer to learn through the eye can learn through the ear or the hand when they are in a training program or class that requires it, though they may complain about it and even lose some learning efficiency. My learning computer programs randomly is in this category.

For a minority, however, learning styles are more firmly set and are therefore more than just preferences. In such cases, the effects of mismatch between style and curriculum or teaching approach are more than a discomfort or minor inefficiency: There may be severe loss of learning efficiency or even inability to learn in that program. If both student and program are rigid, the chances are that the program will label the student as unable to learn languages (and the student may come to believe this of himself or herself), and the student will criticize the teachers and programs for not meeting his or her needs. Many Americans who announce that they cannot learn foreign languages probably suffered from style mismatches when they were taught.

A learning style, then, can run the range from a mild preference ("I'd rather learn by discovering patterns for myself.") through a strong need ("It interferes with my learning when I haven't mastered the grammar patterns first—I have trouble following the material that uses them.") to an out-and-out rigidity ("I have to see it before I can remember it; if I don't see it, nothing sticks at all.").

For John, step-by-step learning is at least a very strong preference. For Kelly, mastery before taking communicative risks is probably a strong preference. Sandy's kinesthetic style proved to be a preference that caused little difficulty when she needed to learn visually, but she was uncomfortable enough with auditory learning that she avoided it (but in class she could learn through the ear when it was supported by text or activity). For none of these three students is their style really a rigidity, though John will need some help with coping with relatively random (free-form) input, and Kelly may need not only some help with learning strategies for dealing with ambiguous material but also perhaps some attention to her self-confidence as a language learner to become more flexible.

4.2.4 Learning Styles and Learning Aptitude

When I do presentations and workshops about learning styles, I am often asked which styles represent the best ways to learn. This is a difficult question to answer, because people of every learning style can learn and learn well. The more important individual variable is probably the learner's flexibility. If a learner can shift styles to meet circumstances (the educationese term is *style flexing*, and it refers to both students and teachers), he or she is at an advantage in most learning situations. Few learners are completely flexible, though. For most, a more relevant issue than the "best" style is the match between the learner's style and the setting: teacher and program.

In an effort to address this issue, I came up with a metaphor that describes learning activities as if they were ground transportation routes. They go from the most closely structured to the least. Box 4.1 presents the four levels of this model. (It is discussed in detail in Ehrman, 1995.) No program is all one or all the other. Most programs represent varying mixes of activity types. Thus, for instance, an audiolingual program of the sort popular in the 1960s probably had a very heavy amount of "railroad" and relatively little "open country" (though in good programs there was always some of the latter). On the other hand, in many communicative programs today, the amount of railroad is very much less (but not necessarily missing altogether), whereas activities that use or simulate open country are considerably more common. The intermediary stages, "highways" and "trailways," also appear in different quantities in different mixes.

Clearly, there is likely to be a relationship between some of the learning styles and the activity types. For example, a sequential learner such as John indicates that he is more comfortable with railroads and highways than with trailways and, especially, open country. Other learners may reject railroads altogether.

If there is any connection between learning style and language learning aptitude, it is that real language use requires open country activities and techniques associated with coping with open country. Learners who cannot cope with open country are at a severe disadvantage in language learning. Many currently used language tests, such as the Oral Proficiency Interview (OPI) of the American Council on the Teaching of Foreign

Box 4.1. Learning Situation Taxonomy (Transportation Metaphor)

Railroads: The traveler gets on at one point and makes few if any choices until reaching the destination. It is also unlikely that one can get from door to door by rail alone: Other forms of transportation must be used in addition. Maximum external structure and control.

Examples of railroad-type activities include defined dialogues for memorization, mechanical and some meaningful drilling; reading and listening matter designed to use lesson material.

Major Highway System: There are a number of options and choice points, but they are limited to marked exits for the most part. One drives one's own car rather than being driven. On the other hand, one follows the roads that have already been built and does not make new roads, and maps are readily available.

Examples of highway-type activities include oral interaction closely linked to lesson material; some meaningful but largely communicative drilling; controlled conversation, edited texts, and edited listening passages that may be based on authentic material.

Trails: It is necessary to find one's way in a network of paths, which are, on the one hand, clearly delineated as paths but on the other hand may lack a map. Some trial and error and exploration may be needed to find one's way. An individual can establish a new trail but seldom a new roadway. Thus, there is less external structure and more freedom.

Examples of trailway-type activities include free conversation, heavily guided by the teacher to include repetition of previously learned material but with room for considerable student initiative, especially in subject matter; generally authentic reading and listening material, but with considerable teacher or curricular guidance in the form of advance organizers, outlines, and other guides.

Open Country: The only guidelines are natural signs, which the traveler must learn to recognize and read. One finds one's own way, blazes one's own trail—maximum freedom.

Examples of open-country-type activities include open-ended conversation, topics, subtopics, and branchings, nominated and branched by both student and teacher; authentic material for reading and listening; student development of his or her own strategies for coping.

SOURCE: Adapted from Ehrman (in press) by permission of Georgetown University Press.

Languages, require the ability to cope with some open country as well. Thus learning styles that facilitate coping with open country are helpful; those that hinder the ability to cope with authentic, unpredictable, ambiguous language are not helpful.

Language is ambiguous and unpredictable. Outside the classroom, it is truly open country. For this reason I have come to see that the ability to tolerate ambiguity is a key to language learning success at higher levels of proficiency. This topic is so important that I will devote considerable discussion to it in Chapter 6.

4.3 Learning Style Categories

Learning style models are different ways of representing a common domain. It is therefore not surprising that there is some overlap among them. Each dimension, however, contributes a different perspective on individual differences and, therefore, on learning difficulties. Thus, for instance, though sequential-random on the one hand and analytic-global on the other have considerable overlap, they are not exactly the same. Each of the dimensions and personality disposition variables is similar to a different stain used by a histologist to reveal a variety of tissue structures. One stain displays a certain set of structures, whereas to show another set on the same tissue, a different chemical must be used.

4.3.1. Simple and Compound

In addition, learning style dimensions can be viewed as "simple" or "compound." Most of the bipolar scales discussed in this section are simple, representing a convenient lowest, indivisible level for most uses. Some scales in composite models such as the Kolb system (Kolb, 1985), 4MAT (McCarthy, 1987), the Myers-Briggs system (Myers & McCaulley, 1985), or the Gregorc model (Gregorc, 1982a) can often be analyzed into the simple components and thus may be considered compound because they are made up of more than one simple category. An example is the Myers-Briggs Sensing-Intuition scale (Chapter 6), which includes concrete-abstract, sequential-random, some degree of analytic-global, a certain amount of field dependent-field independent, and so on.

4.3.2. Cognitive and Personality Dimensions

Another distinction that can be made by those who prefer to make such analyses is that between cognitive processing styles (e.g., concrete-abstract) and personality styles (e.g., extraversion-introversion). Cognitive processes are usually considered apart from feelings and relationships with other people; they are more similar to computing. In fact, some current models of how people think are built on analogies with computers. Personality styles reflect more in the way of feeling and interpersonal relationships. Thus, sequential-random is relatively cognitive in that it is related primarily to data processing, whereas extraversion-introversion affects feelings and relationships and is in turn affected by them.

This distinction breaks down often. For example, the ability to extract and focus on something apart from its context, known as *field independence*, represents a cognitive learning style if it also generates a preference for a certain kind of learning. At the same time, Witkin and Goodenough (1977, 1981) found a close relationship between field independence and a kind of personality style that is more focused on task than personal relationships (more on this construct in Chapter 5). Sequential and random processing are often accompanied by certain personality characteristics (see the discussion in Chapter 6 of Myers-Briggs *intuition* and *perceiving*).

Variations in Learning Style Models

Not all learning style variables are bipolar. For example, there are at least three preferred sensory learning channels: (a) *auditory*, (b) *visual*, and (c) *kinesthetic*. Kinesthetic is sometimes further specified as *haptic* (touch) or *emotive* (relating to emotions, which often manifest as body reactions). But at the very least, sensory channels are three-way. Furthermore, they are not mutually exclusive. Many people learn comfortably through more than one channel; relatively few so strongly favor one channel that they cannot learn through the others.

There are many learning style dimensions or scales that have been designed to examine one aspect or another of individual processing differences. I do not attempt to address all of them. Instead, I have selected a few here that are commonly used in language teaching and have added a few others that are less well-known but which I have found useful in understanding learning difficulties among the adult language learners with whom I work. I will begin with sensory channels, then go on to the relatively cognitive style dimensions in the rest of this chapter. Because the field independence construct has emerged as very important in this book, it has a chapter of its own. Then, in Chapter 6, I will treat a personality dimension, ego boundaries, that I have found illuminating in my work with people learning new languages and cultures. Under the rubric of personality-based learning style, I will also describe the Myers-Briggs composite model in the same chapter, along with a model of learning based on some of these style dimensions.

For each dimension treated in the following and in the next chapters, there is a brief description, some information about the most likely kind of trouble related to it, and a few suggestions for remediation. There is illustrative case material for most. Each section ends with a description of instruments used for assessment of the learning style dimension addressed in the section.

4.4 Sensory Channel Modalities (Auditory, Kinesthetic, and Visual)

More students, especially adults, are aware of this learning style dimension than any other except possibly the "right and left brain" metaphor. Students will often tell you "I'm a visual learner," or "I need to hear it to learn it." (Relatively few adults say that they are kinesthetic learners.) By this, they usually mean that they prefer to have either visual support such as writing on the board, handouts, or textbook material when they hear unfamiliar language, or they prefer to hear what they read. A few have almost rigid preferences, to the point where if they cannot learn through the designated modality, their learning may stall.

Most of the learners with whom I deal put visual learning first, kinesthetic second, and auditory third, after a discussion of this dimension. Relatively few consider hearing their main learning channel, though of course they must rely on it when in natural language learning settings. These proportions may differ with other groups of American students and with students from other cultures.

It seems likely that the paucity of students who are aware of kinesthetic learning preferences is a consequence of socialization from the earliest grades in school. Most who have some kinesthetic learning preference have been taught to try to suppress their need to move and to sit still, and to be vaguely ashamed of pursuing this way of learning.

The following is some interview material from *Karen*, who is experiencing unusual difficulty learning to read a language written in a different alphabet from that of English:

> *Interviewer.* What seems to have worked well for you in the past?
>
> *Karen.* When I was studying a previous language, we had to close our books and learn dialogues by repeating after the teacher. This worked very well for me. I learn from sound. The language I'm studying now isn't comfortable for me to read, and I can't bring in sounds when I read.
>
> *Interviewer.* You need to associate sounds with what you read.
>
> *Karen.* Yes, what works best for me is to use the new language as much as possible and not be inhibited and only learn from books. I like a lively teacher who encourages us to talk and not just take in language and build a large base of words we understand but can't use.
>
> *Interviewer.* So your learning comes from hearing yourself and other people talk in natural ways?
>
> *Karen.* Yes, that's right. Books are ok, but I need to read them aloud so I can hear the sounds and how they relate to the words on the page.

Kelly describes her visual learning preference as follows:

> I review words in the book or from my flashcards first before I listen to the tapes. For grammar, I do the same kind of thing: I look at the patterns in the book, then I do oral drills. Listening comprehension in class is hard, especially when there is no visual support. I like reading much better. Actually, I remember that in school I've always learned without much effort, especially in reading and with written materials.

We have seen that Sandy is a kinesthetic learner. Another indication of this is that she strongly endorses a statement on a learning activities questionnaire (Ehrman & Christensen, 1994; see also the questionnaire in Appendix C) that says that she can work better when she can move around. Here is *Ellis*, describing himself in learning situations:

> I hate to sit still. I have to walk around. I tap my fingers or feet all the time. I'm always moving. I can't sit still unless I'm concentrating on something, and certainly not for a whole class period. I really get bored after a while, just listening and talking once in a while. It really helps to have frequent breaks. Field trips give me some action, so I can go out and use the language. Sometimes I've wondered if I'm hyperactive.

Frequently students will tell you what their sensory preferences are, at least with respect to visual and auditory input. With only a minimal invitation to talk about kinesthetic preferences, you can often find out about these too. The trick here is to convey that you do not think a kinesthetic learner is ill-mannered, fidgety, or "dumb," all of which terms many such learners will have heard often. They will have learned caution about exposing this preference. In some cases, they may not even see it as a preference but as a deficiency. (Ellis, for example, wondered if he had a psychiatric disorder: hyperactivity.)

It is often possible also to get some idea about preferences just by listening to the metaphors people use. Visual people will talk about "seeing" ideas, for instance—"I see what you mean." An auditory person might be likely to indicate understanding by saying, "I hear what you're saying." Kinesthetic preference might be represented by phrases such as "I get it," or "I can grasp that."

Visually oriented students may reject tapes, want their books open, need to write things down. Auditory learners may need to hear written text material, ask for tapes or passages to be read out loud, prefer oral practice without books, and so on. Kinesthetic preferences will often lead to behavior that looks like fidgeting or tics, flipping pages, doing something else while the lesson is going on, and even "spacing out" when the boredom level gets too high.

Sensory channel style preferences are fairly straightforward to address. Most communicative language classrooms have a considerable amount of auditory and visual content. The difficulties are likely to occur when teaching methodology is inflexible: The crudest example of this is "everyone close your books now." When there are strong auditory or visual preferences, it helps to provide some options (e.g., "You can either use the tapes or this alternative set of techniques that works from the book"). In that real language use will require everyone to manage auditory and visual input, it will help those with extreme preferences to begin with low-risk activities in the nonpreferred modality and work up to more challenging and realistic ones. Many learners are likely to use nonpreferred techniques in roleplays and simulations without realizing it, because they get caught up in solving the problem or managing the situation and so will do whatever works.

The most difficult adaptation for most teachers is kinesthetic/haptic, for several reasons. The first has to do with the kind of social conditioning described above—that classroom activity is in some way immature and "grown-ups" sit still. In addition, many classrooms are crowded, making activity difficult. Many kinesthetic activities are based on realia and props, which add an additional logistic burden. Yet the truth is that almost all students enjoy and benefit from well-done kinesthetic activities. Even the most abstract students enjoy field trips, simulations, and roleplays, which often have a high kinesthetic component and are well received when they do not require too much risk. Activities informed by the Total Physical Response methodology can enhance the work done in relatively conventional classrooms. Physical response activities work well in delayed production curricula.

Assessing Sensory Channel Preferences

There are several questionnaires that look at the preferred sensory modality. The Edmonds Learning Style Identification Exercise or ELSIE (Reinert, 1976) is probably the classic such instrument. The four dimensions of the ELSIE—visual image of an object of activity, visual image of a word spelled out, sound of a word, or kinesthetic reaction—served as the base of several of the scales on the composite Learning Style Profile (LSP) put out by the National Association of Secondary School Principals (NASSP; Keefe, Monk, Letteri, Lanuis, & Dunn, 1989). The perceptual response scales (auditory, visual, and emotive) and the manipulative preference scales of this instrument also address sensory channels. The

Learning Channel Preference Checklist (O'Brien, 1990) and the Perceptual Learning Style Preference Questionnaire (Reid, 1987) assess these factors, too. Dunn, Dunn, and Price, in their composite Learning Style Inventory (1978) and Productivity Environmental Preference Survey (1979), the latter for adults, also address sensory channels among other dimensions.

All of the above are self-report inventories of sensory channel preference. The Barbe, Swassing, and Milone (1979) Swassing-Barbe Modality Index addresses the three sensory modalities through performance in response to instructions in the three channels. This instrument appears to be used much less often than the pencil-and-paper questionnaires.

I have used several of these instruments. They have not worked very well for me for information on sensory channel preferences; I now rely primarily on information elicited in interviews and on inferences made from items in the Motivation and Strategies Questionnaire (MSQ), which is in Appendix C. Even the items in the MSQ that reflect sensory channels need to be checked out with the student; they are unreliable as direct indicators. This may because of the nature of the students with whom I work: older, well-educated, and usually fairly flexible. It may also be a consequence of the fact that sensory modalities are often situation-dependent. Most learners are aware of using more than one modality, particularly when the demands of the learning situation change. I find, therefore, that responses to questionnaire items on sensory channels usually serve as the basis for a discussion that leads to more than a simple set of percentage scores can. On the other hand, the standard questionnaires appear to be useful for others; they may work better with school and college populations than they do with adults in foreign affairs careers.

4.5 "Cognitive" Learning Styles

The remainder of this chapter treats the sequential-random, concrete-abstract, and deductive-inductive dimensions. It also addresses the commonly used left-right hemisphere metaphor. All of these bipolar dimensions are somewhat related in that, in a general way, the first member of the pair is the one that primarily seeks structure and clarity, whereas the second is the one that is more comfortable with—even seeks—ambiguity.

They thus overlap in significant ways, but at the same time, they put the spotlight on usefully different domains of learning.

4.5.1 Sequential-Random

The sequential learner wants to learn step by step, following a logical order, usually that provided by the curriculum and the textbook. An extremely sequential learner is likely to become frustrated with very open-ended classroom activities such as extensive free conversation. Many sequential learners say that they prefer to master one thing before going on to the next; most want the sense of a firm base before moving on. These learners often want repetition offered overtly in the form of drilling and other exercises in which the variables are controlled. Sequential learners seldom miss important points, because they make sure that all the material is covered; they are often systematic and, at their best, good planners.

Random learners, in contrast, tend to find their own learning sequence, and it may vary from time to time and subject to subject. In fact, most random processors are very systematic learners, but their systems are often idiosyncratic, and their approach seems random to the outsider. This is one of the reasons for this label; the other is that such learners treat the learning process much the way a computer finds data, through a process called random access. This means that the data are stored in various places, and the computer can find them quickly, no matter in what order they are requested. A random learner does something very similar in finding information and making connections between new and old knowledge. Random learners tend to tolerate ambiguity relatively well and embrace surprises that might disrupt the learning of others. They are usually well equipped for navigating open country (see Section 4.2.4 and Box 4.1).

More learners in my experience seem to prefer sequential learning. In an unfamiliar situation (such as foreign language learning for most Americans or a new country and culture for immigrants), it often seems safest to follow a set of steps that must presumably have worked for others because they are being taught. It is one form of control: reducing the likelihood of surprises that may tax the learner's ability. Furthermore, we are taught sequential processing strategies in our schooling. On the other hand, the apparently rarer random learners can have a strong preference for nonsequential learning even in very unfamiliar circumstances. In a way, it is also a form of control, different from that of the sequential learners: Random learning can be a means of making sure of finding a way to count on one's own resources even in an unfamiliar or ambiguous situation.

John, whom we met in Chapter 1 and at the beginning of this chapter is a strongly sequential learner. *Shirley*, a very sophisticated learner, is also representative of highly sequential processors. She tells us a teaching sequence that has worked well for her:

> In class, new material is practiced *with* the teacher. We *repeat correct* patterns *provided* by the teacher and with *immediate* correction as we try to use the new pattern. The teacher has us repeat the correct patterns. The next step is to try to develop or use the new pattern ourselves. This is done in class so that the teacher can make corrections and repeat the correct pattern as needed, *immediately.* Older material is worked on in class periodically, too, and only after correct patterns are quite firm do the students work at home on the material. Most of us work at home with carefully structured tapes so we are carefully guided to learn and reinforce *correct* patterns from which we can use the language, rather than making things up "from scratch" and learning it wrong. [Emphasis is Shirley's]

Shirley also describes approaches that have caused her difficulty:

> I have a lot of trouble with exercises that test an intellectual understanding of a grammatical point, but change all elements each time so that it does not effectively reinforce basic patterns at the beginning stages. When we ask for something to be repeated, it may be repeated once or twice, but not more, even if students are still getting it wrong. Much more often, the teacher offers six to ten *different* ways to say the same thing. [Emphasis is Shirley's]

In contrast, *Janet* criticizes a course for opposite reasons. Janet is a relatively random learner, though not extreme. (We will meet more extreme random learners later.)

> Overall, Janet liked the textbook as a compact way to get the basics. However, she would have liked a lot more problem-solving activities such as roleplays and simulations. She found helpful the brief sum-

maries of news or other topics that they were asked to do sometimes, in which there was not always a lot of time for preparation. She experienced too much classroom routine and predictability as unhelpful, even stultifying. Her view was that she should do in class only what she could not do by herself, whereas much of the teaching in the course relied on repetitious drilling, which was not a good use of class time for her. When the teacher was willing to let students use the language with him and was flexible as student needs changed, she learned better. On the job, using the language, she has continued to learn, even though she is no longer taking formal classes.

Karen, whom we met earlier, is also a relatively random processor, who describes herself as a good "osmosis" learner. She says that sequential material often interferes with what she calls her "intuitive approach." Karen, on the other hand, Karen also recognizes her need for a well-organized program. She is not so random that she wants to design her own program, as the more extreme random learners do.

Sequential learners are likely to run into trouble when they have to cope with unstructured activities or unsequenced input, unless they feel well prepared with a foundation of well-mastered material. They may perceive a program that does not provide the kind of support that Shirley described as disorganized and even counterproductive. They may feel overwhelmed by chaos, especially if they are not self-confident learners with a history of previous learning success. Skilled and flexible sequential learners can make good use of sequenced materials to maximize the efficiency of their learning.

Random learners are subject to boredom in conventional classes, if skilled. If not so skilled, they may overestimate their ability to cope with unstructured input and wander into a swamp of material with which they cannot cope. Karen, for instance, has learned of this danger and avoids it. For the skilled random learner, on the other hand, the open country they enjoy is not a morass but an entertainment park. Random learning is high risk and high gain. Random learners who follow their own paths may be perceived by more sequential classmates and teachers as disruptive. Random learners who lack sequencing skills may also be judged as not very bright, because they do not put their learning in an order that is clear to the outside evaluator.

To help the sequential learner, find a set of good materials and either follow them in class or provide assistance to the student in pursuing the materials as part of the homework. The same assignment can be handled differently for the two styles: The random learner can be given a fairly general objective, whereas the sequential learner is given a procedure for coping with reading passages, for example. Some predictability in class structure, timing, order of exercises, and expectations will add substantially to the comfort of the sequential learner; at the same time, well-supported and guided adventures will increase their readiness for the much more random "real world."

The random learner should be given as much freedom as she or he can handle, and support should be provided in a way that does not undermine the learner's sense of self-efficacy and autonomy. When the learner wants to strike off in a new direction, let him or her do it and follow along, to the degree that it does not disrupt the work of the rest of the class. Again, differential assignments and projects will make a big difference. Build in some unpredictability into the class; if not overdone, the sequential learners will enjoy it, too.

Assessing the Sequential-Random Dimension

There is one instrument that addresses this dimension directly and as sole focus, the Problem Integration Strategy Test (Weinstein, 1978). It has never, as far as I know, been published. This instrument describes sequential processors as *line integrators* and random processors as *point integrators* and evaluates them through a set of addition and multiplication problems of varying difficulty that respondents are *not* asked to solve. Instead, they are asked to list the order in which they would solve the problems. An adaptation of this instrument is provided in Appendix B.

I usually use the Problem Integration Strategy Test for teacher training. It works well as a starter for discussion of learning styles, using the sequential-random dimension as a base. The question about checking one's work can serve as a window into the reflective-impulsive dimension. I also use the questionnaire to address anxiety, because so many people are made anxious by the sight of arithmetic problems. Indeed, the anxiety (or impulsivity) is sometimes so strong that respondents actually do the problems, despite instructions not to do so.

I have not used this tool with students, both because of the anxiety factor and because the information is available inferentially from the

Myers-Briggs Type Indicator (MBTI, Myers & McCaulley, 1985) and the MSQ (Appendix C).

The Problem Integration Strategies Test uses performance on a task to gather data on style preference. The other questionnaires available for this dimension use self-report of preference through questions on a pencil-and-paper questionnaire.

The only other instrument to address the sequential-random scale directly is the Gregorc Style Delineator (1982b), one of whose two scales is sequential-random. In Gregorc's model, however, the scale is interpreted only in combination with the other scale, concrete-abstract, to yield a set of four types whose wholes are greater than the sum of their parts. Nevertheless, the Gregorc questionnaire provides a means of assessing sequential-random preference if you find a way to work with the score on that scale alone, despite the lack of interpretation.

Other instruments can be used to make inferences (that must be tested) about sequential or random preference. The MBTI sensing-intuition and judging-perceiving scales (Chapter 6) usually include aspects of the sequential-random dimension; so, for example, for a person who prefers sensing and judging, my first guess is sequential, whereas I would be more cautious about an intuitive judger.

One useful way to check is to use specific items on the MSQ (Appendix C) that in fact directly address sequential learning activities. A student who says, for instance, that taking lessons step-by-step is almost indispensable is probably indicating a sequential preference.

One final instrument addresses sequential learning. There is a section on the NASSP Learning Style Profile (Keefe et al., 1989) that tests sequential processing *ability*. This is distinct from sequential processing *preference* and is treated in Chapter 9, in the section on ability tests.

4.5.2 Concrete-Abstract

A concrete learner needs direct sensory contact with the language and its meanings. A concrete learner needs to relate what is learned to direct experience. This means that he or she will prefer activities that involve using the language to do something, not just talk about it.

> *Lonnie*, who is a very concrete learner, likes to play learning games in class, read aloud, have many examples, interview other students to

get information, do transformation drills, read about topics of interest, take field trips, learn dialogues by heart, do roleplays and simulations, drill pronunciation, participate in cooperative learning activities, talk as much as possible, do classroom activities that use his hands, use audiotapes and videotapes, write things down, and visualize pictures. This looks like a wide range of activities, but each of them involves doing something concrete to learn. What Lonnie dislikes and finds a waste of time is revealing, too. He actively rejects classroom discussions of abstract topics like the economy or politics, where the emphasis is on expressing opinions and backing them up. Explanations in the target language leave him behind, and he gets little out of grammar rules. He also gets little out of exercises that require him to read or listen to material that is over his head, with material that he does not know. He needs to see a speaker to follow what is being said.

Students with a concrete orientation are likely to seek real language use. On the other hand, they may have trouble with learning rules, with discussion of abstract topics, or with dealing with language as a system, all of which help in classroom learning and contribute to increasing accuracy in real-life language use situations. They often have difficulty answering "what if" questions, instead bringing the response back to their direct experience.

A preference for abstract learning is likely to show up in a preference for grammar rules, systems, and discussion of abstract topics. A very strong preference for abstract learning may mean that a student gets lost in theory and never gets to the point of language use. (Focus on systems and rules can also be a way of defensively avoiding the risks of real language use.)

Betty, an adult learner with a strong interest in political science, is tripped up by her strong preference for the abstract. You interview her and check her records, finding out the following:

Betty has just left a job as an upper-middle manager, where she played a central role in all the activities of her office that were related to her area of expertise. She took special pleasure in her wide circle of contacts and access to officials at all levels. She is deeply interested in the subject of political science and takes pride in her expertise. There are few if any professional problems she cannot solve quickly and creatively. The beginning part of language class didn't seem too demanding because all the students were asked to do was listen to a lot of the target language without having to say anything in it. It was later that the language really started to get tough for Betty. After some conversation with her about what's going on, this is what you have found out:

Even though she had felt pretty confident of her ability to understand during the first week, which was all heavily reinforced comprehension, now that she actually has to speak and answer questions in the target language, she has a really hard time understanding what her teachers are saying to her. What makes it worse is that the other students don't seem to be having this trouble. And she seems to be able to understand what the teachers are saying to her classmates. She admits that she sometimes starts thinking about a word she has heard or about how the language is put together, rather than just using it.

You have checked her scores on a language learning aptitude test, and she has an above average rating, with no specific areas of weakness to be seen in any of the parts of the test.

Betty has begun to express frustration at the piecemeal approach to introducing grammar in her training program; she says she can't tell how the system hangs together. She also admits that she sometimes has a tendency to bite off more than she can chew, such as choosing more difficult news articles to report on in class. As a result, she often makes more than her share of mistakes. She says that this is because she wants to deal with political science matters, though she knows that she hasn't the language to handle such subjects yet.

Abstract learners, in contrast to concrete ones, are likely to pay attention to issues of accuracy and learn and apply rules. They will tend to respond to a wide range of conversational topics. They can also make their learning overly complex, however (Betty did this to herself by wanting to talk in a sophisticated way about politics before she had the tools), and thus set up unrealistic expectations for themselves. They may avoid real language use because they become overly concerned with accuracy or because they find the system more interesting than actual communication.

Most concrete learners also tend to be sequential, perhaps because this permits them to make sure that the language they learn is directly related to experience. On the other hand, the relationship is not one to one; it is possible to find a concrete and random learner, though these seem to be relatively rare.[2]

Helping the very concrete learner manage some abstractions can be done more or less gradually and in a context in which the "payoff" for using the abstraction is very clear. For the most part, these learners do best when what they learn is closely related to their experience and needs. Sometimes a concretizing metaphor is helpful. For instance, one concrete and very able learner likened the grammar of the language he was learning to an engine, which could be taken apart and put back together. I sometimes use the metaphor of weight training to help concrete learners understand how they can gradually stretch their areas of nonpreference.

Abstract learners will want to feel that their intellects are being challenged, and that they are not limited to "baby stuff." Betty, for example, could be provided with some political content and then given an opportunity to use it within her linguistic knowledge or even encouraged to use it to take a few linguistic risks. Community language learning techniques (see Note 1) could be especially helpful for students such as Betty because they enable students to talk about what interests them (see Curran, 1978 for more information about this approach).

Assessing the Concrete-Abstract Dimension

Questionnaires that address preferences for concrete versus abstract processing include the Kolb Learning Style Inventory (1985), the Gregorc Learning Style Delineator (1982b), and the MBTI (Myers & McCaulley, 1985), especially the longer version of the MBTI called the Type Differentiation Indicator (TDI, Saunders, 1989).

The Kolb Learning Style Inventory (1976) has two scales, active experimentation-reflective observation (processing) and concrete experience-abstract conceptualization (perception). The latter scale addresses the concrete-abstract dimension to some degree, but, as with the Gregorc Learning Style Delineator, these two scales are usually only interpreted in combination with each other. For both the Kolb and Gregorc instruments, abstract and concrete seem to refer less to taste for abstract thinking than to a need to apply concepts to real life.

The MBTI comes closer with the sensing-intuition scale to what is usually meant by concrete and abstract processing. Sensing types tend to be oriented to facts and the tangible; intuitives tend to gravitate to theory and the imaginative. For users of the MBTI, there is bad news and good news. The "bad news" is that the sensing-intuition scale is a composite of a number of dimensions, such as sequential-random, as well as concrete abstract, so it may be difficult to sort out which components are active for a given individual. The "good news" is that two scoring systems used with a longer version of the MBTI called the Expanded Analysis Report and the

Type Differentiation Indicator (Saunders, 1989) extract the concrete-random dimension as one of five sensing-intuition subscales. These more detailed versions of the MBTI can help differentiate among different kinds of sensing type, intuitive, introvert, feeling type, and so on. They must be machine scored, but if there is enough time to wait for the roughly two weeks that machine scoring requires, they can be very informative. (See Chapter 6 for more on the MBTI.)

There are some tests that assess the ability to reason abstractly; they are usually designed for use in neuropsychological testing of individuals who may have some form of brain damage. They generally investigate flexibility of assigning stimuli to categories and are probably not suitable for looking at concrete-abstract language processing for normal students.

4.5.3 Deductive-Inductive

Another dimension that we have seen mentioned in some of the case material previously discussed has to do with the direction of study. Deduction begins with a rule and applies it to specific cases. Induction begins with the data and seeks the generalizations that can be extracted. In general, deductive processing tests a theory (e.g., a rule or generalization) against the facts. Inductive processing seeks to find a theory (rule, generalization) by looking for patterns in data. Most of us use both approaches at least some of the time. In learning, however, we have preferences. I suggest you take a look at the case material in this chapter and try guessing at which style each of these learners favors before reading further. Not all the selections will have evidence, but in those cases, take a guess and try to think about what made you guess that way (you may learn something about your own intuition).

Sandy might be inductively oriented: She prefers not to be given explanations. Janet's random style meshes well with inductive learning—so well that they are closely linked though not identical. Karen, despite her needs for some structuring, prefers to learn from hearing people talk in "natural ways," an inductive way of going about things. Kelly, with her orientation to form before meaning, on the other hand, might favor deduction. Chances are John, who prefers well-structured input, will be more comfortable with a deductive approach, as will Shirley. What is your guess about Betty and Lonnie and other learners whom you have met? (Reminder: You can use the case index at the end of the book to find them.)

For the most part, helping a very deductive learner involves some of the same techniques as were suggested for sequential learners: Help them make use of the language they read and hear to keep learning when they do not have a teacher or book to structure their learning for them. Some inductively oriented learners may use their time inefficiently and may flounder around in ineffective trial and error. Assistance with when to make good use of deductive techniques will save them time and effort.

Assessing the Deductive-Inductive Dimension

This dimension is inferred from items on the MSQ (Appendix C) such as comfort with inducing grammar rules, failure to endorse teacher explanation as highly necessary, and so on. I am not aware of any questionnaire or test in which this is a scale.

4.5.4 Left and Right Hemisphere

Many references that address learning styles mention left and right hemisphere styles (e.g., Brown, 1994). Because that model is so widely used, I have included it in this discussion, though it should not be taken literally—real brain research shows a much more complicated situation than the binary model suggests.

The left-right dimension comes from a simplification of findings from some of the research done on epileptics who were subjected to surgery that severed the link between the two brain hemispheres. *It is more useful as a handy metaphor* than as a literal reference to biological brain function, though there is some relationship to hemispheric specialization. As shown in the lists in Table 4.1 (adapted in part from Brown, 1994), there is considerable overlap between this dimension and many of those previously described, as well as some of those that will be described in the next two chapters. This is perhaps why the hemisphericity model, for all its overgeneralizations, is so convenient as a unifying and organizing metaphor for many of the learning styles. In some ways, however, it is so general that it reduces the amount of information about the learner. For this reason

Table 4.1 Characteristics Associated With the Left and Right
Hemisphere Metaphor

Left	Right
Verbal	Pictorial, images, gestures
Sequential	Simultaneous
Analytic	Synthetic, global
Names	Faces
Control feelings	Express feelings
Parts	Wholes
Classification	Generalization
Deduction	Induction
Literal	Metaphoric
Spotlight	Floodlight

and because of its inaccuracy with respect to real brain research findings, I rarely use it. In this book, I will use the other dimensions previously described and those described in Chapters 5 and 6.

Assessment for the Left-Right Metaphor

There are three questionnaires that are most commonly used to determine preference on this dimension. The most readily available are *Your Style of Learning and Thinking* (SOLAT, Torrance Reynolds, Riegel, & Ball, 1977) and the Hemispheric Mode Indicator (McCarthy, 1987). The other is the Hermann Participant Survey (Hermann, 1984), which must be administered by a trained examiner and machine scored. Both assess "hemisphericity" by asking about a range of preferred activities and thinking techniques that can be related to the list in Table 4.1.

4.6 Practice

To familiarize yourself with the learning style dimensions and the process of making hypotheses (an inductive process, to be sure), I suggest you go back through the cases presented so far and examine them for the characteristics described in the above sections. Do some evince more of the characteristics on the "left?" Who seems to be to the "right?" Are some balanced?

More exercises for the auditory-kinesthetic-visual, sequential-random, concrete-abstract, deductive-inductive, and left-right style dimensions are provided at the end of the next chapter, in combination with the field independence and field-sensitivity scales.

4.7 More Information

H. Douglas Brown (1994) includes a section describing some of the research on the effects of learning styles on language learning. Brown provides a number of useful further references. He also discusses research on several of the dimensions described in this chapter. Other usefule references on learning styles are described after Chapters 5 and 6.

Notes

1. Several language teaching methodologies are mentioned in this chapter. The oldest of those mentioned is the *audiolingual methodology* of the 1950s and 1960s, which was based on a belief that practice that would "burn material into the brain" was the key to language learning. It was characterized by a tightly controlled curriculum that consisted of memorized dialogue material and extensive oral grammar drilling. In the 1970s, methodologists became more aware of the contribution made to learning by conscious reasoning and student feelings. Two important approaches that came from this period were *community language learning* (CLL) and *total physical response* (TPR). The former was based on a larger theory called *counseling-learning* that based learning firmly in the affective and interpersonal; the latter was an attempt to minimize native language input and maximize body learning. CLL was heavily based on lessons that came from what the students wanted to be able to talk about. TPR (crudely described) was based on students' doing things (large or small, simple or complex) based on target language commands. The so-called *communicative approach* is a catchall term for a variety of curriculum innovations that became important in the 1980s that involved including as much real communication as possible, including working with material designed for native speakers of the target language. One subvariant was to encourage students to delay speaking for a short time until they had some reading and listening comprehension ability in the language: This is called *delayed production*.

2. Note that the terms *concrete, abstract, sequential,* and *random* are used as the names of the two dimensions in the Gregorc learning style system (Gregorc, 1982a), in which many learners have a concrete-random style. The terms do not, however, have the same meaning: A concrete-random learner in Gregorc's system may be very comfortable in the realm of abstractions but prefer to learn randomly for goal-related purposes

of his or her own, with an emphasis on the possibilities that learning opens up. In contrast, a concrete-random learner as described here is likely to prefer to learn in hands-on ways about specific, relatively tangible topics, though he or she will be rather flexible in the sequence that things are learned. In the Gregorc system, an abstract-random learner is oriented to interpersonal relationships, and an abstract-sequential seeks intellectual understanding of underlying systems. A concrete-sequential, on the other hand, is very similar to the combination of concrete and sequential as used in this book.

Field Independence and Field Sensitivity

This is the second of three chapters treating learning styles and personality differences. It is devoted to the construct of field independence and field dependence. To account for a wider range of learners than this construct usually covers and to cope with some difficulties in the usual model, I have divided the single construct into two continua, field independence-field dependence, and field sensitivity-field insensitivity. The two continua are combined to yield four learner types that will be used throughout the remainder of the book. The chapter concludes with an assessment of field independence and field sensitivity both as learning styles (preferences) and abilities.

5.1 The Field Independence Construct

Bert is an unusual student: He really likes the study of grammar. He has bought references and frequently comes up with predictions of how a grammatical form he has never seen will look, much to the surprise of his instructor. He is less comfortable with conversational activities that go at a normal pace because he cannot take the time to do the analysis and synthesis that provide the precision he seeks. He participates in activities such as field trips, but he does not find them particularly enjoyable. He has told you that he is much more interested in the language as a kind of puzzle to solve than he is in the people and culture, though he certainly wants to get along with native speakers.

In contrast, *Sylvia* bubbles with enthusiasm for the culture and loves to interact with the people who speak the language. She communicates readily but often inaccurately. She does not worry much about her errors, because she assumes that if her relationships are healthy, her interlocutors will be patient enough for the important meanings to be negotiated. Sylvia is a leader in activities whose main purpose is real or simulated communication, such as simulations, roleplays, and field trips, and she learns a lot from these activities. Her mind wanders, though, when the class focus is on grammar or other material that is out of communicative context.

Both of these students can be considered at least average learners, though their styles are clearly different. Each has strengths, and each has weaknesses. We will see that Bert is probably field independent: he is adept at dealing with language that may be out of context, but he is less comfortable with the kind of global processing that can cope with a lot of things going on at once. Sylvia, on the other hand, manages the rapidly changing context of real language use with considerable aplomb, but she seldom focuses on any aspect of the language in a way that will afford her the precision needed at high levels of proficiency. She can be described as field dependent, needing to learn through material embedded in a context. Because she is also able to use the context to learn, often without knowing how it happened, I am also describing her as field sensitive, to indicate an ability as well as a lack. We will learn more about Bert, Sylvia, and other students later in this chapter.

Many investigators of foreign or second language learning have used a dimension called *field independence-field dependence*. This dimension addresses the degree to which an individual focuses on some aspect of experience and separates it from its background. (The word *field* or *ground* is used for this kind of background; the term *figure* is sometimes used to indicate what receives focus and is thus pulled into the foreground.)

Every natural experience consists of a great range of perceptions: auditory, visual, kinesthetic, olfactory, and so on. All of us have the ability to discriminate and focus to some degree on a stimulus that is important to us, such as a physical object, a certain sound or sequence of sounds, an idea, or a grammar rule. The term *field independence* refers to that kind of activity as at least a preference and at most an ability. Many scholars extend the concept to refer to the ability to conduct abstract cognitive operations on the material that receives such focus (Chapelle & Green, 1992).

The term *field dependence* can mean a relative absence of such discrimination, either as a behavioral tendency or as a lack of an ability. When it is measured, it is invariably through tests of field independence. Thus when addressed as a result of the usual measures, field dependence can safely be defined only as absence of field independence. (I know of no direct measure of field dependence.)

At the same time, all of us need to be able to tell what is going on in the background as well, at least to some degree. Such behavior is especially important in navigating complex social situations (which are often involved in real language use). Some investigators use the term field dependence to refer to a tendency to react more to the general background than to specifics that are singled out from it. Thus field dependence is used with at least two meanings: a negative absence of field independence and a positive presence of responsiveness at some level to the surrounding background. I am now using the term field sensitivity for the latter.[1] As is the case for field dependence, I know of no established measure of field sensitivity, poor performance on which might be considered field insensitivity, though observation and experience tell us that there are many learners who can be aptly characterized by this term.

A field independent learner such as Bert is adept at focusing a spotlight on data, distinguishing and focusing deeply on some specific aspect of the material being learned. Such a learner can look at the forest and find exactly the kind of tree in which she or he is interested. In contrast, a field sensitive learner such as Sylvia makes skilled use of a floodlight. This kind of skill is aimed at staying aware of the whole forest, registering the presence of birds in the trees and chipmunks in the grass (quiet, don't move for a moment!), or a change in the kind of underbrush. Both skills are useful but probably difficult to apply simultaneously. Some learners can apply both, though probably alternating between them (sometimes quite rapidly).

It was at least in part because of a connection with personality that Witkin (see Witkin & Goodenough, 1977, 1981) called the field independence-dependence "psychological differentiation." Witkin found that people who were field independent on the performance tests he used also were often characterized by social detachment, task orientation, and lack of interest in what is important to most others. Field independence sometimes also meant independence of the social field, as well as ability to use internal rather than external cues to perceive an upright rod or to select a geometric figure from a complex background. People who did not test as field independent were called field dependent, and Witkin described them as often global in approach and socially sensitive.

5.2 Field Independence and Field Sensitivity

Field independence is often thought to be in opposition to field sensitivity. I have found that in working with students, it seems to make more sense to separate them into two scales. I now view field independence as one continuum, which indicates more or less of an ability, and treat field sensitivity as another, similar continuum. This division (to the best of my knowledge, original to this work) permits the same individual to be both field independent and field sensitive.

The two dimensions are graphically displayed as coordinates in Figure 5.1. Each quadrant indicates a different type of learner. This four-type model will be used throughout the rest of the book.

	Field Sensitivity	
Field Independence	High	Low
High	Type 1	Type 2
Low	Type 3	Type 4

Figure 5.1. Field Independence and Field Sensitivity: Two Related Dimensions

In the best case (Type 1), a learner can be both field independent and field sensitive, so that he or she can both discriminate what is important from the background and also be aware of the cues in the context that modulate language use. In the worst case (Type 4), a learner is both field dependent and field insensitive—unaware of the important points and unaware of environmental signals. Some learners are field independent and field insensitive (Type 2): These are probably good at analyzing language but not so adept when the language must be used in a sociocul tural setting. Finally, the field sensitive and field dependent person (Type 3) gains many cues from the environment but often does not know how or why he or she knows what he or she knows. This last kind of student may be an excellent communicator but is often inaccurate and may "fossilize" (cease to learn any more language other than vocabulary).

As shown in Figure 5.2, there is much variation possible within each of the subtypes. Again, as pointed out in section 4.1, an individual does not operate at the same point on any continuum all the time and under all circumstances. The field independence and field sensitivity scales are no exception, which means that there is even more variability in fact than Figure 5.2 shows.

The terms *analytic* and *global* are frequently used to refer to certain permutations of the field independence-field sensitivity cluster (e.g., Oxford, Ehrman, & Lavine, 1991). A global learner appears to be a field sensitive learner. The weakness of a global learner who is in trouble is field dependence. An analytic learner is very similar to a field independent learner; when this learner gets into trouble, it is probably through field insensitivity. Another way of describing the difference is that field independence is probably an ability (usually finding a geometric figure in a complicated design), whereas analytic learning style is a preference. Similarly, field sensitivity can be viewed as an ability, whereas global learning style is a preference for perceiving the world. Field independence and field sensitivity are described in terms of "more" and "less." Global and analytic are paired opposites, which are usually described in terms of "either-or," though of course they, too, could be described as paired continua.

Type 1 learners (field independent and field sensitive) seem to have relatively few language learning difficulties because they use both of these two styles. With access to the best of both worlds, they can usually adapt to multiple teaching styles and curricula. If they have a strong preference

Field Sensitivity

Field Independence   High   Low

	High	Low

High	A B C
	D Type 1
	  E F
		G
		    Type 2 H
		I J K

Low	L M Type 3 N O P	Q R Type 4 S T U

Figure 5.2. Variations on Learner Types
NOTE: Letters indicate individuals.

in one of the other learning style dimensions, though, a mismatch between strong style and unyielding environment may cause some difficulty, as may a program that constrains the learner's ability to take advantage of multiple ways to learn. *Vanessa* is probably a Type 1 learner. Though she is not having trouble, the following is included to provide a flavor of a Type 1 learner (*Alice* and *Miriam*, whom you will meet later, are also representatives of Type 1 learners).

> Vanessa is oriented toward verbal subjects and the cultural world (as opposed to the scientific world). She says, "I'd say I'm an average learner, and overall I'm doing ok. My present class is mostly auditory, and in it, I'm helped by my good memory and ability to plan my studying, but it's not the best way to learn for me. I would prefer to learn more through reading—a balance between the two would serve me better. I would say overall that I take an observer stance in new situations; in fact, this is my first foreign language, and I'm taking it as a skill that will enhance my work with immigrants. I'm open to other cultures, but I don't anticipate assimilating into them—language is really a skill to enhance other purposes for me. Overall, though I try to stay open to what comes, new words, concepts, grammar patterns, and cultural values, I don't get overwhelmed by it all. I'm able to keep my culture and the new culture and language

separate without trouble. I can keep interested in everything, but I also like solving puzzles and zeroing in on something that seems important or especially interesting or challenging. It's true, though, that if I can't form a certain amount of personal connection with a task—make it mine—I don't get into it very well. One way to make a task mine is to organize my understanding of it in my own way, not the traditional one that is presented in the book or that we are taught in school. That way I can do what needs to be done, make my associations between new and old things, and build my memory networks. I start by experiencing the new lesson or new experience as a whole, then I break it down."

Vanessa rejects mechanical exercises and prefers open-ended classroom activities such as discussions, simulations, and field trips. She especially likes roleplays because they make language personal and contextual. Perhaps part of why Vanessa prefers open-ended activities is that she "is attracted to finding patterns" and is comfortable with inductive learning. She can multitask, doing more than one thing at once.

Not everything Vanessa says is related to field independence and field sensitivity. We do see, though, that she takes a field sensitive approach when she stays open to everything and in her strong preference for learning new things in context, especially a personal one. Also consistent with a global, field sensitive approach is her preference for taking in a new experience as a whole first and her comfort with open-ended, highly contextual activities.

She also shows her field independent side with her ability to select and focus and to plan her work (which requires her to discriminate among tasks and set priorities). Connected with analytic style and field independence are also her pleasure in puzzles and pattern analysis, her comfort with inductive learning (which requires discrimination), and her relatively detached stance toward the language and culture.

Type 2 learners (field independent and field insensitive) are often good classroom learners but may be less successful outside. They may alienate others, including their teachers, classmates, and native speakers of the language and thus be cut off from interactions that help them learn more. They may sense this rejection at some level and become inhibited in reaching out and making opportunities to continue learning. Bert is a case in point.

Bert has some suggestions related to his learning approach. He likes a conceptual framework to attach other things to. He likes "structure" in his course, by which he means knowing what he is responsible for, as well as a mental framework to which he can attach new words, idioms, cultural information. He usually uses the grammar of the language as such a framework. He sometimes freezes up when he cannot follow everything that is said in class and becomes uncomfortable with inaccuracy. He would rather write than speak. Bert sometimes sounds bookish; he's been slow to learn the conversation management words and "fillers" that make interactions go more naturally; he says "they don't interest me." Bert has also said that he finds it difficult to know what others want of him, though he would like to meet their expectations, and so he's uncomfortable when he feels he's under interpersonal judgment.

Type 2 learners need not be as socially uncomfortable as Bert. *Roger* is very personable and at ease with new people, but as a learner, he is strongly field independent and rather limited in his access to field sensitivity in language learning. Roger is an engineering major with a strong quantitative background. He brings his comfort with analytic processing to the language learning process, telling us up-front "My learning style relies heavily on deduction and reasoning" in a biographic background questionnaire. He may be affected also by a relatively low orientation toward subjects with high verbal content. If Roger and Bert were shown in Figure 5.2 as different kinds of Type 2 learners, Roger would probably fall more or less at *I*, whereas Bert would probably show up more in the *H* position.

Those who are field sensitive and field dependent—the Type 3s—are almost the polar opposites of the Type 2s. These people often go overseas, have a wonderful time, can be highly successful in their work and their interactions with host country nationals, but avoid situations that require precision of language or use communication strategies to bluff their way through such situations. As seen in Figure 5.2, there are multiple combinations of high field sensitivity and low field independence that can be classed as Type 3. Other learning style variables can interact with field independence and sensitivity: For example, *David* (introduced below) and Sylvia are distinguished by the concrete-abstract dimension, yet both are Type 3. David is a good example of a concrete Type 3 learner; Sylvia represents the more abstract variety of Type 3.

David has completed secondary school, where his favorite subjects were woodworking and shop. He is attracted to a military career. He has been in a language class for some weeks, now, and he is feeling stressed out and frustrated with the experience. He calls himself a slow learner and describes himself as "hanging in there by his fingernails." He has compared the language learning experience to being in combat. He feels a very strong need for order and structure in the classroom, and he isn't getting enough. He admits that he has a low tolerance of ambiguity and is easily "turned off" when he thinks the classroom material is not relevant for him, which happens frequently. As he describes the class, there is too much time spent "analyzing the instructional materials—dotting the i's and putting in the commas" and not enough spent on "giving tools to students to work with." He thinks the textbook is good, but the teachers don't follow the instructions; they seem to concentrate on grammar rather than on communication. Every evening, David feels completely exhausted and ready to go to bed early. David finds rote learning helpful and prefers to finish a classroom activity completely before moving on to another. He is used to using memorization and practice to achieve his goals; he makes little use of analytic strategies.

David is field dependent. He makes little use of analytic learning strategies and relies on rote learning and mechanical practice instead. He wants to learn in practical contexts and for communicative use, though he limits his ability to learn globally by his quick closing off of things he finds impractical or irrelevant. His concrete preferences show up in his interest in hands-on activities, his "surface" approach to learning tasks, and his desire for "tools" not abstractions. Sylvia, who is interested in working in cross-cultural settings, is a different kind of Type 3 learner.

I've been very frustrated, though over the past few days I've become more accepting of the need for me to do more on my own. I've been feeling for a long time that my needs weren't being met in my class. I come from a family of teachers, and I was a member of a future teachers society before I started this class, so I'm really interested in how my learning is working. I also have to work on appropriate assertion so that I can get a chance to practice speaking. When I get feedback from my teacher, she says that I need to try to say things more simply, and I just can't do it. Is the problem my attitude or the situation? I feel devalued when there is a change in teacher or I get feedback after a test. Sometimes I feel written off.

When I'm doing drills, I don't learn much new, but in free conversation, I make mistakes and keep getting corrected. It leads to a lot of frustration. There isn't enough speaking or drilling time, and that's what I need. I hate drills—they're boring and mechanical, but I know I need them. When other students take a confrontation approach in debates, it gets in my learning space, and I don't function well.

Sylvia, unlike David, does not seek order and structure in her life. She is, however, very much affected by her surroundings, often taking things personally and taking into herself what her classmates do. She needs linguistic context, and she is very much affected by the social context (the latter is affected by personality dimensions described in Chapter 6 but also by her sensitivity to her environment). Sylvia prefers open-ended activities in which she can take advantage of her strengths, but she also gets overwhelmed by the amount of input that she cannot sort out and prioritize. This is at least one reason why she says she needs drilling. She has difficulty structuring her own learning which is something of a field independent skill.

Holly is a Type 4 learner. This appears in her description of some of her frustrations and some classroom interventions that helped her. She has neither the discrimination skills and analytic orientation associated with the field independent learner, nor the ability to learn globally of the field sensitive student.

I've had a lot of trouble with the lack of structure and lack of reinforcement of material in my class. The teachers have been making some helpful changes, though. Now they're writing more on the board in the language. They give pop quizzes and more review—I was really feeling they were piling it on without giving me a chance to check what I'd learned. They're doing a better job now of reinforcing structures that are clearly identified, written down, and maintained for review. Things have gotten better, but I still don't feel I've mastered the basic vocabulary set, because I'm always on the edge of overload, if not in it. I wish they'd help me identify the really basic vocabulary I need. I would like some training in how to make flashcards; they'd help me with sound-symbol matches. Above all, I really need tests and evaluation: Tell me how I'm doing! I need feedback, consistent and regular. Distinguishing between sounds is hard for me—give me a chart, and then give me intensive practice that goes "bing-bing-bing." Drill me, lots.

Holly is disadvantaged on both scales. She does not have the ability to pull out what's important and set her own priorities readily—she is field dependent. On the other hand, she also does not learn by osmosis from the language around her; she cannot manage complicated contexts by either strategy. She is the kind of student who most needs support from her training—scaffolding while she builds her own internal structures and skills. She has very articulately given us a description of what she needs, though in addition she should have guidance and gradually more challenging tasks to help her learn more autonomously down the road.

Type 1 learners are often helped best by being given a lot of learning space. Too much external structure may cramp their ability to use both spotlight and floodlight. If their field independence is very strong, it may be accompanied by some of the same kind of social independence that I have described for certain Type 2 learners. When this becomes a problem, it may involve classroom management as much as the student's individual learning. Type 2 learners may benefit from some help seeing the forest if they tend to get caught up in the specifics of the trees. Type 3 learners, in contrast, may need help sorting out the trees and making discriminations and setting priorities. It is not all equally important now! Holly has given us good advice for assisting Type 4 learners; I would add that we also have an obligation to give them as many tools for self-sufficiency as they can manage.

5.3 Assessment of Field Independence and Field Sensitivity

In contrast with the other learning style dimensions treated in this book, these constructs partake at least as much of ability as of preference. In Chapter 6, I discuss the connection between preference and skill—that we tend to do more of what we find comfortable, and the more we do something, generally, the better we get at it. It is also true that we also may come to prefer things that come easily to us, whose performance adds to our sense of self-efficacy. Thus there is probably a reciprocal relationship between ability and preference. Both motivate us to practice and thus develop skill.

The learning style (preference) aspect of field independence and field sensitivity is probably a product of this kind of relationship. Field independence as an ability probably leads to preference for learning in field independent ways (focused attention and analysis of material). Field sensitivity is similar (use of peripheral learning and global relationship to target material). Personality characteristics of autonomy and task focus for field independence and social adaptability and global approach for field sensitivity may also result from relative comfort with behaviors associated with each "ability."

5.3.1 Field Independence and Field Sensitivity as Preferences

From the point of view of preferences and styles, there is no one instrument that seems to say definitively "field dependent" or "field sensitive." However, I use the Hartmann Boundary Questionnaire (HBQ; Hartmann, 1991) and the MBTI to make inferences about field sensitivity. The HBQ and the MBTI are described in considerable detail in Chapter 6. Relationships between the these two instruments and the field independence and field sensitivity constructs are also addressed in that chapter.

For field independence, I also make inferences from responses to MSQ items that imply comfort with cognitive restructuring activities—for example, guessing from context and learning grammar inductively. In addition, I make inferences from the Myers-Briggs Type Indicator (more on this in the next chapter, after the MBTI scales have been described).

5.3.2 Field Independence as an Ability

The field independence construct originated in attempts by Herman Witkin and his colleagues to assess individuals' ability to perceive the vertical through internal cues, especially proprioception. Original measurement was through such devices as a specially built tilting chair and a rod and frame assembly in which the relationship between the rod and the frame changed. These were found to correlate with a pencil and paper instrument well enough that the latter, more widely available means came into use. At the same time, the construct expanded from a physical ability to perceive the vertical dimension to a cognitive ability to reconstruct mental schemata and to a personality dimension of autonomy and focus on instrumental factors opposed to conformity and generalized receptivity to social cues (Witkin & Goodenough, 1981).

The standard form of assessment for field independence is through some form of disembedding a geometric figure from a complex background—for example, the Embedded Figures Test (EFT, Witkin, 1969). This test must be administered individually to subjects; more practical for many purposes is the Group Embedded Figures Test (GEFT, Oltman, Raskin, & Witkin, 1971), which can be administered to a group, though it still requires a time limit. There are other varieties of this kind of instrument, such as the Hidden Figures Test (Educational Testing Service, 1975), but they all address essentially the same construct. Another commonly used measurement of cognitive restructuring of visually presented geometric figures is the block design subtest of the Wechsler intelligence tests. This is a manipulative as well as visual test: Examinees must place blocks with colored patterns to match a sample.

Brown (1994) suggests that we have only one scale, field independence and its absence, because the available instrumentation measures only field independence. On the other hand, Witkin and Goodenough (1981) describe psychosocial research that suggests that a low score on an EFT is related to greater social receptivity, rather than representing simply an absence of a positive quality that is assessed by a high score. As described previously, I have felt that the construct is made more powerful (i.e., can account for more variation) by treating field independence and field sensitivity as two separate scales.

None of the usual measures of field independence provides a means to assess directly the personality dimensions that Witkin and Goodenough hypothesize. There is also considerable room for question as to the degree to which a test of proprioception or of visual disembedding reflects the kind of cognitive restructuring of verbal material required in language learning.

There are several ways to assess field independence, and in Chapter 9, I will describe my exploration of the Modern Language Aptitude Test (MLAT, Carroll & Sapon, 1959) for this purpose. But how do we assess field dependence, other than as an absence of field independence? Such a definition deprives us of all the interesting variation possible among "field dependent" people.

Another issue is that, although there are good correlations among the rotating chair, rod-and-frame, and embedded figures modalities, they are far from unity. It also seems likely that there are differences between ability to disembed and restructure geometric images on the one hand and the ability to cognitively restructure verbal material on the other.

5.4 Practice

1. What hypotheses about learning style do you make on the basis of the following statements? (More than one style may apply.) Reminder: The style dimensions that have been addressed so far in this and the preceding chapter are: (a) auditory-kinesthetic-visual, sequential-random, (b) concrete-abstract, (c) deductive-inductive, (d) left-right, (e) field independent-field dependent, and (f) field-sensitive-field insensitive.

a. I can't imagine what I haven't seen.
b. I discover grammar patterns for myself.
c. We learn dialogues by heart so we will have a firm base when we try to speak.
d. Classroom discussions about controversial topics help me learn.
e. The instructor systematically follows a textbook or syllabus.
f. I like to use audiotapes at home; they help me more than the book does.
g. I wish the class would take field trips to places where we can use the language outside the classroom.
h. It is useful and challenging to read (or listen to) material that is over my head, with a lot of material in it that I don't know.
i. I can remember something better when I write it down.
j. I liked to interview native speakers of the target language and report on the interviews.
k. I daydream in long classes and lectures.
l. I want to learn something well before we move on.
m. I like it when the teacher explains a rule and then gives examples of it.
n. Let's do a simulation or a roleplay!
o. There are chances to get up and move around the classroom.
p. I can cope with "fuzziness" as long as it's clearly delineated. (A student really said this!)

2. Look at all the cases treated so far and see whether you can find evidence for each of the dimensions described in this chapter and the

preceding one. For instance, what evidence can you find for sequential and random processing in the case material provided at the earlier chapters, at the beginning of Chapter 4, and in sections treating other learning style dimensions than sequential-random?

3. Based on what you have read so far, write yourself up as if you were one of the cases in the book. What are your preferences? What helps you? What hinders your learning? What are some of your favorite learning techniques? How do they reflect your learning style preferences?

5.5 More Information

For those who are interested in knowing more about the history and theoretical underpinnings of field independence-field dependence, Witkin & Goodenough, (1981) provide a readable and clear overview of Witkin's construct, which he calls "psychological differentiation." Chapelle and Green (1992) is a thorough overview of the application of the field independence construct in foreign language learning research; Griffiths and Sheen (1992) provide a critical review of the research using the construct to Chapelle (1992) responds in a rebuttal article, and to which in turn Sheen (1993) responds. Brown (1994) also treats the field independence-dependence dimension.

Note

1. Although used with a somewhat different meaning in the present work, the term *field sensitivity* is borrowed from Ramìrez and Castañeda (1974), who use it as a synonym for field dependence. Their description of the field sensitive child emphasizes sociability and attachment. Such a child prefers to work with and help others, is sensitive to others' feelings, expresses positive feelings for and wants to become like the teacher, seeks teacher guidance and rewards, is motivated by working with the teacher, and is helped when curriculum objectives and outline are clearly explained, concepts are presented in narrative format and are related to personal interests and experience. Ramìrez and Castañeda describe the field independent child as follows: prefers independent work, competition, achievement of individual recognition; task orientation to exclusion of the social environment when on task; rarely seeks physical contact with teacher, interactions with teacher restricted to tasks, likes to try new tasks on own and to begin and finish quickly, seeks nonsocial rewards; deals well with math and science; and is helped by a curriculum in which details of concepts are emphasized (parts have meaning on their own) and which is based on a discovery approach.

Personality Models

Chapter 6, the third of three chapters treating learning styles, addresses models that involve personality dispositions as well as cognitive styles. The chapter begins with a description of Carl Jung's model of personality as adapted by Myers and Briggs. This powerful system combines some dimensions addressed in Chapters 4 and 5 with personality characteristics, resulting in a model that accounts for introversion, extraversion, information gathering, decision making, and need for order or flexibility in one's lifestyle.

Next, the construct of ego boundaries provides the foundation for a discussion of tolerance of ambiguity, which in turn underlies an original model of learning based on personality differences. The chapter ends with a discussion of how to apply an understanding of learning styles.

6.1 Dimensions Combining Personality Dispositions and Cognitive Learning Styles

The previous chapters introduced some commonly used learning style dimensions that are oriented primarily toward cognitive processing. Some of these dimensions also relate to personality and have personality correlates. A good example is field independence, which has personality features.

In this chapter, the emphasis is reversed. The focus here is on personality dimensions that have cognitive style correlates. I will first treat the Myers-Briggs model, then a personality dimension that addresses ego boundaries. The ego boundaries scale is helpful in looking at the construct of tolerance of ambiguity that I discuss next. All these concepts are used to build a model of learning. I conclude with a discussion of style matches and mismatches.

In section 4.3, I enumerated several "composite" learning style models: Kolb (1985), 4MAT (McCarthy, 1987), the Gregorc model (1982a), and the Myers-Briggs model (Myers & McCaulley, 1985). All four of these frequently used models are built on the theories of the Swiss psychiatrist Carl Jung (1971) about conscious functioning. Each adds something to that theory: Kolb uses concepts from Piaget, and McCarthy (building on Kolb) adds the left-right hemisphere metaphor. Gregorc reinterprets the Jungian functions in terms of orientation to time and order. Myers added a fourth dimension to Jung's three original categories, originally to elucidate theory, but the dimension took on a life of its own. The remainder of this discussion addresses Jung's categories through the lens of the Myers-Briggs model, which I have found particularly useful. I go into it at some length so it can be used in discussions in the remainder of the book.

6.2 The Myers-Briggs Scales

The Myers-Briggs model works with four dimensions: (a) extraversion-introversion, (b) sensing-intuition, (c) thinking-feeling, and (d) judging-perceiving. *Sensing, intuition, thinking,* and *feeling* are mental "functions" in this model, whereas *extraversion, introversion, judging,* and *perceiving* are described as "attitudes," to distinguish them from the four functions.

Jung was the first to bring the concepts of extraversion and introversion into wide use. (In the Myers-Briggs world, extraversion-introversion is called an *attitude,* in contrast to the mental functions.) In addition, Jung posited two bipolar functions. One of these functions is oriented toward experiencing the world; the dimension is called the *perceiving function.*

The other function is oriented toward making decisions and taking action in the world; it is called the *judging function*. Most people prefer one of the two possible perceiving functions *and* one of the two possible judging functions. The other two functions are also part of each of us, but we ordinarily have much less conscious access to and control of them.

Perceiving Functions. These are the two information-gathering functions. Jung called the two perceiving functions sensing and intuition.

Sensing takes in information through the well-known five senses, and it comes to consciousness with relatively little further processing. Thus a person who prefers sensing and typically deals with the world through the sensing function is aware of and interested in the physical world around him or her, in all its rich detail. It is not surprising that such a person may be quite concrete in orientation because the here and now are of interest and are salient.

Intuition, too, takes in information through the five senses, but something more happens to the perception on the way to consciousness. The person who prefers intuition to perceive the world is oriented toward meaning, patterns, possibilities, and generalizations. Detail is often irrelevant to the intuitive, and so is the present. The future is where the action is, and that is where the person preferring intuition focuses. With an interest in patterns and the meanings of things, unsurprisingly the intuitive tends to favor abstract processing.

Judging Functions. There are also two decision-making functions. Jung called these two functions thinking and feeling. His choice of words sometimes causes confusion because he meant both of these terms in a specialized way, rather than the way we use them every day. It is important to keep in mind that so-called thinking types have feelings, deep ones, and so-called feeling types can think and think well.

Thinking in Jung's and Myers' terms means decision making based on logical principles. A thinking judgment attempts to exclude subjective or illogical criteria from the decision-making process. In fact, a thinking approach sometimes attempts to exclude the emotional dimension from life altogether, unless one's own and or others' feelings are part of the cause-and-effect chain. In crude terms, judgments are made on a pragmatic, makes-sense-or-not scale with the head. Although they can be very appreciative, thinking types can express more criticism because they believe that what is good is self-evident and improvement comes from assessing and describing needs. Truth and fairness are very important to thinking types.

Feeling, on the other hand, is a process of making decisions based on values and what is important to oneself and others. In very crude terms, judgments are made on a like-dislike scale with the heart. Feeling types may reject analytic processing; they are often strongly oriented to the interpersonal and assume they know what is important to the other (even when the other does not claim the feeling). Unlike thinking types, feeling types, who can in fact be extremely critical but are slow to voice it, tend to be quick to express appreciation of others and what others do. Interpersonal harmony is very important to feeling types.

Energy Direction. Much of Jung's classic work *Psychological Types* (1921) is devoted to working out the concept of *extraversion* and *introversion.* These complex constructs are interpreted in the Myers-Briggs model as referring to how one's energy flows. If people can be likened to storage batteries, extraversion stores energy by contact with the outside world in all its multiplicity; introversion stores it in solitude or with one or two trusted friends. In the other direction, too much interaction or activity in the outer world "drains" the introvert's battery, whereas too much time alone or in concentrated solitary activity drains the extravert.

Each can learn to operate successfully in the other's milieu, but sooner or later some recharging time is needed. For example, as an introvert, I can gain great stimulation and pleasure from an academic conference at which I speak, meet new people, interact with old acquaintances, and so on. I have found, however, that to fully benefit from the conference, I have to find some time to read or work by myself. Only a few hours of "introvert time" will do it, but if I do not get them, I lose perspective and behave in ways I regret later. Similarly, extraverts can study, write books, and enjoy time alone, but sooner or later they are likely to find themselves needing to seek some external stimulation, whether a conversation or just a dose of television news.

Extraverts generally seem to be vulnerable to understimulation. Introverts, on the other hand, appear to be vulnerable to overstimulation. Extraverts tend toward impulsivity and action; introverts tend toward reflectivity and contemplation. Extraverts on at least one measure prefer auditory and oral activity; introverts prefer visual and written work (Saunders, 1989). At least in the United States, introverts tend to report higher anxiety levels. There is fascinating work being done now that suggests physical bases in levels of brain arousal for introverts and extraverts and for sensing types and intuitives (Newman, 1995).

Need for Structure in Life. Extraversion-introversion, sensing-intuition, and thinking-feeling were Carl Jung's original personality dimensions. In an effort to find a way to determine which of the four functions (sensing, intuition, thinking, feeling) was the most important one for each individual (the so-called dominant function), Isabel Myers worked out a fourth dimension, which she called *judging-perceiving.* (The Myers-Briggs model also calls this an *attitude,* similar to extraversion-introversion.) This dimension proved so useful that it took on a life of its own in the Myers-Briggs model. It is called judging-perceiving.[1]

This name sometimes causes confusion. It may be helpful to keep in mind that judging or perceiving when used by themselves are attitudes; when they are used as adjectives before the word *function* (e.g., judging function), they tell us which of the function scales is under discussion.

Judging types tend to seek an orderly, predictable life. They seek to plan their work, their travel, and their other activities. They also seek closure; because they deal with the outside world through their most preferred judging function (thinking or feeling), they seek to resolve ambiguity and bring processes to an end and a decision. Judging types often prefer sequential processing, especially those who prefer sensing. They are often product oriented. Judging types are the "getters-done."

Perceiving types, on the other hand, want to keep their options open. They at least tolerate and often thrive on surprises and ambiguity. They often resist closure; they also can resist efforts of others to impose order on their lives. Instead, to deal with the world with their most preferred perceiving function (sensing or intuition), they try to keep information channels open and keep collecting data until they are satisfied that they know as much as they need to activate their judging function. They are often "random" processors, especially if they prefer intuition. Perceivers value process and flexibility.

6.2.1 Putting the Myers-Briggs Scales Together

The four Myers-Briggs scales, in the order they are usually described and with their usual abbreviations, include the following:

1. Extraversion (E)-Introversion (I)
2. Sensing (S)-Intuition (N)
3. Thinking (T)-Feeling (F)
4. Judging (J)-Perceiving (P)

(N is used to abbreviate intuition, because I has already been used for introversion.)

In that these are bipolar scales in which an individual is assumed to have a preference on one side or the other, there are 16 possible combinations, which are called types. They are usually referred to by a shorthand that uses the abbreviations so, for instance, an extraverted sensing thinking judging type is called ESTJ. An introverted intuitive feeling perceiving type is called INFP. The 16 types are conventionally displayed in a four-by-four matrix called a type table (Figure 6.1). Characteristics associated with each of the four scales are summarized in Table 6.1. When they come together in one of the 16 types, they are more than the sum of the parts, as can be seen in Figure 6.2, which shows the brief descriptions of all the 16 types that are usually provided when one takes the questionnaire that is most often used to assess psychological type, the Myers-Briggs Type Indicator (MBTI, Myers & McCaulley, 1985).

The type table can be divided in a variety of ways. For example, one common model looks at the two letters that come in the middle of the type name (S or N and T or F), the function pairs. People can be described as ST, SF, NF, or NT; each has its associated characteristics that are both the sum of the parts and more than the sum of the parts. The function pair model is useful for looking at learning styles. Another commonly used model is called "temperament." Its scales of interest are SJ, SP, NF, and NT. It is particularly useful for describing behaviors and values. An important book on the Myers-Briggs model and learning styles used the four "quadrants" of the type table—IS, IN, ES, and EN—to look at learning differences (Lawrence, 1993). Some work on organizations looks at the perceiving function together with the judging-perceiving attitude: SJ, SP, NJ, and NP.

ISTJ	ISFJ	INFJ	INTJ
ISTP	ISFP	INFP	INTP
ESTP	ESFP	ENFP	ENTP
ESTJ	ESFJ	ENFJ	ENTJ

NOTE: Guide to the type table: (a) introversion in the top half, extraversion in the bottom half; (b) sensing in the left half, intuition in the right half; (c) thinking in the two outer columns, feeling in the two inner columns; and (d) judging in the top and bottom rows, perceiving in the middle two rows.

Figure 6.1. The MBTI Type Table Array

The Myers-Briggs model posits that each of the poles of the four scales is normal and healthy. (For this reason, when I administer the MBTI, I tell respondents that it is a "no fault" questionnaire because there are no right or wrong answers or good or bad types.) However, some preferences and some types are more comfortable in certain social settings, and people of whom they are characteristic tend to self-select into these settings. For instance, people who prefer a very structured life may choose a military career. (This is why the MBTI is very useful in career counseling.)

Similarly, behavior associated with some preferences will receive more social approval than others in a given setting. Behavior such as outgoingness that tends to be associated with a preference for extraversion, for example, is usually more accepted in the United States than is that associated with introversion, which may be interpreted as reclusiveness or shyness. Overall U.S. norms appear to favor extraversion, sensing, thinking (women experience pressure to behave in ways associated with feeling), and judging. On the other hand, in universities, introversion and intuition are rewarded in the arts and sciences, so settings make a difference. The model itself is nonjudgmental, but settings and other people do not always withhold judgment, which can mean stress when the individual's preferences are out of harmony with environmental norms.

The psychological type model is predicated on the idea that the four scales that combine to make each of the 16 types are preferences (see

Table 6.1 Characteristics of the Four MBTI Scales

Extraversion	*Introversion*
Outside world	Internal world
Action	Introspection
Interaction	Concentration
Gregarious	A few people at a time
Seeks to find stimulation	Seeks to manage or reduce stimulation
Impulsivity (at extreme)	"Paralysis by analysis" (at extreme)
Auditory	Visual
Talkative and expressive	Reflective and contained
Likes study groups	Likes to work alone

Sensing	*Intuition*
Relatively direct from five senses	Further processed before becoming conscious
Physical world	Meanings
Sequential (especially if with judging)	Random (especially if with perceiving)
Experience	Inspiration
Specifics	Generalizations
Detail	Big picture
What is	What could be
Concrete	Abstract

Thinking	*Feeling*
Head	Heart
Seeks objectivity	Values subjectivity
Logic	Values
Truth	Tact
Fairness	Harmony
Expresses critique	Expresses appreciation
Analytic	Global
Cost-benefit	Like-dislike

Judging	*Perceiving*
Planned	Open-ended
Closure	Options
Decisions	Flexibility
Sequential (especially if with sensing)	Random (especially if with intuition)
"Vertical" filer	"Horizontal" filer
Conscientiousness	Autonomy
Product	Process
Seeks certitude	Tolerance of ambiguity

SOURCE: Adapted from handout materials used at the Foreign Service Institute, School of Professional Studies, 1986.

	Sensing Types	Sensing Types	Intuitive Types	Intuitive Types
Introverts	**ISTJ** Serious, quiet, earn success by concentration and thoroughness. Practical, orderly, matter-of-fact, logical, realistic, and dependable. See to it that everything is well organized. Take responsibility. Make up their own minds as to what should be accomplished and work toward it steadily, regardless of protests or distractions.	**ISFJ** Quiet, friendly, responsible, and conscientious. Work devotedly to meet their obligations. Lend stability to any project or group. Thorough, painstaking, and accurate. Their interests are usually not technical. Can be patient with necessary details. Loyal, considerate, perceptive, concerned with how other people feel.	**INFJ** Succeed by perseverance, originality, and desire to do whatever is needed or wanted. Put their best efforts into their work. Quietly forceful, conscientious, concerned for others. Respected for their firm principles. Likely to be honored and followed for their clear visions as to how best serve the common good.	**INTJ** Have original minds and great drive for their own ideas and purposes. Have long-range vision and quickly find meaningful patterns in external events. In fields that appeal to them, they have a fine power to organize a job and carry it through. Skeptical, critical, independent, determined, have high standards of competence and performance.
Introverts	**ISTP** Cool onlookers—quiet, reserved, observing and analyzing life with detached curiosity and unexpected flashes of original humor. Usually interested in cause and effect, how and why mechanical things work, and in organizing facts using logical principles. Excel at getting to the core of a practical problem and finding the solution.	**ISFP** Retiring, quietly friendly, sensitive, kind, modest about their abilities. Shun disagreements, do not force their opinions or values on others. Usually do not care to lead but are often loyal followers. Often relaxed about getting things done because they enjoy the present moment and do not want to spoil it by undue haste or exertion.	**INFP** Quiet observers, idealistic, loyal. Important that outer life be congruent with inner values. Curious, quick to see possibilities, often serve as catalysts to implement ideas. Adaptable, flexible, and accepting unless a value is threatened. Want to understand people and ways of fulfilling human potential. Little concern with possessions or surroundings.	**INTP** Quiet and reserved. Especially enjoy theoretical or scientific pursuits. Like solving problems with logic and analysis. Interested usually in ideas, with little liking for parties or small talk. Tend to have sharply defined interests. Need careers where some strong interest can be used and useful.
Extraverts	**ESTP** Good at on-the-spot problem solving. Like action, enjoy whatever comes along. Tend to like mechanical things and sports, with friends on the side. Adaptable, tolerant, pragmatic; focused on getting results. Dislike long explanations. Are best with real things that can be worked, handled, taken apart, or put together.	**ESFP** Outgoing, accepting, friendly, enjoy everything and make things more fun for others by their enjoyment. Like action and making things happen. Know what's going on and join in eagerly. Find remembering facts easier than mastering theories. Are best in situations that need sound common sense and practical ability with people.	**ENFP** Warmly enthusiastic, high-spirited, ingenious, imaginative. Able to do almost anything that interests them. Quick with a solution for any difficulty and ready to help anybody with a problem. Often rely on their ability to improvise instead of preparing in advance. Can usually find compelling reasons for whatever they want.	**ENTP** Quick, ingenious, good at many things. Stimulating company, alert and outspoken. May argue for fun on either side of a question. Resourceful in solving new and challenging problems, but may neglect routine assignments. Apt to turn to one new interest after another. Skillful in finding logical reasons for what they want.
Extraverts	**ESTJ** Practical, realistic, matter-of-fact, with a natural head for business or mechanics. Not interested in abstract theories; want learning to have direct and immediate application. Like to organize and run activities. Often make good administrators; are decisive, quickly move to implement decisions; take care of routine details.	**ESFJ** Warm-hearted, talkative, popular, conscientious, born cooperators, active committee members. Need harmony and may be good at creating it. Always doing something nice for someone. Work best with encouragement and praise. Main interest is in things that directly and visibly affect people's lives.	**ENFJ** Responsive and responsible. Feel real concern for what others think or want, and try to handle things with due regard for other's feelings. Can present a proposal or lead a group discussion with ease and tact. Sociable, popular, sympathetic. Responsive to praise and criticism. Like to facilitate others and enable people to achieve their potential.	**ENTJ** Frank, decisive, leaders in activities. Develop and implement comprehensive systems to solve organizational problems. Good at anything that requires reasoning and intelligent talk, such as public speaking. Are usually well-informed and enjoy adding to their fund of knowledge.

Figure 6.2. Characteristics Frequently Associated With Each Type

section 4.2.1 above), not abilities. As with other learning styles based on preferences, however, there is a relationship. It comes from the inclination that we tend to do more of what we are comfortable with. The more we do it, the more comfortable with it we become. In addition, in that we tend to get better at what we practice, we often develop skill at activities associated with the preference. The nice thing about this phenomenon is that it is never too late to increase our skills in those things we prefer less. If our preferred hand becomes incapacitated, we can learn to do many things with the other hand, though probably not as fluently.

Expertise in any of the learning style models is useful for making sense of the raw data of experience, observation, and interviews. It is so useful that I often am asked by teachers how they can get access to the Myers-Briggs Type Indicator, which is what I usually use in workshops that determine participant styles (more on the subject of questionnaires in Chapter 9). I usually say that although questionnaires are useful, there is a great deal that can be learned from observation and interviewing techniques such as those described in Chapters 2 and 3.

Learning style categories, such as those of the Myers-Briggs model, can function as sensitizing concepts as described above in section 2.3.1, always of course on condition that they do not prevent us from seeing what does not fit the sensitizing concept. (Many of my best insights have come from figuring out information that did not fit in.) Observation scales are also useful: Lawrence (1993) includes one for the type table quadrants (IS, IN, ES, EN). The questionnaire results must be checked with the respondent, and they are not always accurate. People may show a different facet of themselves depending on circumstances, including their relationship with you. Even very experienced "type watchers" make mistakes when they guess people's Myers-Briggs types. So every observation and inference about psychological type or other learning style dimension *must* be treated as a hypothesis, though it may become a very strong hypothesis.

As mentioned in Chapter 4, MBTI scales include some of the cognitive learning styles. The probability is high that a person who prefers sensing and judging will also prefer to learn sequentially, and equally so that an intuitive-perceiving type will prefer random learning when confident with the material. (Intuitive-feeling-perceiving types may want more external structure than do intuitive-thinking-perceiving types because intuitive-thinking types are often inclined naturally to attempt cognitive restructuring of material for themselves. Thinking types, on the other hand, tend to appreciate an organized presentation of material or curriculum.) Sensing-perceiving types usually tolerate both sequential and random input, whereas intuitive judging types are less predictable. I usually have to inquire further for the intuitive judging types.

6.2.2 Examples of MBTI Scales in Case Material

The following case material is designed to illustrate how the Myers-Briggs scales may show up in students. (Again, the case index is available for tracking the people we are meeting.) Most of the material used in this section is taken from the preceding chapters, though in a few instances I introduce new information about a learner we have already met. Information that supports the hypothesis is highlighted. None of the vignettes below gives an exhaustive picture of all the behavioral correlates of the Myers-Briggs preference it is intended to illustrate. Some of the vignettes reflect other preferences as well because, as mentioned earlier, the preferences work together to make complex wholes.

Extraversion and Introversion.   The following is some more observation information on Betty, whom we met in Chapter 4. Betty is an *active participant* in class. She can find something to say about most topics, and she *likes to think aloud*. Often she'll *jump right into* a new task. She has already taken a *leading role in inviting professors* who are native speakers to give presentations to the students in the target language and organizing a field trip or two. To the best of your knowledge, she has *wide contacts* among the teachers and other students in the program.

Betty exhibits a number of common behavioral correlates for extraversion. She is active, thinks aloud, and is sometimes impulsive; she likes at times to learn by trial and error. She finds it natural to reach out and make connections with people (e.g., with the visiting professors) and organize outings. Her range of contacts is wide. Betty is also likely to get edgy if she has to study in a concentrated way for a long time.

Interviews have told you more about Bert. He *feels shy about "performing" (speaking in class)* unless he knows his audience; he likes to feel he's "in it together" with the others. *Being under the spotlight is stressful* for him, especially if he has not had *the opportunity to think something through before he says it*. His relations with classmates and teachers are *low key* but easy. He is *not gregarious* but is friendly, *especially if there is some common ground:* He has a special bond with a teacher who shares his enjoyment of fine points of grammar.

Typical of many introverts, Bert likes to think something over before he has to say it (or "perform"), especially if there are a number of people present. He tends not to be a networker. He is more likely to form a bond if there is a common interest. Bert would rather study alone than in a group or even in a pair, though he will do it if it is part of the classroom structure. He has excellent powers of concentration.

Introversion and extraversion have not made a difference to learning success in small, relatively stable classes (Ehrman & Oxford, 1995). In larger groupings, however, extraverts are likely to get more "airtime" because they are not only more willing to talk in a group but they also may need to talk. It remains to be seen if extraversion is of advantage in natural language use settings—extraverts will make more contacts more readily, but only a few interlocutors can be enough for the language exposure needed, so introverts should be able to do well too.

Sensing and Intuition. We have seen that Vanessa *rejects mechanical exercises* and prefers *open-ended* classroom activities such as discussions, simulations, and field trips. She prefers roleplays because they make language personal and contextual. Perhaps Vanessa likes open-ended activities partly because she "is attracted to *finding patterns*" and is comfortable with *inductive learning.* She can multitask, doing more than one thing at once.

Vanessa prefers intuition. This shows in her preference for open-ended, nonmechanical learning and her interest in patterns. She likes inductive learning because it permits her to find the patterns she enjoys and to make associations in her own way.

In contrast, David feels a very strong need for *order and structure in the classroom,* and he is not getting enough. He admits that he has a *low tolerance of ambiguity* and is easily *"turned off" when he thinks the classroom material is not relevant* for him, which happens frequently. As he describes the class, "there is . . . not enough [time] spent on giving *tools* to students to work with." David finds *rote learning* helpful and prefers to finish a classroom activity completely before moving on to another. He is *used to using memorization and practice* to achieve his goals.

Students who prefer sensing, especially when combined with judging, tend to want external structure from a curriculum, syllabus, or lesson plan. They are often intolerant of ambiguity and want to learn in a highly concrete way (e.g., David's tools). Rote learning is more comfortable for sensing types than for intuitives.

Sensing and intuition are the learning style dimensions par excellence. After all, what is taking in information but learning? Perhaps for this reason, as well as the fact that this scale includes several of the scales described above in Chapter 4 and relates in some ways to field independence, the sensing-intuition dimension has more impact on overall learning than any other MBTI dimension. Sensing types tend to be overrepresented among students who do poorly in intensive, communicatively oriented training that seeks to bring students to a high level of proficiency. I have found that it is probable that sensing is more disadvantageous to learners than intuition is advantageous (Ehrman, 1994a, 1994b)—after all, many other things can go wrong for intuitives despite their otherwise favorable learning predispositions, which reduces what advantage they may have. On the other hand, I cannot emphasize enough that there are excellent learners of every MBTI type. Many students who prefer sensing do very well indeed at language learning—they can take advantage of their highly developed observation skills and increase their tolerance of ambiguity.

Thinking and Feeling. One manifestation of thinking appears in the description of Roger. We saw that he is an *engineering* major with a strong *quantitative* background. He brings his comfort with *analytic processing* to the language learning process, telling us up-front "My learning style relies heavily on deduction and *reasoning."*

Engineering is a field that appeals overwhelmingly to thinking types. Thinking types gravitate to analytical processing, and like to take apart and recombine ideas, if they prefer intuition, or things, if they prefer sensing). They are inclined to trust reasoning above all other ways of knowing.

Vanessa, said earlier that she "especially likes roleplays because they make language *personal* and contextual." The need for a sense of personal relationship with people, ideas, and events, is very characteristic of a feeling type. We can thus take a guess that Vanessa is an intuitive feeling type.

The preferences do not always manifest in entirely helpful ways. Sylvia, also a feeling type, is a case in point. She says "I also have to work on appropriate *assertion* so that I can get a chance to practice speaking. When I get feedback from my teacher, she says that I need to try to say things more simply, and I just can't do it. I *feel devalued* when there is a change in teacher or I get feedback after a test. Sometimes I feel written off. *When other students take a confrontation approach in debates, it gets in my learning space, and I don't function well.*"

The down side of the personal relationship that feeling types want to establish with everyone and everything is that sometimes they take personally what is not meant that way. Consequently, Sylvia takes personally a routine change of teacher or standard test feedback. Her learning is also disrupted by classroom friction, because of the feeling type's need for interpersonal harmony. Need for harmony can also lead feeling types to accommodate more to others' wishes than they are really satisfied with and then harbor resentment.

Thinking types are less vulnerable to the kinds of distress that Sylvia describes. Instead, they are especially subject to performance anxiety because so much of their self-esteem is tied up in tasks and competence. They may, if not mature, experience unnecessary friction with classmates and teachers that makes them less well liked. As a result, they may not receive the benefit of the doubt and the little breaks that are given to those who are better liked, and native interlocutors may not be as patient with them.

As learners, intuitive feeling types in particular often take a global approach to learning (see section 5.2). Thinking types are often analytic in their learning style though the kind of analysis is more concrete for sensing thinking and more abstract (hypothesis testing) for intuitive thinking. David is probably a sensing thinking type and concretely analytic; Roger is likely to be an intuitive thinking type and operates by deduction and what he calls "reasoning," that is, hypothesis formation and testing.

Judging and Perceiving. In her interview, Kelly's way of learning suggests a preference for judging:

Interviewer. So you like to get *control of the form*, then think about what it means.

Kelly. Yes, most of the time. I really like studying reading—the foreign alphabet is really interesting to learn. What's really hard is comprehension in class, especially if I haven't seen it in writing or on the blackboard. I just get lost. It goes too fast, and I can't keep up with it.

Interviewer. You can manage the reading and enjoy it, but in-class comprehension just gets out of control.

Kelly. Yes, I *just never know what to expect* in class when I have to listen.

A judging type tends to like to learn sequentially and control one thing before going on to another. Unpredictability is a source of discomfort to the judging type, who seeks predictability in his or her life and dislikes ambiguity.

Janet, on the other hand, has told us that she would have preferred a lot more problem-solving activities such as roleplays and simulations in her class. She found helpful the brief summaries of news or other topics that they were asked to do sometimes, where there was *not always a lot of time for preparation.* She found *too much classroom routine and predictability* unhelpful, even stultifying. When the teacher was willing to let students use the language with him and was *flexible* as student needs changed, she learned better.

Dislike of classroom routine and predictability is suggestive of a preference for perceiving. A perceiving type is likely to value flexibility in self and others, so this was a positive feature in Janet's teacher. Perceiving types are often energized by last-minute preparation and thinking on their feet. They often prefer to work in bursts. For younger perceivers in particular, leaving things to the last minute can cause them trouble. Well-developed, more mature perceivers can usually calculate the risks of waiting until the last minute quite accurately and act accordingly.

Judging is correlated with sensing, and perceiving is correlated with intuition at the .30 to .40 level in most samples (Myers & McCaulley, 1985). This level is high enough to indicate that the SJ (sensing-judging) and NP (intuitive-perceiving) combinations are more common than SP (sensing-perceiving) and NJ (intuitive-judging), but low enough that there are plenty of SPs and NJs. Kelly is probably an NJ, whereas Janet is probably an NP. Both judging and perceiving types have strengths and weaknesses.

Judging types tend to get their work done in an orderly way; they are often natural time managers. Their downside is sometimes intolerance of ambiguity and a need to control the uncontrollable. These characteristics may be intensified if they prefer sensing. Perceivers are usually more tolerant of ambiguity and willing to "go with the flow." On the other hand, they can suffer from lack of "push" and may resist external structure that could be helpful to them. As mentioned, they often prefer to "wing it" with minimal or last-minute preparation. A preference for intuition may intensify these perceiver characteristics.

6.2.3 Assessing Personality Type With the MBTI

This learning style model is closely linked with the instrument that was designed to assess it, the Myers-Briggs Type Indicator (MBTI). Although it is possible to hypothesize an individual's psychological type preferences through observation or by interview ("typewatching"), one can get the individual's own perception of his or her own preferences through a properly administered and interpreted MBTI. The MBTI can be used to test your typewatching hypothesis about the individual's personality structure.

The MBTI must be purchased by and should be administered and interpreted by a qualified professional. Qualification requires training in tests and measurements, and specialized training in the special features of the MBTI is strongly recommended. Those who are not qualified can call on qualified colleagues or counseling staff to administer and interpret the MBTI for them.

Depending on the version of the MBTI used, you can get a little or a lot of additional information from the scores. Most MBTI practitioners use the standard Form G, which takes 20 to 40 minutes to fill out. This version provides consistency scores for each of the preference scales; these consistency scores are interpreted as strength of preference. That is, a higher "preference (consistency) score" is inferred to mean greater expressed preference for that pole of the scale (not necessarily possession of more of the qualities associated with that pole of the scale). Thus, for instance, a person who has a high preference score for intuition is someone who "voted" consistently for intuition most of the time the choice was given to him or her, but this individual is not necessarily a "strong intuitive" with well-developed intuitive skills.

The two longer versions of the MBTI, Forms K and J, provide five subscales for each of the preference scales. These can provide considerable information about what kind of feeling type or judging type a person is and can help us understand why, for instance, one ESFP is not like another ESFP you know. These two forms are used with two scoring systems, the Expanded Analysis Report (EAR, Kummerow & Quenk, 1992) and the Type Differentiation Indicator (TDI, Saunders, 1989), also mentioned in section 4.5.2. The EAR provides 5 subscales for each of the 4 main preference scales. The TDI provides the same 20 subscales as the EAR, but it also includes 7 subscales that belong to two grouping categories simultaneously. One of these two categories is a main preference scale, such as EI or SN. The other category to which each of these 7 subscales belongs has to do with how comfortably one is adjusted to one's milieu. For this reason these 7 subscales are called *comfort-discomfort scales*. The TDI is particularly helpful when Form G of the MBTI (which yields only the four main scales) is ambiguous or contradictory. Form J is machine scored; consequently, the time lag in scoring makes the EAR and TDI somewhat impractical when help is needed quickly.

The psychological types of the case examples above were all assessed by the MBTI.

6.3 The Ego Boundary Construct

Another very useful personality dimension with cognitive effects comes from the world of sleep research. Ernest Hartmann became interested in the differences between people who suffered from nightmares and those who rarely experienced them. He posited another bipolar scale and designed a psychological test, the Hartmann Boundary Questionnaire (HBQ) to measure this dimension (Hartmann, 1991). At one extreme of the scale fall tendencies to make clear separations among internal states (such as states of wakefulness) and to keep categories clearly delineated in daily life. People at this end of the continuum tend to be relatively meticulous and orderly; they may not be very receptive to new information. The name for such characteristics is "thick ego boundaries."

Hartmann's prototypes for such people were naval officers (Hartmann, 1991).

In contrast, at the other end of the continuum is the tendency to make few distinctions among internal states, so that, for instance, thinking and feeling are not necessarily always distinct processes. Such people may claim to have had extrasensory perception experiences. Sometimes these people let everything in—almost as if they had no skin—and can become overwhelmed by it all. They are often very creative. This end of the continuum is referred to as "thin ego boundaries." Hartmann's prototypes are art students and psychotherapists.

Although at either extreme there can be some dysfunction associated with thick and thin boundaries, this is another model of normal functioning. One can have rather thick boundaries and be a solid, contributing citizen through such occupations as engineering, the law, or plumbing, for instance. On the other hand, one can be an equally contributing member of society with thin boundaries, in the arts, as a psychotherapist, or as a language teacher, to cite a few examples. Thick boundaries correlate moderately with MBTI sensing, thinking, and judging; thin boundaries correlate with MBTI intuition, feeling, and perceiving (Ehrman, 1993), Hartmann (1991) found younger people and females to have somewhat thinner boundaries than older people and males.

Keith and *Jenny* are prototypical thick and thin boundary students. Both are more or less average on a test of language learning aptitude, but both are having trouble (These two cases are adapted from Ehrman, 1993).

Keith wants to know the grammar first, do exercises, and be well prepared before he engages in the more communicative activities his language class requires. He wants his tasks clearly defined. He is spending many, many hours on his studies and feels guilty when he takes time off, because he feels strongly that he should do perfect work. His difficulty comes especially in the constant unstructured class activities such as debates or round-robin storytelling, where it is certain that language he has not learned will come up. He majored in engineering, and this is his first language learning attempt. He is probably a Type 4 learner (field dependent and field insensitive). Keith has "thick" ego boundaries

Jenny, on the other hand, really enjoys learning through content-based materials. She had some exposure to another language in a previous overseas assignment and enjoyed learning it "by the seat of her pants." She dislikes it when the flow of content is stopped by unfamiliar structure or vocabulary. She wants everything she is to learn to be out on the table at once, so that she can try to integrate it. Her difficulty can be summarized as "things just mush," and she gets overloaded quickly. She is a literature major and probably a Type 3 learner (field dependent and field sensitive). Jenny has "thin" ego boundaries

Hartmann himself speculated that thinner boundaries might confer an advantage in which shifts of mental set or new ways of thinking are required. He specifically mentioned philosophy, theoretical mathematics, and learning foreign languages "as native speakers do" (Hartmann, 1991, p. 221). I did find a general advantage for thinner boundaries (though again, there are many, many exceptions). A student such as Jenny, however, is not helped by her thin boundaries because she lacks discrimination skills. Thin boundaries—perhaps analogous to field sensitivity—are of help in getting the information in and possibly tolerating the contradictions that are likely in large masses of information. Keith does not even get this far—he does not let much enter his mental systems in the first place. The trouble is that Jenny cannot cope with setting priorities, chunking information to make it more manageable, and pulling out various aspects to focus on more or less systematically—skills that are more related to field independence.

6.3.1 Using the HBQ With Other Models

The exemplar of Type 1 (field independent and field sensitive), Vanessa has averagely thin boundaries. She is very similar to the average in Hartmann's sample. Her access to both field independence and field sensitivity may be related to her more or less middle position in the ego boundaries model. It is also possible for a learner to be a Type 1 and considerably thinner than Vanessa. Roger, one of the Type 2 exemplars (field independent and field insensitive), is also more or less average on overall boundaries, but he is low on field sensitivity.

Their profiles are somewhat different. The Hartmann Boundary Questionnaire yields twelve subscales, which are divided into those that refer to internal boundaries among states of mind within the individual and external boundaries between the individual and the environment:

Roger is more or less balanced throughout all the HBQ subscales, coming out near Hartmann's average on each. Vanessa, on the other hand, reports thick boundaries between internal states but rather thin ones relative to the outside world. In my study of this dimension (Ehrman, 1993), thin external boundaries turned out to be relatively advantageous, whereas very thin internal boundaries were linked with anxiety. Vanessa is representative of an HBQ profile that may have an advantage in learning.

The previous discussion illustrates how interrelated most of the learning style dimensions are. They cover overlapping domains in many cases—hence, their many intercorrelations. They also may work together to provide a clearer picture of an individual. *Ellis* and *Miriam* illustrate this point. Both are INTP (introverted intuitive thinking perceivers) on the MBTI, and their descriptions show similarities that are related to their shared psychological type. Both are visual and kinesthetic learners. On the other hand, they are very different on the ego boundaries dimension: Ellis reports thick boundaries, whereas Miriam's scores on the HBQ represent relatively thin boundaries. As you read the cases, look for the similarities (and try to relate them to what you know about the Myers-Briggs dimensions involved); also look for the differences and see how they might relate to thick and thin boundaries.

Ellis was a physics major who became a military officer some years ago. His initial adjustment to military culture was difficult, but he has found ways to succeed in it. He learned some of a Western European language in high school and in informal experiences with native speakers of that language. Although he describes his vocabulary as very limited, he uses what he knows flexibly to get his points across, though he understands better than he can speak. He says "grammar is not a problem for me." He describes language learning as easy for him, though he does not experience much desire to integrate with the society of the people whose language he is studying. He is motivated by task and by the fun of learning. His very deliberate, careful approach to problem solving affected his performance on the highly speeded portions of a language aptitude test, though he described the items as "easy." Even with his relatively low scores on the highly speeded portions, his overall aptitude score is quite high. He did better on the quantitative portion of the SAT than on the verbal part. Ellis entered his language class somewhat anxious about the new experience, but the anxiety soon dissipated. He expresses enthusiasm for activities involving direct communicative use of the language, activities outside the classroom, and open-ended activities, where he is forced to use everything he knows and cope with much he does not know. He rejects rote learning, perfectionistic correction by the teacher, group study, and mechanical drilling. He also expresses discomfort with overt attention in classroom activities to student feelings.

Miriam is an organizational psychologist whose BA was in linguistics. An experienced learner of both Western and non-Western languages, she finds the study of a new language very exciting. She has never met a foreign language she didn't like. After exposure to practically every teaching methodology there is, she has discovered that she has learned best if allowed to operate in a largely "random" fashion, where she develops her own practice in interactive contexts with native speakers (both teachers and nonteachers). When in a setting with nonteacher native speakers, she has become adept at enlisting her interlocutors to become informal teachers. She copes with social events and small talk, which she does not usually enjoy, by turning them into language lessons. Her interlocutors readily adopt the teacher role, and thus the small talk becomes a vehicle for language learning. Miriam says she wants to assimilate into the culture and society of the people whose language she is studying to the degree possible for a foreigner and in keeping with her tendency for interpersonal detachment. Miriam has a very high score on the Modern Language Aptitude Test; she is able to perform on speeded tests in a fast, accurate way. Her verbal SAT score was above her quantitative score. Miriam sometimes becomes anxious if she thinks she has transgressed socially. She is outspoken about considering rote learning, mechanical drilling, and meaning-free activities a waste of time for her. On the other hand, she enjoys context-free grammar analysis, but will describe it as sterile if it isn't turned into real language use. She expresses a strong preference for open-ended language use activities, the more open-ended the better. She appreciates recognition of feelings in the classroom, as long as it does not interfere with the learning task.

Ellis is probably a Type 2 learner; Miriam is almost certainly Type 1. We can see that there may be a relationship between the ego boundaries model and the concept of field sensitivity: The differences between Ellis and Miriam may be described by either the boundary model or their difference in field sensitivity.

Table 6.2 presents the differences (related to ego boundaries) and similarities (related to psychological type) for Ellis and Miriam. The MBTI and the ego boundaries construct, together, provide a fuller way to under-

Table 6.2 Ellis and Miriam: Differences (Ego Boundaries) and Similarities (Psychological Type)

Ellis	Miriam
Contrasting thick and thin boundaries	
Choice of military career	Choice of career as a trainer
Little or no assimilative motivation	Considerable assimilative motivation
Reflective style (acquired?)	Impulsive style (usually fast-accurate)
Quantitative	Verbal
Little ongoing anxiety	Anxiety related to social errors
Rejects classroom attention to student feelings	Values attention to student feelings

Similarities that may be type-related

Task orientation
Intrinsic motivation (will do it if it's fun)
Enjoyment of/comfort with analytic activities
  (hypothesis formation and testing, grammar)
Dislike of rote, mechanical learning
Desire for open-ended learning (stronger for
  Miriam than for Ellis)
Intellectual risk-taking
Relative uninterest in social small-talk
Prefer to do it MY way (Miriam more than Ellis)
Both are adults with successful careers

stand these two learners than either one does alone. In general, both of these learners are well equipped for contemporary language classrooms and unlikely to have much learning trouble. On the other hand, either of them could run into trouble. How might their learning styles result in difficulties for each of them in classrooms you know?

6.3.2 Assessing Ego Boundaries With the HBQ

The ego boundaries model is assessed through the Hartmann Boundary Questionnaire (HBQ; Hartmann, 1991). It has 12 subscales, most of which fall into two factor-analyzed categories, and a total score. The subscales relate to boundaries between states of wakefulness, between thinking and feeling, among memories of earlier ages, as well as to experiences of ESP, sensitivity to slights, interpersonal receptivity, need for neat surroundings, preference for sharp or fuzzy lines in visual images, opinions about various age groups, lines of authority, ethnic groups, and abstractions such as beauty or truth. The factors are for boundaries among states of mind and for boundaries between the individual and the outside world.

The questionnaire is available in Hartmann's book, but I strongly recommend that if you want to use it, you take several steps first.

1. Read Hartmann's book carefully and review the material on the ego boundaries construct in this book.
2. Delete some of the items that were clinically valid for Hartmann but that may sufficiently bother your students that they reject the questionnaire (primarily those about marijuana and body parts).
3. If the student still expresses discomfort, listen, respond nondefensively, and explain why you are using the questionnaire.

I usually agree that there are some odd items in the questionnaire, explain that it was designed for investigating nightmare frequency and not for language learning, and then say that I use it because it has proved useful as a measure of tolerance of ambiguity, which is an important factor in language learning. This approach usually succeeds in disarming resistance, but if the student still objects, I let it pass and do without the HBQ.

6.3.3 More on Assessing Field Independence and Field Sensitivity

The HBQ works best in combination with other instruments, which it helps elucidate. The preceding section looked at its interaction with the MBTI. In combination with the MLAT, it can be used to make inferences about the field independence and field sensitivity constructs.

Thin ego boundaries on the HBQ together with MBTI preferences for intuition, perceiving, and especially feeling suggest field sensitivity. The MBTI works together with the HBQ in that intuitive feeling and thin boundaries are likely to suggest peripheral learning especially through social means. Feeling types often fall into Type 3 (global and good at peripheral learning, not analytic, as described in Chapter 5 above). Sylvia is an intuitive feeling Type 3 learner, whereas Sandy, whom we met in

Chapters 2 and 3, is a sensing-feeling Type 3 or possibly a low-level Type 1 when she is not under stress.

On the other hand, an intuitive thinking type with thin boundaries is likely to be a Type 1 learner (field sensitive and field independent). Such a student uses peripheral and global learning, but frequently in the performance of tasks of interest to the individual. Alice (whom we will meet in Chapter 7) and Miriam are learners of this sort. Not all Type 1 learners are intuitive thinking types. Vanessa is a Type 1 learner who prefers feeling but has nearly automatic access to field independent skills.

MBTI intuition has been shown in a number of research studies to correlate with field independence, and thinking on the MBTI has correlated with field independence in other investigations (Ehrman, in press). I therefore begin with a hypothesis that intuitives are likely to be field independent, especially intuitive thinking types. In yet other reports of research, introversion has been linked with field independence, thus I am most likely to make an initial hypothesis of field independence about an INTJ or an INTP.

The chances seem rather small that a person with self-reported thick boundaries on the HBQ will be field sensitive, though he or she may be either field independent (Type 2) as is Roger (INTJ) or field dependent (Type 4) as is Holly (ISTJ). Based on the correlations between the HBQ and the MBTI scales (N, F, and P with thin boundaries; S, F, and J with thick ones), I hypothesize that the most likely of the sensing types to be field sensitive is -SFP; the least likely is -STJ. Used in this way, the HBQ can serve as a signpost if not a direct measure of field sensitivity, and the MBTI can suggest more detail about the way in which this quality appears: either abstract (N) or concrete (S) and either socially embedded (F) or autonomous (T).

6.4 More on Learning Styles

6.4.1 Other Learning Style Dimensions

Many who use learning styles use other dimensions. They are also useful in working with students to enhance their learning efficiency. For the sake of space, I will only offer a brief description of a few other dimensions from among the many available, though much more information is available elsewhere.

A commonly used learning style approach (Dunn & Dunn, 1978) looks at the physical environment, including such factors as light level, temperature, size of group, time of day for study, relaxed or erect posture, and whether one likes to eat and drink while studying. Awareness of such preferences and appropriate adaptation to them can make a difference to learning efficiency. Dunn and Dunn also address persistence and motivation.

Considerable work has been done with the reflectivity-impulsivity dimension, also known as conceptual tempo (Kagan, 1966). This scale consists for two subscales (speed and accuracy) and therefore produces another set of coordinates. Low speed and high accuracy are called *reflective*; high speed and low accuracy are called *impulsive*. High speed and high accuracy are called *fast-accurate*. Low speed and low accuracy can be called either *in trouble* or *novice*. Impulsivity may lead to a lot of guessing. A high proportion of inaccurate guesses suggests that the learner work on developing more reflectivity. Reflectivity may result in very slow processing of material. A student whose reflectivity becomes dysfunctional (as opposed to merely provoking the impatience of a more impulsive teacher or classmates), may need help taking more risks and guessing more. Ellis and Miriam, for instance, probably differ on this dimension as well as on ego boundaries: Ellis is more reflective, though he guesses often and appropriately; Miriam's style is usually more impulsive (though usually accurate—she is a good guesser).

The Dunn and Dunn dimensions are assessed through the Learning Style Profile (Keefe et al., 1989) and the Learning Style Inventory (Dunn et al., 1978). The former includes a section that tests abilities in analytic, spatial, sequential, and simultaneous processing, as well as discrimination skill and memory for visual details. It also assesses preferences for perceptual response, manipulation, and physical circumstances of study. The physical circumstance items of the Learning Style Profile are based on the Dunn et al. Learning Style Inventory, whose scales are oriented primarily toward physical circumstances of study.

Conceptual tempo (reflective and impulsive) is usually assessed through the Matching Familiar Figures Test (Kagan, 1965). In this test, the examinee must choose one of six very similar alternatives as the one that is the same as a stimulus figure.

6.4.2 Linking Learning Style Models

The observant reader has probably seen many ways in which the learning style models overlap. The Kolb (1985), 4MAT (McCarthy, 1987), and Gregorc (1982a) models work with a coordinate system of four quadrants that seem to map onto each other to a considerable extent. For example, the Kolb and 4MAT "diverger" and the Gregorc abstract-random type all are concerned with a human element to learning and want a personal relevance to what they learn. In turn, this shared quality seems very similar to important aspects of the MBTI feeling function. Similarly, the Kolb and 4MAT "accommodator" and Gregorc concrete-random have in common active, future-oriented, calculated risk taking, which is also an important manifestation of extraverted intuition. Figure 6.3 shows my attempt to find the link points for these models.

These models can be assessed in the following manner. The Learning Style Inventory (Kolb, 1985) is used both for Kolb's own model and for the 4MAT model (McCarthy, 1987). The Gregorc model uses the Gregorc Style Delineator (1982b). Both of these questionnaires are short, multiple-choice, self-report instruments.

The case material may also suggest connections between the field independence and field sensitivity model and the Myers-Briggs model. Research has shown moderate correlations between field independence tested by ability to extract figures from a complex visual background and either intuition or thinking, depending on the sample. I believe that the confusion comes from the cognitive aspect of field independence, which correlates with intuition, and the social aspect of field independence (tuning out interpersonal fields), which would probably correlate more with thinking. The analytic quality of field independence would also link with thinking. There is no test that I know of for field sensitivity, unless the HBQ turns out to point toward this direction, but if there were, it might correlate with peripheral perception and awareness of the interpersonal, social milieu. I have included my guess at how the four combinations of field independence and field sensitivity in Chapter 5 might best map into the four quadrants in Figure 6.3, though the fit is only conceptual, probably having many exceptions.

Figure 6.3 is potentially misleading, in that it could imply more overlap among the four models than may in fact exist. As mentioned in

G: concrete random K: Accommodator M: (extraverted) intuition F: Type 1	G: abstract random K: Diverger M: (intuitive) feeling F: Type 3
G: concrete sequential K: Converger M: (extraverted) sensing F: Type 4	G: abstract sequential K: Assimilator M: (introverted) thinking F: Type 2

Key: G = Gregorc; K = Kolb and McCarthy; M = MBTI; F = field independence-field sensitivity.
Type 1: high field independence, high field sensitivity.
Type 2: high field independence, low field sensitivity.
Type 3: low field independence, high field sensitivity.
Type 4: low field independence, low field sensitivity.

Figure 6.3. Relationships Between Major Learning Style Systems

section 6.1, the Kolb, 4MAT, and Myers-Briggs models are all based on Carl Jung's model of conscious functioning. It makes sense that relationships can be found among them, though far from one-to-one. The field independence model came from a different source and may thus be less closely linked to any of the others than those others are to each other.

Perhaps you are asking "Which of these models is the best?" All of them are good. Your choice may depend on which you learned first, in which one you can get training, which one seems to best describe the difficulty with which you are currently dealing, or even which one strikes your fancy. My thinking is influenced by all of them, though not all at the same time. Different individuals make different dimensions important. Field independence may be the issue for one learner, whereas judging-perceiving or very thin ego boundaries may give me the conceptual tools I need to work with another. Yet another model that integrates some of these concepts will be provided in Section 6.6. You may find that one useful, too.

Keep in mind that all models are oversimplifications. Do not expect them to work perfectly, and you will not be disappointed in them. If you use them as signposts for your thinking, not as recipes, you will be using them appropriately.

6.5 Tolerance of Ambiguity

Language learning for real communicative use, especially in situations that demand structural and lexical precision, is an extremely demanding whole-person engagement. It requires the learner to cope with information gaps, unexpected language and situations, new cultural norms, and substantial uncertainty. It is highly interpersonal, which is in itself fraught with ambiguities and unpredictabilities. Language is composed of symbols that are abstract and often hard to pin down. Concepts and expressions in any two languages do not relate one-to-one. It should not be surprising that a key to doing well in language learning aimed at real communicative use is tolerance of ambiguity. The importance of ambiguity tolerance shows up in a number of cases in which students such as John, David, Shirley, and others who lack it are in considerable trouble.

6.5.1 A Tolerance of Ambiguity Construct

Because tolerance of ambiguity is so important to learning complex, fuzzy-edged subjects such as language (or theoretical physics, for that matter), this section looks into the construct a little more deeply. The ego-boundaries concept is very helpful in understanding how it works.

I have come to think of tolerance of ambiguity as consisting of three levels. The first level is admitting information into one's mind in the first place. Thick ego boundaries—especially thick external boundaries—may interfere with this level, so that a learner such as Keith does not even become conscious of the new information, or becomes aware of it in only a very superficial way, without making connections to the learner's other knowledge. In my 1993 paper, I called this level *intake*.

The second level is what I called *tolerance of ambiguity proper* (Ehrman, 1993). This level assumes that intake has occurred, and now the learner's task is to put up with contradictions and incomplete information or incomplete systems in his or her mental system. People with relatively thin boundaries reach this point, but they may become overwhelmed with all the information and treat it all as equally valid or as if it were all at an equal level of abstraction or concreteness.

The third level is the one in which discriminations are made, priorities are set, and hierarchies of information such as level of abstraction are built. At this level, the learner integrates the new information with existing schemata to change the latter and make something new that did not exist before. For this reason, borrowing from Piaget (1967), I call this level *accommodation*. (Inasmuch as the learner also may make changes in the concepts he or she has taken in, there is also some assimilation or adapting new information to existing constructs. Assimilation, however, can also serve as a way to defend oneself from ambiguity and new learning, by saying the new is really similar to the old.) Skills associated with field independence are probably especially important at this level, whereas skills associated with field sensitivity are needed especially at the levels of intake and tolerance of ambiguity "proper."

The three levels of tolerance of ambiguity are summarized as follows:

1. *Intake:* Letting it in
2. *Tolerance of ambiguity proper:* Accepting contradictions and incomplete information
3. *Accommodation:* Making distinctions, setting priorities, restructuring cognitive schemata

The following description of John, some of which you have seen before, represents difficulties at the intake level:

When the curriculum follows the textbook closely, John works steadily and systematically. He readily performs the drills and exercises that fill the text. When asked to participate in more free-form activities such as storytelling or roleplays, John grumbles and stumbles. He becomes upset when too much new vocabulary is introduced in the course of an hour's activities, and he regularly mistranslates because he assumes that every English word will have a close equivalent in the new language. He takes almost no conversational risks in the target language.

We have met Kelly several times before. Here is some more information from her that suggests that she has difficulties with tolerance of ambiguity proper in listening comprehension. She lets the information in, but then cannot hold it.

> I review words in the book or from my flashcards first before I listen to the tapes. For grammar, I do the same kind of thing: I look at the patterns in the book, then I do oral drills. Listening comprehension in class is hard, especially when there is no visual support. I can't keep all the different things I hear in my mind. If you just gave me a list, that would be ok, I could remember that, but when it's ideas and they don't hang together, then I start feeling that it's all a kind of mess and I lose interest in the task. I like reading much better. Actually, I remember that in school I've always learned without much effort, especially in reading and with written materials.

Jenny, you may recall, was the student who enjoyed learning "by the seat of her pants" but for whom things "mushed together" so she could not make discriminations in her intake. Her skills at the middle level (tolerating contradictions and incomplete information) were well developed. Her difficulty came at the level of accommodation. It was hard for her to decide what to focus on, to pull data out of her internal ocean of concepts, and manipulate the data.

6.5.2 Assessing Tolerance of Ambiguity

Section 6.3.2 describes the use of the HBQ, which is my main pointer to tolerance of ambiguity, through thin ego boundaries. Two other instruments sometimes used for assessing tolerance of ambiguity are the MAT50 (Norton, 1975) and the Tolerance of Ambiguity Scale (Ely, 1989). The former is a general questionnaire instrument that addresses ambiguity in a variety of situations (job, interpersonal communication, personal philosophy, problem solving, public image, preference for art forms, for example). Unfortunately, no norms are published for scoring it, so users must build up their own local norms. This means that if you decide to use it, you will have little information to give the first few students who take it about what their scores mean. The Tolerance of Ambiguity Scale (Ely, 1989) was designed specifically for use in assessing reactions to language learning situations, with items such as "It bothers me when the teacher uses a Spanish word I don't know." This questionnaire has the advantage of specificity to the language learning situation, but it is so specific as to serve less as an indicator of a general personality disposition that can work with other scales as does the HBQ.

The MBTI also relates to tolerance of ambiguity. Intuition and perceiving are usually associated with tolerance of ambiguous verbal material. Intuitives generally not only accept but even seek hidden meanings, multiple interpretations, and unclear boundaries. Perceiving types, who by definition prefer to keep their options open, not only enjoy the unexpected but they can also become bored and feel constrained by too much predictability. Extraverts are probably advantaged in socially ambiguous situations, such as parties full of strangers. The social self-confidence exhibited by many extraverts helps them negotiate these situations more comfortably than introverts tend to do.

6.6 Ehrman's Four-Track Model of Learning

Figure 6.4 is an attempt to deal with the fact that relationships among learner variables are complex and yet there seem to be patterns of behavior that often do not show up in correlational studies, where the statistics show only weak relationships at best. Such weak findings belie the clinical experience of people who work with students and see the wide variations among individuals at the same time as they encounter recurring patterns.

The model in Figure 6.4 can be viewed horizontally and vertically. The horizontal dimension goes from relatively deep personality disposition through behavior to outcomes. The vertical dimension displays four "tracks" or primary learning approaches, each of which is an outgrowth of different personality dispositions.

Reading horizontally, the model begins with what seems to be the most fundamental style dimension addressed here: ego boundaries. The

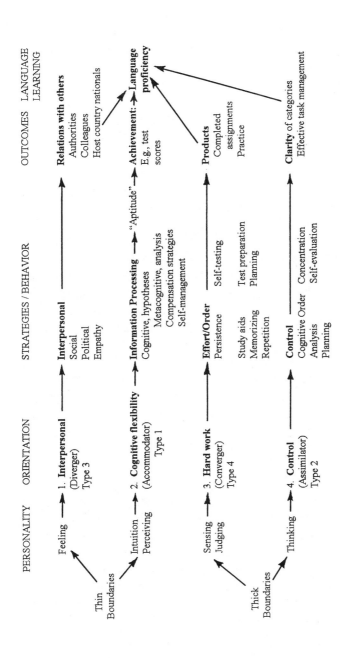

PERSONALITY   ORIENTATION   STRATEGIES / BEHAVIOR   OUTCOMES   LANGUAGE
LEARNING

Relations with others
Authorities
Colleagues
Host country nationals

Feeling ⟶ 1. **Interpersonal**   **Interpersonal**
(Diverger)   Social
Type 3   Political
Empathy

Thin
Boundaries

Intuition ⟶ 2. **Cognitive flexibility** ⟶ **Information Processing** ⟶ "Aptitude" ⟶ **Achievement:** ⟶ **Language proficiency**
Perceiving   (Accommodator)   Cognitive, hypotheses   E.g., test scores
Type 1   Metacognitive, analysis
Compensation strategies
Self-management

Products
Completed assignments
Practice

Sensing ⟶ 3. **Hard work**   **Effort/Order**
Judging   (Converger)   Persistence   Self-testing
Type 4   Study aids   Test preparation
Memorizing   Planning
Repetition

Thick
Boundaries

Thinking ⟶ 4. **Control**   **Control**
(Assimilator)   Cognitive Order   Concentration
Type 2   Analysis   Self-evaluation
Planning

Clarity of categories
Effective task management

Note: Type 1, Type 2, Type 3, Type 4 in the "Orientation" column refer to the field independence types (Chapter 5).

Figure 6.4. A Four-Track Model of Learning

next level to the right is that of the psychological functions in the Myers-Briggs model.

The following column represents overall orientation, so feeling, for instance, is associated with an interpersonal approach. Primary strategy categories are the next column to the right; this column shows some specific techniques, strategies, and attitudes characteristic of each row. The column labeled "outcomes" shows outcomes associated with each row. In addition, arrows show that all the rows contribute to the general outcome "language proficiency," in the rightmost column. (The proficiencies of different individuals may have varying characters, depending on the track(s) emphasized in reaching them.)

Reading vertically, the model begins with a dichotomy, thin and thick ego boundaries (although they are really a continuum, ego boundaries are treated as a dichotomy for purposes of clarity). Each of these two initial tracks divides again at the next level to the right to make four tracks. Thin boundaries are associated with feeling and intuition (which in turn is associated with perceiving). Thick boundaries are associated with thinking and sensing (which is in turn linked with judging). At the level of "orientation," each track is named after the primary approach on which it relies: Track 1 is interpersonal; Track 2, cognitive flexibility; Track 3, hard work and persistence; and Track 4, control. Each of these approaches is also listed with the most appropriate term from the Kolb model, so the thin, feeling, interpersonally oriented learner is likely to be a "diverger." (Very simply, the diverger wants to know for what social purpose he or she is learning; the "assimilator" wants to know what it is that is being learned; the "converger" wants to know how to do it; and the "accommodator" is interested in what new thing or idea can be made of what is learned.) I also include the field independence-field sensitivity type that is most likely to rely on this strategy: Thus a Type 3 is likely to make heavy use of an interpersonal approach, for instance.

The tracks affect each other. For example, being perceived as a good student contributes to achievement through effects that begin with the well-known "halo effect" and go through being given special privileges and more attention. Diligence and hard work, as well as effective interpersonal relations with teachers and classmates, contribute to this image, sometimes at least as much as the learning success brought about by cognitive aptitude. Outside the classroom, good relations with others often result in opportunities for language exposure and practice.

Between the "strategies/behavior" column and the "outcomes" column is the word *aptitude*, which refers to the kind of abilities usually tested by learning aptitude tests. These tests tend primarily to address cognitive flexibility and so go with Track 2. For classroom learning, all the tracks contribute, but probably Track 2 (cognitive flexibility) is the most needed, as suggested by the discussion of tolerance of ambiguity and the field independence-field sensitivity types. In most classrooms, an adept Track 2 student who is weak on the other tracks can achieve well, whereas students whose strengths come from the other tracks but who are weak on Track 2 are not likely to achieve as well, no matter how diligent, metacognitively adept, or personable they are. Conditions outside the classroom may permit these students to exploit more of their strengths and depend less on other tracks.

Some of the cases we have addressed so far can be readily associated with one or more of these tracks. (You can find case descriptions in Appendix E and locations in the case index.) In most instances, the first Case Index entry has the most information about the case.) For example, John works largely in Tracks 3 (hard work) and 4 (control). He has some access to Track 1 (interpersonal), largely through extraversion. He is relatively weak in Track 2 (cognitive flexibility). Track 1 stands him in good stead because his teachers want to find ways to help him.

Vanessa is particularly strong in Track 2 (cognitive flexibility). She also makes considerable use of strategies associated with Track 1 (interpersonal)—this is a major skill area for her, in fact—and some use of Track 4 (control). She relies least on Track 3 (hard work) but does what is needed, though probably not a lot more unless it is interesting to her.

Bert probably makes roughly equal use of Tracks 2 and 4 (cognitive flexibility and control). He seeks clarity of understanding, but he also uses the kinds of cognitive strategy that help him adapt to the unexpected. Track 1 (interpersonal) is available to Bert, but he does not favor it; as with Vanessa, he operates in Track 3 (hard work) enough to accomplish what is needed and what he is interested in.

Typical of learners who rely heavily on Track 1 (interpersonal) is Jenny. Global communication strategies such as skillful circumlocution (from Track 2) and adept interpersonal relations get her a long way, especially in a communicative classroom and in an environment in which the language is used. Because she is unskilled at the accommodation level in the tolerance of ambiguity sequence, Jenny does not access the more field

126 UNDERSTANDING SECOND LANGUAGE DIFFICULTIES

independent strategies associated with Track 2 (cognitive flexibility) and the analytic approach that may be associated with Track 4 (control). No matter how hard she works (Track 3), without some field independence her ability to use the language with precision will be limited, and she may stay confused. She may do very well in real interactions so long as they do not require too much accuracy, but she may need a lot of assistance to pass a rigorous language proficiency test.

6.7 Applying Learning Styles

What use can we make of learning styles? One important application of all the models we have investigated is what happens when a student is "out of sync" with the methodology, the teacher, or the other students in the class. There are other consequences when the match is too good. Learning styles may be illuminating across cultures, and they may help us understand differences between strong learners as well as those having trouble. Finally, there are some quick fixes that can be made when adaptations are needed.

6.7.1 Learning Style Matches and Mismatches

What happens when Janet is in a class taught by Holly and with a syllabus designed by Keith? Chances are, Holly teaches very much the way she prefers to learn, and Keith has designed a syllabus that would be helpful to him. Take a moment to place Janet, Holly, and Keith on the Four Track Model (section 6.6). What points of friction can you predict based on what you know about these three individuals so far? (If you need to review your knowledge about them, Janet is introduced in 4.5.1 and 4.5.3; Holly appears in 5.2, and Keith appears in 6.3.)

Janet has a very different learning style from that of Holly and Keith. Holly is probably quite satisfied with Keith's curriculum, and she cannot understand why Janet is constantly complaining or tuning out. She may even be telling her colleagues that Janet is not a very good student; Holly may even have let Janet know that she thinks this. Janet, on the other hand, is having trouble getting enough open-ended activity to satisfy her and probably feels that she is wasting a lot of time in class. If something does not change, Holly will end the year unsatisfied, and Janet at best will not have learned as much as she could and at worst might get a bad grade or start labeling herself as a poor language learner.

Suppose the roles are switched, and Janet is the teacher, using Keith's materials. She really is uncomfortable with all the drills and discrete point testing. To make the class bearable for herself and promote the kind of learning she believes in, she may skip a lot of the material in the syllabus or even throw it out altogether if she can. At the very least, she will add a lot of open-ended activities because she believes that students cannot spend all their time on the railroad or even the highway system (see Box 4.1), and it is her duty to prepare them for the open country they will encounter outside her classroom. In the meantime, Holly, the student now, may be so frustrated that she has gone to Janet's supervisor to say that she is not the only one who feels this way—at least three quarters of the students agree with her, Holly.

Meanwhile, two other students in the class are also having a hard time with each other. (Review Shirley, sections 4.5.1 and 4.5.3 and Karen, sections 4.4, 4.5.1, 4.5.3. Place them on the Four Track Model.) Here is what Shirley says about Karen:

> Karen is really frustrating to have in class. She's really random and scattered. The teacher can't control her; she's just all over the place. We can't ever just work through a lesson systematically, even for as little as 20 minutes at a time. I wish she would be more interested in repeating correctly and letting us get through material so I can get the systematic repetition and buildup I need. She wants to do grammar and let vocabulary take care of itself, and I want to work on building up my vocabulary systematically. I really need the basics, and Karen's constant tangents get in my way.

Karen, on the other hand, says that

> Although I want to have a solid foundation before I stick my neck out too far, I don't want to wait as long as Shirley does. She wants such a systematic approach that there's no opportunity to try things out. Learning a language is much more than just learning rules and amassing a lot of words that we can't use, even if we understand them. Let's learn a little and then try it out. Shirley should trust her ability to learn more indirectly, too. Everything doesn't have to be formally introduced and covered thoroughly in class. Shirley wants everything

spelled out and done one step at a time. That really gets in the way of my learning after I've got the basics. But don't forget—I still need to get control of what I'm learning first."

If you were the teacher of this class, how would you handle this situation? This issue is addressed in section 6.7.3 and at greater length in Chapter 10 (section 10.4).

6.7.2 Across Cultures

Is the concept of learning styles a peculiarly American invention? Much of the early work on the style dimensions was done in the United States, but on the other hand, some of it is also based on gestalt psychology, which originated in Germany. So the concept is Western European in origin.

Does the construct work for different cultures? Certainly. If you teach English as a Second Language (ESL) and have a number of students from a single culture, you have probably observed that there are certain *behavioral patterns* that are similar among them—these come from cultural norms. On the other hand, if you have come to know your students, you have almost certainly discovered that they do not all *prefer* to learn the same way. It may take an atmosphere of trust and openness for certain such students to move from behind the cultural mask, but once you get a chance to see the preferences, the differences are there. For example, when you first meet a class with Asian students in it, you may think they are all introverts who need a great deal of structure from the teacher. After you get to know them, you will probably find the range of variation that I have been describing. A recent research project looked at six readers, each from a different culture, with a range from Europe through North America to China. Every one of the six was very different in style, and the Chinese, for instance, was not at all like the stereotypes we hold of that nationality (Tyacke, 1995). Most of the students you meet in the case material in this book could be members of a multicultural ESL class.

6.7.3 Coping With Different Styles

Adapting teaching and curriculum to different learning styles does not have to be a major undertaking, nor does it have to be done all at once.

Often a minor adaptation or change is enough to let a student know that you recognize his or her needs. I have had sensing-perceiving students, who tend to be very kinesthetic learners, satisfied just with being given encouragement to get up and move around when they need it. The permission is often enough, and then they do not take advantage of it. (For some, of course, more than just permission is needed, and they do get up and move as needed.)

Most students also understand that a teacher and a program have to meet the needs of many students who are different from them. They are usually willing to accept partial solutions. The main thing is that they feel that their needs are validated and taken seriously. Again, there are exceptions to this generalization, but even these "squeaky wheels" are usually satisfied once they believe that serious efforts are being made to meet their needs and if the needs are correctly assessed. Later, we will look at some cases where the wrong assessment of needs (diagnosis) led to a great deal of preventable frustration on the part of student and teachers.

The best approach is to gradually build in an increased array of options for classroom work and homework assignments. Guidance to students in structuring their own homework along lines that begin in their comfort zones and gradually stretch them out of the comfort zones is generally well received.

Another fact that should make your job easier: Usually, a well-designed program works for the majority of students. For instance, at the Foreign Service Institute, years of designing language training programs to meet the needs of the U.S. government foreign affairs community have led to a program that works well for roughly 70% of the students. The remaining 30% need varying amounts of individualization, ranging from minor changes to major program restructuring. The more flexible the faculty and curriculum become, the fewer such cases there are because options are increasingly built into the program.

The main difficulties are likely to occur when the teaching methodology is rigid. Sometimes it is because of your style; other times it may have to do with external constraints on the program, such as a required textbook. If it is your style, get to know what you are comfortable with first, then, as with students, work on stretching it. If the constraints are external, there are usually ways to adapt the activities you do in the classroom and the work you give students to do outside.

If you are interested in preparing your students to deal with open country language, you are probably already looking for ways to make them more independent, paying attention to preferred learning styles and their associated strategies, and seeking ways to help your students expand their repertoires. To do this, though, you usually need to start from where they are, not where you think they should be. Then find ways to help them begin small and increase their skills (I sometimes talk of letting them start to swim at the shallow end of the pool and work up to diving into the deep end).

Task-based activities are a good way to find something for everyone. Preparation for the task can be done in ways that satisfy the students such as Shirley and the ones such as Miriam. Both want preparation but will go about it in different ways. A range of options will help. Actual enactment of the simulation or similar task engages students of multiple styles. Collaborative learning techniques help students take advantage of each others' strengths.

Teachers with large classes point out that they cannot meet everyone's needs. I tell such teachers that the difficulty is more in their expectations of themselves than in the task. They are the only ones who are expecting the miracle of meeting everyone's needs at once. Why not select one category of style or learning difficulty to focus on at a time? Work up techniques and options for that set of preferences, then move on to another. In the meantime, be as responsive as you can to the needs of the other kinds of student, without exhausting yourself.

There is a place for railroad activities, just as there is a place for open country ones (Box 4.1). Different class groups and different students will need different mixes of these alternatives. The needs will differ from time to time and stage of learning as well.

Almost inevitably, when I do a learning styles workshop for teachers, I am asked, "Should we try to put people with similar learning styles together?" Before you read further, think for a moment about how you would answer this question.

The first answer is that doing so is almost impossible. If you choose a major dimension such sensing-intuition or thick and thin boundaries, there are so many other learning style variables at play in addition that there will still be substantial variation in any group you set up. We have seen in the cases of Ellis and Miriam that even when students are matched by the full four-dimension psychological type (both were INTPs, remember), there is considerable difference among them. No model of cognitive functioning can pick up all the important differences among individuals.

Secondly, when students are only with students who are similar to them, they get too comfortable. A little friction is energizing. A little difference teaches new ways to solve problems. Students learn different learning strategies from watching each other tackle problems with which they may have some difficulty. Grouping by style may deprive them of this opportunity.

Does this mean that students should never be in style-alike groups? No. It may be appropriate for certain activities to let students group themselves by how they would prefer to approach a task or assignment. If you give options, then students can decide for themselves when they need the support of like-minded classmates, and when they do not.

Finally, though this book is about learning difficulties—multiple ways to do badly—do not lose sight that there are multiple ways to do well, too. These are describable using the same dimensions as have been used in Chapter 4 and 5 and this chapter. The Four Track Model is a representation of strengths as well as weaknesses. Your students in difficulty have strengths: Build on them. It may help to keep in mind that what is described as learning aptitude is often simply a fortunate coming together of learner skills and preferences with circumstances. If you cannot change the learner, maybe you can change some of the circumstances (you the teacher, the program, etc.). This kind of change may surprise you by enabling the student to change himself or herself.

6.8 Practice

1. Skim the descriptions and case material for the various learning style models treated in this chapter. Add to the description of your learning style that you started in exercise 3 in Chapter 5. Where do you come on the Four Track Model in Figure 6.4? Based on this model, what are your learning strengths and weaknesses? How do your preferences affect your learning? Are your preferences somewhat different under different circumstances?

2. Describe the kind of student you most enjoy teaching. How similar to you is such a student? How would this kind of student be different from you? Use the Four Track Model to describe this kind of student.

3. What kind of student is most difficult for you to deal with? Why? How does this relate to your own preferences? Use the Four Track Model to describe this kind of student.

4. Analyze cases in this and the preceding chapters. What do you think their MBTI types are? (You will probably not be able to guess at all four dimensions for most of the cases, but look for whatever evidence you can find and take a guess where you can.)

5. Do the same for the thick-thin boundary dimension. What is your evidence in each case? What more might you ask if you had the opportunity?

6. Try placing the students who appear in the case material on the Four Track Model.

7. Try evaluating your own class. If you are a teacher, what are the learning style trends you observe? If you are a student in a class, what are the areas in which you and your teacher match and mismatch?

8. What learning style dimensions do you find in the following vignettes? What is the evidence? What more would you want to know?

   a. You have made vocabulary tapes for your students to use. A couple of them come back and tell you that the tapes are boring. They cannot learn words out of context. Can the tapes not be made more interesting?

   b. You have asked some intermediate students to watch two videotaped discussions on related topics. You asked them to identify the discourse style of the interaction (formal, informal, etc.). Back in the classroom, some of the students seem to have become absorbed by the subject matter and found it difficult to do the task you assigned.

   c. One of your students tells you that she has been trying to read newspapers in the target language regularly, but she is quite frustrated. She is using a dictionary to find the meaning of every word. It takes a long time, and not every word is in the dictionary.

   d. A couple of your students have complained that you do not assign enough homework. They would like a more directive approach on your part.

   e. One of your students tells you, "I feel unusually good about the class we had yesterday. We had a native-speaker visitor, and we interviewed him in class. We really handled the situation well. We understood everything he was trying to tell us, and he understood us. I wish you would arrange for more of these real-life situations."

   f. A student says, "I make many mistakes and would appreciate it if you would correct me every time. I've said this before, but I'm still not getting corrected all the time. How can I improve if you don't force me to speak correctly all the time?"

    g. Another student comments, "I came to class already knowing the language a little and using it informally. I was feeling pretty comfortable with my language use. But since I've been in class, I've been corrected so much that I'm afraid to open my mouth. The teacher keeps interrupting my flow of speech and train of thought."

9. Try keeping a journal for a week or so, recording situations such as the ones in the cases or in these vignettes. Go back and use the conceptual frameworks provided here to make hypotheses about your observations.

6.9 More Information

The description that I have provided above of the Myers-Briggs model and how the functions and attitudes work together is highly condensed. For those who want more information about the MBTI, refer to Myers (1980), Keirsey & Bates (1978), Kroeger & Thuesen (1988), and two very recently published works: Bayne (1995) and Myers & Kirby (1994). The *MBTI Manual* (Myers & McCaulley, 1985) is unusually readable for a technical manual and is full of good information.

There is much more about the Kolb, 4MAT, and Gregorc models in Kolb (1985), McCarthy (1987), and Gregorc (1982a).

Brown (1994) treats recent research on reflectivity-impulsivity, as well as several other style dimensions addressed above. More general works that treat many learning style dimensions, including some not addressed in this book, are the two books put out by the National Association of Secondary School Principals in 1979 and 1982, Guild & Garger (1985), and, for those who would like to go deeply into the subject, Tyler (1965). A recently published compendium of research on learning styles in English as a second language is Reid (1995).

Information about the ego boundaries construct is available in Hartmann (1991) and Ehrman (1993).

A particularly readable and relevant work that describes and discusses seven very different learners (who happened to be good learners, but they had their weaknesses as well) is Earl Stevick's (1989) *Success with Foreign Languages: Seven Who Achieved It and What Worked for Them.* (The person who is called *Gwen* in the Stevick work is the same person as the one who appears as *Miriam* in this book.)

Note

1. A theoretical note about the MBTI judging-perceiving scale: In MBTI theory, a judging type is one who deals with the outside world through thinking or feeling (and thus uses sensing or intuition in the introverted attitude). Similarly, a perceiving type is one who uses his or her sensing or intuition function in the extraverted attitude, and the judging function is used in the interior world. For extraverts this works in a straightforward way, because part of what it means to be an extravert is that one's most preferred function is used in an extraverted way. For introverts, there is another step in understanding: For the introvert, the most preferred function is by definition used in the inner world, in the introverted attitude, and does not show up to others as readily as the second-most function (called the auxiliary function), which is used in the extraverted world. Thus, for instance, an extravert whose dominant function is feeling will use it in the extraverted attitude and will seek to organize the world by imposing harmony on it. Secondary will be either sensing or intuition, which will be used in an introverted way and may not appear clearly to others. Conversely, an introvert whose dominant function is feeling will use it in the introverted attitude, perhaps putting much energy into clarifying his or her own values as a lifetime project. This may not show in the outer world; what others see would be the auxiliary (second-best) sensing or intuitive function, which is used in the outer world. All four of the functions can be dominant or auxiliary, but in most cases if the dominant is a perceiving function, the auxiliary will be a judging function, and vice versa. Similarly, if the dominant function is introverted, the auxiliary is usually extraverted, and vice-versa.

The Affective Dimension

Motivation, Self-Efficacy, and Anxiety

S tudent feelings have as much power to affect their learning success as their styles and strategies. This chapter treats the impact of student motivation, sense of self-efficacy as a learner, and anxiety. The discussion stresses the importance of managing one's expectations of oneself and the damaging effects of perfectionism. Everyone uses a variety of ways to defend him- or herself from anxiety, but sometimes these "defense mechanisms" become dysfunctional. This chapter addresses some of these mechanisms in the context both of student anxiety and of teachers' feelings, which also have an important impact on the learning and teaching process.

7.1 The Power of Feelings to Affect Learning

Angela has finally reached the point where she feels the need to ask for some help because words she learns are not sticking with her. You are having an initial interview with her. The following is part of it, after some discussion of specifics of her difficulty with retaining vocabulary, even on topics of interest to her.

Interviewer. In general, what's it like for you to be in language class?

Angela. Well, I know I won't have a lot of use for this language after I'm finished. I'm just trying to meet requirements so I can graduate. If I didn't have to pass this class, I'd be out of here!

Interviewer. What effect does that have on your motivation to study?

Angela. It affects it a lot! I'm finding it just depressing to have to study, when my only reason for being here is to meet a requirement. (Harsh tone of voice)

Interviewer. You sound downright angry!

Angela. That's right! It really annoys me to have to waste my time on this, when I could be learning something I'll use after graduation. And then I start worrying about the final test, and whether I'll make it at all.

Interviewer. It must be hard to keep a lot of new words in your head with all that going on inside.

Angela. It is. There was a time I stopped being angry for a couple of weeks, and I didn't feel so bad about all the new words, but now I'm mad again; I've been upset since the midterm, when I made so many mistakes. The pressure's just too much for me!

This is a clear description of how feelings can have a strong impact on learning. Angela has a generally good aptitude for language learning. She is a Type 3 global learner (ENFJ), who has access to a reasonable number of field-independent skills. From what she said at another time in the interview, the teaching style is fairly well matched to the way she learns.

It seems likely that the issue for Angela is that she did not want to be in class in the first place, which she freely states. She attributes her vocabulary deficiencies to "the pressure" of class input and wonders if there is something wrong with her. In fact, because she did not wish to learn the language, she did not learn it, and this set up a downward spiral in which she became increasingly anxious about meeting the impending graduation requirement. The anxiety, in turn, interfered even more with her learning, which intensified both the anxiety and the anger. During the interview, she made a number of comments that confirmed her low level of motivation, such as "I'd rather be learning more about social issues than be in this language class."

In Chapter 3, we learned that when you are trying to listen effectively, you find that most messages include both cognitive content and feelings. Often it is feelings that you will experience first when you meet with a student having difficulty. Even if you do not, sooner or later some element of the affective dimension—feelings—is likely to show up as a cause of the difficulty, effect of the problem, or both. Sometimes the feelings are a smoke screen for something else: In every case, though, they constitute an important signpost to what is going on with the learner.

Every imaginable feeling accompanies learning, especially learning that can be as closely related to who we are as language learning is. There can be positive feelings such as joy, enthusiasm, satisfaction, warmth. This book is more concerned with some of the less pleasant feelings that are associated with learning difficulties: frustration, anger, anxiety, lack of self-confidence.

In looking at student difficulties, I have found it useful to think about feelings using a conceptual framework of attitudes related to the learning event. The three elements in the framework are motivation, self-efficacy, and anxiety.

Motivation is the perceived "payoff" for the student's investment of time, energy, and effort. It has to do with why the student is there in the first place and what keeps him or her working. The motivation may be positive, or it may be negative. There are a lot of factors that bring students to given learning settings and keep them there.

Self-efficacy is the degree to which the student thinks he or she has the capacity to cope with the learning challenge. I limit the use of these terms to the domain of learning. A learner can experience a sense of self-efficacy in one domain (e.g., physics or language learning) but not in others (e.g., social interaction with strangers), though often a sense of effectiveness in one or more areas of skill can overflow into how one feels about him- or herself in general, too.

Anxiety relates to the response a student has to a perceived threat to his or her sense of security or self-esteem. The threat may be direct, such as a bad grade on a test, or more indirect, such as having to give up cherished beliefs about the uniqueness or superiority of one's own native culture, or even deeper, a threat to the perceived integrity of one's identity.

In general, learning aptitude is related to how much language a student can learn in a given time, all other things being equal; learning styles indicate how students most effectively use their resources; and the affective dimension affects how efficiently students can use what they have. For instance, strong motivation tends to help students marshal their assets and skills, whereas low motivation or intense anxiety interferes with their ability to use their skills and abilities. Angela's situation is a good example of this phenomenon.

7.2 Motivation

7.2.1 Kinds of Motivation

People undertake language learning—and persevere in it—for a variety of reasons. Some of them are interested in the language and culture, some seek the challenge, and others may want a tool for increased interaction with interesting people. For such people, language learning is something they do for their own reasons and for internal satisfactions. This kind of motivation is called *intrinsic*. It contrasts with *extrinsic* motivation, which represents the desire for some kind of external benefit, such as increased pay, job enhancement, getting along in a foreign society, or meeting an organizational or academic requirement. Passing a test is also a kind of extrinsic motivation. Angela's motivation is clearly extrinsic.

Extrinsic and intrinsic motivation are not mutually exclusive. Many students begin language class because they have to, but then they find that there is considerable personal satisfaction in the content, getting to know the people who speak a language, or mastering a new area of intellectual endeavor. On the other hand, intrinsic motivation may lead people into academic majors or careers in which a language is required.

In organizational or academic settings, it is probably advantageous to be able to tap both kinds of motivation. Intrinsic motivation is very powerful and is likely to lead to deep learning because an intrinsically motivated learner will take every opportunity to satisfy the motivation-driven needs to expand and deepen knowledge. Miriam's statement that she finds language study exciting and that she never met a language she did not like is a good example of intrinsic motivation. On the other hand, an exclusively intrinsically motivated learner may not pay sufficient attention to the program or organizational requirements to pass necessary hurdles or to take full advantage of the resources of the teaching program.

An exclusively extrinsically motivated learner, on the other hand, is vulnerable to the kind of disaffection that we see in Angela, whose motivation appears to be entirely extrinsic. This is probably especially the case when the motivation is the result of perceived coercion. Angela is so angry about having to be in class in the first place that she has not permitted herself to activate much intrinsic motivation. Language learning has ended up being a worse than joyless exercise for her; it has became a threat to her perception of her own competence.

A simple way to look at intrinsic and extrinsic motivation is that people tend to put their cognitive and emotional resources where their interests and values are. Sufficiently powerful circumstances can force them to allocate personal resources to other tasks, but not necessarily in a lasting way.

Intrinsic motivation is not always positive, nor does extrinsic motivation imply a lesser kind of inspiration. Guilt and shame represent internal processes and thus may generate a kind of intrinsic motivation, but they also arouse anxiety, which can interfere with efficient mobilization of learning resources. Extrinsic motivation can be very powerful and positive: A desire to enhance one's effectiveness at one's work is largely extrinsic, and it is also constructive.

The field of language teaching has been influenced for many years by a model that came from studies of language immersion in Canada. Robert Gardner (1985) described two forms of motivation, instrumental and integrative. Instrumental motivation refers to learning to accomplish a task, such as passing a course, getting better pay, and so on. It is very similar to extrinsic motivation. Integrative motivation, on the other hand, has to do with the desire to become part of a target language community. It seems to have components of both extrinsic motivation (desire to join a community) and intrinsic motivation (satisfaction of affiliation needs). Brown (1994) suggests that instrumental motivation can also be intrinsic—for instance, learning to enhance a career that one values.

Miriam's desire to at least partially assimilate to the target culture partakes of integrative motivation. This may be related in some degree to her thin ego boundaries (section 6.3). Vanessa, with neither thin nor thick boundaries also takes a middle ground on integrative motivation; her motivation seems more extrinsic-instrumental. She told us the following:

> I'm open to other cultures, but I don't anticipate assimilating into them—language is really a skill to enhance other purposes for me. Overall, though I try to stay open to what comes, new words, concepts, grammar patterns, and cultural values, I don't get overwhelmed by it all. I'm able to keep my culture and the new culture and language separate without trouble.

Recently researchers have been expanding the concept of foreign language learning motivation the beyond he original Gardner model by including other concepts from various branches of psychology (Crookes & Schmidt, 1991; Dornyei, 1994, Oxford & Shearin, 1994). Among these concepts are intrinsic-extrinsic motivation, hierarchies of need (from safety to self-actualization), need for achievement, expectancy of good results, valence (subjective value associated with an outcome), attribution of causality (internal to the individual or external), level of goals set for oneself in relation to difficulty and specificity and differential cognitive development (related to the kinds of rewards sought). Gardner and his colleagues have expanded their model to include many of these concepts (Tremblay & Gardner, 1995).

Theories of motivation have influenced teaching methodologies: One example is the audio-lingual methodology especially in vogue in the 1950s and 1960s. Its heavy reliance on memorizing, drilling, and repeating came from a theory of learning and of motivation that relied on the concept of behavioral reinforcement as both a mechanism and a motivator.

All of these theories contribute something useful to our understanding of motivation, though, as with the learning style models treated in Chapters 4, 5 and 6, the motivation models address overlapping terrain. It is not in the scope of this book to deal in detail with these models, though you may find one or another of them particularly helpful as a sensitizing concept. For the most part, I have found the intrinsic-extrinsic model helpful. I also look to see if some form of integrative or assimilative motivation is present because of its implications for the directions of student interest.

Another important element of motivation is that it is sensitive to success and failure. If one succeeds at a task, he or she is usually energized to do it some more. On the other hand, failure may lead to avoidance of the challenge. (For some, failure may lead to redoubled effort, but only temporarily. Effort with no payoff in the long term leads to discouragement.) In fact, motivation to undertake a task or even a career is often related to a history of past successes. Many people who have found that they had a talent for baseball have sought to become professional athletes; many who have discovered a gift for languages have entered careers in which they could exploit the gift. A case in point: I have a great absence of the former talent and considerable of the latter; as a result I have avoided competitive sports and have become a professional foreign language trainer, which gave me the opportunity to learn quite a few languages.

7.2.2 Dealing With Motivation

The greatest challenge to you in dealing with motivation difficulties is when there is not enough. The second greatest challenge is when there is too much. *Matthew* is interesting because he seems to have both low motivation to learn language but high motivation to achieve. He was referred for consultation because of a persistent inability to respond in class that appears related to in-class tension. As you read about him, what would you want to tell him?

> Matthew is entering a career in foreign relations, for which he was motivated by a desire to travel and to solve interesting problems. He wants to be a well-rounded generalist with the opportunity to help people. He says that one of the biggest deterrents to his undertaking this career was the prospect of having to learn foreign languages because he'd had difficulty with academic English grammar, but he's gritted his teeth and is now in language class. Although he made a good start, he now feels he is losing ground and trailing most of the other students. He says that he likes to be the best in sports and his classes and usually has been able to achieve this without intense effort and without acting in a way that he would describe as aggressive. He has always looked down on "grinds." A persistent fantasy that he will fail, wash out of his career, and end up selling shoes is a paradoxical source of relief: There will then be no more stress, the ordeal will be over.

Matthew is an ISTP with thick ego boundaries. His tested language learning aptitude is good. There is no evidence of a learning disability or learning style mismatch. Instead, his ambivalent motivation seems to be interfering with his ability to produce the target language. He seems torn between his interest in a foreign relations career and his reluctance to study language because of the threat it poses to his self-image as an effortless achiever. He is strongly motivated to achieve well; indeed, need for achievement is an integral part of his personality. He fears, however, he is unable to achieve in this important domain of effort. Like Angela, he is experiencing increased anxiety, which in turn is making his lack of achievement something of a self-fulfilling prophecy.

Those who work with ESL students may discover that there is anger about the implicit coercion of having to learn English to succeed in the United States or other English-speaking country. This kind of anger may not be expressed as directly as Angela was able to state it. Instead, it may appear in negative comments about the target culture, expressions of homesickness, and so on. Instrumental factors may drive the student so hard that he or she may not be aware of the impact of contrary motivations.

In working with students such as Angela or Matthew, it is useful to try to help them clarify their goals. If they decide that a larger goal is really important (e.g., graduation, a foreign affairs career), they then need to come to terms with doing what it takes to achieve the goal. It may be important to listen to their anger at feeling so constrained. They will also need to find ways to manage their anger (e.g., by seeing the glass as half full rather than half empty) and their anxiety. Listening to the anger, tension, and mixed motivations is the first step. If the student can stop defending against the negative feelings, he or she may be able to examine and cope with them. In addition, it will go a long way if you can help them find something in their study to activate intrinsic motivation. One simple way to do this is to ask straight out what they enjoy about their class. Another is to find out what their interests and hobbies are, then work with them to find ways to bring these pleasurable activities into language class.

Because Angela's anger was limited to the situation, which was time limited, she found it helpful to try to suppress some of her anger and work on "self-talk" to help herself see the situation in a somewhat different light. Matthew benefited from some fairly elementary suggestions for anxiety management such as relaxation exercises and stopping damaging thoughts and trying to replace them with something more pleasurable. In both cases, some modifications were also made in their learning activities so that they felt that their needs were taken seriously.

The single most important thing to do is to find ways to build in success, on the principle that most of us are motivated to do what we experience ourselves as being good at. If you are a teacher, you can do this through classroom and homework assignments; any consultant, including teachers, can also work with students to help them structure some of their own study to build in success.

The following is a different kind of problematic motivation that many of you may run across. *Mari* is a native-born American whose grandparents were immigrants.

Mari has been in language class for several weeks now. She is compliant with classroom requests and does her homework regularly. She is an average student, neither outstandingly good nor outstandingly bad. Somehow, though, she lacks enthusiasm. She has come to you to talk about her performance in class, with which she is not satisfied. As you talk with her, you learn that she has signed up for this class because it is the language of her grandparents. She has always regretted that she could not speak easily with them, and there has always been some pressure on the children of her generation not to lose touch with the motherland's culture. Her parents and surviving grandparents were delighted when they heard that she had enrolled in the course. Mari is majoring in a subject for which this language will not be useful, and, truth to tell, she doesn't much like the class or the language. However, she feels that if she drops the course, she will disappoint her entire family. It is now too late to drop the course without penalty.

How would you work with Mari?
How can she get the most out of her language class?

7.3 Self-Efficacy

We have seen that there is a close relationship between a sense of self-efficacy (the belief that one can cope and succeed) and motivation.

Enhanced self-efficacy—that is, more expectation of good results—tends to increase motivation. It also increases willingness to take learning risks. Students who consider themselves poor learners are likely to want to learn in settings that reduce risk by reducing options and imposing external structure. They tend to want railroad and highway training (see section 4.2.4). Too much of this kind of program, of course, does not contribute to their ability to deal with the open country that is outside the protected classroom.

Self-efficacy is often an issue for students of nontraditional age. *Linda* is a case in point.

> Linda is 55 years old. She is an ISFJ, a learning style that is sometimes associated with difficulty in communicative classrooms like the one Linda is in because of a strong need for external structure and sequential learning. Linda herself relates her personality type to "detail-oriented perfectionism." The difficulties she is experiencing in this case are having an effect on her sense of self-efficacy, such that mid-course she is indicating little confidence in her ability to master the language. Linda describes herself as an achiever, who began as a secretary and worked her way up to officer level in a large organization. Here's what she says:
>
>> French defeated me. This (other Western European) language seems easier. But I'm with younger, better educated classmates. I really feel inadequate. When we go on field trips, I'm afraid I'll be out of my depth in the language. I hate to make mistakes and seem as if I'm not smart. At first I was afraid I was holding the others back, but that seems not to be the problem. Language learning just makes me feel inadequate. It's like playing bridge—I have to learn to let myself make mistakes. But I know I'm just not a good language learner.
>>
>> In my family, women never had careers—even becoming a secretary was a kind of rebellion for me. I never married and had a career instead. I sometimes think I have a mindset that came from the envy of my family and high school classmates. It made me try to do everything perfectly, so that even one of my teachers told me I'm my own worst enemy.

Linda seems to understand her difficulties well. She also has good insight into what she needs to do to help herself: judge herself less seriously and manage her expectations of herself. Without getting into issues that are better handled in psychotherapy, Linda can be helped to see that the envious members of her family and from her home town are not present in her language classroom.

Language learning difficulties constitute a particular assault on the self-esteem of people such as Linda who have had success in other aspects of life or other academic subjects that require different skills and often less tolerance of ambiguity. Such people must change their expectations of themselves and their performance. Linda, for instance, can be helped to see that she does not have to get 100% to do well. (This is a common but particularly self-defeating point of view for language learners, in that 100% mastery of real, open-country language is simply not possible for most learners in classrooms.) Linda needs to see how effective she is in many ways in her language learning without losing a realistic picture of her limitations.

Expectations of self are a particular case of the beliefs a student has about learning. Students may believe that languages are difficult to learn or only certain kinds of people can learn languages or that there is a "right way" to learn. All of these beliefs can have an effect on a student's sense of his or her ability to learn. Teachers often have beliefs, too. Many of their beliefs and assumptions are similar to those of their students. Others have to do with proper teaching, the teacher's role and relationship with students, and so on.

Lack of self-efficacy can lead to very dependent behavior by a student. The following is what *Corwin's* teachers say about him.

Corwin has been having difficulty with grammar rules and memory for vocabulary. His pronunciation is so poor as to be intrusive and difficult to understand. Although he is not a fast learner, he has convinced himself that he is worse than he really is. He is often grouped with another learner who has been having some trouble. Corwin complains about being with such a slow student, describing him not only as "stupid" but narrow-minded. He attributes his very slow progress to the fact that he is so often with this other student. He has requested to be put in more advanced groupings, but he does not realize that the others have explicitly requested that he not be in their learning groups. Corwin has expressed satisfaction when his teacher is very "demanding" and imposes a lot of learning structure on him, checking his homework and guiding him step-by-step in both daily class activities and in homework. He had studied before with a teacher who in his opinion was insufficiently strict, so that Corwin did not feel obliged to study at home. (The earlier teacher has described efforts to "empower" Corwin to manage more of his own learning.) Corwin has been performing at the same level with both teachers. He says that he is a person who needs strict guidance and direction and that if he had had this all along, he would have done better. He says he is terribly bored in class and can't wait to leave.

Corwin, a rather dependent learner, needs what can be called "appropriate support." This means the right amount of external structure, but no more and no less. Corwin has convinced himself that he can never stand without a cane, instead of recognizing that, whereas sometimes he will need a prop, with practice and mastery he can do without the prop until the next new thing comes along. Helping a student such as Corwin develop a sense of self-efficacy does not mean requiring him to deal right away with unlimited "open country". That would have a contrary effect on his sense of self-efficacy as a language learner. Instead, for him, it will probably be a good idea to let him spend most (though not all) of his time on railroad and highway activities at the beginning of the course. He will probably need to learn the material in new lessons similarly, and follow the same routine for each. He can be challenged, however, with carefully selected and limited bits of authentic material in which success is built in. He can also be given help in developing strategies for setting learning priorities, planning his study, and evaluating his learning.

Self-esteem is precious to all of us, and we go to considerable lengths to defend it. Self-esteem is often built on a sense of self-efficacy. Some students, for instance, focus on their expectations of success in interpersonal relations. This is especially true of those who emphasize Track 1 in the learning model discussed in section 6.6. In fact, the Four-Track Model can help in establishing hypotheses about the area in which the student finds most of her or his self-esteem. In classrooms, most students also hope to gain some sense of their own effectiveness as learners. Lack of success deprives them of this important source of self-esteem, so they may seek other avenues. John, whom we have met a number of times, provides an example of such behavior.

John was upset by a change to a new class and wanted to remain with his previous classmates. He believed that he should be in class along with the "best and brightest" students, as well as people in more senior positions, so he could be stimulated and challenged as well as associate with those closer in occupation. He asked to be returned to his original class and was counseled that he would do better in a class which moved ahead at a less pressured pace, so that he could get a solid base in the language. He went along with this advice and continues to work in the slower-moving class, but he socializes actively during the breaks and outside class with his previous classmates. He thinks his current classmates are overly laid back and do not take their language learning seriously.

We have also seen that John reacts to the threat implied by activities that do not match his preferred learning style and at which he knows he will be less successful.

When the curriculum follows the textbook closely, John works steadily and systematically. He readily performs the drills and exercises that fill the text. When asked to participate in more free-form activities such as storytelling or roleplays, John grumbles and stumbles.

If you understand some of the fear behind behaviors such as those shown by Corwin and John, perhaps you can deal with them more effectively. Many behaviors are defensive of emotional equilibrium and self-esteem. If they are understood in that light, they may be less problematic. The next section will have more on the subject of defense mechanisms.

Perception of oneself as unable to learn can cause self-fulfilling prophecies. Students who perceive their own ability as low and who believe that ability is fixed also tend to limit their own achievements. Corwin is a good case in point. Linda is in danger of doing the same thing.

A sense of self-efficacy is usually helpful. When it leads to overconfidence and rigidity, it is not helpful. A student who is convinced that she or he is right and that you are wrong is unlikely to change how he or she goes about the learning task, even when it is not working very well. Some personality types are characterized by this kind of assurance of their rightness, and they can be quite stubborn. In other cases, closed-mindedness that seems to reflect self-efficacy may in fact be based on quite the opposite feeling, and the student is making desperate efforts not to have to face his or her own sense of inadequacy. In dealing with apparent overconfidence, both hypotheses should be tested.

7.4 Anxiety

Motivation, self-efficacy, and anxiety are closely linked. Satisfactory self-efficacy contributes to maintenance and even enhancement of motivation. There is usually little cause for debilitating anxiety. On the other hand, disappointment with one's performance can lead to reduced self-efficacy and also to reduced motivation; it can also result in anxiety that gets in the way of learning. Anxiety is often linked to fear that one will fail in some way: on an assignment, speaking in class, on a test, in the final grade, in competition, maintaining one's position in a community, in interactions with native speakers, or on the job. Sometimes the anxiety is localized to only one kind of activity. In other cases, it is aroused by the entire learning situation.

Psychologists differentiate between *trait* anxiety, which is a stable part of a person's personality, and *state* anxiety, which is related to specific events or situations. Research has shown that introverts tend to experience more anxiety than extraverts (Ehrman, 1994b; Myers & McCaulley, 1985). Thin ego boundaries are also associated with trait anxiety. We saw that the "thin" exemplars Jenny and Miriam experienced some anxiety, whereas the "thick" exemplars Keith and Ellis reported none. Perhaps trait anxiety is *state* anxiety extended over many more situations. For purposes of working with students having learning difficulties, it may be a good strategy to treat all anxiety about learning as if it were state anxiety. In this way, both you and the student can perceive the anxiety as manageable, not inevitable.

Another important distinction is between *debilitating* and *facilitating* anxiety. The anxiety previously described is debilitating. It gets in the way of learning. Facilitating anxiety mobilizes resources to accomplish a task.

Some researchers believe that no anxiety is ever helpful, and others believe that facilitating anxiety exists for some people but not others. The phenomenon could be called tension or arousal, but because anxiety appears in fact to be a component, together with tension and arousal, I will continue to use the term *facilitating anxiety* here.

The function of facilitating anxiety is to build up just the right amount of arousal to get onto a task and mobilize one's cognitive and affective resources. When I have a writing task, I generate a little anxiety to get me out of my natural tendency to procrastinate—just enough anxiety, but no more than needed. Once I have started the task, I turn off the imaginings that mobilized me, because the unfinished task usually energizes me from then on. Good teaching relies on the facilitating anxiety implicit in challenges to the student that are just a little beyond what they can do but not too far. An appropriate level of competition between students can also stimulate facilitating anxiety or task arousal. The phenomenon of too much or too little anxiety at either extreme and an optimal level somewhere in the middle is referred to by psychologists as the *Yerkes-Dodson Law*. This generalization can be represented on a graph, with anxiety on the horizontal axis and performance on the vertical axis. The resulting shape is usually an inverted U, and the high spot represents the peak performance. Depending on such variables as task, self-perception, time available, and so on, the location on the horizontal axis of the peak of the inverted U varies. In practical terms, this means that only for individuals in specific circumstances can we determine (a) the point on an imaginary curve at which relaxation turns into optimal arousal and (b) the point at which optimal tension becomes debilitating.

7.4.1 Manifestations of Anxiety

When working with students having learning difficulties, you are likely to see much more debilitating anxiety. Sometimes you will not get a direct expression of anxiety; instead, you will be able to infer its presence from the behaviors that are used to avert it. If we look at the students we have already met in this chapter, we can see indications of debilitating anxiety among them. Angela, Matthew, Mari, and Linda express their anxiety directly and in words. Corwin and John tend to express their anxiety less directly. Corwin's boredom in the class and John's grumbling about activities he does not feel confident with both suggest anxiety. (The statements about Corwin and John are inferences and must be tested.)

Sometime the anxiety is unmistakable: It reaches nearly panic dimensions. The following is a teacher's description of such a student.

Celia is very worried about reaching the goal of working proficiency that she needs to get a job she wants. She is panicked at the idea of not making her goal. She made a major scene when her schedule to take a test was changed. When she was offered a compromise, she turned splotchy red and became "hysterical." She has no tolerance for her own mistakes, which drive her into a downward spiral. She is drastically more anxious than the other students in the class, and it's clearly affecting her concentration. I keep hearing "I'm not making my goal, this program isn't helping me, and what are you doing to help me?" All that unproductive worry and anxiety makes me wonder if she's trying to sabotage her success.

Celia's issue was related to her fear of failure. As it turned out, she was indeed sabotaging herself so that she would have an excuse for not meeting her goal. If she did badly, she could say to herself "if I'd really tried, I would have succeeded." The result was that her anxiety was a protection of her self-image as competent through setting things up so she could not succeed, but at the same time it also produced a threat to her self-perception.

We have also seen that Sandy has extremely strong emotional reactions. She cries, snarls, and loses her temper. She is aware that she is doing it, but she seems to be unable to control it. These eruptions are almost certainly related to sudden rises in Sandy's level of anxiety, but her teachers are baffled about what brings them about. As far as they can tell, they are interacting with her and using materials just as with other students. We will return to Sandy in a future chapter to explore this question further.

Anxiety is not always just about learning. Sometimes it has to do more directly with relations with others. Bert has expressed such concerns fairly directly.

> He finds it difficult to know what others want of him, though he wants to meet their expectations, and so he is uncomfortable when he feels he is under interpersonal judgment. He *feels shy about "performing" (speaking in class)* unless he knows his audience; he likes to feel he's "in it together with" the others. *Being under the spotlight is stressful* for him, especially if he has not had *the opportunity to think something through before he says it.*

Bert's social concerns affect his learning, of course. He suffers from inhibition about performing that is a result of feeling in the spotlight and judged by others.

7.4.2 Defenses Against Experiencing Anxiety

As mentioned in section 7.3, we protect our emotional equilibrium and our self-esteem in a variety of ways. The technical term for these is *defense mechanisms*. All of us use defense mechanisms. They are part of normal life for every one of us. Without them, we would be emotionally defenseless, quite literally, in a world where some defenses are needed. Defense mechanisms are essential for softening failures, protecting us from otherwise overwhelming anxiety, and maintaining our sense of personal worth. The mechanisms themselves have been classified by some scholars as more or less mature (Vaillant, 1977), but every normal person uses all of them—immature or mature—in greater or lesser degree all the time. Much of the time, we use defense mechanisms appropriately, but they do have a less functional side in that they involve a degree of self-deception and reality distortion. When inappropriately used, they do not produce realistic adaptation, and sometimes they involve others in inappropriate ways.

Each of us has our own preferred means and patterns of defense against anxiety, but ultimately, defense mechanisms can be seen as involving some form of avoidance of discomfort, whether directly or by some sort of substitution. They compose a variety of behaviors, thought processes, and manipulations of our feelings; they are ordinarily used unconsciously. We can categorize the various common defense mechanisms as (a) flight or withdrawal behaviors, (b) aggressive or "fight" behaviors, (c) group manipulation behaviors, and (d) compromise behaviors. A number of defensive behaviors are presented in Box 7.1 under these four categories, together with examples of how each might appear in a language classroom.

In the group of students we have seen in this chapter, there is a range of defensive behaviors. Corwin withdraws his emotional energy; John puts his energy into socializing with students whose company enhances his sense of his worth. Angela, too, refuses to invest emotional energy in language learning when she can find no intrinsic motivation in the activity. Vanessa's cool distance from overinvolvement with the new culture protects her from disappointment and loss. Matthew's fantasy of failure and Linda's assumption of inadequacy are defensive maneuvers. Celia and Sandy act out. Bert's inhibitions may well be at least partly defensive in nature.

Box 7.1   Defense Mechanisms

Flight Behaviors (Moving Away, Direct Avoidance)

Intellectualization (emotional insulation): One deals with emotions in an "objective" way so that it is never necessary to come to grips with feelings. This may include overpreoccupation with details or paying attention to the inanimate or the external to avoid dealing with people and feelings.

Generalization is closely related: A statement such "People can get really anxious when there are long silences" may really mean "I am very anxious about this silence."

Repression: this is most simply described as forgetting. One may forget an assignment, learned material, an appointment, and so forth.

Denial: Failure to be aware of some aspect of external reality. For example, "If I'm just friendly enough, all those do's and don't's won't matter" is a denial of the real importance of sensitivity to cross-cultural differences.

Withdrawal: Pulling away. May show up as lateness, absences, silence, unresponsiveness, boredom, or even physical removal of oneself from the class. "Nomadism" and fantasy are special cases of withdrawal.

Nomadism: The "geographic cure." Inability to stay in one place, frequent changes of class group, even need for frequent change of content or materials.

Fantasy (escape from reality): All of us probably daydream from time to time, but when we live in a fantasy world to the exclusion of job, family, class, assignments, and so forth, this defense has gotten out of hand.

Rationalization: An attempt to justify maladaptive behavior by substituting "good" reasons for real ones—for example, "I'm not getting much out of this class because what I really need is vocabulary about X," or "I can't do the reading because I have other responsibilities too!"

Reaction Formation: Behavior diametrically opposed to an unacceptable wish. For example, one might take care of classmates when one really wishes to be taken care of, or express very strong dislike for some aspect of a foreign culture that represents fulfillment of inappropriate wishes.

Aggressive (Moving Against, Substitution)

Projection: Attribution to others of characteristics that are unacceptable in oneself. For instance, someone competing for "airtime" in class might attack another person for taking more than his or her share of the class time. This may involve strong suspiciousness of others' motives and collecting injustices to which one believes one has been subjected.

Competition With the Teacher (or classmates): One who attempts to control the class or "out-do" the teacher may be trying to demonstrate superiority to avoid a feeling of incompetence or shame.

Displacement: Redirection of feelings toward an object (person, animal, thing) toward which one feels less strongly than about the person or situation arousing the feelings. Scapegoating (the program, classmates) is a form of displacement; anger with learning a certain skill (e.g., I hate reading) might be a displacement from "I hate feeling out of control when I don't know all the words."

Cynicism and Negativity: Belittling the program and its goals, teacher, other students, the assignment. Scapegoating the language program as a way of avoiding looking at one's deficiencies is both a form of negativity and a form of displacement.

Interrogation: A barrage of questions keeps others on the defensive. Constant cross-examination of others, or consistent focus on asking questions about the language might be efforts to keep the spotlight safely away from oneself.

Identification: All of us identify with others; it is a key element of learning, especially of languages and cultures. But it may be harmfully defensive if one identifies with someone who is cynical, who resists learning, for example. Identification with the aggressor is a common source of hostile behavior.

Acting Out: Action to avoid awareness of the feelings associated with an underlying wish or impulse. This may involve fidgeting and other motor activity, displays of temper, impulsive acts and statements, certain kinds of failure, or chronically giving in to impulses to avoid buildup of tension (e.g., blurting whatever is on one's mind all the time in class).

Passive-Aggressive Behavior: Passive aggression is a special case of acting out. It is aggression toward others expressed indirectly (and often ineffectively) through passivity or against the self, and this can include procrastination, clowning, illness, nonfulfillment of promises.

Group Manipulation Behaviors

Forming Subgroups: Class members seek out one or two supporters and form an emotional subgroup alliance in which they protect and support each other. This may be done by projecting onto and belittling others, or simply by exclusive closeness.

Rescuing: This may occur both within or outside subgroups. In conflictual or confrontational situations, one member mediates for another who seems to be under fire, with the assumed contract that the other will return the favor. When unsolicited, this can interfere with the other person's learning.

Focusing on One (Scapegoating): A class may spend excessive time and energy on one individual (or the program). By keeping the spotlight on one person, others can become passive or keep the action away from themselves.

Compromise Behaviors

The following are generally considered to be relatively "mature" or constructive defenses, but even these can be overused or misused.

Anticipation: Realistic expectation or planning for future inner discomfort. Includes goal-directed but sometimes overly careful planning and worrying, premature grieving for loss or "pre-living" of other discomfort.

Sublimation: Reflection of wishes that one may not feel comfortable with through activities that do not have either adverse consequences or marked loss of gratification. This includes expression of aggression through constructive competition, artistic expression, making a game of a task, and so forth.

Humor: Overt expression of ideas and feelings with appreciation for their inherent contradictions, without individual discomfort or unpleasant effect on others. This may include some games and playful regression (laughter in the classroom). In contrast, wit is often a form of displacement, distracting one from what is painful, whereas humor looks directly at what may be painful.

Altruism: Vicarious but constructive and personally gratifying service to others, including benign reaction formation (see above), philanthropy, and even well-paid service to others. Tutoring others in one's class is a clear example of altruism.

SOURCE: Based on material from Pfeiffer and Jones (1972), Sapountzis (undated), and Vaillant (1977).

The following is material you have seen about Sylvia.
How would you characterize her defensive behaviors?

I need to try to say things more simply, and I just can't do it. Is the problem my attitude or the situation? I feel devalued when there is a change in teacher or I get feedback after a test. Sometimes I feel written off.

When I'm doing drills, I don't learn much new, but in free conversation, I make mistakes and keep getting corrected. It leads to a lot of frustration. There isn't enough speaking or drilling time, and that's what I need. I hate drills—they're boring and mechanical, but I know I need them. When other students take a confrontation approach in debates, it gets in my learning space, and I don't function well.

Comments such as these are probably not unfamiliar to many of you. They represent a number of ways of externalizing—Sylvia perceives her difficulties all coming from outside herself.

When you come up against these behaviors, perhaps understanding that they are ways of coping with fear and anxiety may help keep you from getting caught up in reacting to them in an equally defensive way. When we are faced by accusations, withdrawal, acting out, for example, we experience anxiety and defend ourselves against them in our own ways. This means that we do not have the ability to work effectively with students. To the degree that we can accept that even scapegoating of the program and our teaching is not really aimed at us personally, we can better address the things that are causing the anxiety against which the student is defending himself or herself.

7.5 Assessing the Affective Dimension

In this chapter, three categories of feelings important to language are described: motivation, self-efficacy, and anxiety. Scholars doing research on motivation in the language learning field have tended to rely on questionnaires designed specifically for their investigations, so there is no standard instrument currently in use for language learning motivation. For self-efficacy, educational research also uses a variety of instruments, many of them specific to the domain (on the grounds that global self-efficacy does not necessarily predict self-efficacy in a specialized area such as language learning or mathematics). There are also more standard instruments in use for areas related to self-efficacy, such as internal versus external locus of control (Rotter, 1966)

Similarly, there are a number of anxiety instruments available, many addressing a specific domain. One of the best known for general anxiety is the State-Trait Anxiety Inventory (Spielberger, Gorsuch, & Lushene, 1970), which addresses anxiety both as a stable personality trait and as a response to specific situational pressures. In the language learning world, a standard is the questionnaire provided in Horwitz, Horwitz, and Cope (1986). This questionnaire was designed for use with university students and treats a variety of classroom stimuli that may arouse anxiety.

I have used two questionnaires for motivation, self-efficacy, and anxiety as a language learner, both developed for my use. One is the composite Affective Survey (Ehrman & Oxford, 1991), which includes items for motivation, self-efficacy as a language learner, and various categories of anxiety. It was developed primarily for research purposes, though scores on it have sometimes been helpful in student consultations. The other instrument is Part I of the Motivation and Strategies Questionnaire (MSQ, Appendix C), which addresses these categories more simply. Part of the MSQ may be more suitable than the Affective Survey for counseling work with the usual run of students because it points the way to fruitful topics for exploration in interviews at the cost of very little time.

7.6 The Teacher's Feelings

Although this book is not about the teacher, your own feelings have an effect on your ability to work well with students. I mentioned just above that teachers—human beings just as students are—display defense mechanisms to protect their equilibrium and self-esteem in the face of situations that challenge them. Teachers have needs and anxieties, many of them about their effectiveness and the degree to which they are needed. They can feel friendship, fear, anger, enthusiasm, and so on about their students. We saw, for example, that Sandy's teachers felt upset, intimidated, and angered by her unpredictable eruptions. The following are some other students who have aroused feelings in their teachers.

As you read about them, notice how you feel as you read. What are your reactions to these students? What if they were your students?

Alice says, I've realized after several unsatisfactory classroom languages that the fundamental problem is that I have to work with a teacher. Teachers feel that they have to teach; they feel a duty and responsibility for your learning, and that gets in the way. At first, I thought it was a question of activities, not having enough autonomy, but now I realize that even with that autonomy, I would want to do it myself, without someone else's needs, suggestions, and desires impinging on me.

In my most successful learning, in the Peace Corps, after about 10 to 12 weeks of audio-lingual pattern-parroting (which I treated as a game and I'm good at it because I have a good short-term memory and can analyze quickly), I couldn't say a word when I got to the country. When I decided I wanted to speak the language because I liked the country and the people, I got myself a teach-yourself book with all the morphology and syntax in it and read through it a couple of times for the overall framework of the language (I did not control any of it). Then I started to listen to people, read what I could, talked with children and with a close friend. It went from there. I got a native language boyfriend and pressured him to talk only his language with me. That's how I learned the language.

If I could get the teacher to feel comfortable with just being my friend, that my learning or not will be no reflection on her, that I will take care of it, then I will feel comfortable. I do well in classes because I play those games well, but I don't feel I learn very much that way. If I don't like the people or country—and that has happened—I don't learn the language to a very high degree of proficiency.

Let me be responsible for my learning. I want to do this, I can do it, I have done it, and this is the only way I'm going to give *good* results—meaning more than just a high score on a proficiency test. You get into the culture; you get a new skin. The same thing was true for my other educational experiences.

What can you say about Alice's motivation? Her self-efficacy? What makes her anxious? How would you deal with her if you were her teacher? Would you work with her differently in a one-to-one class and a group class?

Suzanne is bright, articulate, and very demanding of her teacher's time. She is having difficulty learning the new language, and since there are important extrinsic incentives depending on her achievement in the course, she feels great pressure to succeed. She considers herself a good language learner. Every week Suzanne complains about something new. First, she thought that the reason she was not doing well was because the class was too big. When arrangements were made for her to work in a smaller class grouping, she didn't want to go because she thought the students were less able than she. Next she complained that the teacher spoke too fast and never explained anything clearly. The schedule and the class activities, in her opinion, were geared more toward the other students' needs. She also complained that the textbook did not have enough grammar explanations. She could not use the language laboratory because it was too noisy. In short, Suzanne was miserable and let her teacher and classmates know it. In addition, she has recently been sick and missed a number of days of class. The program has tried to accommodate Suzanne's needs whenever possible, but it has also been necessary to tell her that she is in danger of not reaching her proficiency goal. Suzanne is very upset and has been making very negative remarks about the course and the teacher. She's even mentioned going to her teacher's supervisor.

What is your guess about what is happening with Suzanne?
If you were her teacher, how would you be feeling?

Until recently, *Logan* seemed very upbeat about his language class. He seemed to be progressing well in his first non-European language and was showing a lot of potential to succeed at learning this difficult language. Now he seems much less happy in general. Logan's teacher is also uncomfortable. For some reason, he feels that Logan is trying to take over the class. Here's how the teacher described the situation:

> Logan apparently thinks the class is going too slowly and the activities are boring and confining. As a result, he is bringing into work into class that he has done that was not assigned, or starting up conversations or activities that interfere with my plans for the day. He always has some suggestion on how the class could be taught and is beginning to stir up trouble among his classmates. For instance, the other day, he suggested that I divide the class into two groups. While one group would stay

with me, the other would prepare an activity to be presented in class, then the two groups would switch roles.

The new teacher feels that this kind of suggestion is preposterous. He has to follow his program and the book closely. Splitting the class into groups would be disruptive, and who knows what would happen if he, the teacher, were not there to help. Based on his many years of teaching, he is convinced that students should not go off on their own, or do whatever they wish, and then come back to class and dictate to the teacher what they want to do. In his opinion, Logan does not understand that the teacher is paid to be in charge and is responsible for the success or failure of the students.

How would you account for the change in Logan? What do you think Logan would say about the role of a teacher? Do you agree? If you had to help Logan and his teacher come to an understanding, what would you want to say to each of them?

The following is what his teachers say about Corwin (section 7.3), who was presented as a very dependent learner.

Although he is not a fast learner, he has convinced himself that he is worse than he really is. He likes it when his teacher is very demanding and imposes a lot of learning structure on him, checking his homework and guiding him step-by-step in both daily class activities and in homework. He interpreted efforts to provide him more latitude as slackness on the part of another teacher and says that because he needs strict guidance and direction, he would have done better if he had had such close guidance all along. He says he is terribly bored in class and can't wait to leave.

What is your emotional reaction to Corwin? How would you like to work with him?

Difficulty, even friction, between teacher and student can come from a number of places. Suzanne is letting us know that something is going very wrong for her, and her teachers are having difficulty getting it clear enough that they can address it. Putting out the little fires that keep coming up is not dealing with their source. The source may be in the classroom, but it is also possible that it is not the language class or the teacher's inadequacy where the difficulty lies. More information is needed.

The difficulty for Alice and Logan seems to be much more related to a fundamental disagreement about the proper role for the teacher. When I train teachers, I use these cases to help teachers understand that their value as teachers is not only as orchestrators of student learning. They discover that there are many, many other roles that students such as Alice and Logan need them to play, but direct control and direction of such students' learning are not among them. At the same time, it is important for Logan to take a responsible role as a member of the community to which he belongs as a member of the class (this is less an issue for Alice, who has accurately pointed out that she can "can play those games well").

It is common for teachers and students such as Corwin to end up in a kind of collusion to keep the student dependent. This is not done consciously or with malice. In fact, it is based on a lack of self-confidence on the part of both parties. The student does not trust that he or she can learn without the teacher's close support; the teacher fears that if the student does not need the teacher to orchestrate the learning, the teacher will not be needed.

It is probably a good idea when a student arouses discomfort in you to take a good look at what may really be going on with the student. Stepping back and trying to describe the behavior without interpretations of motive or otherwise is a good first step. Then list your current interpretation of the behavior along with as many other alternative interpretations as you can think of. (A less involved friend or colleague may be able to think of even more alternatives.) Try them on for size. Perhaps one or more fit as well as your original interpretation. Try these as hypotheses, using the techniques described in Chapters 2 and 3 and using some of the concepts in the rest of the book. Maybe one of these alternatives will end up enabling you to work more effectively with the student.

As part of this process, it is also a good idea to take some guesses about which of your own insecurities are activated by this student. For instance, you may be feeling unliked—even unlikeable—or incompetent. You may wonder "Who's in charge here, anyway?" You may wonder if you are pulling your weight. Awareness of your own anxieties and expectations of yourself and your assumptions about your role as a teacher may help you reinterpret what is happening between you and the student.

7.7 Practice

1. When you have learned foreign languages (or other subjects of importance to you), what has your motivation been? How did your successes and failures affect your motivation?

2. How would you describe your level of self-efficacy when you were learning? What enhanced it? What detracted from it?

3. What made you feel anxious when you were learning? How did you cope with it for yourself? What kinds of help did you get to cope with your anxiety? How did you get it?

4. McDonough (1981, p. 143) lists several indicators of motivation: (a) energy, (b) willingness to learn, (c) perseverance, (d) interest, (e) enjoyment of lessons. Look in the case material you have encountered so far for examples of these.

5. Think of several of your students. Which of the motivation indicators in Question 4 do you see in them?

6. For the same students, describe their self-efficacy. What detracts from it? What enhances it?

7. Again for these students, describe what makes them anxious. How do they show their anxiety? In which cases do you have to infer anxiety? In such cases, what is your further evidence?

8. What defense mechanisms do you see these students using?

9. The following is a statement from Kelly. Based on what you have read in this chapter, what can you add to what we already know about her?

    I need visual support. I can't keep all the different things I hear in my mind. If you just gave me a list, that would be ok, I could remember that, but when it's ideas and they don't hang together, then I start feeling that it's all a kind of mess and I lose interest in the task.

10. Consider a student who makes you feel uncomfortable. (Choose a case from this book or a real student you know.) Describe the discomfort for yourself. What is the behavior that elicits your discomfort (try to describe it without interpretation). What are the interpretations you make of the behavior? What alternative interpretations could you make? Do any of them fit? If one or more fit the facts well, would adopting that interpretation make it easier for you to deal with the student?

11. In Day (1990, pp. 54-57) there is a detailed description of classroom interactions over 45 minutes. Use this or some other description of classroom interactions to seek evidence of motivation, anxiety, and defensive behavior.

7.8 More Information

For more information about the Gardner model see Gardner and Lambert (1972) or Gardner (1985). Other models of motivation are addressed in two books, McDonough (1981) and an edited collection of articles (Oxford, 1996), as well as the articles cited in the section on motivation: Crookes & Schmidt (1991), Dornyei (1994), and Oxford and Shearin (1994). An expansion of the Gardner approach using some of the models from general psychology is to be found in Gardner and Tremblay (1994a, 1994b) and Tremblay and Gardner (1985).

If you are interested in evaluating the degree to which your teaching enhances intrinsic motivation, there is a useful checklist in Brown (1994, pp. 188-189).

Language learning anxiety is thoroughly addressed in Horwitz and Young (1991). This edited collection describes research on foreign language learning anxiety, ways to assess it, and suggestions for helping students deal with it. MacIntyre (1995a) provides a comprehensive review of the place of foreign language anxiety in general psychology and of current research on the subject.

A very readable treatment of defense mechanisms is Vaillant (1977). The main flaw in this work is that it is based on a longitudinal study that only included males. Vaillant's more recent (1993) book on defense mechanisms treats both sexes.

Biographic Background Information and Student Learning Strategies

This chapter presents the last of the major dimensions of individual difference—biographic background and learning strategies. Biographic background includes sex, age, native language and culture, socio-economic status, educational background (including exposure to other cultures and languages), subject matter interests, and career focus. All of these have an effect on motivation, preparedness for language classrooms, and ability to make use of both internal and external resources.

Learning strategies—activities and behaviors we use to learn—are a kind of internal resource. Previous background is likely to affect the learning strategies used by a student. This chapter also treats the even stronger effect of learning styles on learning strategy use, as well as the effects of different kinds of motivation to learn.

Learning styles are often linked with personality and therefore difficult to change. On the other hand, the learning strategies associated with the various styles are more malleable. This chapter also addresses the topic of helping students learn new strategies that may help them go outside their preferred styles when needed. Finally most of the factors treated in Chapters 4 through 7 appear together in a student case.

8.1 The Role of Biographic Data

Although the topic of biographic background information has been left for relatively late treatment in this book, when you actually are working with students, it should be one of the first things at which you look. Section 3.2.1 indicated that background information can be a useful way to start an interview. Just asking for this kind of material can break the ice between you and the interviewee. In any event, background information constitutes one of the basic question types in an interview (section 3.4.1).

Your student's previous history will color much of his or her experience in language learning. The older the student, the greater the number of biographical categories that come into play. A high school student will not have a long educational experience nor, usually, much of a work history. Relatively few high school students have the opportunity to declare and experiment with a major subject, though they may have well defined interests. Older students, on the other hand, may have rich histories that provide good information about how they approach a variety of tasks, academic and otherwise.

8.1.1 Career, Major Study, Interests

When I begin work with a student, I like to look at the person's occupation and college major. If the student is in high school or has not yet declared a major, I ask about career aspirations, favorite subjects, and outside interests. When I do this, one of the main things I am looking for is the person's orientation toward verbal learning and activities that call on verbal skills. Students of this sort are more likely than those who have a more quantitative or practical orientation to find classroom language learning comfortable.

Literature and humanities majors, people in the social sciences and other liberal arts usually call on a substantial amount of verbal processing. People who prefer using words and symbolic thinking are often attracted to these subjects. On the other hand, hard sciences and practical majors such as business and criminal justice tend not to call on the same kinds of verbal skills (though they certainly require other abilities). The chances of finding a student with strong verbal abilities in these kinds of majors is reduced, and I make an initial "hypothesis" that such students may find many of the language classroom activities somewhat alien. They may well have difficulty with the verbal ambiguities of communicatively taught foreign language.

At the very least, a quantitatively oriented student is likely to favor analytic processing over global and may be a Type 2 learner such as Roger (field independent and field insensitive, see Chapter 5). You may remember that Roger is an engineering major with a strong *quantitative* background. He brings his comfort with *analytic processing* to the language learning process, telling us up-front "My learning style relies heavily on deduction and *reasoning*." A practically oriented learner such as Lonnie (section 4.5.2) may have more difficulty. Many such learners are best described by Type 4 (field dependent and field insensitive) and are so concrete (section 4.5.2) as to have difficulty with the abstractions entailed by classroom language learning.

Adult career histories provide information not only about the student's orientation but also suggest such characteristics as persistence, proactivity, and other important traits. A learner who has been successful in a career may have difficulty with the loss of status involved in becoming a student—we saw this in the case of John, the business executive. On the other hand, John brings a history of getting results and of persistence; these are of help to him as long as they are not overdone. Moreover, lower-ranking employees and people who have worked their way up through the organizational ranks sometimes experience diffidence about their educational backgrounds that affects their self-confidence and assertiveness in class.

8.1.2 Educational Level, Grade Point Average, and Socioeconomic Status

To get an idea of how comfortable a learner is with the classroom setting and how he or she handles academic demands, I also look at previous performance history. For high school students, this is the grade point average. If they are available, grades in specific subjects can give information similar to that described in the previous section, indicating differential interests, aptitudes, and so on.

For adults, the level of education achieved also tells me something about the likelihood of comfort in a classroom and with academic activities. The students with whom I usually work have an average age of 40, so many have been out of school for a long time. In such cases, I usually ask when their most recent training or study activity was and how it went. Other information can come up unexpectedly in an interview.

> *George*, a mature student, was talking about how he had learned more tolerance of ambiguity in the course of his life. One key event was being laid off, which happened for ostensibly financial reasons. In fact, the underlying reason that he was considered dispensable despite a high level of professional competence was that he had developed political trouble with a ranking executive. An INTJ who valued intellectual competence over most other traits, George had made no secret of his lack of respect for the executive's intelligence and judgment.

This little piece of history suggested the possibility that George might choose confrontational ways of reacting to classroom policies with which he might disagree and opened up the topic of effective ways for him to get his needs met.

Socioeconomic status (SES) may have affected the opportunities available for a person's education and occupational choice. Low SES (or very high SES) may mean lack of familiarity with appropriate learning techniques. SES may affect motivation. A student may be the first in his or her family to reach this level of education; that fact may mean either very strong support from the family and community of origin or opposition to the student's educational aspirations. This kind of information can come out in an interview and provide useful context for what is going on with the student.

Previous evidence of learning disability is an important element of background. Students usually know if they had difficulty with learning to read, write, or spell. Sometimes they have been diagnosed with some form of dyslexia or other learning disability. In other cases, they have developed such good coping skills in their native language that mild learning disabilities may not surface until they take their first foreign language, and their coping strategies are overwhelmed by the learning task. The subject of learning disabilities will come up again in Chapter 11.

8.1.3 Native Language and Culture

In Chapter 7, we saw that Mari's family background and culture of origin had an effect on her feelings about her language study (section 7.2.2). She was studying the language of her family's origin more out of a sense of duty than for reasons related to her own interests or career development. (This kind of situation is common in undergraduate education.)

Mari's was a case of foreign language learning. ESL teachers in the United States are likely to see various effects of native language and culture constantly. The reasons for learning—survival, career enhancement, or sheer interest in English—will make a great difference to all the student's feelings about the learning process. A student who is a member of a stigmatized ethnic group is likely to feel very different about forming an "American self" than one who feels no stigma. For the former, learning English may be associated deeply with fear of loss of the original cultural identity. For the latter, because the original persona is not perceived as being under attack, learning English is a welcome opportunity. For students of the latter sort, it is probably safer to expand their range of personality and let more language and culture through their ego boundaries (section 6.3).

Cultural differences affect the learning in a less profoundly personal way, too. They influence level of class participation, need for achievement, and preferred learning approaches. Many students from overseas are socialized by their schools and families to stay quiet in class. For such students, production of language in a large class group may not be the way to go for some time, if ever. The cooperative learning that is the norm in certain countries may be misinterpreted by Western teachers as cheating. Some reframing of the teacher's perception is in order here. Some cultures are notorious for the pressure their members experience to get high grades and achieve in their careers; others may reject too much such achievement. Such influences are likely to affect level of effort by individual students and also result in motivations that either enhance or interfere with deep, associative learning of the sort that promotes retention of new material (more on deep learning below, in section 8.2.1).

Studies have found that learning style variables can be said to characterize cultural groups. For instance, there is a low level of field independence reported for one of the immigrant groups that is commonly met in the Washington D.C. area. This has a distinct effect on their level of achievement in conventional academic settings, and it may affect their learning of English beyond the level of basic functioning, as well.

8.1.4 Sex and Age

Who do you think are better language learners: males or females? The vast majority of studies have found that females do better in most language classrooms, from high school through university. I know of one investigation of a program designed for college graduates in which males achieved higher proficiency than females in formal language training, but it turned out that most of the males were at least college graduates, whereas the females were mostly high school graduates (reference unavailable). My own findings with a group of students receiving long-term intensive training for jobs related to foreign affairs were that there were *no* differences between the two genders in achievement as measured by end of training oral proficiency tests in speaking and reading.

What do these contrasting findings suggest? Language courses in schools, unless required for other purposes, are heavily populated by females. They are part of the complex of subjects that tend to differentially attract women (and feeling types, see section 6.2.2, above), in contrast to subjects such as science and engineering, in which males (and thinking types) cluster. Language is a means of communication, an instrumental goal for many females.

In contrast, all the students in my investigation of students heading for foreign affairs jobs are selected and self-selected for similar careers. Their interests, backgrounds, and learning styles tend to be quite similar. Their instrumental purposes are also pretty much the same. They have about the same high level of interest in communication. Thus most if not all of the moderating variables that may determine the usual difference between the genders are removed. What is left is no difference. This all suggests that although in most settings females can be expected to have something of an edge in language learning, attention to variables such as interests, culturally determined gender roles, sex-related personality differences, and learning circumstances may suggest ways to enhance the language learning success of both males and females.

Do children learn languages better than adults? Most people believe this to be the case. It is certainly true that young children can sound similar to their new-language classmates very quickly and if young enough can become native speakers of the new language, with all the cultural background that implies. It is also very rare that adults gain the depth of cultural background that makes a real native speaker of a language.

There are a number of ways in which adults are advantaged and children disadvantaged. Young children speaking a new language still speak it like children: relatively small vocabulary, relatively simple grammar, and generally concrete topics. Adults, contrastingly, have a level of cognitive development, knowledge of the world, and experience of how to learn and cope that permits them to reach high levels of language proficiency in remarkably short periods of time.[1] Few adults need more than the ability to interact flexibly and precisely with new-language interlocutors; they usually do not need to become full-fledged members of the new culture. Most do not want to do so: The identity of origin is of considerable importance to most of us, though we may be cognitively flexible enough to put it aside temporarily.

Most studies have found that there is an advantage for younger learners in adult classroom learning situations. My own work has been with learners two thirds of whom are between 30 and 50 years of age. Many of them are excellent, even superb language learners, achieving high levels of speaking and reading proficiency in multiple foreign languages in short periods of time. Statistically, even among these students, there is a moderate probability that younger students will do better in their language classes. On the other hand, many individuals who have reached middle age do extremely well, and some younger students experience great difficulties.

The conventional wisdom that older people do not learn languages well is widespread and can be detrimental. This myth may keep some people out of language learning who might succeed nicely. Others who undertake language study start out with lowered self-efficacy. When they run into trouble, they may attribute it to their age, when it is really something else that can be remedied. For example, consider Betty, whom we first met in Chapter 4 as a highly abstract learner.

Betty is in her 50s. She is painfully aware that she is probably the oldest student in her class; indeed she was a little shocked to find out that she is old enough to be the mother of some of the younger class members. She wonders if the trouble she is having with her language class is because of her age.

In fact, some decrease in working memory may have affected Betty, but her difficulties proved to be much more related to her inappropriate expectations of herself. The effects of age were secondary, but Betty's awareness of her age got in her way.

For older students, I have found that the real key is whether they have learned how to learn languages. Some learning styles are advantaged in classrooms at any age (for instance, Type 1 learners who can use both field independent and field sensitive strategies or intuitives on the MBTI who are shown in study after study to have an edge in reading). In general, as with so many other aspects of life, it seems also to be a matter of "use it or lose it." As with muscular strength, cognitive power and flexibility last longer when exercised regularly.

Older learners are also affected by a phenomenon that Charles Curran (1978) called "adult resistance." Curran believed that the development of adult resistance begins in adolescence, together with increased self-consciousness. Adult resistance has to do with the rejection of learning because it requires the individual to admit that he or she is deficient in some way. As we become more invested in what we know and our own competence, it becomes increasingly difficult to accept that there is something we do not know and to accept the need to be taught. This concept is at the heart of Curran's Counseling Learning philosophy, which emphasizes the need for it to be safe for a learner to admit and accept ignorance and the impact of adult resistance on the relationship between learner and "knower" throughout the learning process. Adult resistance is almost certainly active in everyone who is past puberty. It contributes to the difficulties adults and older learners may have with learning new languages and accepting new cultures.

Chapter 7 (section 7.4.2), described defense mechanisms that protect a learner against anxiety and lowered self-esteem. The concept of adult resistance is closely related to this phenomenon. Adult resistance can either be seen as a form of defensive behavior or as a source of it or both.

Adult resistance may be a factor in the desire of adults to speak like adults. Betty is a good example of an adult learner who was impatient with her inability to speak about her specialty in her new language as well as she could in English. Her frustration contributed substantially to her learning difficulties. She was helped a great deal by coming to look at the learning process in a new way (reframing). She came to see that her task was no longer to solve political problems but to solve linguistic ones. When she started getting her necessary sense of achievement from linguistic coping, she had much less difficulty with her language program.

8.1.5 Previous Exposure to Languages and Other Cultures

I have mentioned that it is helpful to have already learned how to learn. This is probably the main benefit from previous language learning, and it is a big one. If the previous language is related to the new one, there may also be some transfer benefits because of lexical and structural similarities. For instance, learning one Far Eastern language makes learning how to describe quantities of things much easier, because languages from Northeast to Southeast Asia have come to use a similar system. This kind of advantage tends to be greater in the earlier stages of learning a new language.

Much more important than transfer of linguistic specifics such as noun classifiers is the mind-set that tends to develop after one has learned one or more languages. One stops expecting the new language to correspond more or less directly to the native (or previously learned) one. When something appears to be too similar to the native language, the experienced language learner reacts with healthy suspicion. Surprises are (paradoxically) routine. Knowledge that learning has ups, downs, and plateaus and that the learning curve seems to level off after the early stages helps the experienced learner keep emotional equilibrium in the face of the long time it takes to reach real proficiency. Experienced language learners have learned what works for them. Alice and Miriam, for example, have discovered the most efficient ways for them to master what they need to know. They are supremely self-confident when they can make use of their self-knowledge and preferred learning strategies.

Learners such as some of those we will meet later in this chapter, on the other hand, are hindered by their inexperience. They do not know how to learn, and they do not have the knowledge base of how languages work that so helps Alice and Miriam. A good example of such a student is Holly (5.2), who has difficulty not only because she is a Type 4 learner (field dependent and field insensitive) but also because this is the first foreign language she has learned. (In fact, the two factors may be related, in that Type 4 learners may avoid language classes unless forced to take them.)

Previous learning in other subjects may contribute to learning effectiveness. On the other hand, it may also get in the way. Students who have learned linguistics, for example, may have tremendous tools for analysis and understanding new linguistic features, and yet they may be seduced into overemphasizing analysis over more global learning when the latter is appropriate. Former language teachers may know a great deal about learning strategies, language learning theory, and what has worked for their students. They must resist the temptation to waste energy second-guessing their teachers and criticizing the program because it is not structured or executed as they would do it.

Almost any other subject can make a contribution to learning as well in the form of world knowledge, topics for conversation, study techniques, or interests to follow up for reading practice, for example. The main drawback from previous study of other subjects that I have seen is that many lend themselves to 100% mastery. One can learn all the available information about a historical document and pass a test with a perfect score. Unless language is broken down into unrealistically small, limited units, this seldom is the case for language learning. Expectations of 100% mastery interfere seriously with coping with a body of knowledge and experience that will probably always be known approximately.

Exposure to other cultures, such as through previously learned languages, is usually helpful. It tends to promote openness to the unexpected and reduction of solipsistic beliefs. Coping with one culture may provide skills for engaging with the next one. As with languages, there may be similarities that can be used to bridge to the new culture. On the negative side, experience of culture shock or other trauma may make the student shy of too much exposure to another new culture. There may be aspects of the new culture that conflict with important values the student holds. In particular, for ESL students in the United States, acceptance of American culture may (to them) imply rejection of their culture of origin. It is a sad fact that it often takes a high level of sophistication and maturity to see differences among people as opportunities, not threats.

8.2 Student Learning Strategies

Calvin is running into difficulties with memorizing vocabulary and remembering the meanings of words when he hears them. He does not feel comfortable interrupting the flow of conversation or narrative to request clarification, with the result that he constantly feels lost. He works regularly with audiotapes. Here's how he goes about it: first he reads the textbook on which the tape is based. Next he plays the tape, one small bit at a time, trying to equate the target language and English. Then he rephrases the target language, trying to find a new way to say what was on the tape.

Calvin is on the right track insofar as he is giving himself repeated exposure to the material on the tape, and he is doing it in a way that is not entirely mechanical. On the other hand, there are improvements that could be suggested in how he goes about the task that would enhance his retention and recognition of vocabulary in real-time use. Calvin's approach is limited to the material in the textbook and on the tape, and it does not give him practice in what he needs to do with the language. Even rephrasing the target language material may be dangerous, if he is making it similar to his native language and thus preventing himself from getting authentic input and practice. He has not considered his strategies in the light of developing functional, practical language, nor in terms of effective learning processes.

8.2.1 Deep and Surface Processing

Long-term learning (storage and retrieval) usually is a result of what is called *deep processing*. This refers to an active process of making associations with material that is already familiar, examining interrelationships within the new material, elaborating the stimulus through further development of it, connecting the new material with personal experience, and considering alternative interpretations. The learner may use the new material to actively reconstruct his or her conceptual frameworks. (This is very similar to the process of "accommodation" that was treated in section 6.5.) The process involves seeking personal meaning in the material and active engagement with it.

Deep processing is contrasted with surface processing. In the latter case, focus tends to be on completion of the task with minimum conceptual effort. Surface processing is often characterized by memorizing and by limiting the domain of activity. The task may be seen as externally imposed and to be accomplished as expeditiously as possible. Personal meaning is seldom considered relevant. Activities are often mechanical; reorganization and reinterpretation do not occur.

The relationship between extrinsic-intrinsic motivation (Chapter 7) and surface and deep processing approaches seems fairly clear. Intrinsic motivation can be expected to lead for the most part toward deep processing strategies. Extrinsic motivation alone may promote more surface approaches, as part of an effort to meet requirements and no more. For the most part, these are the tendencies we can expect when the student has the option of using either approach. Some students, however, do not have the choice of using deep processing. For example, they may have never learned to make use of deep processing strategies. This may be a result of poor educational background, lack of learning aptitude, learning style, or inexperience. Some students may have learned to apply deep processing strategies in one domain of knowledge but have difficulty transferring it to a new domain.

Calvin's approach is largely at the surface level. He does not seek personal meaning, link what he is learning with his own experience, elaborate what is presented, and challenge or expand what he is given in the text and tapes. There is little evidence of cognitive restructuring as a result of his tape study.

Furthermore, on the age-old principle that we get better at what we practice doing, Calvin needs to set up his study so that it provides opportunities to work on the area he needs to develop: recognizing vocabulary, retrieving its meaning, and integrating the meaning with the ongoing discourse in real time as an interaction or narrative is taking place.

Calvin's teacher suggested that he seek to link and associate the words and constructions in his study materials with what he already knows, associating to the meaning of the message not just the surface pattern. He was urged to try to rehearse some of the material in real-life scenarios. He was encouraged to work with authentic audio materials, such as tapes of news broadcasts. Above all, he was urged to break down the task into manageable chunks, selecting what he thought would be most important for him to use in class and not make himself responsible for the rest. To get repetition and keep the task within reasonable bounds, it was also recommended that he use the same topic over several classes to "recycle" the vocabulary on which he was working.

These suggestions were aimed at helping Calvin make more use of deep processing and practice activities that would simulate at least part of the real-world task with which Calvin was having difficulty. Choosing what to focus on required another kind of "deep processing:" He had to think about the material in order to determine what was most immediately valuable to him. Setting priorities and chunking material down can be conceived of as a form of deep processing. It entails active engagement with the material in the light of what is important to the student.

Are some learning strategies better than others? I have suggested that deep strategies are more likely to result in long-term retention and more efficient retrieval of information. On the other hand, there are sometimes tasks or situations in which surface learning is either necessary or appropriate. When learning a new language with a different writing system, I almost always begin by learning the letters, sounds, and rules for letter combination, even before I have learned much, if any, of the spoken language. Much of this is direct memorization. There are a few associational strategies available (e.g., "Oh, that's the one that looks like a cat's head" or "those two look alike, but the one that has a longer tail is the one that is pronounced *th.*"). I also rely on a lot of repetition once the symbols have been learned—earlier learning means more exposure and practice with the symbols and in increasingly meaningful context. These are largely surface strategies. In general, though, the more meaningful cognitive activity entailed by the study, the better.

Certain learning strategies tend to be associated with various of the learning styles described in Chapters 4, 5, and 6. Deep and surface processing strategies can, for instance, be introverted or extraverted (you may wish to review the material on the Myers-Briggs Type Indicator model in Chapter 6). Introverted strategies are probably contemplative ones in which mental models are built, internal narratives are created, or there is a kind of internal dialogue. A more extraverted way of developing associational links would be to experience the linguistic item in interactions with others, engage in debates, or experiment in a trial and error way. Needless to say, we can and should make use of both approaches at different times and to meet different needs, but each of us may have a preference for one or the other if all other circumstances are equal.

Perhaps one of the reasons that the links between learning styles and learning success are not even stronger is that it is possible to find both deep and surface processing approaches that fit with most of the style dimensions. An introvert and an extravert can both deal with material superficially—for instance, the introvert might only review a word list for vocabulary, whereas the extravert may think that a once-over in a study group is enough. The introvert might achieve a deeper engagement with new material through reading or listening to tapes; the extravert might seek more extensive conversational contexts for the new material. Another example: A sensing type may operate in a surface way by looking only at the facts and not what they mean or in a deeper way by experiential use of the language. An intuitive may look only at the "big picture" in overview and decide that he or she understands, yet have only a superficial grasp of the issue or else engage with the details in a way that enriches the overview already achieved.

All the previous discussion yields three principles that may be helpful in working with students who have weak study skills. (The principles that emerge in the course of this chapter are presented together below.)

> *Principle 1:* Whenever possible, seek a deep processing strategy over a surface technique. Find an element of meaning that brings about links with other knowledge or experience.
> *Principle 2:* Bring the learning activities as close as possible to simulating the real-life tasks they are preparation for. To the degree possible, students should practice what they expect to do with the language.
> *Principle 3:* There is no correct set of learning strategies. Learning strategies should be chosen to meet the demands of the learning task and in line with the learner's style. Most goals can be reached by multiple routes; some people prefer to go through town, whereas others prefer to take the suburban or country route. All three will get them to their destination.

Students often conceive of learning as an accumulation of information or perhaps the ability to make use of a skill. (So, for that matter, do some teachers.) It is true that these operations are components of learning. Perceiving relationships within material and between new material and experience and using knowledge to reinterpret one's view of the world are, however, much richer forms of learning that build on knowledge and skill. Effective language learning is very much a process of reinterpreting one's view of reality using alternative perspectives.

8.2.2 Student Responsibility and Independence

A teacher can help a student learn in all of the ways described in the preceding section, but the ultimate responsibility to learn, and learn actively, is the student's. Some students insist on taking this responsibility—for example, Alice. Others are more dependent. Corwin (section 7.3) is a good example of a relatively dependent learner. He said that he wants a very demanding teacher who imposes a lot of learning structure on him, checking his homework and guiding him step-by-step in both daily class activities and in homework.

Our goal as teachers should be not only to provide students with content but also to enable them to continue to learn in our area of knowledge after they leave us. This is especially important for language learning in which the skill is likely to be applied in settings where there is no teacher. Learning strategies are a way for students to reach the point where support can be withdrawn. Appropriate strategies are the techniques students use to become independent learners. For this reason, effective teaching includes helping students learn how to learn.

Let us return to Holly, whom we met as a Type 4 learner (field dependent and field insensitive). Holly wants her teachers to write on the board, give her pop quizzes instead of piling on the material without punctuation, and reinforce structures that are clearly identified and maintained for review. Some students take care of these needs for themselves. They write material for themselves (and may check spelling either on their own or with a teacher), decide for themselves what is important and break the material into manageable chunks, find ways to test themselves, and decide on the vocabulary and structures they want to review and make sure they come up. Holly, however, has not learned to do this for herself and is distressed at not knowing what to do to study her current lesson material.

Advice to Holly included having her go through the vocabulary covered so far in the book and find a set number of items from each lesson that will be her "core" vocabulary and to do the same thing for each new lesson.

She was given suggestions about how to make and use flashcards. (I usually recommend that students make their own flashcards even when sophisticated commercial ones are available, because it creates and activates another set of associations and brings in some kinesthetic input.) Holly was also urged to negotiate with her teachers for time out and some review when she started feeling overwhelmed by the amount of material that was coming at her. A schedule of systematic activities to cover new and current lessons and to review was worked out with Holly so her time could be used in a way she would experience as productive.

These activities were designed to encourage Holly to do as much deep processing and simulate open-ended language use as possible, but for the sake of reducing her anxiety, the more open-ended activities were built up to through a series of more mechanical drills. She was strongly urged, however, not to omit the "culminating" deep and realistic exercises that were less comfortable for her learning style. Thus the first two of the principles (deep processing and realistic practice) were set up in a way that Holly could manage. The third principle was honored in the effort to find a way to start where Holly was comfortable and let her build up to activities that are necessary but difficult for her. She had neither the experience nor the cognitive skills to design her own learning effectively.

Dennis has even more trouble with managing his own learning. His difficulties are compounded by an attitude that "it's not my job to do it but the program's job to do it."

> Dennis is in a class whose teacher assigns very little homework directly, assuming that the students will follow their own preferences in working out ways to learn the material that comes up in class and in the textbook. Dennis says the hardest thing is to figure out how to spend the weekend in that little work is assigned. He feels he has to guess what is to come the next day and prepare on his own. The class seems to move very fast, with no time for the material to "soak in." To cope, Dennis has come up with a mishmash of activities that he follows inconsistently: He listens to tapes, often while he is driving to work, reads the textbook trying to "semi-memorize" dialogues, he writes a paragraph a day in a diary that he sometimes shows a teacher and recites aloud in front of the mirror.

This is a good description of a learner who, as with Holly, needs a lot of appropriate support before he can become an independent learner. He will probably never be as independent as Bert or Vanessa, let alone Alice. On the other hand, he can be encouraged to build the skills and sense of self-efficacy that will permit him to structure more of his own learning than he feels capable of doing now.

8.2.3 Appropriate Teacher Support

Some works on learning strategies describe external structure (such as mechanical drilling and close guidance by the teacher) that is used while a student is building skills as "scaffolding." This is a nice metaphor that suggests that some kind of external structure is needed while construction of knowledge is underway. When a physical construction can stand on its own, however, it is time to take away the scaffold. The same is true of learning.

The issue of appropriate support carries over from the beginning of the learning process, at which time more scaffolding is probably needed, to the advanced stages, in which less is likely to be needed because more skills have become automatic. It also applies at more of a microlevel, for each new lesson or even each new chunk of learning. The process of giving the right amount of external support is thus recursive—it comes up over and over again and at different levels of learning, from the smallest to the largest units. Alice, Holly, and Dennis show extremes of need for such scaffolding: Alice needs next to none, whereas Holly and Dennis need a lot as they begin each new learning task.

One of the teachers who had taught Corwin (7.3) had tried to empower him and make him more independent. Corwin resisted this attempt. Perhaps the well-intentioned teacher withdrew support too soon. Corwin probably needed much longer with an external scaffold to build his linguistic edifice than his teacher thought he did. For him, appropriate support would mean a longer period of direct guidance and low-risk learning activities than he was getting. It would probably be possible to help Corwin reach a point of more independence in limited domains, but it would take a while.

The sequence described for Holly in which she begins with a great deal of closely structured practice and is led to move out into what for her are riskier activities is a good example of appropriate support. A student such as Alice has such well-developed learning strategies that the most appropriate support for her is *no* support in the form of external structuring. For her, external structure interferes with her successful learning approach. For most students, however, some amount of external structure is helpful or even necessary. The issue is what kind of structure, how much of it, when to give it, and above all, when and how fast to remove it. Most need more than Alice but less than Holly or Dennis.

Dennis, who was having difficulty with structuring his own study, was given suggestions that helped him make use of all the materials he had in the course in a systematic way. He was urged to use his diary to practice writing using material he selected as especially interesting or challenging for him, and to use it as a "dialogue journal" in which he communicated with his teacher in writing (mostly in the target language). Listening to tapes from old lessons was recommended as a way to review, practice clearly achievable comprehension, and demonstrate to himself the progress he was making. Dennis was offered ways to get the repetition he wanted outside class through reading and study groups. When he felt he was trying to manage too many variables at once, he was given suggestions for how to use simpler sentences, with fewer thought units per sentence, as a coping device. Together, he and his teacher worked out a routine for him to follow as he worked through new lesson material and reviewed old material. He was encouraged to list words and constructions on which he wanted to work and check them out with the teacher every few days. This way, he began to practice setting his own priorities, but at the same time he was not abandoned entirely to his own devices, in which he had little confidence at first.

From this discussion, emerges another principle related to learning strategies and study skills:

> *Principle 4:* Learners need different amounts of independence and external structure. For a student to become more independent, he or she needs the appropriate level of support or scaffolding.

The issue of appropriate support is closely linked with the relationship between teacher and student. A teacher who takes a relatively nurturant approach to students is likely to provide substantial support. The danger for such a teacher is intrusion into the student's learning space and creating or prolonging dependency. A teacher with a more competence-building approach, on the other hand, may move readily into withdrawal of scaffolding; the danger is that support may be taken away prematurely, resulting in a feeling of abandonment by the student.

8.2.4 Helping Students Develop Deeper Strategies

Students with weak study skills often have difficulty in the areas of planning and evaluating their own study, a category called "metacognitive strategies." (The term "metacognitive" refers to thinking about one's own thinking processes.) Such students often have difficulty setting their own priorities. They experience everything that comes up in class for them as an expectation they must meet. They feel responsible for every word, whether in the lesson materials or introduced in response to a classmate's question. No wonder they soon feel overwhelmed and even despairing of mastering the language.

Sometimes the difficulty with setting priorities is simply that the student does not feel "authorized" to make such decisions for him- or herself. In such cases, it is fairly straightforward to help the student understand that picking and choosing from all the input that comes in is not only permissible, it is necessary.

Other students may accept the permission to select what is most important for focused study, but they may lack the skills to make use of that permission. We have seen that many field dependent students are like this. Students who have trouble with the last level of the tolerance of ambiguity model ("accomodation," 6.5) let a lot of information in but do not pick and choose or set hierarchies of importance and of relationship within the information. Such students are likely to need more guidance and gradually more challenging practice opportunities as they build skills that are outside their usual learning style.

Some students lack adequate memorization strategies. They do not have the little tricks that help them associate sounds or images to new words; they do not link the new and the familiar. Students may use flashcards in a mechanical way that does not test their knowledge or challenge them, but rather uses a surface approach. Straight word lists run the danger of being used in a surface way. Again, students who lack these skills can be taught to use them, though it may take a considerable amount of time before they have automatic, fluent access to them. I usually encourage such students to begin in the sensory channel modality with which they are most comfortable and use the less comfortable modality only after developing some sense of mastery through the more favored channel. The principle applies to other learning style dimensions:

> *Principle 5:* Let students begin something new and challenging in their most comfortable learning style, and challenge them to "stretch" only after they have a sense of some security and mastery with the new material.

A number of scholars have classified the many, many learning strategies that can be listed. For convenience, I will use the six-category taxonomy developed by Rebecca Oxford (1990). Her scheme has the following strategy categories:

Memory	Metacognitive
Cognitive	Affective
Compensation	Social

Memory strategies are the techniques used to get material into our long-term storage. Cognitive strategies include practice and repetition, as well as intellectual processing. Compensation strategies are those that are used to fill or compensate for gaps in knowledge or skill, such as circumlocution. Metacognitive strategies have to do with goal setting, planning work, and evaluating it. Affective strategies are those that are used to manage one's feelings, such as "positive self-talk." Finally, social strategies involve other people.

Every kind of learning strategy can be a way of elaborating and deepening knowledge. Memory strategies make sound, image, location, or experiential links. Cognitive strategies may make use of intellectual, logical constructs to establish a kind of association. The necessity to use compensation strategies often provides experiential associations that greatly enrich the associational network of the language. Affective strategies link learning with feelings, a powerful influence on storage and retrieval. Social strategies bring others into the associational network through group study, getting help, pairwork, and so on. They often activate affective strategies, too.

Affective self-management is so important that it is worth another principle of its own. As discussed in Chapter 7, feelings can either enhance or inhibit one's access to one's cognitive and personality-style resources. Management of one's feelings is vital for reaching, maintaining, and restoring access to learning abilities. Discouragement often leads to lowered intrinsic motivation, which in turn may result in decreased use of deep processing strategies:

> *Principle 6:* Management of one's feelings is at least as important as the cognitive strategies one uses. Discouragement can subvert any set of techniques. A sense of self-efficacy promotes the persistence language learning requires.

Commonly suggested techniques such as working on material that is about a common theme or putting one's own words into drills or sample dialogues are classic ways to link new material with old. They also provide ways for students to "spiral" their learning, getting review without boredom and building new associations.

Most lists of learning strategies and techniques put most of their emphasis on direct and conscious techniques. They encourage directed attention to one's own production and that of others, especially native speakers. These are valuable suggestions. On the other hand, some of the most effective learning comes peripherally, "out of the corner of one's eye," so to speak. One of the great advantages of content-based language learning is that it enables this kind of process. To make it work, though, the learner needs to stay open—keep ego boundaries between self and the outside world somewhat thin—and trust that learning is really taking place, even though it is not directly controlled. You can help your students come to value and trust this kind of process at the very least by making it legitimate for them:

> *Principle 7:* Encourage students to develop trust and skill in peripheral learning as well as the kind of directly focused learning that most lists of learning techniques promote. If they can keep their boundaries open, students can get some of their best learning when their direct attention is on something else.

It is difficult to give hard-and-fast rules on how to study. Learning style, level of independence, area of difficulty, goals for learning, and relationship with teacher (among other factors) make each instance different. Needs and solutions are often highly specific. We can see this in the case of Calvin, in sections 8.2 and 8.2.1. He has sought help for a particular learning difficulty: retrieving vocabulary for use in real time. He wants help in a specific domain of preparation: using audiotapes. The techniques recommended are equally specific and related to Calvin's own level of independence, existing skills, and learning style.

For this reason, working from general principles is a fruitful approach. You can use the principles in Table 8.1 to evaluate the strategies that you hear the students describe themselves using. Are they resulting in active engagement with the language? Are they promoting practice that at least simulates real language use? If not, you can use the principle that was "violated" to design a replacement strategy to suggest to the student.

For example, Calvin limits his work with audiotapes to the text and lesson material. This approach not permitting him to practice the skills he needs when he is actually using the language for communication. To give him that kind of practice, you have him listen to tapes of authentic material designed for native speakers as a way to give him practice in a real task, becoming so comfortable with listening to language beyond his full mastery level that he has the cognitive space to retrieve vocabulary as he needs it. This intervention is based on Principle 2, having students practice what they need to do in the language.

I usually prefer to explain the principle of deep processing as well, so students can begin to use it to evaluate their own strategies and design new ones. I encourage students to look at the goals for the activities they develop for themselves.

8.2.5 Assessing Student Learning Strategies

General inventories of learning strategies take either of two approaches. One is a list of activities that are then classified into categories of activity types. A widely used example of such a questionnaire is the Learning and Study Strategies Inventory (LASSI, Weinstein, Palmer, and Schulte, 1987), which provides scores on the following categories:

Attitude and interest
Motivation, diligence, self-discipline
Time management

Table 8.1 Principles for Addressing Study Skills

1. Whenever possible, seek a "deep" processing strategy over a surface technique. Find an element of meaning that brings about links with other knowledge or experience.
   a. Seek or develop personal relevance
   b. Use advance organizers to get initial familiarity before plunging in
   c. Connect the new with the old—link with previous knowledge or experience
   d. Recombine new material
   e. Analyze (e.g., find the parts of a word)
   f. Construct hierarchies of information, don't let it just be a "flat" mishmash
   g. Guess and evaluate the response to the guess
   h. Build images related to the new input (pictures, sounds, diagrams, word constructions, etc.)
   i. Associate material with at least one context (more are better)
2. Bring the learning activities as close as possible to simulating the real life tasks they are preparation for. To the degree possible, students should practice what they expect to do with the language.
3. There is no correct set of learning strategies. Learning strategies should be chosen to meet the demands of the learning task and in line with the learner's style. Most goals can be reached by multiple routes.
4. Learners need different amounts of independence and external structure. For a student to become more independent, he or she needs the appropriate level of support or scaffolding.
5. Let students begin something new and challenging in their most comfortable learning style, and challenge them to "stretch" only after they have a sense of some security and mastery with the new material.
6. Management of one's feelings is at least as important as the "cognitive" strategies one uses. Discouragement can subvert any set of techniques. Self-efficacy promotes the persistence language learning requires.
7. Encourage students to develop trust and skill in peripheral learning as well as the kind of directly focused learning that most lists of learning techniques promote. If they can keep their boundaries open, students can get some of their best learning when their direct attention is on something else.

Anxiety and worry about academic performance

Concentration and attention to tasks

Information processing and reasoning

Selecting main ideas, recognizing important information

Use of support techniques and materials

Self-testing, reviewing, preparing for classes

Test strategies, preparing for tests

Probably the best-known learning strategies instrument for language learning is the Strategy Inventory for Language Learning (SILL, Oxford, 1990), which asks for responses indicating frequency of use for a variety of learning techniques, grouped by Oxford's learning strategy taxonomy (section 8.2.4). There is a version for English speakers learning a new language, and another version for non-native speakers of English learning English. In addition, Oxford's book provides a wide range of checklists usable by both learners and teachers for assessing day-to-day strategy use. The SILL has been translated into multiple languages and is in use around the world.

Questionnaires such as the LASSI or the SILL, which have very heterogeneous items, can be useful in at least two ways. One is to use the existing subscales that represent items that are grouped together, usually on the basis of intercorrelations among the items. In this case, an analysis of how the student learns and discussion with him or her is about categories of learning techniques. For many students, it is also helpful to look at specific items that they either endorse or reject. This type of use can help students try out new learning strategies and it can reveal patterns of learning activity that are obscured by the subscale grouping that comes with the tests.

The other form of learning strategies instrument groups learning approaches by the purpose of learning. An example with which I have been experimenting is the Study Processes Questionnaire (Biggs, 1992), which addresses motivation and learning strategies in three categories: (a) surface (to get a task done with little personal investment), (b) achieving (to succeed in competition and get good marks), and (c) deep (to learn with personal investment in the task). Self-report of surface motivation or surface strategies as the main approach can be a good sign that the learner may have weak study skills. Endorsement of achievement strategies alone suggests a level of expedience that may not result in lasting learning. A student who relies on deep strategies alone may learn what he or she wants to learn, but failure to adapt to social reality in the classroom may result in friction with the teacher and other students and lower marks than the student deserves. Probably the most successful combination is that of deep and achieving strategies, though surface strategies should not be rejected altogether because sometimes they are appropriate to the situation or the learning task.

In addition to the SILL, Part 2 of the Motivation and Strategies Questionnaire (MSQ, Appendix C) provides a list of classroom learning activities that has proved useful in working with students having difficulties. A number of the activities correspond with learning style and aptitude dimensions, as suggested in Appendix D. Generally I look at the items in this section that have been marked as either essential or a waste of time and check them out with the student, verifying the standard hypothesis (Appendix D) or one that I have built in the light of the information I have already gained about the student. This technique is similar to the second method just described for using surveys such as the SILL or LASSI.

8.3 Putting It Together

We have looked at learning styles, personality dispositions, motivation, self-efficacy, anxiety, biographic background, and study skills (learning strategies). For each, we have seen examples from real students, but we have not yet seen all of the categories of interest in one student. *Beverly* illustrates all the major dimensions.

Beverly is a 24-year-old graduate student in an international relations master's degree program. She majored in Russian studies as an undergraduate. In addition to Russian, in which she has intermediate proficiency, she also learned some French in high school and college. She has traveled to a number of countries. She enjoyed her previous study of foreign languages and also took pleasure in putting them to use when traveling. Now, however, she is learning a Far Eastern language with a difficult writing system, and she has run into trouble. She has become discouraged and focused on the degree to which the teacher favors another student with previous background in Asian languages. She says the following:

Beverly. I feel as if I'm falling behind. The teachers go so fast through the material, and I'm just running as hard as I can to keep up.

Interviewer. You'd like a pause to catch your breath.

Beverly. Yes! And furthermore, the presentation seems to leap around from topic to topic. Every hour the teacher starts something new, and it's not always related to what came before. I get so confused.

Interviewer. There seems to be no continuity for you to hold on to.

Beverly. Yes, I'm just accumulating a lot of material, but it isn't sticking very well. I don't really feel I understand it, and I really need some review. I just had a really frustrating week. We learned the negative imperative, and we didn't use it enough. Then we went on to the next lesson, and we went through that in two days. So then I got requests, which are complicated. I know a little about negative imperatives, and I know a little about requests, but I can't really use either one.

Interviewer. Sounds as though you feel as if you're trying to drink the ocean.

Beverly. That's for sure. It really helps when the teacher speaks using mostly language we've already studied. When she starts talking more naturally, we can't understand her at all. Also, a lot of material is introduced in class, and I for one would really like a written handout to go along with the book. It's hard to remember all the things that come up in class, and then I have to know them.

Interviewer. Part of that drowning feeling comes from the fact that you can't see all the new material?

Beverly. Yes, that's right. I can memorize things when I have a chance to visualize the words. You know, I used to think I was a pretty good language learner, but now I'm wondering if I'm up to it.

Interviewer. This is really pushing your limits! How have you been studying up to now?

Beverly. Well, I look at the vocabulary every night, and I read the current lesson and review material from the one before. I listen to the tapes a few times while looking at the book. Sometimes I try a few tricks to memorize words, like finding rhymes for them in English or Russian. I practice the drills at home every night. Sometimes I exchange a few greetings with my neighbor, who comes from that country. What's so difficult is that it is never clear that I have done enough or if I'm on the right track. Give me some concrete rules and examples, and I can work on them at home. Worksheets would really help. Above all, let me know when I do things right, as well as wrong!

Before reading further, make some hypotheses about Beverly.
Look at various dimensions of her learning style, what her
feelings are and how she handles them, and her study strategies.
How would you characterize what is going on?

As you pursue your work with Beverly you learn that she is an ENTJ, and her ego boundaries are not especially thick or thin. The interview has already suggested that she has a strong preference for visual processing and gets overwhelmed by too much auditory input without visual support. She is somewhat deductive and concrete in approach. When she is not overwhelmed by more input than she can handle, she learns well in communicative contexts, but she is not field independent. She is thus probably a Type 3 learner. Because she does not impose her own structure on material, she feels the need for external structure and sequential processing of lessons.

Further investigation reveals that this field dependent learner is in a program that up to now has been so selective that it could limit its students to those with strong analytic, field independent skills who do very well on a standardized language aptitude test. The teaching approaches that have been developed in the section and the expectations of the teachers are premised on students who can cope with a lot of material out of context and who can impose their own structure on the mass of information the teachers deliver. Recently, however, there has been more diversity in the kinds of students who enter classes in this language, and the program has been slow to adapt to them. The teachers perceive field dependent students as "poor learners."

At the same time, there are some changes Beverly needs to make as well. She came to this class from previous experiences in which her learning style and study approach permitted rather easy success. The inadequacy of her previous approach came as a shock to her when she began this notoriously difficult language. For the most part, Beverly describes learning strategies that rely largely on surface processing. Beverly's study at home, though regular and diligent, is not active in the sense that she is elaborating, recombining, making rich networks of associations, or attempting to come as close as possible to practicing language in context. Beverly needs to combine developing her cognitive strategies with management of her feelings about herself and the language learning process. She is not exploiting an exceptionally valuable resource: her neighbor. She also needs to make use of a special kind of social strategy: assertion and respectful negotiation with her teacher to get her needs met.

Pause for a moment. If you were asked to do so by Beverly and her teacher, what suggestions would you make to each? Use the principles in Table 8.1 to design study suggestions for Beverly.

Although it is not the purpose of this book to offer prescriptions, here is a partial list of the suggestions that were made to Beverly and to her teacher. First, after a discussion with her about her learning style and what is likely to help and not help her, she was urged to make a list of the two or three most important changes her teacher could make that would help her learn more effectively. She was encouraged to bring those up with her teacher, making suggestions that would not disrupt the learning of the others in the class or put unmanageable burdens of preparation on the teacher.

Second, Beverly was encouraged to learn as much as possible in context. She was introduced to the idea of deep processing, and she and the interviewer explored some possibilities for her to use to make her engagement with the material more active, including the use of external resources such as her neighbor. She was provided with some elementary techniques for planning her learning and for setting priorities. To set priorities, she needed to be able to structure the material she was learning in simple hierarchical relations, so she was given some help in this area as well. Some stress management techniques rounded out the picture, particularly related to performance anxiety, which is often a source of special difficulty to intuitive thinking learners.

Beverly's teacher was introduced to Beverly's learning style profile, with suggestions for how to maximize her strengths (contextual learning, good analytic skills when not overwhelmed, disciplined study habits, willingness to take conversational risks if enough of a knowledge base). The teacher was also introduced to the concept of appropriate support and in this vein was urged to provide more guidance to Beverly (and others) about what was important and what could be ignored. She was encouraged to write more on the board, prepare more handouts (other students would also benefit from these), make explicit the purposes of the various activities, and build in more opportunity for review and somewhat more continuity, or at least to make some of the connections clear to the class that seemed so obvious to her. She was also strongly urged to seek opportunities to give Beverly positive messages about her performance as well as negative ones.

8.4 A Taxonomy of Areas Affecting Learning

Table 8.2 summarizes the categories addressed so far that may help in diagnosing language learning difficulties. They are organized more or less as they have been presented in this book. Most of the categories are related to the student as an individual. No student, however, learns in isolation from his or her environment. The last major category in the list therefore treats the student in relation to his or her setting: style mismatches and the appropriate amount and kind of support to give each student at varying times. Those who work with students having learning difficulties are strongly encouraged to examine the program, the teacher, the curriculum, and the interaction between the student and all of these aspects of the learning environment. In Chapter 10, you will meet some students in situations in which there is such a mismatch between student needs and their programs. This kind of situation will be addressed in more detail at that time.

For most students, information from all of these categories works together to help build a coherent picture of a learner. Sometimes there are contradictions. I have found that I learn the most from the datum that will not fit in, or the internally contradictory evidence. I often have to hold the contradictions in mind until more information comes in (often about another student) that helps me understand the inconsistencies in a new light. Frequently, one category gives a lot of information, and the most of the others are either redundant or only marginally informative. I could simplify my list, except that what is important in working with one student may be of no help at all with others, and a category that gives little information for the first student may be the key to understanding the next one.

Table 8.2 Taxonomy of Areas Affecting Learning

1. Biographic Background
   a. Age
   b. Sex
   c. Cultural background
   d. Socioeconomic status
   e. Career history
   f. Education
      1. Level
      2. Subjects of study
      3. History of learning difficulties
   g. Interests and hobbies
   h. Previous language learning history
   i. Previous exposure to other cultures
2. Learning style
   a. Preferred sensory channel (auditory, kinesthetic, visual)
   b. Cognitive style
      1. Sequential-random
      2. Concrete-abstract
      3. Field independence and field sensitivity
      4. Deductive-inductive
      5. Left and right hemispheres
   c. Personality dispositions
      1. The Myers-Briggs Type Indicator
      2. Ego boundaries
      3. Tolerance of ambiguity
3. Affective factors
   a. Motivation
      1. Extrinsic-intrinsic
      2. Instrumental-integrative-assimilative
   b. Self-efficacy
   c. Anxiety (facilitating-debilitating)
   d. Defense mechanisms
   e. Beliefs about language learning (who can do it, what it takes to do it).
4. Learning strategies
   a. Deep and surface strategies; active learning
   b. Simulation of real language use (to the degree possible)
   c. Planning and setting priorities
   d. Different strategies for different styles, tasks, and stages of development
   e. Levels of learner independence
   f. Strategies for managing feelings
   g. Promoting "peripheral" learning
5. Learning aptitude
6. Interaction between student and environment
   a. Mismatch between student and teacher and/or program
   b. Need for appropriate support from program

8.5 Practice

1. The following are some language learners. What are their probable assets and liabilities as language learners?

    N is a college freshman, learning his first foreign language.

    O has been in the United States for 6 months and is in an ESL class.

    P was the child of a foreign service couple and spent many of her growing years in a variety of countries.

    Q is a 55-year-old middle manager who began her career as a secretary. She is beginning her first foreign language in preparation for work overseas.

    R majored in linguistics but has never learned a foreign language in depth.

    S grew up in an immigrant family in which a cognate language was spoken, but he received all his schooling in English.

2. When you have to learn something new, do you consider yourself a relatively independent or dependent learner? What relationship do you prefer to have with your teacher? What roles do you want him or her to take with you?

3. What are your favored learning strategies? Were there some that did not work well for you in the past? Why do you think they were unsuccessful?

4. When do you use surface learning strategies? What are some of the deep strategies you use as a learner?

5. Table 8.3 is a list of learning strategies suggested in a well-established and successful language teaching program. Evaluate the strategies in it from the point of view of the principles in Table 8.1. Which if any of the items would you change? Which would you remove or add? Why?

6. Observe or interview a student or two. What strategies are they using? Are they effective? Why or why not?

7. Simon has come to you for assistance. He says the following:

    I'm having trouble in class when there are spontaneous conversation activities. What's really hard for me in those classes is listening comprehension, word recall, and remembering material that comes up in class. I'm spending 3 to 4 hours a day doing homework, but it just doesn't seem to be working very well. My study includes scanning new lessons, reviewing old ones, listening to lesson tapes, and especially listening to tapes of news broadcasts that we get once a week. I also try to keep up with the new vocabulary that comes up in class—I write it down and make flashcards, but I can't keep up with all of it. In order to get the reading assignments done, I went out and bought

Table 8.3 A List of Some "Study Tips" (For use in practice activity
8.5.5)

Pronunciation
1. When listening to tapes, (a) listen first without repeating; (b) listen again,
   repeating silently; (c) repeat aloud.
2. When you are familiar with the content, practice saying the lines *along with* the
   voice on the tape. This will help you become fluent and aid in improving rhythm,
   intonation, stress and pauses.
3. Look in a mirror while pronouncing certain words or sounds that are particularly
   difficult for you. Make certain that your lips and face muscles actually move.
4. Record your voice and compare your pronunciation with that on the tape.
5. Try to practice troublesome words and sounds within a context that will help you
   to remember, such as in a song, proverb, or idiomatic expression.
Grammar
1. Study language samples, whether in the form of dialogues, narratives, or other.
   Pay attention to such things as word order, "little words" (e.g., articles, pronouns,
   prepositions), word endings, and agreement. You may thus arrive at some
   tentative "grammar rules" of your own.
2. Be aware of differences between the way a particular idea is expressed in the new
   language as opposed to your own language. Focus more on the differences than on
   the similarities.
3. *After* you have made the above observations, read grammatical explanations in
   your textbook and make sure you understand them. If you have any questions
   regarding the explanations, ask.
4. Become thoroughly familiar with specific "rules," guidelines, or explanations.
5. To remember a specific rule, try to find illustrative examples and memorize one of
   these to which you can refer as a model.
Vocabulary
1. *Always* begin your study of new words in specific contexts. This will help you
   remember their meaning. You might then study them in isolation. You should *not*
   reverse this process.
2. Try to associate words with pictures or images to avoid dependence upon
   translation. Practice with flash cards that have a picture on one side and the word
   or phrase on the other.

a dictionary, so now at least I can look up all the words I don't know
when I read. But I can't use a dictionary when I'm listening. What can
you suggest for me?

Decide what is going on with Simon's learning strategies based on
the principles in Table 8.1. In light of the same principles, what
would you suggest he do differently or additionally?

8. Consult with a colleague about one of his or her students who is
   having difficulty. (I suggest starting with someone else's student

Table 8.3 Continued

3. To retain better, group words by semantic content such as professions, foods, clothing, political terms.
4. Write words out several times, saying them out loud as you write them.
5. Make flash cards with words used in sentences.
6. Try recording vocabulary lists that you would like to memorize. Listen to them and repeat several times.
7. Try out new words as often as possible in meaningful contexts. Make new words part of you and your way of speaking.

Managing a Conversation

1. Learn the polite expressions for beginning and ending conversations, including telephone interaction.
2. Learn some standard expressions that show you are paying attention to the conversation (e.g., "You don't say," "Really," "How interesting," etc.)
3. Learn expressions to "control the native speaker," that is, how to interrupt gracefully. This is troublesome in that the rules are often more cultural than linguistic ("could you clarify that?" "Did you say . . .?" "Excuse me, please . . ." "If I understand you . . .").
4. Learn appropriate "filler" expressions, such as "well," "What I was trying to say was . . ." or "That's it, yes, now I see." These will not only make the conversation flow more smoothly but will also give you time to think of what to say next.
5. Learn hesitation devices to sound as if you are searching for a thought rather than a verb ending.
6. Do not neglect the study of the cultural context of your assignment; for effective communication, you must know why and when to say things in addition to how to say them with accurate grammar, vocabulary, and pronunciation.

SOURCE: Zappala, S. (1995). *Roadmap to Communicating in Italy: Information for Students Entering Italian Language Training* (Unpublished handout). Arlington, VA: Foreign Service Institute.

because the task may be easier if you are less emotionally involved.) Try applying the material you have learned from this book, working collaboratively with your colleague. What is the information you think you will need from your colleague to begin the diagnosis process? What are the sensitizing concepts (categories on which your attention is focused, described in section 2.3.1) that organize how you listen, ask for further information, and make hypotheses?

9. Try the same kind of thinking as in activity 8 with one or more of your own students. Perhaps you could think about one of the students whom you selected as a focus in the activity at the end of Chapter 1.

8.6 More Information

You can learn more about the effects of various ages and language learning in Lightbown and Spada (1993). Curran (1978) and Stevick (1980) go more deeply into the concept of adult resistance and apply it to language learning.

A very thorough treatment of deep and surface processing, along with other valuable contributions to learning strategy theory, is to be found in Schmeck. (1988). In fact, the entire book in which that article is to be found has excellent material on learning strategies in general (not just for language learning). Stevick (1996) approaches long-term memory in another, useful way.

For treatments of language learning strategies, consult the following excellent books, among others. Chamot and O'Malley (1994), Oxford (1990), and Wenden & Rubin (1987). Chamot & O'Malley have an extensive taxonomy of learning strategies and a very useful model of scaffolding and appropriate support. Oxford offers not only her convenient taxonomy of learning strategies but many excellent exercises for working with them and a widely used questionnaire for assessing strategy use, the Strategy Inventory for Language Learning. Wenden and Rubin offer a comprehensive overview of theory and research on learning strategies up to the mid-1980's; most of it is still relevant.

There has been considerable investigation of programs to teach learning strategies to students, with mixed results; Dornyei (1995) provides a comprehensive overview of the subject. Both Chamot and O'Malley (1994) and Oxford (1990) are excellent starting places to find information on strategy-teaching techniques that have had success. Indeed, teaching of learning strategies is the focus of the Chamot and O'Malley work.

Lawrence (1993) offers considerable information on language learning strategies and the psychological type (MBTI) dimensions. Ehrman (1989) has substantial detail on learning strategies reported by foreign language learners representing all eight of the MBTI preference poles; some of this information is summarized in Ehrman and Oxford (1990a, 1990b).

Both students and teachers can make productive use of books designed to help learners do a better job of language learning. A representative and useful selection of such books is composed of Brown (1991), Cohen (1990), Fuller (1987), Marshall (1989), and Rubin & Thompson (1994). Willing

(1989a, 1989) has a variety of activities that are aimed at teachers that they can use to help students learn how to learn. Each of these books has a slightly different emphasis, but all of them list strategies that will be of help to both learners trying to find better ways and teachers looking for suggestions to help learners. Jackson (1994) reviews these and other works.

Finally, Stevick (1989) is replete with techniques and strategies described by the seven gifted learners in that book. Because the learners are so different, there is a great range of strategies, illustrating vividly Principle 3 in Table 8.1 (there is no one correct set of learning strategies).

Note

1. An adult in intensive full-time language training can achieve professional levels of proficiency in a new language that is closely related to the native language in as few as 600 hours of classroom instruction. In contrast, Lightbown (1985) states that " 'A conservative estimate of the number of hours young first language learners spend 'acquiring' their first language is 12,000-15,000' " (quoted in Larsen-Freeman, 1991, p. 336.).

Using Information From Questionnaires and Tests and Language Aptitude

Chapters 2 and 3 described data gathering through observation and interviewing. This chapter completes the coverage of data collection. It treats the complex subject of tests, surveys, and questionnaires. Tests have great advantages, but they can also be very misleading, so the chapter begins with a discussion of how best to use such information, how seriously to take it, and how to relate it to data gathered by other means. Much of the chapter is devoted to the subject of general and language learning aptitude and the tests designed to measure it. There also is a short section devoted to testing language achievement and proficiency. The chapter ends with an effort to relate data derived from questionnaires and tests to classroom needs. Several cases illustrate how the information these instruments provide can enhance understanding of individuals.

9.1 Tests and Questionnaires as Data Sources

Up to now, the discussion has mostly assumed that you are working only with information from observation of the student or interviews.

Perhaps you have had the student fill out a biographical background questionnaire, similar to the example in Appendix A. For some of you, this is the only way you will be able to assess the learning style dimensions if you do not have access to questionnaire and test data.

Many of you, however, will have access to questionnaires and tests, or at least the results of them. For these readers, this chapter will explore the uses of information from standardized instruments—tests and questionnaires.

Information from instruments such as the Modern Language Aptitude Test (MLAT) can be very helpful indeed. It can serve as a shortcut to finding out things that would otherwise take much longer to discover. Furthermore, some of the information offered by tests and questionnaires cannot be gathered by other means, and tests or questionnaires provide excellent hypotheses on which to build.

Test and questionnaire data can also be misleading. They are relatively concrete and are usually reported in the form of numbers. Numerical data tend to have instant credibility in Western society, even when they are built on weak foundations or omit important information. These characteristics may lead us to attribute value to questionnaire data over the evidence of our eyes and ears. We may be led by the ready availability of information from questionnaires and tests to skip getting data by the other means. This can be a mistake, as will be shown in Chapter 10.

The best information is that which comes from multiple sources. Each source sets up hypotheses that you can use the other sources to test. If all sources seem consistent, your hypothesis is supported. If there is contradiction among the data sources, you will need to come to conclusions carefully and try out different interventions to see which work and which do not. The good side of contradictory data that can otherwise be so frustrating is that they give you the opportunity to make new discoveries about your student and about your conceptual frameworks.

Questionnaires work together. In the same way as information from observations, interviews, and questionnaires can either be convergent or so divergent that they challenge your interpretive skills, so multiple tests with overlapping domains can provide similar convergence and divergence.

An example is our pair of INTPs who differed on the Hartmann Boundary Questionnaire (HBQ), Ellis and Miriam (6.3.1). Thin boundaries on the HBQ tend to correlate with intuition, feeling, and perceiving.

In this case, however, the usual correlations for thinking worked for Ellis (thick boundaries) and those for intuition and perceiving did not, though Ellis is clearly an intuitive and a perceiver. On the other hand, for Miriam (thin boundaries), the correlations for intuition and perceiving worked in the expected direction (thin), whereas those for thinking did not, although her preference for thinking is very clear. If it were not for this kind of situation, there would be very little value added by the HBQ to the MBTI.

Tests and questionnaires are called *instruments*. This term is meant to indicate that they are "tools" for solving problems. They are also tools for helping us give shape and substance to our intuitions. A psychological test such the Rorschach inkblot test serves as a framework for making clinical intuitions real in the hands of a skilled practitioner; it is a powerful vehicle for crystallizing deep insights about the person who took the test. Similarly, the much less invasive instruments described here have served well to help me crystallize my intuitions about language students. These or others may do the same for you, with practice and thought.

A note on terminology. I reserve the term *test* for instruments that probe abilities, that have right and wrong answers, such as the MLAT. I use the term *questionnaire* for inventories of preference, such as the MBTI or the HBQ, in which there is no right or wrong answer. This distinction will be made throughout.

Questionnaires are usually based on the individual's report about himself or herself. There are a few questionnaires (as I am using the term) that look at preferences through performance, but most use self-report. They thus share with interviews the weakness of being subject to wishful thinking, defensiveness of self-esteem, or even conscious distortion. They may be subject to a form of influence called "social desirability response bias"—that is, the wish to appear in ways that the person thinks are socially approved. Some questionnaires and psychological tests have special scales designed to sort out "faking good" or "faking bad" (malingering). In general, however, I have found that most respondents try to give an honest picture of themselves when they understand the value to themselves of doing so and when they feel secure that the questionnaire findings will not be used against them in any way. Assurances of confidentiality, some interaction on my part with the individual so a little rapport is formed before they fill out the questionnaires, and exploration of surprising or inconsistent findings in a feedback interview all help to minimize response bias.

Tests, on the other hand, that are meant to investigate abilities, usually rely on performance of tasks meant to elicit the ability. An intelligence test, for instance, requires the individual to solve problems. A language proficiency test elicits samples of language use. Most psychological "tests" of personality use self-report, but as mentioned above, they often include ways to assess the amount of distortion there may be in the responses.

The following sections are not meant to be exhaustive but to describe instruments that are representative or that I have personally found useful. The battery of questionnaires and tests that I currently use consists of a biographic background questionnaire, the Myers-Briggs Type Indicator (MBTI), Hartmann Boundary Questionnaire (HBQ), Modern Language Aptitude Test (MLAT), the Motivation and Strategies Questionnaire, and such other instruments as I may be experimenting with at the time. The set is the result of a combination of availability, theoretical exploration, experimentation, and relative payoff for my purposes. I have also experimented with others, including some that are described in this book. If you should be in a position to design your own set of questionnaires, you may well find that a different group of instruments meets the demands of your circumstances and your own style.

9.2 Language Aptitude Tests

The MLAT is one of several language aptitude tests that emerged from the tradition of psychometric test development and efforts to predict language learning achievement. Other important language aptitude tests developed out of the same tradition include the Pimsleur Language Aptitude Battery (Pimsleur, 1966), the Defense Language Aptitude Battery (DLAB; Petersen & Al-Haik, 1976), and VORD (Parry & Child, 1990).

The MLAT is based on a factor analysis of a large number of individual characteristics thought to contribute to language learning (Carroll & Sapon, 1959). These were grouped into four main categories: (a) phonetic coding ability (distinguishing sounds and reflecting them graphically), (b) grammatical sensitivity (recognizing and using syntactic relationships), (c) memory (rote and contextualized), and (d) inductive language learning. All but the last of these four are directly addressed in the five parts of the MLAT (see Box 9.1).

The Pimsleur addresses the ability to deal with sounds and symbols also, but it differs from the MLAT by including a portion directly addressing the ability to infer language structure from an artificial language stimulus, in addition to segments assessing phonological and grammatical sensitivity. The DLAB consists primarily of such induction-testing items using an artificially adapted version of English. VORD was designed to test the ability to cope with the grammar of languages in the Altaic family (Parry & Child, 1990) and has items that focus largely on grammatical analysis. All four, including the MLAT, have similar predictive validity (Parry & Child, 1990).

Other components listed by scholars of language aptitude include motivation and knowledge of vocabulary in the native language (Pimsleur, 1966), the ability to hear under conditions of interference (Carroll, 1990), the ability to "handle decontextualized language" (Skehan, 1991), and the ability to shift mental set and cope with the unfamiliar (Ehrman, 1994b). (The hypothesis that coping with the unfamiliar and tolerance of ambiguity strongly affect language learning success are behind a new test that is being developed through a joint research project by the Foreign Service Institute and Yale University.)

Previous correlations for the MLAT with performance measured by tests of actual language use ranged between .42 and .62, with outliers of .27 with non-Indo-European languages at the Army Language School and .73 with FSI language instructor performance ratings (Carroll & Sapon, 1959). More recent tests of the MLAT are quite mixed, with various subscales, also called part scores, found predictive of differing aspects of learning performance, such as listening comprehension or for learners in one kind of setting rather than another (for more information on some of this research, see Ehrman, forthcoming).

Most of the research cited addresses the use of the MLAT (and other aptitude measures) as predictors of learning success, and indeed this is an important consideration for many programs. The MLAT, however, is also used for *placement* in a program (Wesche, 1981) and *diagnosis* of learning difficulties, for counseling students, and for tailoring programs to their needs (e.g., Demuth & Smith, 1987; Lefrancois & Sibiga, 1986, Sparks, Ganschow, Kenneweg, & Miller, 1991). These applications have received far less attention in the literature.

Box 9.1   The Modern Language Aptitude Test and Its Subscales

Part 1—Number Learning: This subtest requires the examinee to learn four morphemes and interpret them in combinations that form numbers; it is entirely orally delivered. The subtest is described in the Manual (Carroll & Sapon, 1959) as measuring part of memory and "auditory alertness," which play a part in auditory comprehension (showing how well one understands what one hears) of a foreign language.

Part 2—Phonetic Script: This subtest requires the examinee to select a written equivalent (in Trager-Smith phonemic transcription) for an orally delivered stimulus. The MLAT Manual describes the subtest as dealing with the ability to associate a sound with a particular symbol, as well as how well one can remember speech sounds. In addition, the subtest is described as tending to correlate with the ability to mimic speech sounds and sound combinations in a foreign language.

Part 3—Spelling Clues: In this entirely written subtest, an English word is presented in a very nonstandard spelling. The examinee must select the correct synonym. Vocabulary items are progressively more difficult, though the most difficult is probably within the repertoire of a college graduate. According to the Manual, scores on this part depend largely on how extensive a student's English vocabulary is. As in Part 2, it measures the ability to make sound-symbol associations but to a lesser degree.

Part 4—Words in Sentences: The stimulus is a sentence with a highlighted word or phrase. The examinee must indicate which part of another sentence matches the designated part. The subtest is entirely in writing. It is described as dealing with the examinee's sensitivity to grammatical structure and thus expected to provide information about the ability to handle grammar in a foreign language. No grammatical terminology is used, so scores do not depend on specific memory for grammatical terms.

Part 5—Paired Associates: The examinee is presented with 24 foreign words with their English equivalents and given some time to learn them. The words are then tested. This subtest is said to measure the examinee's ability to memorize by rote—a useful skill in learning new vocabulary in a foreign language.

Raw Score Total: Total of all five subscales.

Source: Descriptions are based on material in the MLAT *Manual* (Carrol & Sapon, 1959).

9.2.1 Using the MLAT for Diagnosis

In my own work, I have used the MLAT primarily for diagnosis of learning style and learning difficulties. As suggested in some of the sections above, it has proved very useful for this purpose. From the point of view of learning styles, it appears that the MLAT may provide a window on field independence and dependence (more on this in section 9.2.3). Interviews of students about what actually went on when they were performing a task on which they did especially poorly or especially well also provide invaluable information about their processing preferences and their learning strategies.

The MLAT does not operate in isolation in the collection of instruments I use. The following are the variables with which it correlates. Students who do well on the MLAT in general tend to have had more previous language learning experience. They express preferences for introversion and intuition on the MBTI and for perceiving on one MBTI/TDI JP subscale that addresses letting things happen without trying to control them. The research subjects who do well on the MLAT report relatively thin ego boundaries on the HBQ, especially in the form of dislike for too much neatness and order and of clear-cut separations among visual images. They also show greater ability at simultaneous and sequential processing of visual images on the NASSP Learning Style Profile. Box 9.2 presents some of the learning activities correlates, generally indicating a relationship between high MLAT and endorsement of open-ended learning activities. Of all the research instruments I have used, the MLAT also is by far the best predictor of success on an oral proficiency interview and an interactive reading proficiency test (section 9.4). Details of MLAT correlations are available in Ehrman (forthcoming).

In student counseling work, I use the variations in part scores to initiate hypotheses to examine how the student learns. Each of the MLAT factors probably represents a set of abilities. For example, Part 3 has proved particularly fruitful in the hypothesis generation and testing process with students. It is highly speeded and requires considerable cognitive restructuring. The items require examinees to select among five choices for a synonym to an English word that is unconventionally spelled, but in a way that reflects its pronunciation. Among the possible task requirements of these items are the following:

Box 9.2   High MLAT Scores and Learning Activity Categories

- High MLAT Total and *all* part scores
    Self-efficacy as a language learner
    Tolerance of ambiguity (low-structure activities and input)
- High scores on the Total and Parts 2, 3, 4, and 5 are correlated
  with
    Acceptance of/preference for use of authentic material for
      reading and listening
    Authentic conversation
- High scores on Parts 3 and 4[a] (and relatively low ones on the
  other parts) are correlated with
    Analytic learning
    A sense of organization in the curriculum
- The combination of high Total and a high score on Part 2 (and
  somewhat lower scores on Parts 3 and 4) are correlated with
    An experiential, kinesthetic approach (e.g., field trips and
      learning experience activities)
- A high score on Part 2, with low scores on Parts 3 and 4, suggests
    A relatively global learner
- High scores on the Total and Parts 2 and 4 correlate with
    A preference for directing one's own study.

NOTE: These findings apply to learners at the Foreign Service Institute. They should be tested
with other students.
a. This effect was slightly stronger for Part 3; students who rejected a "touchy feely" approach
on one item (the only such item) also tended to be high scorers on Part 3.

Gestalt processing of the whole word

Sound-symbol processing

Rapid hypothesis testing of sound-symbol possibilities

Shift in mental set between conventional and this repre-
sentation/semantic evaluation

Puzzle solving

Closing out distractions

To come up with an accurate interpretation among the several possibilities usually requires an interview of the student. Diagnosis of the

causes of weak performance on an MLAT part suggest implications for the student's study approach and for the classroom. For example, the following cases represent six possible reasons for weak performance on Part 3, together with some implications for learning and the classroom.

1. One student might have done poorly on Part 3 because of difficulty with the kinds of analytic activities often described as "field independent." This student is likely to have difficulty with analytic activities, often the kind of thing involved in induction of rules and patterns, and is likely to respond better to such material in a meaningful context.

2. Another might do poorly on the same part because of a weak English vocabulary (among the possible causal factors: poor education, low intelligence). This student, if a native speaker of English, may have difficulty with vocabulary learning (among other things) because of lacking concepts and background. The classroom may have to include activities to help this student build content background as well as language.

3. A third experiences difficulties reorganizing schemata or with gestalt processing or shifting mental set. In extreme form, this may represent a lack of ability to think abstractly, as manifested by difficulty with categorizing and recategorizing stimuli. Part 3 makes considerable demands on a person's ability to shift mental set. Such a student may be more comfortable with relatively predictable activities and less so with open-ended ones and may need help in developing skills to cope with the latter.

4. Yet another might have a phonetic coding difficulty (relating sounds and symbols) of the sort described by Sparks et al. (1991). He or she is likely to have corresponding low scores in Parts 1 and 2, which also require decoding of sounds. Such a student may be handicapped in both speaking and reading and will need more time to absorb material. Kinesthetic input is likely to help this student.

5. For some students there may be a distractibility factor. That is, a strongly extraverted student who is drawn to interpersonal interactions might not be as adept at the kind of focus that the puzzle-solving aspect of Part 3 entails as one who tunes out the world more readily. Study strategies and setting up conditions to maximize concentration, including frequent breaks, might help a student with difficulty concentrating.

6. Finally, a person who is reminded by Part 3 items of crossword puzzles and dislikes them has had an *affective* reaction that interferes with

ability to use cognitive resources. Alternatives to puzzle-solving activities would probably help the sixth student, or perhaps cooperative learning when puzzlelike activities are part of the curriculum. The teacher would need to be alert to the affective impact of such activities.

Yet other students have reported that they simply became tired. The highly speeded nature of this subtest is likely to disadvantage strongly reflective learners, for example. A student might suffer from several of these difficulties, complicating the consultation further.

Overall total score on the MLAT gives a crude measure useful at the scoring extremes: A very low score indicates weakness in all the factors; a very high score suggests strength in all the factors. In the middle, it becomes useful to examine the "peaks and valleys" of the part scores. I usually do this by looking only at the student's performance on the part scores. Calculations of the percentage correct for each subscale (part score) give me a very quick idea of where the high and low points are for that student. In addition, in more absolute terms, very high percentages (e.g., above 90%) or very low ones (e.g., below 50%) are also signals.

Analysis of the MLAT subscales is based on correlations with other variables of learning style, preferred learning activities, and tested end-of-training proficiency in speaking and reading. Such analysis suggests links of some of the parts with learning style variables. The following are my current working hypotheses:

> *Part 1—Number learning:* No clear associations so far, and no diagnostic hypothesis. (When I ask students what happened while they were taking this part, many—especially those who did well on it—say that they took notes during the aural presentation of the test numbers, then referred to the notes to fill in the answer form. Perhaps this part, in a way unintended by the developers, in fact assesses willingness to use whatever strategy works in defiance of the apparent structure of the task.)
>
> *Part 2—Phonetic script:* Global processing perhaps because of need to integrate auditory input and visual stimuli.
>
> *Part 3—Spelling clues:* Analytic processing, developed English vocabulary, puzzle-solving, shifting mental set, pattern analysis.
>
> *Part 4—Words in sentences:* Analytic processing, developed knowledge of English grammar, sensitivity to syntax and grammatical categories, pattern analysis and matching.

Part 5—Paired associates: Weakness may indicate poor mnemonic strategies, as well as deficiencies in metacognitive strategies because coping with the paired associates task requires some planning of the whole task.

The above discussion will be most useful to people who have access to the MLAT. On the other hand, for those who do not, it may serve as an example of how you can build and test hypotheses about the meanings of scales of tests to which you do have access. The process takes time and careful interviewing, but the payoff is high, once you have some reasonably solid hypotheses.

9.2.2 Language Aptitude, Intelligence, and Predicting Success

There is ongoing controversy about the role of intelligence in language learning. This section addresses the question and relates it to the MLAT.

Does it help to have high intelligence to learn languages? Popular wisdom has tended to say that intelligence is unnecessary for language learning. In a way, this is true. Very dull people learn their native languages, and rather unintelligent people can become functional in foreign languages and can cope with many of life's demands in the foreign language if they are living where the language is used regularly or if they are members of cultures in which language learning is expected.

On the other hand, most such people probably do not speak with much lexical or grammatical precision or read very demanding material. Learning to speak as an intelligent adult in one's native language requires intelligence, and so does learning to speak as an intelligent adult in a foreign language. This is even more the case when the learning must be done in a short time in a classroom, without all the motivational and peripheral learning advantages of a target-language-speaking environment.

Vocabulary is considered the best single overall measure of intelligence (Anastasi, 1988). Vocabulary is a product of (first) language learning. It is thus reasonable to assume that ability to achieve lexical precision in a second language is also related to intelligence. That is, although motivation and good learning strategies unquestionably play an important role, sheer cognitive power and flexibility is a tremendous asset in language learning to higher proficiency levels and to rapid learning at lower proficiency levels.

As a general predictor of performance on oral and reading proficiency tests, the Total Score is the most useful of the MLAT variables. Of the part scores, Part 3 is the strongest predictor. Part 3, with its dependence on knowledge of English vocabulary as well as ability to solve puzzles, may also be an indirect indicator of general intelligence, in that general vocabulary, which has already been mentioned as the single best stand-in for overall intelligence, represents crystallized intelligence (based on well-learned material) and the kind of cognitive restructuring it requires represents fluid intelligence (solving unfamiliar problems).

Links among the MLAT and other individual differences suggest an expanded definition of aptitude that includes both cognitive aptitude (measured specifically for languages by the MLAT and more generally by cognitive aptitude tests) and personality factors that predispose a learner to cope with ambiguity and apparent chaos. All of these become especially important in the relatively unstructured learning setting of communicative teaching approaches. A number of features that help in communicative language learning seem related to fluid intelligence:

Cognitive flexibility (may include ability to cope with the unfamiliar)
Random (vs. sequential) learning
Orientation to meaning over form
Ability to cope with surprises (linguistic and pedagogical)
Openness to input and tolerance of ambiguity
Ability to sort input, analyze as appropriate, and organize into mental structures

Absence of these characteristics appears to disadvantage the learners with whom I am familiar, perhaps more than their presence advantages them (Ehrman, 1994b).

Correlations between the MLAT and personality variables suggest a role for the disposition to use one's cognitive resources in ways that go beneath the surface and that establish elaborated knowledge structures. Those who are open to new material, can tolerate contradictions, establish hypotheses to be tested, focus on meaning, and find ways to link the new with previous knowledge structures seem to have an advantage in managing the complex demands of language and culture learning. The weakest students appear to be overwhelmed by the chaos they encounter; the strongest meet it head on, may even embrace it to a degree.

9.2.3 The MLAT, Field Independence, and Field Sensitivity

As mentioned in Chapter 5, I have been experimenting with the MLAT as a way of assessing field independence and field sensitivity in the verbal domain. Subscales 2, 3, and 4 seem promising. Scale 2 (Phonetic Script) may point to field sensitivity, based on some of the correlations described previously and on my experience with students. Parts 3 (Spelling Clues) and 4 (Words in Sentences) may indicate a verbal form of field independence. Needless to say, these relationships and the following described profiles, are hypothetical and in need of continued testing.

The following are additional specifics on the profiles I hypothesize to relate to field independence and field sensitivity. Low scores on MLAT subscales 3 (Spelling Clues) and 4 (Words in Sentences) seem to indicate potential difficulties with activities associated with field independent cognitive restructuring. High scores on these two subscales appear to indicate abilities that are closely related to field independence.

When subscales 3 and 4 are low and subscale 2 (Phonetic Script) is high, I suspect some element of global learning, which may be associated less perhaps with lack of field independence than positively with the construct of field sensitivity described in Chapter 5. With this MLAT subscale configuration as a cue, I examine the HBQ and MBTI as described above in section 6.3.3 to look for evidence of field sensitivity. That is, MLAT Parts 3 and 4 low, Part 2 high, HBQ thin boundaries, and particularly though not exclusively intuition and feeling on the MBTI strongly suggest a global, field sensitive learning Type 3 learner.

In addition to providing a signpost to field sensitivity, the MLAT also indicates field independence in the medium of interest to us—that is, language rather than visual disembedding. As described in section 6.5, for tolerance of ambiguity to result in better language learning, the learner must impose some kind of order on intake and set priorities. These are cognitive disembedding and restructuring tasks, which is the essence of the field independence construct. Following Piaget, I called this kind of activity *accommodation* in section 6.5; it is also closely allied to field independence. High scores on MLAT Parts 3 and 4 suggest field independence, at least in the verbal domain.

9.3 Tests of General Abilities

The usual test of general ability is the well-known and much-maligned intelligence test. As an example of this kind of test whose scores you may run up against, I will briefly describe the Wechsler Adult Intelligence Scale-Revised (WAIS-R). Another instrument —not an intelligence test— that tests specific abilities that apply generally—is the NASSP Learning Style Profile. Finally, there is further discussion of the field independence construct as an ability rather than as a learning style.

9.3.1 The Wechsler Tests

If you work in a school or if you work with students who are dyslexic or otherwise learning disabled, you are likely to come across either the WAIS-R or one of the versions of the WISC (Wechsler Intelligence Scale for Children), which is used up to the late teens. Although these tests must be administered and interpreted by trained and qualified personnel, the scores on them are often available to teachers and administrators. Most people are familiar with the composite "bottom line" score, the Full-Scale IQ, for which the average is 100, and roughly two-thirds of a general population fall between 85 and 115. Like the MLAT, though, the Wechsler intelligence tests consist of subscales. There are two sets of subscales, called *verbal* and *performance*. Verbal subscales assess world knowledge, vocabulary, and the ability to do arithmetic word problems. Performance subscales investigate various visuo-spatial and kinesthetic tasks. For an individual, there may a considerable difference between the Verbal IQ and the Performance IQ, or they may be very close.

There are a number of other ways to analyze the Wechsler subtests. One of the most common is to distinguish between those that measure crystallized abilities and those that assess fluid abilities. Crystallized abilities, as mentioned in section 9.2.2, are those that are built on developed skills, including vocabulary, world knowledge, and so on. Fluid abilities require coping with tasks that are relatively unfamiliar and thus demand problem solving. Some of the verbal subtests call on crystallized skills, whereas performance subtests draw largely on fluid abilities. We have seen in the discussion of the MLAT that both crystallized and fluid abilities are helpful in language learning, but the cognitive flexibility implied by fluid intelligence is especially important.

9.3.2 The NASSP Learning Style Profile

As mentioned in 6.4.1, the NASSP composite Learning Style Profile (LSP) includes several scales that measure ability, as well as a number that assess preferences. The examiner's manual (Keefe & Monk, 1986) describes them as follows:

Analytic Skill—To identify simple figures hidden in a complex field.

Spatial Skill—To identify geometric shapes and rotate objects in the imagination.

Discrimination Skill—To focus attention on required detail and avoid distraction.

Categorizing Skill—To use reasonable vs. vague criteria for classifying information.

Sequential Processing Skill—To process information sequentially and verbally.

Memory Skill—To detect and remember subtle changes in information.

Simultaneous Processing Skill—To process information globally and non-analytically. (p. 5)

The LSP scales are very short and may not adequately challenge college graduates, though they may work very well with the intended high-school audience. Several of them (analytic, discrimination, and what is named "sequential processing") appear to address characteristics associated with field independence.

9.4 Language Achievement and Proficiency Tests

A test of the target language itself is not only a measurement of how much language the student knows. It can also be an opportunity for direct or indirect observation of how the student goes about the learning task.

While the test is going on (especially if it is an interactive test of language use), you can observe various processing strategies, some of which might be inefficient or counterproductive. You can use your observations of how the student goes about coping with the demands of the test as a way to infer learning styles. After the test, in discussions with the student, you can look at what happened during the parts that went well and those that did not go so well, as I have described for the MLAT in section 9.2.1. Discussions of tests may elicit new information about affective factors—for example, motivation for learning, demotivators about which you can do something, or sources of anxiety.

As with any of the individual difference instruments described previously, a language test is a good stimulus for data collection. Any kind of test you use in your classroom can be used in this way. A test is a special kind of opportunity for observation, as described in Chapter 2, though it is likely to be affected by student anxiety.

A test can be as simple as a vocabulary quiz or as elaborate as the Oral Proficiency Interview as practiced by examiners trained by the American Council on the Teaching of Foreign Languages or from the various government language schools. Specific achievement tests may be a relatively easy place to start, because the number of factors to interpret are limited. On the other hand, an oral interview test provides much richer information and relatively realistic data on a learner's coping strategies. As with any other interview, you can make it easier to interpret by selecting sensitizing concepts to focus your attention. You do not have to manage all the information right away for every test. In fact, if you are working with a student you already know to be having difficulties, you are likely to have a set of working hypotheses to test when you observe or discuss a test, no matter how complex.

9.5 Putting It Together

9.5.1 Relating Instruments to Classroom Activities

Certain kinds of classroom activity will call on greater or lesser of various individual difference variables. Box 9.3 shows how individual difference variables relate to activities categorized under the "ground transportation" metaphor introduced in section 4.2.4 and Box 4.1. If your student is having difficulty with memorizing, Box 9.3 suggests that you look at MLAT Part 5 (Paired Associates) and at SILL memory strategies as starting points. You can also work in the other direction. If, for example, your student does poorly on MLAT Part 3, you may find it useful to observe how he or she copes with target language idioms or points in which semantic sets do not work the same way in the native language and the target language. Low endorsement of compensation strategies on the SILL might suggest that the student could become stuck in conversations when his or her proficiency is exceeded by only a little or else have trouble reading authentic material written for native readers of the target language.

Please note that Box 9.3 is meant to help you generate the hypotheses that are so useful when you work with students having learning difficulties. It is not meant to provide hard and fast answers.

9.5.2 Using Questionnaire Results for Individuals

This section looks at the questionnaire and test information that is available for several of the students you have already met as cases. Not all the instruments are represented for each of these learners, but we will look at how to put together what there is for each of them. Chapter 10 begins with an extended case in which information from tests was both helpful and not so helpful.

* * *

Lonnie
Age: 19
Major subject: Mathematics, GPA 3.25
Occupation: Student
Previous history: 6 months of Spanish, which was very hard for him
MLAT: Part 1 (Number Learning)—82%; Part 2 (Phonetic Script)—57%; Part 3 (Spelling Clues)—12%; Part 4 (Words in Sentences)—46%; Part 5 (Paired Associates)—46%; Total—51%
MBTI: ENTJ, low consistency score for intuition
HBQ: Internal Boundaries—thick; External Boundaries—thick. Strongly rejects messy surroundings. Total—thick
MSQ: Rates self as below average to poor relative to other learners; highly motivated, and fairly anxious about this class

Strongly *endorses* transformation drills, correction of all errors, hands-on manipulative learning; use of all possible resources (tapes, classmates, etc.),

writing material down to remember it, using charts, and sticking to the basics until mastered before moving to more complex material
Strongly *rejects* classroom discussion of controversial topics, reading or listening to material that is "over his head," background music while studying, using vague words or hands to compensate for a word he can't think of, mind wandering in class

Lonnie presents a consistent picture of a person who handles verbal material in a concrete way. He has clearly emphasized the quantitative in his education (and done respectably well at it). His MLAT total is just about average relative to the American population at large but fairly weak for the more selective program in which he is currently enrolled. The MLAT parts show a distinctive and very dramatic weakness in Part 3 (Spelling Clues), suggesting concrete thinking and field dependence. The consistently thick boundaries he reports on the HBQ indicate that he is also not field sensitive, thus he is probably a Type 4 learner (field dependent, field insensitive). The TJ preference on the MBTI is consistent with the thick boundaries. A past history of difficulty with Spanish has already made him lose confidence in his ability as a language learner and become quite anxious about his present language class. Consistent with the rest of his profile is his desire for considerable external support in his learning and need for a very systematic, sequential approach to his studies. He rejects activities that are very open-ended, probably does not do more than one thing at once (suggested by rejection of background music, need for silence while studying), and has difficulty with information gaps (not using vague words and gestures to compensate).

The one inconsistent datum is Lonnie's stated preference for intuition on the MBTI. Intuitives are usually not as concrete and structured as Lonnie is. When interpreting the data, then, there are a few further questions. Is the preference for intuition an expression of social desirability or how Lonnie would prefer to be? Are there indications in the MSQ among the items that were not strongly endorsed or rejected that Lonnie is not entirely concrete sequential? As it turns out, the latter is true. Lonnie has endorsed as helpful "We help design the program as we go along," and "I discover grammar patterns for myself." These inductive approaches are consistent with MBTI intuition. Lonnie is thus probably a Type 4 learner, concrete and sequential in approach, who has a preference for the big picture and making connections when he can do so.

Box 9.3 Learning Situations and Learner Variables

1. Characteristics listed are at least desirable and often necessary for success in each of the following four environments. The instruments listed offer insight into relative presence or absence of that characteristic.
2. Each level includes those that precede it—for example, *trail network includes roadway system* and railroad.
3. Probably no classroom programs operate entirely at any of these levels.
4. Affective factors moderate access to abilities, skills, and available "processing" capacity.
5. Interpersonal skill enhances performance at every level, but especially highways, trails, and open country, and most especially learning in the host country.

1. *Railroad:* Defined dialogues for memorization, mechanical and some meaningful drilling; reading and listening matter designed to use lesson material.

Skill	Learning Characteristic	Instrument
All	Motivation	Affective survey items
	Affective self-management	SILL affective
	Good study habits, self-discipline	MBTI judging, SILL meta-cognitive (esp. practice)
	Prefers closed-ended learning activities	MSQ, HBQ, MBTI sensing, judging
	Lack of Ethnocentricity	HBQ?
Conversation	Ability to memorize	MLAT V, SILL memory
Reading	Phonetic decoding	MLAT I, II, III
	Sound-symbol decoding	MLAT II, III
Listening	Phonetic decoding	MLAT I, II, III

2. *Roadway System:* Oral interaction closely linked to lesson material. Some meaningful but largely communicative drilling; controlled conversation, edited texts and listening passages that may be based on authentic material.

All	Abstract processing	MBTI intuition, MLAT III
	Metacognitive skills (planning, evaluation)	MBTI thinking, judging, SILL, metacognitive, MLAT V
	Analytic skills	MLAT III, IV
	Deep processing strategies	SILL cognitive (conceptual), MSQ
	Acceptance of external guidance	MBTI sensing, judging

Box 9.3 Continued

3. *Trail Network:* "Free" conversation, heavily guided by the teacher to include repetition of previously learned material but with room for considerable student creativity especially in subject matter. Generally authentic reading and listening material but with considerable teacher or curricular guidance in the form of advance organizers, outlines, specific tasks, and other guides.

Skill	*Learning Characteristic*	*Instrument*
All	Global/simultaneous processing	MLAT II (sound-symbol)
	Random processing	MBTI intuition, perceiving
	Combination of cognitive abilities	MLAT total
	Recombination of old material	MLAT III
Conversation	Coping with information gaps	SILL compensation
Reading	Gisting skills	MLAT III
Listening	Gisting skills	MLAT III

4. *Open Country:* Open-ended conversation, topics nominated and branched by both student and teacher, very open-ended tasks, authentic material for reading and listening, student develops own strategies for coping.

All	Tolerance of ambiguity	HBQ total, external boundaries
	Flexible shift of mental set	MLAT III
	Preference for open-ended learning	MSQ, MBTI intuition, perceiving
	Moderation of affective arousal	Affective survey
	Independence (high-level meta-cognition & affective self-perceiving	MLAT total, MBTI intuition

SOURCE: Adapted from Ehrman (1995) by permission of the Georgetown University Press.

This unusual profile made it difficult for Lonnie to work comfortably in a class in which the activities were either comfortable for the concrete sequential learner (toward the railroad end of the continuum in Boxes 4.1 and 9.3) or for the more abstract and random learners (approaching trailways and even some open country). He was helped greatly by being able to spend quite a lot of time working on his own with a substantial array of interactive video programs and regular "check-ups" with a teacher.

This took away the pressure of working with the class in modes that were difficult for him and allowed him to exercise his preferences and skills as they were appropriate for him.

* * *

Jenny
Age: 30
Major subject: Literature, GPA 3.5
Occupation: Former teacher of literature, new foreign service recruit
Previous history: College German and Spanish, travel in Germany
MLAT: Part 1 (Number Learning)—87%; Part 2 (Phonetic Script)—89%; Part 3 (Spelling Clues)—42%; Part 4 (Words in Sentences)—45%; Part 5 (Paired Associates)—78%; Total—57%
MBTI: INFP, low consistency score for introversion
HBQ: Internal boundaries—very thin; External boundaries—thin; Total—very thin
MSQ: Not available

Jenny's profile is very consistent. Her college major and initial occupation, her MBTI type, and her thin boundaries are all of a piece. Her MLAT, together with the MBTI and HBQ suggest a Type 3 learner, and what we already know of her (from section 6.3) confirms this hypothesis. Jenny relies heavily on learning Track 1, the interpersonal track. Jenny is distinctive because she reports extremely thin boundaries, thinner than 99% of her new foreign service colleagues. Weak scores on MLAT parts 3, 4, and the total suggest that she will have a very difficult time sorting out all the information that she gets in class and out of it, and that she may be very vulnerable to overstimulation. This hypothesis is supported by her preference (though relatively weak) for introversion, which also suggests the need to manage external stimulation. She is likely to need help with metacognitive and some cognitive strategies having to do with setting priorities and organizing information. Elaboration strategies probably come fairly naturally for her. If she is finding language learning discouraging, some assistance with affective self-management is also in order.

* * *

Sandy
Age: 24
Major subject: International Relations
Occupation: Student
Previous history: College Italian and Japanese; has used language as a tourist. Finds language learning not especially difficult or easy

MLAT: Part 1 (Number Learning)—90%; Part 2 (Phonetic Script)—88%; Part 3 (Spelling Clues)—77%; Part 4 (Words in Sentences)—81%; Part 5 (Paired Associates)—75%; Total—84%
MBTI: ISFP, low consistency scores for sensing and feeling
HBQ: Internal Boundaries—thin; External Boundaries—average in thick direction. Total—average for her group
MSQ: Rates self as an above average learner; highly motivated, and initially not anxious about this class or about speaking in class

Strongly *endorses* speaking in the classroom and at school as much as possible, classroom exercises that use her hands (drawing, pointing, etc.), audiotapes, roleplays and simulations, reading without a dictionary, writing things down to remember them, being free to move around while learning, and looking at someone who is speaking

Strongly *rejects* classroom fill-in exercises, one-by-one reading aloud, transformation drills, correction of all speaking errors, rote memorization of dialogues, teacher having main responsibility to see that student needs are met, hearing directions for a task, mind wandering in class, and writing down ideas in order not to forget them

Sandy is the student we met in Chapters 2 and 3 who was very upset and whose teachers were at their wits' end because her motivation had dropped drastically and because she is so volatile in class (sections 2.2 and 3.1). As you look over the material just presented, do you find anything that you think would help us understand what is going on with Sandy?

Much of the evidence suggests that Sandy has the cognitive equipment and inclinations to do fairly well in language training. She has majored in a highly verbal subject, her MLAT is good across the board (though not stellar), she appears to be a flexible learner who is at home with relatively open-ended activities. She does not appear to need much external structure in her learning, and she is not perfectionistic, both of which are consistent with her preference for MBTI perceiving.

She has a preference for visual learning, which makes her fairly typical, but she also has a clear kinesthetic preference, which is less common in higher education. This might be a source of some of the difficulty, if she has to sit still too long, or the classroom activities are exclusively visual and auditory. We also note that her internal boundaries are thin and she prefers introversion, which may indicate some vulnerability to overstimulation. The preferences for sensing and feeling, neither of which is strong, could reflect some difficulty with field independent activities, contrary to the good performance on MLAT Parts 3 and 4. It is not certain whether she is field sensitive. The high score on MLAT Part 2 (Phonetic Script) and the preference for MBTI feeling indicate field sensitivity, but the low-average external boundary score does not support that conclusion.

A working hypothesis for Sandy based on what we know of her now might be that she has some field sensitivity when she is not on the defensive, but she is also vulnerable to emotional disruption resulting from overstimulation. In addition, if the weak preference for MBTI sensing is accurate, she may not always cope with linguistic abstractions and cognitive restructuring when necessary, despite her ability to solve the rather limited puzzle presented by the MLAT Part 3 items. Sandy's field independence and field sensitivity are probably about equivalent. When circumstances are exactly right for her, they function well together, and Sandy can look something like a Type 1 learner, though without the speed and range of an Alice. When something goes wrong in her life or class, however, Sandy's access to her skills is disrupted and she looks more like a Type 4 learner. We shall return to Sandy later and see if these hypotheses are valid.

* * *

Victor
Age: 17; in the United States for 3 years
Major subject: Sociology, top 10th of secondary school class. Likes statistical analysis
Occupation: Student
Previous history: Twelve years of English in school in native country, but little opportunity to speak it. Not in an ESL class now, though he had a couple of years of ESL in high school
MLAT: Part 1 (Number Learning)—68%; Part 2 (Phonetic Script)—57%; Part 3 (Spelling Clues)—62%; Part 4 (Words in Sentences)—71%; Part 5 (Paired Associates)—87%; Total—68%
MBTI: INTJ
HBQ: Internal Boundaries—thick; External Boundaries—average; Total—average
MSQ: Rates self as an average language learner; sufficiently but not strongly motivated, and initially not anxious about this class or about speaking in class

Strongly *endorses* conversation practice in dyads, interviewing target language-speaking people and reporting in the target language in class, classroom discussion of controversial topics, field trips, chances to move around in the classroom, extensive correction of both speaking and written errors, discovery of new grammar patterns for himself, using the language both in and outside of school, completing one task before beginning another, writing

things down to remember them, background music when studying, moving around when studying, introduction to new material by reading about it
Strongly *rejects* reading aloud one by one after the teacher, looking up words from a teacher-given list and copying translations, choral transformation drills, hands-on manipulation exercises, group study and cooperative learning, roleplays and simulations, jumping into tasks without instructions, hearing instructions for a task, using vague words and his hands to fill in when he can't think of a word, and remembering verbatim material

Victor may be a Type 2 learner. Although the MLAT is not really valid for non-native speakers of English, when one does as well as Victor has, it is an indication of considerable ability, either in what the MLAT tests, or in test-taking skills, or both. Elevations in Parts 3 and 4, with their considerable basis in English vocabulary and grammar, may represent a combination of field independence and a solid academic background in formal (written) English. Victor's interest in statistical analysis, which would be an unappealing part of a sociology major for a more global learner, supports a guess that he is field independent, as does endorsement of such activities as discovery of new grammar patterns for himself and rejection of group study. A peak on MLAT Part 5 (Paired Associates) suggests good memorization and planning strategies.

Information indicating field sensitivity is harder to find. His MBTI type gives a mixed picture: Intuition can go with field sensitivity, especially if the HBQ points to thin boundaries. In this case, it does not. Thinking and judging, however, militate against field sensitivity. The activities endorsed on the MSQ also give a mixed picture. An interview would help us understand if Victor uses such relatively open-ended activities as interviewing native speakers for instrumental or for more integrative purposes. The latter could suggest more field sensitivity.

The expression of preference for learning sequentially and systematically also suggests that Victor is not really a global learner and will probably cope with global tasks such as discussions and roleplays (which he does not find useful) in an analytic way. The INTJ type often greets new ideas and activities with overt skepticism; an awareness of this fact will help his teachers give him the space to "buy in" on new concepts and exercises. He will probably cope well with the limited ambiguity of a class that has mostly highway and trailway activities (Box 4.1), but he will probably find too much railroad boring and too much open country confusing, eliciting a withdrawal to activities in which he can use his focused cognitive skills.

Apparently a strong visual, secondarily kinesthetic and lastly auditory learner, he will also be handicapped in classes in which the input is almost entirely aural and may have less auditory working memory than some of his classmates.

9.6 Practice

The first few practice items consist of some data from various instruments. For the purposes of this practice, think of yourself in the role of an outside consultant—a teacher trainer, supervisor, or counselor. The assumption is that you have not yet had an opportunity to observe or interview the student, but you do have some paper records. Use the information you have to make a working hypothesis about the student. For each case, respond to the following questions, *providing the evidence for your hypothesis.* (You may not have enough information to answer all the questions for each case—that is the way it often is in the "real world.")

a.   What are the student's sensory channels?

b.   How does the student come out on the field independence and field sensitivity dimensions? Other dimensions such as sequential-random, concrete-abstract, left-right, deductive-inductive?

c.   Based on what you know of the MBTI and psychological type, how would the student's personality type interact with the guesses you have already made?

d.   What is the student likely to do well?

e.   Where would you expect the trouble spots to be for this student?

f.   What are you still uncertain about?

g.   What would you look for in an observation of this student?

h.   What would you want to find out in an interview?

1. Beverly has made an appointment with you in frustration about her classroom language learning. The following is what her records say:
   Major subject: Eastern European Area Studies
   Previous history: Russian and French in high school and college. Hebrew as child, after school, until age 13 and can still read it. Generally likes foreign language learning and using it when traveling. Has been out of formal classes for five years

MLAT: Part 1 (Number Learning)—95%; Part 2 (Phonetic Script)—90%; Part 3 (Spelling Clues)—74%; Part 4 (Words in Sentences)—73%; Part 5 (Paired Associates)—50%; Total—78%
MBTI: ENTJ
HBQ: Not available
MSQ: Not available

2. Matthew's teacher is concerned about him. So far, this is all you know, until you look at the papers on Matthew.
Major subject: Engineering, Navy ROTC
Previous history: A semester of college Spanish. Had a childhood stutter that emerges again when he is nervous
MLAT: Part 1 (Number Learning)—93%; Part 2 (Phonetic Script)—100%; Part 3 (Spelling Clues)—58%; Part 4 (Words in Sentences)—53%; Part 5 (Paired Associates)—96%; Total—76%
MBTI: ISTP
HBQ: Internal boundaries—thick; External boundaries—thick; Total—thick
MSQ: Rates self as an average language learner, whose motivation is mostly extrinsic and instrumental, to meet external requirements. He does not experience much anxiety about language learning but does get anxious about speaking aloud in class. On another survey, he endorsed a lot of negatively phrased items about motivation. Has said that he feels deprived of free time by language study

Strongly *endorses* getting material mastered before moving on, step-by-step learning, being corrected so he will have perfect speaking, pronunciation, and writing, completing one task before beginning another, and writing things down to remember them
Strongly *rejects* reading and listening to material that contains a lot of unknown material, too much "free" conversation, group study and cooperative learning, roleplays and simulations, jumping into tasks without instructions, background music when studying, and using vague words and one's hands to fill in when he can't think of a word

3. The following information is about Bernice, who is struggling hard.
Major subject: Business. GPA 3.0
Previous history: Foreign born. Came to United States in her early teens. Many years of learning English in formal classes; it was not one of her best subjects. Now in ESL classes
MLAT: Part 1 (Number Learning)—average; Part 2 (Phonetic Script)—average; Part 3 (Spelling Clues)—low; Part 4 (Words in Sentences)—very low; Part 5 (Paired Associates)—very high; Total—average. (Take appropriate care in interpreting the MLAT for a non-native speaker of English. Bernice took it as part of routine intake processing.)
MBTI: ESTJ

HBQ: Internal boundaries—thick; Sensitivity—thin; External boundaries—
thickish average; Total—thick to average

Study Processes Questionnaire: surface motive and strategies average;
achievement motive and strategies high, deep motive and strategies high

MSQ: Rates self as an average language learner; very strongly motivated,
though she is anxious about this class and about speaking aloud in class.
Although she indicates some competitiveness and instrumental needs
for the language, she also endorses all the intrinsic motivation choices

Strongly *endorses* systematically following a syllabus, interviewing native
speakers, transformation drills, correction of all oral and written errors,
immersion trips and shorter field trips, being forced to use what she
knows, pronunciation drills, audio- and videotapes, writing things down
to remember them, talking about things to remember them, taking a lot
of notes, working in a quiet place, visualizing textbook pages, and doing
one task at a time

Strongly *rejects* jumping in and doing things without instructions, just talking about things, background music, visualizing images, and talking herself through tasks

4. Angela is coming to see you in an hour. She sounded a little angry on the
phone. There is no time to check with her teacher, but you have the following information on her.

Major subject: English literature

Previous languages: High school French

MLAT: Part 1 (Number Learning)—91%; Part 2 (Phonetic Script)—90%;
Part 3 (Spelling Clues)—66%; Part 4 (Words in Sentences)—84%; Part 5
(Paired Associates)—48%; Total—80%

MBTI: ENFJ. Preference scores for E and N are strong. On the TDI, reports
herself as polyactive (doing more than one thing at once) but more plan-
ful than open-ended and somewhat methodical

HBQ: Internal boundaries—average; External boundaries—quite thin;
Total—thin

Affective Survey: Rates self as a slightly above-average language learner; sufficiently but not strongly motivated, and anxious about her final rating
but not about speaking aloud in class. High level of endorsement of negatively phrased motivation items

NASSP Learning Style Profile: Strong in analytic, spatial, simultaneous
processing skills; high average in categorization and sequential processing skills, average in discrimination skills, and low average in memory
for changes in visual details (leveling/sharpening)

5. Which tests and questionnaires are available for you to use? Can you actually administer any of them? For which ones can you get information, even
if you cannot administer them yourself?

6. Under what circumstances can you imagine wanting data from question-naires and tests?

7. What changes would you make in the MSQ (Appendix C) to make it more applicable to your setting? Why?

8. What (if any) ideas do you get from the MSQ for things to try out yourself?

9.7 More Information

General information about psychological testing is to be found in Anastasi's (1988) comprehensive treatment of the subject. This book provides excellent information about intelligence testing, including the Wechsler tests. If you are interested in any of the instruments described in this book, check in the sections above that address them for references to documentation, as a starting point.

Most of the tests and questionnaires come with some form of manual or other documentation. The MBTI is one of the best documented instruments, with an exemplary manual (Myers & McCaulley, 1985) and countless books and journal articles about it. Substantial information about the HBQ is in Hartmann's (1991) *Boundaries in the Mind*. The references for John Carroll are good starting points for information about the MLAT, as well as an article I have recently drafted (Ehrman, forthcoming). For extensive information about learning strategies and the SILL, begin with Oxford (1990). A number of style surveys are to be found in Reid (1995). The MSQ is not yet documented.

10

Students in Context

This chapter presents five extended cases in which it is appropriate to look beneath the surface and at the same time address the student and the learning context together. In these longer case treatments, all the available data are integrated and used to help us understand complex learning situations. The cases are intended to consolidate all the many variables addressed in the preceding chapters.

The first case, Elsa, has to do with the degree to which information from formal tests can be helpful or misleading: Questionnaire data can be both a boon and a bane. In the next case, we finally find out what is going on with Sandy, the student who was having mysterious emotional outbursts. Next comes Sheldon, whose learning setting put limits on how far a counselor's intervention can go. Students learn in the context of other students as well as teachers and curricula. The interaction of Janet, Karen, and Shirley is used to look at some of the complications brought about by interstudent relations. Finally, Mark's case illustrates the importance of understanding what is behind a student's panic and working with both the student and the classroom teacher to implement interventions based on the diagnosis.

Unlike the preceding chapters, this chapter has no separate practice section. Instead, the cases that constitute this chapter are designed to provide practice as you work through them. As you read the cases, try to make hypotheses. I suggest that at each stopping point, you pause and consider the questions asked at those points before reading further.

10.1 Keeping Test
Information in Perspective *(Elsa)*

10.1.1 About Elsa

Elsa, 23, is a recent graduate from a first-class university who has recently entered graduate school in a program that requires language proficiency. When she entered, she was tested to find her proficiency level in previously studied languages, as are all new graduate students in the program. She received proficiency ratings in French and Polish; the French rating was stronger than the Polish. The problem was, though, that she had had a very bad experience with French in college, and she feared that she would be required to use French in her program. What she really wanted was to find a way to build on her knowledge of Polish by working on it or another Eastern European language.

It turned out that Elsa's fears were realized. She was indeed required to do work that would require a good proficiency in French. This meant French language classes. Elsa was so upset by the whole matter that she was referred for special counseling before she even began classes. The following is what she said in that session.

She had studied French in both high school and college, and it was a very difficult experience from beginning to end. She did so badly in her classes, which were fairly traditionally taught, with focus on vocabulary and grammar exercises, that her teachers decided she could not learn languages. She was referred to her university counseling center, where she was given a battery of tests, including the Modern Language Aptitude Test and other verbal learning tests. A year later, her difficulties continued, and she was given a battery of neuropsychological tests by a psychologist, who diagnosed her as having a formal language learning disability. The neuropsychological battery had shown some minor deficits in working memory and other processing relative to Elsa's overall ability, which is in the superior range. In passing, Elsa also added that if she did not feel comfortable with her teacher, she did not learn well.

Elsa completed a biographic background questionnaire, the Myers-Briggs Type Indicator, the Hartmann Boundary Questionnaire, and the Motivation and Strategies Questionnaire. The following is Elsa's profile follows.

Biodata:
>23 years old
>Native speaker of English, American born
>Recent B.A. from good university in international relations
>Two languages on entry into graduate school
>Diagnosed as dyslexic and "language learning disabled" while in university

MLAT: Part 1 (Number Learning)—93% correct; Part 2 (Phonetic Script)—83%; Part 3 (Spelling Clues)—40%; Part 4 (Words in Sentences)—56%; Part 5 (Paired Associates—29%; Total—63% (average for the program she is in).

MBTI: Preference (consistency) scores were very low, and Elsa strongly resisted committing to any category. Strongest preference, though still weak, was for intuition

Hartmann Boundary Questionnaire:
>Thin boundaries, 1.5 SD above the mean for females in this language program and nearly 1 SD above Hartmann's mean for females. Both internal and external boundaries are thin

Motivation and Strategies Questionnaire (MSQ):
>Rated herself as below average in language ability but expected to perform averagely in class
>Rated herself as not at all motivated in French but very motivated in Polish
>Somewhat more interested in non-Western languages than Western ones
>Really nervous about French, a "fair amount" of anxiety about learning Polish

Strongly endorsed open-ended language learning activities (e.g., discussions), small group conversations, interviews of native speakers, field trips using the target language, correction of written and oral errors, off-site immersion experiences, being forced to use what one knows even if imprecise, using the language as much as possible both in and out of school, and trusting her intuitions.

Strongly rejected learning dialogues by heart, reading aloud one by one after the teacher, hearing grammatical rules explained in the target language, correcting grammar mistakes in writings, discovering grammar patterns for herself, pronunciation drill, studying alone, activities that use the hands, background music, taking a lot of notes, and completing one task before beginning another.

A section of the report on Elsa's psychological tests that diagnosed her as learning disabled states that "One can see . . . how learning a foreign language

would be extremely problematic, even considering her superior intelligence.
. . . For many individuals with this type of language-based disability, learning a foreign language at a proficient level is probably out of reach."

---

*Consider the information I have given you so far. What are
your hypotheses about what is going on with Elsa?
What would your next steps be?*

Here's what happened next: One of the counseling staff is an experienced language teacher of Spanish, her native language, and has also been thoroughly imbued with the importance of individual differences to learning. She arranged to give Elsa some trial training in Spanish so we could see what she could really do. Elsa undertook the experiment enthusiastically. The first hour was spent interviewing Elsa about how she learns, and then the former Spanish teacher gave her a lesson in Spanish. The main thing she did was to make sure that everything she taught Elsa was in some kind of communicative context. She reported that Elsa learned splendidly, and Elsa was equally positive.

When it looked as though there was no way for Elsa to avert the French class, she began to panic. The next step was to try to ease Elsa back into French. The counselor suggested simple, low-threat activities she could try. All of them increased Elsa's anxiety level; she even reached the point where she could not stand to listen to French songs, and they had been one of the few things she could enjoy.

What's your take on the situation now? What would you do?

The next step was to arrange with the French department for a few hours of one-on-one training before formal classes were due to begin. The people working with Elsa asked for a teacher who is skilled at putting students at ease, someone who would put the relationship first, rather than the language. The teacher who worked with Elsa fit the bill well. The first few sessions were distinguished by massive dysfluency. But by the third day, there seemed to be a breakthrough. Elsa came to see her counselors, and she was almost another person. Gone were the shaking hands and trembling voice. Instead, she was relaxed, confident, and a little triumphant at her success. She felt ready to begin French and join an intermediate class.

What do you think now?

Sometimes it is difficult to sort out what is really going on, especially in that cognitive and learning style problems can lead to intense affective reactions, and conversely affective factors can interfere markedly with a person's ability to make use of cognitive resources. Elsa had an intense affective reaction, almost phobic, to French. Her reaction was so strong that it led Elsa herself to become convinced that she could not learn languages, despite evidence to the contrary. Her anxiety was made worse by misleading test data, which were not taken in the context of the individual and the teaching methodology.

Despite the compelling nature of the psychological tests Elsa brought with her, this was not really a case of cognitive dysfunction at its core. Instead, it began with a profound learning style mismatch between a very global (Type 3) learner and programs that insisted on teaching and testing decontextualized language. Elsa became convinced that she was a poor language learner. An affective reaction to a series of failures produced a downward spiral, and increasing energy devoted to protection of self-esteem drew off more and more of Elsa's cognitive resources and made them even more unavailable for language learning. Bureaucratic hang-ups that delayed her relief from the situation at her college made her even more upset. By the time she reached the new language class, all the unpleasant-ness had been generalized to the study of French under any circumstances.

In this case, the information about Elsa's "learning disability" was very misleading. In fact, there was quite a lot of useful information in the report on Elsa's psychological tests, but the interpretation was made based only on the test data, not in connection with the kind of teaching that Elsa was receiving.

Test data can be very helpful. Cautious interpretation and an attempt to get as much information about the student's subjective views and about the student's situation are major factors in making pencil-and-paper instruments work well. I use the information to make hypotheses, which I encourage the student to use with me as we test the hypotheses in the light of the student's experience. The key is to use *all* the information that comes along. For me, for instance, a key was the aside Elsa made on the first day about the importance of her relationship with teachers. Another was the description of how language had been taught (decontextualized, mechanical) and the very clear Type 3 profile.

Most language classes rely to some degree on material that is not embedded in a meaningful context. Elsa's French class was no exception. Diagnosis was only the first step. After that, it was important to make sure her teacher did not slip into traditional memorization, drilling, and vocabulary list techniques. At one point this began to happen, and Elsa's panic began to re-emerge. Negotiation among Elsa, the teacher, and the counselor averted a relapse by bringing the classroom activities back to more communication of meaning. With this kind of adaptation—one that did not interfere with the progress of Elsa's classmates and indeed may have enhanced their learning—Elsa completed the course with flying colors.

10.1.2 Using Instrumentation

Do we really need instruments for student counseling? I find them useful in a number of ways. First of all, they are a crystallization of intuition. For a person without the automatization of expert knowledge, they provide a kind of a crutch in the form of an explicit model.

Even for an expert, who can get much of this information from an interview, test data can be very helpful in defusing the threat posed to students by having to address their problems. In a way, having their responses in print has the effect of reifying, ordering, and depersonalizing often chaotic personal information so the student can work better with it. In a sense, test data provide a kind of "play space," where the student and I together can create a model of how the student works and what will help him or her. This concept is analogous to D. W. Winnicott's (1971) extremely effective use of this concept in psychotherapy.

On the other hand, when I do not have access to questionnaires, I can get most of what I need from interviews that are based on a model in my mind of how people learn languages and what gets in their way. That is, test and questionnaire data are very useful to have, but with some training or experience, a skilled teacher, knowledgeable about what the survey-based research tells us, can do well without them.

10.2 Student and Teacher *(Sandy)*

10.2.1 About Sandy

You have met Sandy in several previous chapters. The following is all the information about Sandy put together. She is in a fairly small class, in a program with experienced and generally very successful teachers. Efforts have been made to tailor the course content to her ongoing needs.

We learn about Sandy from a teacher, who is distressed about her and has come to seek advice.

I am very concerned about Sandy. She seems quite depressed and distressed. The day before yesterday, she came in very angry and started to cry. She cried for nearly two hours and said that she hates this language. I spent most of the time trying to calm her. Yesterday, she was also angry and rude to me. During one of the teaching activities, she burst out crying when there was a mention of her parents and also remarked that marriage is a depressing issue.

She has said many times that she hates this city and is eager to leave it for her new job as soon as she can. She refers to her previous language learning experience as much better and is most complimentary about the culture of the country where the previous language is spoken. It feels as though she is trying to insult my country and language. One of our other students even commented that Sandy was being cruel to me.

I am reluctant to interact with her at any level. I don't even say "how are you?" any more, so she won't erupt. If she does not want to do something in class, I just let it pass. It is hard to have an agenda for the class since it has become hard to predict how she is going to react. The times when I try to explain something, she gets upset, kicks her feet around, and says that if she wants an explanation, she will ask for one. She does not like to listen to the tapes; however, sometimes she seems to enjoy speaking to me in an informal situation.

When she is in an informal and social setting, she appears to be quite bubbly and professional.

Last week, when there was an unexpected change in a scheduled lesson, she lost her temper and became very uncooperative. But every time when she is upset, she says it is her "own stuff" that has messed her up. I am dreading having class with her today. I feel rejected and trampled on. We need some professional intervention.

What are your initial hypotheses about what is happening with Sandy? What further questions would you like to ask her teacher? What are your initial suggestions for dealing with Sandy? If you were her teacher, what do you think the effects of Sandy's behavior would be on you?

You take the opportunity to review Sandy's questionnaire data, which are repeated here from Chapter 9.

Age: 24
Major subject: International Relations
Occupation: Student
Previous history: College Italian and Japanese; has used language as a tourist. Finds language learning not especially difficult or easy
MLAT: Part 1—90%; Part 2—88%; Part 3—77%; Part 4—81%; Part 5—75%; Total—84%
MBTI: ISFP, low consistency scores for sensing and feeling
HBQ: Internal boundaries—thin; External boundaries—average in thick direction; Total—average relative to other students similar to her
MSQ: Rates self as an above-average learner; highly motivated, and initially not anxious about this class or about speaking in class

Strongly *endorses* speaking in the classroom and at school as much as possible, classroom exercises that use her hands (drawing, pointing, etc.), audiotapes, roleplays and simulations, reading without a dictionary, writing things down to remember them, moving around while learning, and hearing words in her head when she reads

Strongly *rejects* classroom fill-in exercises, one-by-one reading aloud, transformation drills, correction of all speaking errors, rote memorization of dialogues, teacher having main responsibility to see that student needs are met, checking her answers in her head before giving them, mind wandering in class, and writing things down in order not to forget

---

Take a moment to try to describe Sandy, using this information
(and without referring to the information about her in
Chapter 9, for now). To what degree does this information
help you think more clearly about Sandy?

The following are the interpretations of the questionnaires repeated from section 9.5.2. Much of the evidence suggests that Sandy has
the cognitive equipment and inclinations to do fairly well in language
training. She has majored in a highly verbal subject, her MLAT is good
across the board (though not stellar), she appears to be a flexible
learner who is at home with relatively open-ended activities. She does not
appear to need much external structure in her learning, and she is not
perfectionistic, both of which are consistent with her preference for MBTI
perceiving.

She has a preference for visual learning, which makes her fairly typical,
but she also has a clear kinesthetic preference, which is less common in
higher education. Here might be a source of some of the difficulty if she
has to sit still too long or the classroom activities are exclusively visual
and auditory. We also note that her internal boundaries are thin and she
prefers introversion, which may indicate some vulnerability to overstimulation. The preferences for sensing and feeling, neither of which is strong,
could reflect some difficulty with field independent activities, contrary to
the good performance on MLAT Parts 3 and 4. It is not certain whether
she is field sensitive. The high score on MLAT Part 2 and the preference
for MBTI feeling indicate field sensitivity, but the low-average external
boundary score does not support that conclusion.

A working hypothesis for Sandy based on what we know of her now
might be that she has some field sensitivity when she is not on the
defensive, but she is also vulnerable to emotional disruption resulting from
overstimulation. In addition, if the weak preference for MBTI sensing is
accurate, she may not always cope with linguistic abstractions and cognitive restructuring when necessary, despite her ability to solve the rather
limited puzzle presented by the MLAT Part 3 items. Sandy's field independence and field sensitivity are probably about equivalent. When circumstances are exactly right for her, they function well together, and Sandy
can look something similar to a Type 1 learner, though without the speed
and range of an Alice. When something goes wrong in her life or class,

however, Sandy's access to her skills is disrupted, and she looks similar to a Type 4 learner.

What changes would you make in your hypotheses about Sandy based on the above material? What more would you like to know?

Another teacher, who sometimes works with the first one, joins the discussion. This teacher says the following:

Fortunately my colleague and I have been in it together and have been able to support each other. I wonder if Sandy is afraid of having two teachers. It has become something of an obsession with me to find out what I can do and how I can help. Sandy erupts and criticizes but never points to anything specific. Her usual statement is "It has been like this since I began here." Yesterday, I tried to make some corrections in a diplomatic fashion, and she strongly objected by saying "I don't know why you are correcting me; I will tell you when I need to be corrected." Whenever we explain something, she says, "I don't know why you are telling me things that I can understand perfectly." What does she need a teacher for, anyway?

I asked Sandy if she feels uncomfortable about alternating teachers, but she said this arrangement does not bother her. I want her to succeed, but I also want our efforts to be successful. It is very difficult to get her to follow our program, which we have spent so much time and effort developing. My colleague and I, as teachers, don't have a solution. She is cruel to us. When I review or reinforce materials, she stops me by saying she knows what it is and does not want to rephrase it. She is a good-looking person, but it is easy to see when she becomes tense—her mouth goes down, her neck muscles stand out, and her hands shiver. I used to count the days when she would finish; now I am counting the hours and quarter hours. I wonder what she will do when she evaluates this course. We have spent so much time developing a program to suit her needs, and she does not seem to appreciate its value at all.

If you were the advisor to whom the teachers went, what would you say to them now? If you were Sandy's teacher, what would you be thinking of trying?

Here's what actually happened. When one of the teachers said that Sandy objected to being given explanations, the advisor asked intuitively, without thinking, "Then why do you need to give an explanation?" The teacher replied in considerable surprise at the question, "That's what I was trained to do." After a fairly extended discussion, the advisor and the teachers came to an agreement that there were many things going on with Sandy, including some things in her life outside the classroom, but that the teachers could only deal with what goes on in their classroom and should put their focus there. When the advisor succeeded in helping the teachers narrow the scope of the responsibility they were feeling for Sandy, then it was time to help them start to look at her in a different way. Up to now, they had made the assumption that she was similar to most of their students. These teachers had been very successful with the great majority of students, who very much appreciated their attention and care to meet the students' needs. Clearly, this was not working with Sandy.

As it turned out, Sandy had been giving very clear messages about her need for learning space. Every time she objected to being corrected or given an explanation, she was saying "Let me do it myself. Give me some space to learn for myself." What most students appreciate as teacher attention caused Sandy to feel as if she was being crowded. Her responses to feeling crowded were not always constructive ones—she was experiencing other stresses, and her coping skills might not have been all that mature even under ideal circumstances. We have seen from her questionnaires that she can make a firm, even tough first impression, but she is in fact vulnerable to emotional disruption.

Sandy's teachers deserve a great deal of credit for continuing to try to help Sandy, rather than writing her off. It would have been natural to avoid her and give her as little as possible to avoid what felt like "cruel" treatment.

Instead, the teachers, with the best of intentions, were responding to Sandy's distress with what usually worked with other students: taking more care of her. By their lights, they were giving Sandy what she was saying she needed through her signals of distress. Unfortunately, they did not realize that these efforts were making things worse.

What would you suggest doing with Sandy now?

The advisor suggested to the teachers that they step back from Sandy. They were urged to rely more on indirect correction and on waiting to give explanations until Sandy indicated a need for them. One suggestion was to offer Sandy some options from time to time, so that she could choose what to learn and how to learn it. The teachers were strongly encouraged to see themselves as Sandy's assistants, as she struggled with the learning task, not always as her leaders. The advisor acknowledged that this whole approach might be difficult for the teachers; they might feel that they were neglecting Sandy or that they were not doing their job—to teach.

The teachers agreed to try this way of working with Sandy. They even thought up a few techniques and activities on their own. A few days later, they told the advisor that they had seen a great reduction in Sandy's outbursts. It was as if they were working with a completely different person. They were most encouraged. Sandy completed the course. She was never a brilliant student, but she ended her training with results that satisfied her and her teachers.

10.2.2 Teachers, Students, and Appropriate Support

I use this case in a teacher training course on enhancing learner independence. It is the key exercise in a segment of this course called "Giving the Student Appropriate Support." There are several points I try to make with the case.

First, strong emotional reactions should not be dismissed as immaturity or bad manners. They can be a good indicator that something is not being heard.

Second, the information about what is going on is often there, if you can get out of the usual mindset you bring to your work. If you go back to the two teachers' statements, you can see indications of what the difficulty was in several places. Her teachers could not hear it because getting out of the way was not part of their view of teaching. To solve puzzles such as the one Sandy prevented, it is vital to stay open to alternative explanations for what is happening.

Third, the student may not be aware of what the problem is. Sandy almost certainly was unaware herself of how much the teachers' "caretaking" was stressing her; she was almost certainly sincere when she ascribed her distress to her "own stuff." There was plenty of her "own stuff" in the picture, and it was misleading to all concerned. The teachers and at first the advisor spent a considerable amount of time on the question of what was going on in Sandy's outside life.

Fourth, it may be tempting to write off a student. The persistence of the teachers in Sandy's case, however, was repaid by their finding a way to work with her. They were professional enough to seek help when they realized that they were stuck. (Some students present difficulties that are beyond the professional expertise of teachers and teacher supervisors. We will look at some of these student types in Chapter 11.)

Appropriate support is giving the student what he or she needs *now*, not what was needed at the beginning of the course, or even yesterday, or what other students need, or what a student who resembles this student may have needed. Needs for external structure, independence, space, or correction vary not only from person to person (learning style) but also within a person from time to time. Most students want and appreciate a lot of direct teacher support when they are beginning something new: a subject, a lesson, a verb form, for example. In most cases, the scaffolding can be withdrawn slowly or fast as the student gains skill and confidence. For some students, the need for space is very great, and for them scaffolding may need to be unobtrusive, if it is there at all. This topic is addressed more completely above in section 8.2.3.

10.3 A Need for Balance *(Sheldon)*

10.3.1 About Sheldon

The following notes are from a counselor's files about an adult student in language training for an ongoing job assignment. The student is a former teacher of ESL and very dissatisfied with the language training program.

Sheldon was referred to me by the principal of the training school because he complained not only to school authorities but also to his own employers. The principal asked me to see what I could do with Sheldon after meeting with him and getting his agreement to call me in. The principal and vice principal experienced Sheldon as hostile and angry. They believe that he has an agenda beyond language learning having to do with career issues.

I immediately made contact with Sheldon's teacher to let him know that I had been asked to become involved and asked for his help in getting in touch with Sheldon. The teacher expressed sympathy for Sheldon's situation but said that he did not think that Sheldon was a very strong language learner. The next day, I had the opportunity to meet with Sheldon himself. This is what he told me:

> He is a former Peace Corps volunteer in the region where the language he is learning is spoken, though in a different country, which uses a different language from the one he is currently learning. He was a teacher of ESL in the Peace Corps. His reaction to the present training program is that it is unprofessional: The teacher is sometimes unprepared and has no idea of how to structure a teaching hour. Sheldon loves languages and language learning and has had previous successes, so the problem is not in him, Sheldon. He is considering paying for a private tutor himself, if things don't improve.

In talking about his goals, Sheldon says,

> I want to feel comfortable when I go into a professional meeting. Now I can only buy fruit in a market. We're just hacking around and have little mastery of the basics of the language. If my work supervisor overseas wants me to accompany him or her and interpret or use the language, I won't be able to do what's needed. My employer thinks I'm getting trained, and I'm not.
>
> I've repeated my efforts to get help many times, to no good effect. The problem keeps getting focused on me, and why I'm the only one in my class complaining. I've tried to be constructive. I've offered my services to help with the program, to edit materials, and will do anything in an appropriate role. But I don't see the will to improve.

The counselor's notes continue: I said that my role would probably be to try to help Sheldon get his needs met within the resource limitations of the program. I also said that anything that could be done would probably be only a partial solution, but that Sheldon and I could work with the teacher to try to get at least some of Sheldon's needs met.

---

*What are your initial reactions and hypotheses? What kind of
learning style do you think Sheldon has?*

The counselor asked, "What has helped you in your previous language learning?" Sheldon said that he learns through a kind of photographic memory. He learns the new script early, and he uses reading as a major learning medium. Unfortunately the weakest portion of the present course is the reading curriculum. He also prefers a clear sequence of things on which they are working. He likes to be forced to use the patterns until mastery is achieved. He likes regular correction. This program seems to him to have no sequence, no syllabus, no organized materials. The method seems to be random exposure—Sheldon has taken to referring to the program as "Learning Language X by Default."

Sheldon does not think he has a personality conflict with the teacher, and the teacher confirms this opinion. The teacher, an educated member of the target language culture, admits that he is untrained and indicates that he is teaching a language for which learning materials are sparse and dated. The program supervisor has been working with the teacher to bring some order into the syllabus and help the teacher with lesson planning and effective use of student time. This process, however, will take a long time to complete, and in the meantime Sheldon is feeling the pressure to learn the language now.

Sheldon has taken the MBTI. He is an INTJ, and all preferences are clear. There are no other questionnaire data available for him.

---

*Give the best description you can of Sheldon's learning style. What
would you currently recommend for him? What can you say about the
teacher's learning style? What would you recommend for his teacher,
in view of the teacher's and program's limitations?*

From the counselor's notes: I proposed that if Sheldon had some time on a one-on-one basis, he might take more initiative in guiding the direction of the course. In that this teacher cannot fulfill Sheldon's expectations of a fully trained teacher, Sheldon should find some ways to make the most of the inevitable and work with the teacher as he might work with an ordinary native speaker who had agreed to help him learn. I gave him a little information on how to work with a nonteacher native speaker.

I proposed to Sheldon and his teacher that some time be set aside for them to work in the ways Sheldon preferred, with Sheldon taking something of the lead and the teacher attempting to follow by finding or developing readings and speaking activities to meet Sheldon's requests. The teacher's supervisor agreed to find funding for this and to take a little time from his very busy schedule to provide the teacher with an introduction to basic lesson planning.

The teacher seemed agreeable at the time, but Sheldon reported that the next day the teacher seemed depressed and a little cold to Sheldon. We discussed the possibility that the teacher might have felt that he had lost face and how Sheldon might help the teacher feel better about him and about the proposed change. He decided to ask the teacher to teach more grammar, a topic in which he is unusually knowledgeable and in which Sheldon feels a real need for help.

Sheldon had come to realize that he could not take a role in teacher training and curriculum design as he had previously offered to do and yet fill in the gaps in his knowledge of the language. He decided that the latter must be his priority. He had begun a plan to start by filling in his knowledge gaps before moving on to new material.

What do you think will happen with Sheldon now? Where would you anticipate the trouble spots will be? If you could design the ideal program for Sheldon, what would it be like?

The counselor writes: A couple of weeks later, Sheldon came in to update me on what was happening. Overall, he is pleased with the way things are working out. He describes himself as doing a "deep regearing" of his language knowledge. He still does not like the absence of a clear syllabus and finds it a strain to have to do much of the program planning, but he also recognizes that this may be the only way for him to get the sequence he wants. I suggested that he might use a textbook for a related language as a guide for sequencing his lessons, following the topics and structural points.

The teacher is not entirely comfortable with the arrangement in which Sheldon has most of the control. From time to time, he tries to take it back and does things that are not very helpful to Sheldon, though they are consistent with the teacher's cultural roles for teachers. Sheldon must then find tactful ways to move the teacher back into the unfamiliar role of consultant and facilitator.

I asked what's not working, and Sheldon said, "I'm responsible, so I have to develop a clear way of doing this. I'm actually enjoying it more than I thought I would. It's the intuitive thinking need for competence. The lack of structure in this language program has been bugging me, but now I have a chance to show my competence, and I'm responsible."

Sheldon worked with the teacher part time in class with the other students and for several hours a week alone with the teacher. He completed the course three months later with mediocre results. He attributed his lackluster performance to having started with a weak program and spending 6 months more or less "spinning his wheels." The teacher said that Sheldon was overconfident and not as good a language learner as he thought he was.

10.3.2 Balancing Competing Needs

This case is a good example of the way things often really are. From time to time, there is a really satisfying intervention such as those for Elsa and Sandy. More often, we have to settle for what we can get.

Sheldon is an experienced language learner with knowledge of the region's cultural patterns. He has a reasonably accurate idea of what works well for him. His learning style is essentially sequential and visual; he is probably more a type 2 learner than any other (field independent and field insensitive). At a guess, his cognitive aptitude is above average but not extraordinary. The new program, in which he took much of the lead, probably would not have worked at all if he had not been (a) self-aware, (b) somewhat field independent, so he could extract both sequence and substance from context, (c) something of an independent learner, and (d) an experienced language teacher himself. It was these factors that led the counselor to guess that he could transcend his strong sequential learning preferences to get something useful from the teacher.

On the other hand, the program is very constrained by the teacher's admitted limitations, the small budget, and an overburdened supervisor. The teacher himself is probably more comfortable with relatively random processing and may be relatively auditory in that he has not given much attention to the reading portion of the course. The teacher's culturally determined expectations of his role as a teacher play a part in what is happening and in his receptivity to the change in Sheldon's training.

In a situation such as this, it is likely that no one will be fully satisfied. Sheldon is not going to have a professional teacher and a well-sequenced program, though the teacher may improve during Sheldon's time with him. The teacher will not have complete control of the program and the amount of supervisory support he needs. The teacher may find the new approach wounding enough that he may sabotage its success in subtle ways; Sheldon may stay angry enough at feeling deprived of a professionally taught program that he in turn may also sabotage the workaround plan. In fact, it is possible that some of this did happen.

On the other hand, Sheldon learned much more of the language and left feeling more confident of his language skill than if there had been no change in his language course. The teacher and program were saved from an end-of-training blast from Sheldon, and the teacher had the opportunity to get some on-the-job training he might not have had otherwise. On balance, then, the intervention seems to have paid off and was worth the energy put into it.

10.4 Students With Students *(Janet, Karen, Shirley)*

10.4.1 About Janet, Karen, and Shirley

In Chapter 6 (section 6.7.1) we were introduced to a class in which three learners we had met before were students: Shirley, Janet, and Karen. They are having a difficult time working with each other. The material on these three learners is repeated for Janet from sections 4.5.1 and 4.5.3; for Shirley, from sections 4.5.1 and 4.5.3; and for Karen, from sections 4.4, 4.5.1, and 4.5.3.

In section 4.4, Shirley, a very sophisticated learner and also highly sequential processor, tells us a teaching sequence that has worked well for her.

In class, new material is practiced *with* the teacher. We *repeat correct* patterns *provided* by the teacher and with *immediate* correction as we try to use the new pattern. The teacher has us repeat the correct patterns. The next step is to try to develop or use the new pattern ourselves. This is done in class so that the teacher can make corrections and repeat the correct pattern as needed, *immediately*. Older material is worked on in class periodically, too, and only after correct patterns are quite firm do the students work at home on the material. Most of us work at home with carefully structured tapes so we are carefully guided to learn and reinforce *correct* patterns from which we can use the language, rather than making things up "from scratch" and learning it wrong.[Emphasis is Shirley's]

Shirley also describes approaches that have caused her difficulty in the following:

I have a lot of trouble with exercises that test an intellectual understanding of a grammatical point, but change all elements each time so that it does not effectively reinforce basic patterns at the beginning stages. When we ask for something to be repeated, it may be repeated once or twice, but not more, even if students are still getting it wrong. Much more often, the teacher offers six to ten *different* ways to say the same thing. [Emphasis is Shirley's.]

In section 6.7.3, I suggest that task-based activities are a good way to find something for everyone. Preparation for the task can be done in ways that satisfy the students such as Shirley and the ones who take an opposite approach, such as Miriam. Both value such preparation but go about it in different ways. Shirley will want to master one thing at a time and will welcome instructions from the teacher on how to undertake her preparation and even how to manage the task, whereas Miriam is likely to resist such instruction and work out her own approach.

In contrast, Janet criticizes a course for opposite reasons to those given by Shirley. Janet is a relatively random learner, though not as extreme as Miriam.

Overall, Janet liked the textbook as a compact way to get the basics. However, she would have liked a lot more problem-solving activities like roleplays and simulations. She found helpful the brief summaries of news or other topics that they were asked to do sometimes, where there was not always a lot of time for preparation. She found too much classroom routine and predictability unhelpful, even stultifying. Her view was that she should do in class only what she could not do by herself, whereas much of the teaching in the course relied on repetitious drilling, which was not a good use of class time for her. When the teacher was willing to let students use the language with him and was flexible as student needs changed, she learned better.

In section 4.5.3, Janet's random style is described as meshing well with inductive learning—so well that they are closely linked though not identical. Dislike of classroom routine and predictability is suggestive of a preference for perceiving. A perceiving type such as Janet is likely to value flexibility in self and others, so this was a positive feature in Janet's view of her teacher. Perceiving types are often energized by last-minute preparation and thinking on their feet. They often prefer to work in bursts. For younger perceivers in particular, leaving things to the last minute can cause them trouble. Well-developed, more mature perceivers such as Janet can usually calculate the risks of waiting until the last minute quite accurately and act accordingly (section 6.2.2).

In section 4.4, we had some interview material from Karen, who is experiencing unusual difficulty learning to read a language written in a different alphabet from that of English.

Interviewer. What seems to have worked well for you in the past?

Karen. When I was studying a previous language, we had to close our books and learn dialogues by repeating after the teacher. This worked very well for me. I learn from sound. The language I'm studying now isn't comfortable for me to read, and I can't bring in sounds when I read.

Interviewer. You need to associate sounds with what you read.

Karen. Yes, what works best for me is to use the new language as much as possible and not be inhibited and only learn from books. I like a lively teacher who encourages us to talk and not just take in language and build a large base of words we understand but can't use.

Interviewer. So your learning comes from hearing yourself and other people talk in natural ways?

Karen. Yes, that's right. Books are ok, but I need to read them aloud so I can hear the sounds and how they relate to the words on the page.

In section 4.5.1, we found out that Karen is also a relatively random processor, who describes herself as a good "osmosis" learner. She says that sequential material often interferes with what she calls her "intuitive approach." She also recognizes, however, her need for a well-organized program. She is not so random that she wants to design her own program, as the more extreme random learners do. She has learned that random learners can overestimate their ability to cope with unstructured input (section 4.5.1). We also saw in section 4.5.3 that Karen, despite her needs for some structuring, prefers to learn from hearing people talk in natural ways, an inductive way of going about things.

You are their teacher, and you are not too surprised when Shirley and Karen come to see you about the difficulties they are having learning together. The following is what Shirley says about Karen:

Karen is really frustrating to have in class. She's really random and scattered. The teacher can't control her; she's just all over the place. We can't ever just work through a lesson systematically, even for as little as 20 minutes at a time. I wish she would be more interested in repeating correctly and letting us get through material so I can get the systematic repetition and buildup I need. She wants to do grammar and let vocabulary take care of itself, and I want to work on building up my vocabulary systematically. I really need the basics, and Karen's constant tangents get in my way.

Karen, on the other hand, says the following:

Although I want to have a solid foundation before I stick my neck out too far, I don't want to wait as long as Shirley does. She wants such a systematic approach that there's no opportunity to try things out. Learning a language is much more than just learning rules and amassing a lot of words that we can't use, even if we understand them. Let's learn a little and then try it out. Shirley should trust her ability to learn more indirectly, too. Everything doesn't have to be formally introduced and covered thoroughly in class. Shirley wants everything spelled out and done one step at a time. That really gets in the way of my learning after I've got the basics. But don't forget—I still need to get control of what I'm learning first.

Shirley and Karen both recognize that Janet gets bored with the drills and practice that they and many of their classmates value. They are conscious that she feels her time is being wasted. They also sometimes experience themselves as pushed into conversational and simulation activities well before they feel ready for them. Janet's approach is more difficult for Shirley than for Karen, who at least can relate to Janet's random style.

Janet has not come to see you about Shirley and Karen or other classmates, but she has asked to be excused from some of the more mechanical practice, and you have agreed because she appears to be learning well without as much drilling as her classmates seem to need. Although she has not said anything about it, you have observed that she brings target-language reading material to work with when you are drilling with the other students, and you are aware that she is eager to use her time productively.

---

a. *What is your initial take on this situation? What more would you like to know before proposing an action plan?*
b. *How do you think the three students come out with respect to some of the information on which there may be questionnaire data (MBTI, ego boundaries, field independence and field sensitivity, overall cognitive aptitude, preferred learning activities, motivation)?*

Your next step is to see if there is anything helpful in the information from questionnaires. Unfortunately there is almost nothing on Janet, except that she is an INFP and has learned French and Arabic to at least a working level of proficiency. There is more about Shirley and Karen.

Karen
Previous history: Strong background in Romance languages. Has not found language learning difficult
MLAT: Part 1—44%; Part 2—63%; Part 3—30%; Part 4—87%; Part 5—88%; Total—58%
MBTI: ISFJ, moderate consistency scores
HBQ: Internal boundaries—average; Neat: thick External boundaries—average; Total—slightly thick (Reminder: High (thin) score on "Neat" really means "prefers things *not* to be very orderly.")

MSQ: Rates self as an above-average learner; highly motivated, and somewhat anxious about this class but not about speaking in class

Endorses no activities strongly, but mildly endorses conversational activities, guessing unknown words, drilling, field trips and longer-term immersion trips, speaking in the classroom and at school as much as possible, moving around the classroom and exercises that use her hands (drawing, pointing, etc.), rote memorization of dialogues, audiotapes, roleplays and simulations, reading without a dictionary, mastering one thing before moving on, and step-by-step learning.

Strongly *rejects* one-by-one reading aloud, looking up words and copying them, correction of all speaking errors, and designing the program as they go along.

Shirley
Previous history: Some background in Romance languages

MLAT: Part 1—91%; Part 2—100%; Part 3—78%; Part 4—76%; Part 5—96%; Total—87%

MBTI: INFP, clear consistency scores. TDI subscale scores (see section 6.2.3) suggest anxiety

HBQ: Internal boundaries—thin; Neat and Edges: thin External boundaries—thin; Total—quite thin. (Reminder: High (thin) score on "Edges" indicates a preference for blurred edges and lines in visual images.)

MSQ: Rates self as an average learner; highly motivated, and very anxious about this class but not very anxious about speaking in class

Strongly *endorses* transformation drills, correction of all written mistakes and a "reasonable number" of oral errors, the teacher has main responsibility to see that she gets what she needs, study alone, and use of audiotapes. Mildly endorses a considerable range of varying techniques.

Strongly *rejects* early pronunciation drill and no other activities.

Where there any surprises for you in these data? What strengths do Karen and Shirley show that you can help them take advantage of? What conflict areas do their profiles suggest?

Karen's profile on the questionnaires suggests a learner who is likely to be relatively sequential (MBTI sensing and judging, low MLAT Part 3—Spelling Clues) and intolerant of ambiguity (somewhat thick on the HBQ, low MLAT Part 3). The first three parts of the MLAT suggest that Karen is probably a Type 3 learner. MLAT parts 4 (Words in Sentences) and 5 (Paired Associates) are quite high, suggesting that she is good at organizing tasks, has good planning and task-organization strategies, and is well versed in formal English (grammar). This profile does not predict her actual approach or her language learning record, which includes two languages learned to a very high level of proficiency indeed. Karen herself says that previous language study has come easily for her.

Karen makes use of a considerable range of learning activities. Those she rejects are largely characterized by mechanical processing with no payoff afterwards in increased language repertoire. Her relatively random preference leads to comfort with the various conversational and other open-ended activities; her apparent recognition that her abilities do not permit a fully random approach has led to an expressed need for external help with the learning task through step-by-step learning while she builds the linguistic base she needs for communicative language use.

Shirley's profile also has some surprises. Her very strong preferences for learning structure and teacher guidance are consistent with what we usually see for students with thick ego boundaries. Her learning preferences as described, both what she likes and what she does not like, would seem to suggest a low tolerance of ambiguity. On the other hand, everything in her MBTI, HBQ, and MLAT profiles would normally indicate a student who is very tolerant of ambiguity, at least as far as accepting contradictions is concerned. A student such as Shirley may well have difficulty at the level of cognitive restructuring; indeed, it is likely that she, too, is a Type 3 learner. Type 3 learners are not usually as forceful as Shirley about their need for external structure, though they often want it. Shirley is also unusual among Type 3 learners in that she appears to reject use of field-sensitive approaches that rely on learning from context.

These two students, both Type 3 learners, thus present some contradictions. Both have learning approaches that belie their responses on the questionnaires and tests they took, and they appear to complement each other. Karen's profile suggests a strong desire for step-by-step learning; instead, Karen often takes a relatively random approach to her learning. Shirley, on the other hand, has a profile that could readily belong to a learner who goes through life using what she knows effectively but often imprecisely, and yet she seeks precision and a great deal of external structure.

I have suggested above that Karen, who prefers random learning, has also learned her limitations and so she seeks external structure to help her set learning priorities. It may be that Shirley is similar: She has come to recognize that an underlying preference for a flexible, fluid lifestyle does not enhance her achievement of productivity goals. As a result, she may have rejected her perceiving, thin-boundary, cognitively flexible style in favor of a safer judging, thick boundary, and cognitively more firmly set style. As noted elsewhere, among intuitives, feeling types often require more external structure than their thinking fellows in any event (section 4.5.1).

This kind of variation in the way the models work with real people is fairly typical. A model offers a probability, not a certainty, of encountering certain preferences and behaviors. Students with profiles like Karen's are more likely than not to learn sequentially, but not all such students. More information, such as the fact that Shirley has found that a global approach gets her into trouble and so has worked hard to build other skills, can often explain some of the apparent contradictions. Individuals' previous experiences interact with their personality preferences to shape their responses to new experiences.

Shirley's profile offers one more piece of information, because it includes the TDI scoring of the long version of the MBTI (described in section 6.2.3). On this questionnaire, Shirley reported herself as worried, defiant, ambivalent, and distractible. All of these are at the discomfort pole of the comfort-discomfort scales, suggesting that Shirley is experiencing considerable distress in her life. Shirley's rather thin boundaries, together with only moderate cognitive restructuring (MLAT scores on Parts 3 and 4) and her TDI discomfort outcomes, may suggest an internal vulnerability and possibly an area of internal conflict that she may protect with a hard and aggressive exterior. Her possible overcompensation for thin boundaries and too much flexibility may have resulted in stylistic rigidity contrary to her own interests in a classroom setting. This is countered by her readiness to make use of a very wide range of learning activities.

Finally, although there are few questionnaire data about Janet, we can note that both she and Shirley are INFP learners. The main difference seems to be that Janet is more comfortable working with the global approach that often characterizes these learners than Shirley is. It seems likely from what we know of Janet that she is also able to access field independent skills; she is probably a Type 1 learner. In this case, it is not surprising that Janet finds drilling and memorizing to be a poor use of her time: She makes use of deep learning strategies that emphasize cognitive restructuring and finds external imposition of structure unnecessary.

Now what is your diagnosis of what is going on? What would
you do to help these students get the most from their class?

There is more information about the learning setting and the learners that you may find helpful as you work out ways to help all three students learn as well as possible in the same class. The required syllabus for the program begins by "front-loading" grammar, on the principle that this will enable students to make full use of communicative opportunities later on in the course. This course organization presents no difficulty for Type 1 and 2 learners, but it can stop others in their tracks. By the time they reach the more communicative portion of the program (or go out into a target-language speaking environment), they may be so thoroughly demoralized by their lack of success in the training program that they come to consider themselves poor language learners and avoid language thereafter. This demoralization is especially a danger for first-time learners, but it also has an effect on more experienced learners such as Shirley and Karen. Such learners may come to dismiss their previous successes by attributing them to the fact that they were learning "easy" languages, but that they cannot learn languages with "real grammar," such as Germanic, Slavic, or non-Western languages.

Examination of how Karen and Shirley have learned their previous languages indicates that both rely heavily on auditory input. Unfortunately, this program emphasizes reading, which is not a preferred modality for either student, and which they anticipate needing less than speaking ability after they complete the class.

Shirley described her previous learning experiences by saying that she was similar to a sponge, learning by listening and interacting, because she catches on quickly. She said that she needs repetition for retention. It is thus possible that Shirley would do very well in a program that offered scope to these more global learning tendencies, as long as she accepted that learning new material does not mean immediate ability to retrieve and reproduce it (at first, simple comprehension is all that should be expected). The emphasis on need for external structure may be a product of a considerable mismatch between Shirley's real learning style and a program that is relying on mostly decontextualized language.

Karen says that when she lived for a short time overseas, the language "just came." Pronunciation was easy to pick up. In a previous classroom she had had good success with a program that made heavy use of the target language but also required memorization of short dialogues. She described the success of that program as coming in part because it began with a comprehension base before production was required. The class was frequently broken into small cooperative groups to perform various tasks.

Use the information you have to prescribe in a way that will meet the needs of all three students. (Table 10.1 summarizes the available information for the three learners.)

10.4.2 Meeting Multiple Needs

Most classes have more than three people with competing needs. Indeed, even in this somewhat simplified case, although we treat the needs of three learners and two of them in particular, other members of the class also have differing styles. On the whole, though, the classroom methodology is working reasonably well for the majority of this class. The challenge is to come up with a solution to the difficulties experienced by Janet, Karen, and Shirley that will not disadvantage the rest of the class.

For Karen and Shirley, there is almost certainly an important affective component. Both are experiencing considerable anxiety because of the way the course is designed, with its heavy visual and initial grammar component. As auditory and probable Type 3 (field dependent and field sensitive) learners, they feel at an immediate disadvantage. They react both with an expressed need for more external structure, which lowers their sense of risk, and by defensive complaining about each other. A useful first step is to address their needs for learning security (Curran, 1978; Stevick, 1980, 1989).

The following suggestions are made to address the learners' needs. Janet has already been helped by being permitted to find alternative ways to use some of her class time, when she feels the general activities are not promoting her learning. The remainder of these suggestions will not get in her way and may help her. Based on what we know now of Karen and Shirley, the following is proposed to help them.

Structure and Predictability. The teacher works with them to come up with a clear agreement on what they are trying to get from the course.

Table 10.1 Summary of Information About Janet, Karen, and Shirley

Janet[a]	Karen[b]	Shirley[c]
	Auditory, kinesthetic	Auditory
Random	Random	Sequential
Inductive	Inductive	Deductive
INFP	ISFJ	INFP
	Some what thick ego boundaries	Thin ego boundaries
	MLAT high Parts 4, 5	MLAT: all parts high, but Parts 3 and 4 lowest
	MLAT low Parts 1, 3	
Type 1?	Type 3?	Type 3?
Little external structure	Some external structure	Much external structure
Wants: Language use	Grammar	Vocabulary
Open-ended activities	Some foundation, then use	Very firm foundation first

a. Janet: Strong previous language learning history (French, Arabic)
b. Karen: Good previous language learning history (Romance languages)
c. Shirley: Some background (Romance language)

The teacher then gives them an explicit syllabus for the course, to which the teacher adheres for the most part. (Some digression is appropriate, but for the most part, the overall progress of the program is predictable.) To the degree possible, the teacher finds opportunities for systematic review of important material. Feedback is explicit, going beyond "you're doing fine."

Language in Context. The program includes communicative, contextual activities from the beginning of the course, even when the students have not yet gained all the knowledge they need to speak with precision. The teacher makes sure all grammar points and vocabulary are treated in context. The program provides more inductive learning opportunities.

Auditory Practice. Teacher and interested students find ways for more auditory practice that can be done outside of class. Some examples include reading aloud, finding audio- and videotapes that are not necessarily linked with textbooks, structuring listening goals so that full mastery is not necessary, listening to conversations between people speaking the target language, retelling orally what is in the readings, and studying with a partner.

Refer back to section 6.7.3 for general suggestions on coping with multiple learning styles. Above all, avoid an all-or-nothing approach. You cannot meet everyone's needs all the time, but you can address some of them most of the time, and you can help students develop techniques for learning in their own styles if they do not already have them.

10.5 A Student in a Panic *(Mark)*

10.5.1 About Mark

I recently received the following message from a colleague:

> We need some immediate help with an extremely difficult student. We seem to be unable to offer him the counsel he needs and would appreciate your help in the matter. His behavior is disruptive to the class, and he is unlikely to reach his learning goals.

What are your initial hypotheses as you read this message?

Mark has traveled widely and has some language background. He has working proficiency in French and Spanish. His languages were learned in country, both through part-time classes and through interaction with host country nationals. He comments "I enjoy being able to watch movies or news in French or Spanish," and describes himself as a good mimic.

Mark originally expected to take a short survival course in preparation for a new job. He began to become anxious when his boss-to-be suggested that he take the full course of language training. His anxiety was raised by the necessity to deal more with grammar in the longer course, whereas the survival course emphasizes low-level functional ability and de-emphasizes grammatical precision. Mark knew there was a lot of grammar in language X, whereas he had been able to "wing it through French and Spanish." He was so anxious that he began to call the supervisor of the language X program before training even began to seek reassurance. The training supervisor said that in the regular program, they tend to teach a lot of grammar so that students will have all the tools they need for the much more communicative later sections of the program, so he was not able to give Mark much reassurance.

Once he began class, Mark found that he was having trouble with "memory," and that he was falling asleep in class because he was so exhausted. He was no longer doing anything but study language X and was beginning to feel deprived of the rest of his life, especially because his study did not seem to be paying off. When I inquired about his study strategies, they sounded reasonable, though I thought he could tighten up his setting of priorities somewhat. He also said he can commit large chunks of his reading (in English) to memory when it is in areas of interest.

His class group seemed to be well bonded, but Mark said "I'm pretty sure I'm the dumbest one in the class, though the others try to help me." He mentioned that one of the other students is good at figuring out structure, and another classmate does nothing but study so is generally accurate. He could not think of much of anything he did well, except possibly pronunciation.

Not only were the teachers concerned about him, he also told me that he was afraid he would have a nervous breakdown in 6 months. He was feeling depressed every morning by what he saw as impending failure. He had sought help from the teachers' supervisor but experienced him as unhelpful because of his very strong task-orientation.

Consider the information I have given you so far.
What are your hypotheses about what's going on with Mark?

I asked Mark to complete the questionnaires I usually use for diagnosis of student learning. The following is how his profile turned out.

Biodata:
Native speaker of English, American born
Has taken college-level courses, no degree
Working level in French and Spanish
MLAT: Total score slightly above average. Part scores not available.
MBTI: ENFP, likes cultural topics, easily disrupted by interpersonal disharmony
Hartmann Boundary Questionnaire: In the middle: Near the mean for males. Exhibits thin boundary behavior, so average scores may indicate strong need for control or social desirability response bias.

MSQ: Rated self as above average in language ability but expected to perform averagely in this class

    Rated self as highly motivated to learn the language and go to the country

    Motivated by job, challenge, use with people, learning something new, pride

    Really nervous about learning language X but not at all about speaking in class

    Strongly endorsed open-ended language learning activities (e.g., discussions) *and*

    Strongly endorsed activities that help him chunk input (e.g., step-by-step program)

    Indicated a preference for kinesthetic and auditory learning, over visual

Affective Survey

Motivation total	Above average
Intrinsic	Average
Extrinsic	Above average
Desire to use language outside class	Above average
Effort	Average
Beliefs about self as a language learner	Below average
Anxiety total (following are subscales)	Above average
Competition	Very high
Use with native speakers	Very high
Comprehension of over-the-head material (listening & reading)	Above average
Self-esteem	Above average
Outcomes (grades, final ratings)	Average
Public performance (speaking in the classroom)	Average
Making errors and being corrected	Below average
Tests	Below average
General discomfort with language learning	Below average
Negatively phrased items (a subset extracted from the above items)	Average

---

Would you modify your hypotheses in the light of this information? If so, how?

The following are the hypotheses I made and proposed to Mark about his difficulties with his classwork:

a. He was using so much mental energy on experiencing anxiety and trying to cope with it that there was not much left for processing the language. He really liked this hypothesis; it put his difficulties into a new perspective for him.

b. He was a very global learner, who learned material through rich contexts, not in isolation. His classmates, on the other hand, and the general approach to training in the language *X* section, were strongly analytic. So there was a considerable style mismatch between Mark and his environment.

c. He was made especially anxious by the prospect of interpersonal disharmony, including the disfavor of teachers whose expectations he was not meeting and classmates with whom he was not keeping up. (The anxiety became so unbearable that it overpowered classroom etiquette and resulted in the emotional outbursts that prompted the original message requesting help.)

What would you do now?

I suggested to Mark that he "lighten up" and undertake some affective self-management—for example, read novels (something he enjoys) or play with his dog. Step away from study (or—mentally—from the class activity) when he gets the overwhelmed feeling. Pick himself up and give himself a pat on the back (figuratively speaking) when he starts feeling panic.

Mark was very critical of himself for being so emotionally labile and "childish". I urged him to accept his lability and work around it and to understand that language class can be a very regressive experience. I also talked with him about the importance of forgetting to learning (i.e., that some forgetting permits relearning in new contexts and reworking of knowledge so that the ultimate web of associations is enriched). We spent a lot of time talking about appropriate self-expectations, and I surprised him by suggesting that his classmates were probably also anxious and sometimes envious of his abilities (mimicry, ability to learn from context).

When he, the language *X* section supervisor, and I met, I pointed out that neither Mark nor the language *X* section, were likely to change, but that we could affect the interface between them. Both the supervisor and I worked with Mark on the nature of foundation laying (messy, slow, and yet essential). We were able also to agree on some alterations in the presentation of the material by the teachers. We agreed that a very accepting and yet down-to-earth senior teacher would become a point of contact for Mark in dealing with the training section.

Do you think this would work? What would you do differently?

I met with Mark after a week. He told me that he had benefited a great deal from working on managing his feelings. Although he still had ups and downs, the downs were much less low, and he found some of the affective self-management techniques that I suggested to be very effective. One of the teachers also helped a lot. Mark had a much increased sense of control because he could recognize when he was beginning to feel overwhelmed. He started to develop activities to cope with this situation by physical action at home and by mental action in class. If in class, when he made a mistake, he told himself "everyone screws up from time to time" and he saw times when he was more successful than his classmates. He visualized and reviewed his successes. He told me that the key is "walking away from it" (physically and mentally). His learning was getting better, and he felt that he was using his time better.

Mark and I agreed that Mark's anxieties were largely about people, not really about learning per se. We saw that he worked well with open-ended, contextual input, but he needed help with chunking the training and appreciated that kind of structure from the program. These observations could help him continue to manage his own learning.

10.5.2 Working Out What Is Behind the Feelings

I learned a great deal about Mark from the interviews; indeed, I had an initial hypothesis from the time I received the initial e-mail message. What did the questionnaire data contribute? Certainly, I got information about learning style and the interplay of a global and largely interpersonal, Track 1 style (Chapter 6) with a need for external structure, something I often see with intuitive feeling students, who are frequently Type 3 (field independent, fiels sensitive learners) as mentioned in sections 4.5.1 and 10.4.

I got useful information about this student's learning style from the MBTI, in particular the intuitive-feeling preference combination, which explained a great deal about the sources of the anxiety and provided a number of working hypotheses that turned out to be accurate. The Affective Survey, in combination with the MBTI, confirmed the probable underlying source of this student's highly disruptive anxiety: interpersonal relations, rather than language learning ability. Doing poorly was related far more to relations with Mark's future supervisor (not disappointing him), his desire to please his teachers, and his wish not to have tense relations with his classmates.

How does this apply to you? You may not have access to questionnaires, and if you do, you may not have the time or training to use them confidently. Furthermore, test data can be misleading if not taken in the context of the whole picture of an individual. The good news is that most of what we have learned about Mark also came out in my interviews with him, though, to be sure, my experience and knowledge of learning differences was of considerable help in developing sensitizing concepts to direct my attention. On the other hand, the test data sharpened my process of generating and testing hypotheses and added useful information to my dialogue with Mark.

10.6 More Information

The learning style dimensions treated in that work overlap largely but not entirely with those in the present book. In addition to the suggestions in sections 6.7.3 and 10.4.2, Betty Lou Leaver (1993) has addressed this question in *Teaching the Whole Class*. In it, she describes some of the same learning style dimensions as are addressed here. She also treats some not covered here, whereas this book treats some dimensions not addressed in the Leaver work.

More case material that treats learners in context is available in Stevick (1989). Although these are mostly good learners, their successes and difficulties fit in well with those of the learners we have met in this book. Another book of cases is Plaister (1993). These short cases are focused primarily on teaching methodology (e.g., "Is Dictation the Answer?"), with a few on ESL program administration; they are set entirely in the ESL domain.

When You Need
Outside Help

You have seen in Chapter 10 that there are limits to what anyone can do to meet every student's needs. For instance, it was too late in Sheldon's program, and the circumstances were too constrained to bring about the changes that would have permitted him to make fullest use of his language class. Karen and Shirley may never be fully satisfied that their needs are being met. The language program that Mark is in may not accommodate much to his learning style.

In this chapter are cases in which expectations are even more limited and in which it may be appropriate to seek outside assistance. This is especially the true when you suspect the presence of learning disabilities. It is also important not to feel that you have to do it all on your own with students who show extremes of feelings such as anxiety or anger. Some other students are so self-defeating that they succeed in nullifying every effort you make to help them. Such students often need assistance from people with specialized expertise.

Most teachers have little training in how to meet the needs of students with learning disabilities. Although this chapter is not intended as a course in the subject, it offers a taxonomy of learning disabilities, some case material, and a few very general approaches that may help you work with students of this sort.

Students with extreme anxiety or who are unable to give up blaming the program for their disappointments also present challenges that go beyond the training most teachers receive. Again, without trying to make you into a psychotherapist, I offer some illustrative cases and a few general suggestions.

11.1 About *Joe*

Joe is beginning a language course in a program that has multiple class sections. He plans to go overseas after the course for the first time in his life. He was born and raised in the Southeast of the United States and has an associate degree in electrical engineering. He has never studied a foreign language before.

Language study is coming very hard for Joe. He is willing, even eager, to learn, but somehow the language simply is not sticking with him. He has been passed from one class to another. He is now in a class of students all of whom are very slow, but he is one of the two slowest even in this class. Nothing the teachers have tried has seemed to help.

The course is grammar based, using a textbook that was written when audio-lingual methodology (dialogues and drills) was the accepted way of teaching. The teaching staff use the book as the basis of a great deal of conversational activity, and there is no lack of "communicative" activity as well. However, the course is sequenced around grammar.

Joe's teacher comes to you in some distress. She is at her wits' end. She does not want to drop Joe from class: He is trying hard and has expressed determination to succeed in gaining conversational ability. Joe has said that he will take all the help he can get, and, at this point, his teachers are feeling the same way.

You interview Joe for the first time. He is very pleasant, eager to please, eager for help. He is willing to undergo any diagnostic procedure you want to try on him. The results of the questionnaires show the following:

Joe is an ESTJ on the MBTI. He is weak on tests of analytic skills (related to field independence), moderately strong in visual memory, and prefers visual over auditory learning but likes hands-on learning even better. Joe likes a physically relaxed, quiet, brightly lit study space.

Joe scores very low on a questionnaire that indicates openness to new information and tolerance of ambiguity. On a questionnaire of motivation and anxiety, he shows high motivation to learn and little anxiety about learning, relative to other students.

On the Modern Language Aptitude Test, Joe's extremely low Total Score falls below the 10th percentile. This overall score indicates that *all* the part scores are also very low: Part 1—33%; Part 2—53%; Part 3—4% (2 correct answers out of 50); Part 4—20%; Part 5—25%;, and Total Score—25%. On a memory test, Joe is somewhat lower than others his age overall and considerably lower on immediate recall for connected text, though he shows little deterioration in delayed recall 30 minutes later. No difference was apparent when connected text was presented auditorily or visually.

On the Strategy Inventory for Language Learning, Joe indicates most use of memory strategies and least for learning with others and managing his emotions. On the LASSI, he relies on concentration, selecting main ideas, time management, and reviewing, and he relies least on reasoning and information processing strategies. There are a few cues that Joe has difficulties with letter transposition when he reads.

In the interview, you learn that Joe appears to have good study skills, at least as far as previewing, studying, and reviewing go. He seems to be willing to guess at unfamiliar words. You are surprised to learn that he acts in plays as one of his recreational activities and so ask how he memorizes lines. He says he has no particular difficulty with this; he just reads them over and over until they stick with him. It seems to help that he practices them with others.

Joe is active in his church and likes organizing activities there. He has met some target-language speakers socially. He likes to read biographies and technical material (about electricity and building houses). He enjoys sight-seeing, roller-skating, fishing, antiques, and watching volleyball games.

What do you think is going on with Joe?

11.2 Possible Learning Disabilities

11.2.1 What Is a Learning Disability?

Leaning disability refers to a dysfunction in one of the components of learning that takes place in the brain. It is variously used to refer to a variety of learning problems that are probably brain related. A strict construction of the term *learning disability,* distinguishes it from *learning difficulty,* stating that "Individuals with learning difficulties may appear to possess the characteristics of a person with learning disabilities. However, it is only when those learning difficulties are so pervasive or severe that they markedly interfere with learning or day-to-day living that a learning disability is suspected" (Lokerson, n.d.,p. 1).

Many authors take a less strict point of view, using the term *learning disability* to refer to a range of difficulties that are more or less likely to be biologically based. A typical such definition is a significant discrepancy between estimated learning potential and actual performance (this definition was used to diagnose Elsa, in section 10.1.1, as language-learning disabled). For adults, who have often developed coping strategies that compensate for learning disabilities, the distinction is very hard to make clearly. In this chapter, learning disability is used for difficulties whose origin is more probably in the neurological structure, whereas *learning dysfunction* is used for difficulties whose origin is less likely to be in brain structure but might be. The distinction is not exact.

One useful taxonomy of the components of learning that are affected by learning disabilities is presented in a pamphlet on attention deficit disorder (Silver, n.d.). Silver's components are input (recording information in the brain), integration (organization and comprehension of information), memory (storage and retrieval), and output (communication or use of the information). Common learning disabilities can be organized according to these categories.

Input

Although we receive input through all the senses, the ones that have the most impact on classroom learning are hearing and sight. More precisely put, learning results from the effects in the brain (i.e., perceptions) of what we hear and see.

Visual perceptual disabilities usually have a spatial aspect. They may appear in the form of problems with subtle differences in position or relationships, for example confusion of *b* and *d.* A 3 could be rotated to appear as an *m.* Visual perceptual disabilities can also show up as difficulties with depth perception, orientation of self in space, judging distances, eye-body coordination, and difficulties focusing on the most important stimulus from among many. A messy desk might cause trouble for such a person when he or she has to focus on a single task.

Auditory perceptual disabilities often cause difficulty with distinguishing differences among sounds. Minimal pairs such as *boil* and *bowl* may be confused or even believed to be homophones. Silver gives the example of a person asked "How are you?" who hears "are as old" and answers "twenty five." (In a child this mismatched response could also be the result of an expectation, because children are so often asked "How old are you?") A student may have difficulty picking out the appropriate vocal stimulus from other sounds and thus be perceived by teachers or others as not paying attention. Such students may be affected by "auditory lag," the result of slower processing of sounds; the result may be that they miss part of what is said.

Integration

After information reaches the brain through perception, it must be ordered (sequencing) and understood (abstraction). Some individuals may have more difficulty with integration of data perceived visually, whereas others may have more difficulty with auditorily perceived information.

Sequencing disabilities appear in difficulties with narratives, particularly managing sequences of ideas or events. Beginning, middle, and end may be mixed up. Spelling errors will show up as reorderings of the letters, all of which may be present, or material may be copied in the wrong order.

Simultaneous processing disabilities are not mentioned in Silver's taxonomy, but they would seem to belong here. They may manifest as the severe inability to do even the kinds of everyday multitasking called on by taking notes while listening to a lecture, for example. Figure-ground problems (finding the appropriate stimulus among other stimuli) are listed as indicators of auditory or visual perceptual disabilities, but they may also represent dysfunction in integration.

Abstraction disabilities may show up as difficulties with making inferences, appropriate categorizing, seeing interrelations, or going from the specific to the general. Problems are likely to show up in making subtle semantic distinctions.

Memory

Along with integration, information must be stored and retrieved. Memory disabilities affect short-term and long-term memory, and they may be related to auditory or visual information.

Short-term memory disabilities are likely to appear when an unusual number of repetitions are needed to put material into memory. A person might have to go over new material 10 to 15 times, whereas most others would need 3 to 5 times.

Long-term memory is usually dependent on successful integration, in my opinion. Most people store information based on associations, categories, and hierarchies of data. Integration is usually even more important to successful retrieval. Difficulties with organized retrieval (speed, precision, and effort required) and ability to transfer what is learned from the original learning context to a new one could suggest long-term memory disabilities.

Output

Once information is retrieved from either short- or long-term memory, it is applied in some way. The usual forms are through language (words) and motor activities (actions). (Output also includes difficulties with computing and calculating, which are sometimes referred to as *dyscalculia.*) Needless to say, our primary interest is in language output.

Language disabilities may occur either in language production or reception, and of course each affects the other. Language production disabilities may show up for spoken language under either spontaneous or demand conditions. Spontaneous language occurs when we initiate a communication and can organize our thoughts and put together the language needed. Under demand conditions language is used in "real time" in a conversational setting, with little delay for internal language processing. Internal processing and speaking are simultaneous. A person with a demand disability may seem normal when speaking if not responding to a question; some such people learn to forestall demand conditions by talking constantly. Responses to questions may be monosyllabic, rambling, or characterized by groping for words.

Language reception difficulties affect listening and reading. Typical such dysfunctions are described above under the headings of input, integration, and memory.

The popular term *dyslexia* is most precisely used to refer to reading disabilities, though some use it as an inclusive term for language disabilities in general. Some of the difficulties that are symptomatic of dyslexia are perceptual, such as the switching or inversion of sounds or letters and confusion of sound-symbol relationships. Others may occur in the area of integration, when information is not further processed in some way.

Motor disabilities may be gross, affecting walking and large movements. They may also appear in difficulties coordinating groups of muscles (fine motor disability); such disabilities may affect writing, speaking, and so on. Thoughts may come much faster than the individual can express them, leading to apparent logjams.

You may also hear the term *attention deficit hyperactivity disorder* (ADHD); attention deficit disorder (ADD) also appears without hyperactivity. Although the symptoms of this disorder are most dramatic among children, there are attentional effects for adults as well, though usually much diminished. Silver (n.d.) defines hyperactivity as "a specific nervous-system-based difficulty which makes it hard for a person to control muscle (motor) activity" (p. 6). Distractibility is similarly defined as specific and nervous system based, in which all stimuli compete for attention and the attention span is short. Behavioral and social problems may appear as consequences of learning disabilities and attention deficit disorder, but they are not part of the disorder.

Learning disabilities tend to be more commonly addressed for children than for adults. This fact makes sense when we consider that children are in structured situations that are focused on how they learn. Adults, on the other hand, usually operate in relatively unstructured situations in which their performance is at issue. If they can find ways to end-run their disabilities and perform satisfactorily, the disabilities may never come to light. It is when they go back to school (as in the case of language courses) or move into jobs that require skills that are affected by their disabilities that the difficulties arise.

Learning disabilities are difficult to diagnose at any age. In adults, the task is complicated by their ability to find ways to avoid situations that tax areas of difficulty or develop compensating strategies. On an everyday level, all of us do some of this kind of thing: I regularly avoid situations that require a lot of rote memorizing, and I have routines that help me remember, for example, which periodicals I have read of the many that I receive and which I have yet to read. The difference for the learning disabled person is that he or she may end up with considerable self-limitation in activities undertaken or may be caught up short because automatic strategies do not work in a certain situation.

Diagnosis is also complicated in that learning disabilities take many forms in varying levels of severity and often with multiple subtypes. They often occur in unpredictable combinations. The taxonomy presented above is a very simplified version of the variations that appear in books about learning disabilities for specialists. When adolescents and adults are aware of learning disabilities, they may be ashamed of them and attempt to hide their disabilities by denial and defensiveness (Hartlage, 1985). An additional complicating factor in diagnosing learning disabilities is the possibility of poor educational background in the native language, fewer cultural opportunities, culture shock phenomena, and low proficiency in the language that is the medium of instruction. This last factor deserves special attention when you are considering whether an ESL student in an English-speaking country may have a learning disability. (For more information on working with learning disabilities in an ESL context, see Lingenfelter, n.d.)

For these reasons, and because a great deal of specialized expertise is needed in the area of learning disabilities, you will do best to seek diagnostic assistance from such resources as school psychologists, university counseling centers, special education teachers, and institutions or organizations that specialize in learning disabilities. Some resources to begin with are suggested in section 11.7.

11.2.2 Learning Disabilities and Foreign Language Learning

Learning disabilities and classroom foreign language learning are a notoriously unpromising combination. Barr (1993) states that "Recent findings show that most students with learning disabilities have inordinate difficulties in foreign language classes" (p. 1). Levine's (1987) exhaustive treatment of learning disabilities states, "No single content area is as commonly a threat to [people] with learning difficulties as is that of foreign languages" (p. 378). Barr (1993) cites Downey (1992) to say that modifications by the instructor are more helpful at the earlier stages of language learning, but that severe language or learning disabilities are likely to prevent attainment of more advanced proficiency.

Impediments to learning are attributed variously to perceptual, integration, and memory disabilities as well as specifically language-related problems such as processing vocabulary and syntax. Ganschow and Sparks (e.g., Sparks & Ganschow, 1995; Sparks et al., 1991) make a strong case for phonological processing problems as the primary culprit. Reading is certainly affected by the ability to link, store, and retrieve sounds and symbols, often referred to as *phonetic coding*.

On the other hand, other researchers believe that Sparks and Ganschow make too strong a case for linguistic coding deficits (especially phonological). Many researchers, though not excluding such abilities as sound discrimination and integration of sounds and symbols, prefer to stay open to a wider range of dysfunctions, both generally integrative (e.g., simultaneous processing) and specifically linguistic (e.g., syntax or semantics). For example, Levine (1987) says that "Attention deficits, language disabilities, specific memory dysfunctions, sequential disorganization, and weaknesses of verbal cognition singly or in clusters deter foreign language learning" (p. 378). I would add that difficulties in simultaneous processing and the various activities covered by the term *abstraction*, including ability to shift mental set, also affect language learning.

Affective factors almost certainly play a role as well. Sparks and Ganschow's strong position on their linguistic coding deficit hypothesis has ignited controversy on this point, too. For example, MacIntyre (1995a, 1995b), representative of researchers who actively disagree with Sparks and Ganschow, says that they "have relegated language anxiety to the status of an unfortunate side effect" (p. 90) in his report on the effects of anxiety on learning.

Adult learners are sometimes surprised by the emergence of difficulties that suggest that they may have learning disabilities. Residual weaknesses that may have been overcome in other subjects and overlearned and thus automatized in the native language are exposed under the multiple demands of foreign language learning. Compensatory strategies no longer work. Many such learners can pick up practical language in the context of real language use in communities where the language is spoken, but it is much rarer for them to achieve much in the way of grammatical or syntactic precision (for an exception to this statement, see the description of Patricia in section 11.2.4).

Several studies have found the MLAT to be an excellent predictor of trouble for university students in foreign language classes, when such trouble may be related to learning disabilities. These students are highly overrepresented among those who seek exemption from foreign language requirements or who petition for alternative learning routes. Very low MLAT scores on Parts 3, 4, and 5 are especially indicative (Gajar, 1987; Ganschow et al., 1991).

11.2.3 Signs of Learning Disabilities

Box 11.1 presents difficulties that appear in adults and that may suggest underlying learning disabilities. It is organized according to the taxonomy of learning disabilities that was described above in section 11.2.1. Again, many of the signs are common to most of us. The issue is how much and how often they appear, and how much impact they have on the individual's life.

Before you read further, I suggest that you return to the description of Joe in section 11.1 and see how many of the signs from Box 11.1 you can find. After that, see how it fits with a little more information about Joe.

On an instrument that asks him to complete the stem "I am . . ." 20 times, he describes himself as honest, religious, neat, caring, a hard worker, a good parent, security-minded, a good husband, a good American, mechanical minded, considerate, compatible, "I'm very patience" [sic], a good father, loyal, and a good employee. He has a high preference for visual learning and heavily prefers spatial to abstract learning. He has a moderately strong score on a test of finding changes in detail on successive versions of a visual image.

It is possible that Joe has a subtle learning disability or a set of them that are related to verbal functioning. He has succeeded in avoiding activities requiring high verbal facility by his life choices, for example his very conventional lifestyle as indicated by his self-description and his limited education, which he undertook in a technical field. He has thus never had to confront his limitations explicitly. In his native language, Joe can use overlearned language to accomplish nearly everything he needs to

Box 11.1 Signs of Possible Learning Disability

Perceptual: Auditory
  May not hear rhyme well
  Figure-ground: difficulty picking out the appropriate auditory stimulus
    from others
  Perceived as not paying attention
  May miss part of what is said by others
  Auditory lag: slow processing of sounds, words, sentences

Perceptual: Visual
  Transpositions and inversions of letters
  Difficulties with copying (see also output: language: writing and
    output: motor)
  Figure-ground: picking out the appropriate visual stimulus from
    others
  Problems with depth perception, judging distances
  Eye-body coordination dysfunctions

Integration: Sequencing & Simultaneous Processing
  Keeping things in order (e.g., months of year, lists of instructions,
    alphabet)
  Doing two things at once, e.g., listening and taking notes
  Difficulties with organizing work, projects, notes, life activities
  Problems working with background noise

Integration: Abstraction
  May not understand humor
  Takes what is said literally
  Misses nuances
  Difficulties with categorizing information and seeing interrelations
  Problems with organizing activities, learned material
  Trouble with generalizing and applying new rules

"Memory"
  Poor short-term auditory or visual memory.
  A quick forgetter as much as a slow learner.
  Difficulties memorizing facts, new terminology, etc.
  Needs a great many repetitions
  Trouble with transferring new information to different contexts

Output: Language—Speaking and Listening
  May take time to mentally process conversation in native language
  Pronunciation problems in native language

Box 11.1 Continued

Problems with word-finding in native language
Difficulty responding to questions in native language (demand
  disability)
Marked dysfluency in native language conversation (demand disability)

Output: Language—Reading
Reads native language slowly
Difficulties with reading comprehension in native language lead to
  problems summarizing
Loses place in a series of readings.
Demonstrates persistent inaccuracies in writing the language

Output: Language—Writing
Severe handwriting problems (dysgraphia)
Demonstrates persistent inaccuracies in writing
Difficulties in listening and taking notes (sound interference and short-
  term auditory dysfunction)
Difficulties with copying (see also perceptual: visual and output: motor)
Severe and persistent spelling problems in native language
Has difficulty putting ideas on paper

Output: Motor Activity
Difficulties with physical coordination
Difficulties with copying (see also perceptual: visual and output:
  language: writing)

"General Functioning"
General abilities and language skills are inconsistent with each other
Level of work varies from day to day; reports "good" and "bad" days
Becomes disoriented, confusing right and left, north and south
Difficulties remembering time, "loses" time
Negative self image (lazy, stupid, careless, etc.)
Seems to "switch off" or reports doing so
Short concentration span
Needs to be given information more than once

SOURCE: Adapted from material in Lee (n.d.-a) and Silver (n.d.).

---

do. He has developed strategies (such as massive repetition for learning
lines in a play) to take care of verbal demands in his life.

Joe may have some dysfunction in his visual perception (transposed letters), but his visual memory seems to be in the average range. On the other hand, there is a suggestion in the data about Joe that he may have more auditory dysfunction. He mishears words in his native language; for instance, he referred to "congregating" verbs. His writing "I am very patience" could be the kind of error people make when in a hurry; on the other hand, in view of some of the other evidence, it might also be diagnostic of some kind of language dysfunction. When I visited his class to observe what was happening with him, I found his auditory short-term memory to be extraordinarily small. He could manage two or three meaning units, and no more.

Joe's MLAT, both total and part scores, are almost rock-bottom. On the Hartmann Boundary Questionnaire he is an outlier at the thick boundary end of the continuum, suggesting low tolerance of ambiguity. These, and his weakness in analytic processing, suggest possible dysfunction at the level of integration, further supporting the hypothesis that Joe has a learning disability, as well as some areas of strength (e.g., perception of detailed differences in visual images). (You can review these tests and questionnaires in Chapters 6 and 9.) If further diagnosis and help were needed to meet Joe's learning needs, I would feel justified in requesting it.

11.2.4 Additional Cases

As you read about Deborah, look for evidence that she may be learning disabled. In what areas of the taxonomy in section 11.2.1 would Deborah's learning problems fall? Come up with some suggestions you might want to make to Deborah of techniques she could use to study.

Deborah is coming for help with some specific difficulties. She says that she is "dyslexic;" she says she became aware of her own dyslexia when her daughter was formally diagnosed as dyslexic. Deborah has developed some strategies for coping with her language-learning difficulties; one of them is to picture words as if they were being projected onto a screen. Today, she tells you that she is having problems with memorizing new words. She can retain them for a short time, but then she forgets them and cannot associate them with any meaning. When she does not hear a native speaker (her teacher, in this case) for a while, she forgets what that person's voice sounds like and feels that her comprehension regresses when this happens. She feels concerned about an upcoming vacation period that will mean that she does not hear her teacher for several days in a row. In addition, Deborah tells you that she is getting frustrated watching videotapes, because she concentrates too much on all the words she recognizes but cannot associate with any meaning. Our only questionnaire information about Deborah is that she is an ISTP.

It is likely that use of the term *dyslexia* in this case is in the broadest sense, meaning language dysfunction, rather than the more restricted meaning of dysfunctional reading. There is little information about how Deborah reads; we know much more about her difficulties retaining auditory input. It sounds as though Deborah may have auditory input problems and difficulty with processing auditory input. It is entirely possible, however, that this is not a case of learning disability at all. Perhaps it is a matter of very strong learning style preference (introversion is often associated with a preference for visual learning), or affective issues (anxiety about dependency matters, for instance). It may also be a combination of all three factors. If you think you need more exact diagnosis to clarify these various hypotheses, it is time to seek specialized assistance.

The concept of low-level, localized learning dysfunction (if not full-fledged learning disability) can help us understand students such as Shirley (section 10.4) and Holly (section 5.2), who make a very strong demand for external structuring beyond what seems reasonable for their level of ability. They may have some low-level learning disability, probably at the level of integration, and more specifically in the domains of sequential and simultaneous processing. If they cannot manage intake and sequencing together, it becomes more important to them to have sequencing provided from the outside, so they can concentrate their resources on intake. Here is another case:

What evidence can you find that might suggest learning disability?
What other hypotheses can you make for what is happening?
If you were Evan's teacher, what would you do for him?
How would you propose that he help himself?

Evan has been referred to you because he is having difficulty making it off a long-standing learning plateau. He began this round of language training with a measurable level of proficiency in the language from previous study in college and one semester in a family stay program in the country where the language was spoken. He had also had overseas sojourns in two other countries and had learned some of the languages spoken there. Of his many language learning experiences, Evan described the present one as the least enjoyable experience of his life, largely because of the "sword of Damocles" hanging over his head in the form of a requirement to achieve a certain level of proficiency to maintain his status in the institution. He has always been a good student: He graduated from college with honors and holds a master's degree in international relations. On the Scholastic Aptitude Test, he scored nearly perfectly in the verbal section (but near the national mean on the quantitative section).

He described two areas of difficulty: (a) discrimination and pronunciation of certain vowel sounds, especially diphthongs; and (b) retaining vocabulary. Evan says he can read well enough, but it's hard to "cough the stuff up," that is, produce coherent language in real time. He is comfortable with reading or listening for gist and does it effectively, but he has much more trouble when he thinks he has to get details. This leads to anxiety that in turn makes things worse for him.

Evan admits that at the beginning of the training program, he wasted a lot of time using poor language learning strategies. He acted as though the program were a classroom language program such as the previous university language courses he had taken, which had focused on grammar. It took a conference with his teacher to help him understand the need to use a different set of learning strategies to cope with the communicative language program he was in now. Even with the change in his learning strategies, he was still having trouble.

In the course of the discussion, it turned out that Evan has suffered some hearing loss and was diagnosed as "dysgraphic" as a youngster (he is about 30 now). This may have led him to some perfectionism and anxiety about errors, perhaps as a result of not knowing whether the error was due to the usual learning mistakes or a result of his hearing loss or dysgraphia.

Evan suggested that his anxiety might be related to the threat to his self-esteem in language learning. He is also frustrated by being one of the few unmarried students—recently he tried to start a study group, but couldn't get it off the ground because of other students' family commitments. In the case of other languages he had learned, it had been "a social thing outside the classroom," but that doesn't seem to be possible here.

On the learning style questionnaires, Evan reports himself as an ENTJ. He falls within the normal range on the Hartmann Boundary Questionnaire, suggesting average tolerance for ambiguity. On the SILL, he favors metacognitive and compensation strategies, and tends to reject memory and affective strategies. At the beginning of training, Evan reported himself as highly motivated for his assignment and for language learning, though somewhat anxious about it. He finds the following nearly indispensable: chances to get up and move around the classroom, field trips and immersion experiences, coping with "over-the-head" language, discovery of patterns, roleplays, constant use of the target language, and frequent use of videotapes. On the other hand, he also makes a strong statement that the teacher has the main responsibility to see that he gets what he needs, and he wants to master one thing before going on to another. Evan's MLAT scaled score is somewhat below average for the language program he is in. His part scores are as follows: Part 1—62%; Part 2—73%; Part 3—44%; Part 4—39%; Part 5—62% and Total Score—54%.

In section 11.2.1, it was mentioned that it is unusual for people with serious learning disabilities to reach high levels of proficiency. Joe, for instance, probably has a substantial learning disability, and he is unlikely to reach professional proficiency no matter how long he studies because of the demands for lexical and structural precision at that proficiency level. Under most circumstances, you should help Joe develop realistic expectations of success, at the same time focusing on what he *can* do. On the other hand, many people who do well in school and in their careers (such as Evan and others) may turn out to have a localized or relatively minor learning disability. This disability may affect the kinds of learning strategies they need and their learning styles. (Conversely, we can also consider people whose learning styles are very rigid to be somewhat dysfunctional at best in the domains of learning affected by those styles.)

Patricia exemplifies learners who reach very high language proficiency levels despite some level of learning disability and some style rigidities. Patricia came for language proficiency testing in German. The examiner is interested in students with learning disabilities and so made the following note for the files.

This student has already tested in reading and speaking in two Romance languages at a very high level of proficiency (equivalent to ACTFL-ILR superior). And the Germanic language in which she was being tested was at the working proficiency level. When we completed the proficiency test, she commented on her reading proficiency (above working proficiency): She was a little surprised because she said she's dyslexic. We asked her to talk more on how she had learned all those languages so well. She has really conquered her reading disability. She said that for one thing, she's a "street learner." She said there's nothing more deadly to her learning than reviewing a verb conjugation on the blackboard. She spent a total of four years in France, being exposed to the language in almost every imaginable context.

On all the language proficiency tests Patricia said the hardest part for her was a portion where she had to read a short passage which served as a stimulus for her to give a monologue, and do it in the very short time allocated. My own notes on the test say that she is a master of getting the most out of the language she controls. She stayed off complex subjects. We suspected that her comprehension was less than it appeared, and we turned out to be right when we checked. Patricia is superb at "winging it," guessing, and using her world knowledge to make the most of her reading and listening comprehension. Her reading fluency was on the low side, but we didn't suspect dyslexia until she told us. She said the size and color of the print (very clear) made a big difference.

The kind of feedback we have received from Patricia about her testing experience suggests ways in which we can meet the needs of learners with localized dysfunctions. In section 11.5, there is some general discussion of steps teachers can take to make it easier for students with learning disabilities to learn languages.

11.3 Extreme Affective Reaction

We have seen some cases in which students came in great emotional distress about their language learning. In many cases, the root of the distress can be traced to learning style mismatches between student and program, as was the case for Elsa (10.1.1) and Mark (10.5.1), and appropriate changes can be negotiated. We met other students in Chapter 7 whose primary issues were in the affective domain. Sometimes, though, it is not that clear. Consider Laurie. What are your hypotheses about what is going on with her?

Laurie, whose parents are immigrants, is a student in a large language program with multiple class sections. She walked into my office, and I could almost feel how tense and intense she was. She immediately told me that she was feeling very anxious in this, her second round of trying to learn this language. The first time, she'd been more relaxed in class, but then she'd been ill and forgot a lot. She felt that she'd never caught up with her class then. When she took a proficiency test a couple of years after using the language overseas, she thought she had lost ground and said, "I was disappointed, and I refused to sign the paper that said I'd received my results. Maybe I was dubbed a rebel, then. Besides, all the feedback was negative. I'd like some encouragement. I used to be a concert pianist and taught music, too. I respond better to positive feedback and tend to shut out the negative." Laurie then went on to talk about herself and her own learning in remarkably negative ways: For instance, she talked about her teacher's help as "baby-sitting" and about being unable to quit comparing herself with her classmates, despite her knowledge that it was unhelpful. She said, "I've never been so self-destructive before in my life. It's as if all possible control has been taken from me. I'm beginning to see people as enemies, not friends any more, even people I really know want to be helpful. It may be in my head, but I see the teachers of this language turning their heads away from me." Laurie described going into a tailspin when she received feedback that she was unlikely to reach her proficiency goal at her present rate of progress. She also reacted to the prospect of the upcoming proficiency test with great anxiety: "thinking of it, it feels cold, like being under a microscope. It makes me go blank."

Laurie was further distressed by the fact that she had spent her lifetime breaking down barriers to her achievement and had never let anything get to her like this. I asked her what she thought was different about this experience, and she answered that she felt that she was getting constant negative judgments that she was not living up to expectations, that she was not expected to succeed. We talked about Laurie's feeling that she had been "written off" by the program. She perceived all the other students as getting affirmation and encouragement and being challenged by the teacher, whereas she felt that it didn't much matter to the teacher what she did. She said, "Most of the teachers are pleasant, but one or two terrify me: They are very critical and won't speak to me in the hallway. I feel stupid and unwelcome. In class I know the strategies to use, but I forget to use them when I begin to get mixed up on grammar points."

We discussed the fact that Laurie feels that she has no control at all, and she's used to being in control and taking control when she needs it. This situation isn't permitting that. As a concert musician, she has had to submit to direction, and it made her feel manipulated and pressured then. She seemed to think that the teachers in the language program were doing something of the same kind of thing as the manipulative, tyrannical conductor. She said of the teachers, "They're nice people, but they get defensive when they teach. Students with problems are dismissed and then feel bad."

278 UNDERSTANDING SECOND LANGUAGE DIFFICULTIES

As the proficiency test approached, Laurie reported headaches and panicky feelings whenever she thought about the test. She was particularly concerned about the timed sections of the test; she has noticed that her performance goes down drastically under timed conditions. On the MLAT, Laurie's overall score was about average for the U.S. population at large but considerably below average for the relatively selective program she was in. No part scores were available. The only other available questionnaire results were the MBTI (ENTJ) and the SILL, on which Laurie reported that she most uses social strategies (learning from and with others) and least used memory strategies.

What is your take on Laurie?

Laurie is in a very difficult and stressful situation. She has had a history of achieving by perseverance, strength of character, social skills, and her wits. She has usually found some handle in which she could take control (necessary for all of us in one way or another, but especially for an ENTJ, whom Keirsey & Bates (1978) nicknamed the "field marshal"). Unfortunately, she is in a situation in which none of her usual strategies is serving her well. The proficiency test is something of an immovable object. Laurie is really in above her head. Her tested aptitude is below average in this program, and thus she starts from behind her classmates. She does not have either the aptitude or the learning strategies to catch up, and her anxiety about her relative position and her prospects of reaching her proficiency goal has mounted up to the point in which it is sapping the cognitive and emotional resources she does have. Additional pressures such as timed tasks interfere seriously with Laurie's ability to think and process.

In addition, Laurie has gone through life getting her sense of her own value from her achievements and believing that others value her for the same things. When she fails at the achievements that she believes have provided her value in the eyes of others, she begins to believe that they cannot possibly value her. (With lesser intensity, this mechanism is characteristic of many intuitive thinking types, who value themselves for their competence.)

The conceptualization that she has nothing that others can value comes to shape Laurie's perceptions of the reactions of others to her, so that she starts to feel written off, disliked. Things begin to be interpreted in the light of this perception, and it is possible that Laurie begins to act in ways that elicit some of the behavior she fears. Her teachers, in the meantime, cannot figure out what is going on.

What would you want to suggest to Laurie's teachers?
What would you do if you were Laurie's teacher?
(We will return to Laurie before this chapter ends.)

11.4 Self-Defeating Students

Sometimes you run across students who seem determined to sabotage their own success. It is bad enough when they only defeat themselves; it is worse when they lash out at the program and the other people in it, as if they wanted to bring everyone down with them. Unfortunately, there are no easy answers for dealing with such situations. Melvin is an example of this kind of student.

Melvin has come to see his program supervisor. He has announced that he needs effective teaching so he can pass his course. He feels he's made considerable progress, but he is stymied by the bad teaching he is receiving. He feels frustrated and angry. When asked what he is doing for himself, he says he is listening to lesson tapes, but their quality is really bad. He goes on for some time about how bad the tapes are, then stops himself and asks, "Am I using defense mechanisms?" (All students in the program have recently had a lecture on how defense mechanisms are often used to avoid learning.) The response to Melvin's question is that whether or not he was using defense mechanisms was less important than whether they were getting in the way of his learning. Melvin sidesteps this point to describe how he did well in classes when the teacher was effective; indeed, he was better than the other students. It was when new material was introduced and he started working with the present, ineffective teacher that things started going downhill. When asked what more he is doing to learn, he says, "It may seem juvenile, but I need to be led." The interviewer comments on how angry Melvin seems, and he says, "Yes! I had a bad start, some of it was me, and the (organizational) system is really messing me up. But I'm finally beginning to pull up even with the class again." We learn that the final test, which is looming large in Melvin's view, is important to him because it will prove to the faculty that he really can learn. After considerable discussion of specifics of the learning strategies he is using, he and his interviewer agree on a set of learning techniques for him to try, along with a considerable emphasis on ways to manage his feelings, which are clearly getting in his way.

Melvin returns for a couple of additional interviews. Each seems to follow a course very similar to the first one. Melvin complains to anyone who will listen to him about how ill-served he is, but he does not try any of the suggestions that have been made to him.

What is going on with Melvin? If you had him in your program, how would you work with him?

It is hard for the supervisor and teachers in the program to be sympathetic to Melvin. His classmates almost certainly wish he were not in their class. It is very likely that Melvin's issues have very little to do with his language class and a great deal to do with feelings he carries around with him everywhere he goes. He has a fair amount of ability, which keeps him "afloat," but he is probably unhappy everywhere he ends up and yet in his view it is the fault of the people around him, who are not meeting his needs. Melvin wants to be taken care of (reflected in "I need to be led") well beyond the point that most adults can expect such caretaking. He seeks help but then rejects it because it does not meet an ideal that he has in his mind. As a result, he is likely to find his desire to be taken care of frustrated regularly, and in turn, he will become angry, pushing away any prospect of getting what he wants.

We have seen a tendency in other students to externalize anger and disappointment, blaming the program, teacher, and classmates. The difference is that for most, the tendency is self-limiting. Most students also make use of the resources the program offers, and while they may not be completely satisfied and may complain a lot, they also learn and can usually experience gratitude as well as disappointment. Melvin, in contrast, seems to have caught himself in a never-ending spiral of frustration.

11.5 Coping

This chapter is about the students you may not be able to figure out on your own. We have met students with learning disabilities, both mild and relatively severe, as well as students whose feelings have made them their own worst enemies and have caused their teachers a lot of concern at the same time. What kind of help would you want to ask for in working with each kind of student?

11.5.1 Possible Learning Disabilities

As mentioned in section 11.3.1, when you think you are dealing with a learning disability, and a firm diagnosis will make a difference to how you go about working with the student, you can turn to special education teachers, school psychologists, counseling centers, consultant psychologists, institutions that specialize in diagnosing and working with learning disabilities, and public service organizations. (Vision and hearing problems should be ruled out before a formal assessment is done.)

Manifestations of learning disabilities are probably even more numerous than the kinds and clusters of learning disabilities themselves. For example, some learning disabilities will lead learners to be very detail oriented, as a way of getting control of the uncontrollable. Others promote a very global learning style. We see this difference in Joe and Patricia. Joe is very detail oriented and has difficulty managing large chunks of information. Patricia, on the other hand, has developed a number of rather global strategies that help her compensate for her difficulty managing details. Joe is almost certainly a Type 4 learner (field dependent and field insensitive). Patricia is probably a Type 3 learner (field dependent but field sensitive). Evan probably has localized dysfunctions and some limitations in his verbal analytic skills, but his record suggests a high level of overall intelligence, a substantial asset in his learning.

While you are waiting for your consultations to be completed, there are some general techniques that you can try. Although there are wide differences among learning disabilities, a number of techniques can help you work more successfully with students who have them. Box 11.2 lists a number of accepted approaches that work for many such students. (A

Box 11.2 Common Approaches to Working With Learning
Disabilities

Work to the learner's strengths and avoid reinforcing failure.
Stretch the weaker functions slowly and with as much built-in
success as possible.
*Make heavy use of advance organizers to help the student organize his or
her time and strategies.*
These can include a detailed syllabus, a calendar of due dates, and
content previews.
Work on one problem at a time.
It is easy for people with learning disabilities to get overloaded.
Give plenty of time.
For perceptual processes, for organizing thoughts, for production.
Provide as much close structuring as the learner seems to need.
Avoid letting go before the learner is ready, but don't hold on any
longer than necessary.
*Remind the learner of a strategy as often and as long as he or she needs
you to.*
It's not "cheating" but providing necessary support.
Calibrate the "chunks" to the learner's intake capacity.
Sometimes they will have to be very small.
Present learning material in a variety of different ways.
It helps with generalization, which many with learning disabilities
find difficult.
Overlearning helps. Practice, practice, practice.
Find different ways so there are more contexts to connect with.
Increase time on task.
This increases the opportunity for learning to take place.
Seek ways to provide multisensory input and practice.
Kinesthetic learning is often of great help; look for ways to build it in.
*Encourage use of technology like computers, calculators, spelling
dictionaries, memory aids.*
Why rub two sticks together when you can throw a switch?
*Appeal to the "right hemisphere" with color, patterns, imagination, and
visualization.*
These enhance the more conventional learning.
Another "right-hemisphere" approach is to give the whole picture.
This will help those with a global style.
*Recognize and discuss the nature of the individual's difficulties with him
or her.*
This helps learners put their condition in perspective and take
control of the learning.
SOURCE: Adapted from Lee (n.d.-b).

promising attempt to teach foreign languages to people with learning disabilities using some of these principles is described in Sparks et al., 1991.) As you try some of these suggestions, treat them as based on another set of hypotheses, similar to the guesses you have been making about the learners you have met in earlier chapters of this book. For example, you may make a guess that a student has some difficulty with simultaneous processing. In that case, you would try conscious application of the principle of working on only one task at a time.

11.5.2 Emotional Reactions and Self-Defeating Patterns

Students who have persistent emotional upheavals or who are self-defeating despite your best efforts can also cause you to expend a lot of energy. Help is also available for such students. The first recourse is your "chain of command." Most teachers work in organizations, which means that they have supervisors, who in turn have their supervisors. In more than a quarter century of working in a bureaucratic hierarchy, I have learned that the chain of command has its uses in helping me do my job. A good supervisor is not only an ear and sometimes a source of helpful advice (because not so deeply involved), he or she can also serve as something of a firescreen when the heat gets too great. The supervisory chain can take a lot of heat for you both from discontented students and their sponsors and from above in your own hierarchy. Your role, though, is to keep your supervisors well informed, keep good records just in case there is a more formal dispute, and do your best to ensure that your supervisors are justified in their support of you.

Sometimes there are events in the students' outside lives that can go a long way to explaining their stressed-out behavior. Students often have work, family, or school constraints in addition to their language study. Family commitments and family problems, personal illness, financial or legal problems, and other personal problems can take away a lot of energy and motivation. These things are not your responsibility, though you may feel sympathy and look for ways to lighten the load (appropriately).

For a student such as Laurie or Melvin, you may well benefit from professional consultation. In the cases of both these learners, after ruling out poor learning strategies, learning style mismatches, and stresses in their lives outside the classroom, explore the possibility of perceptual or cognitive dysfunction, for which the emotional reaction might be a smokescreen. If there is evidence of dysfunction, it may be time to turn to the professional resources mentioned.

On the other hand, if the issue seems truly emotional and embedded in the student's personality structure, and if it is destructive to the student's learning and to others around him or her, look for such resources as employee assistance programs, counseling centers, community mental health clinics, and so on. The first step might be to consult with these resources yourself about their view of what was going on and to find out what services would be available. You can also use these resources to help manage your own stress, so that you will be in a better position to work with the others involved in the matter. Seek guidance on how to encourage the student to make use of the service as well.

Depending on the teacher's own personality structure, the urge to move in and save the troubled student is greater or less. Some teachers can let go of such students quite readily (though they may continue to be concerned about them). Others may want so much to be able to help the student through the crisis that they become overinvolved. Keeping a balance is an important part of taking care of yourself.

For a Laurie, do your best and keep looking for ways to help her with her anxiety and her learning strategies. For a Melvin, keep from letting yourself feel backed into a corner and responsible for Melvin's troubles. There may be some appropriate adjustments you can make in the curriculum and teaching style to meet some of Melvin's or Laurie's needs. Following through on such adaptations is entirely appropriate. The chances are, though, that you will not satisfy Melvin, and Laurie will still be anxious. Your situation will be similar for many others who display some of the difficulties we have been discussing. At a certain point you have to say, "I did the best I could, and that was good enough."

11.6 Practice

1. Which of the approaches in Box 11.2 would you recommend for Joe, Deborah, Evan, and Patricia? Try writing out a short prescription for each.

2. Using the information in Box 11.1, examine some of the cases in earlier chapters. Is there evidence to suggest that any of them might

have learning dysfunctions or learning disabilities as described in this chapter? If so, what would you suggest doing for them?

3. Have you had first-hand experience with learning disabilities or know others who have? If so, what can you add to what is presented here?

4. How can you take care of yourself when you have a difficult student such as Melvin or a student such as Laurie whom you cannot figure out how to help?

5. Have you ever felt similar to Laurie or Melvin, yourself? If so, what would have been helpful for you?

6. What are your local resources for dealing with students whose needs are difficult to address on your own?

11.7 More Information

Information about learning disabilities is available from a wide range of sources. For those who prefer to study in depth, two very fat tomes from among the many resources on the subject will give an in-depth picture of the subject in general: Myers & Hammill (1990) is slightly less theoretical and is more oriented to the classroom practitioner than Levine (1987), whose focus is more toward the medical or psychological practitioner. Both are excellent sources of information. Surfing the World Wide Web will also pay dividends. Boxes 11.1 and 11.2 use material from a Web site (the Dyslexia 2000 Network, at http://www.furturenet.co.uk/charity/ado/index.html). Another useful starting place is Learning Disabilities and Foreign Languages Treasure Chest (http://www.fln.vcu.edu/ld/ld.html). Either of these sites contains valuable material and links that allow exploration of related topics and other relevant sites.

Specific material on learning disabilities and foreign or second language learning is somewhat less available. A number of articles address the subject; those cited here such as Gajar (1987) and Ganschow et al. (1991, 1993) are good starting points for further investigation of research findings on learning disability and foreign language learning. Vickie Barr's (1993) Eric Digest summarizes the reports in a conference on foreign language and learning disability that took place in 1992. In the second language realm, Lingenfelter (n.d.) applies knowledge about learning disabilities to the ESL population in Canada and at the same time provides a wealth of information about the nature of learning disabilities, ways to recognize and test them, and some ways to address the needs of learning disabled students both in general and with limited English.

A very readable but at the same time profound look at factors that cause emotional reactions in classroom settings is Salzberger-Wittenberg, Henry, and Osborne (1983), *The Emotional Experience of Learning and Teaching*. Review of the works about defense mechanisms that were described at the end of Chapter 7 would also be helpful. Again, insights in Stevick (1980), *Teaching languages: A way and ways*, bear directly on the emotional interactions between student and teacher.

The following are some resources related to learning disabilities, most from Lokerson (n.d.):

Adult Dyslexia Organisation (ADO)
336 Brixton Road
London, UK SW97AA

(0171) 924 9559 (telephone)
(0171) 274 7840 (fax)
e-mail: adorg@ibm.net
http://www.futurenet.co.uk/charity/ado/index.html

American Speech-Language-Hearing Association
10801 Rockville Pike
Rockville, MD 20852-3279

800-638-8255, 301-897-5700 (telephone)
301-897-0157 (TTY)
301-571-0457 (fax)

Children with Attention Deficit Disorders (CHADD)
4999 N. W. 70th Ave., Suite 309
Plantation, FL 33317

305-792-8100 (telephone)

Division for Learning Disabilities (DLD)
The Council for Exceptional Children
1920 Association Dr.
Reston, VA 22901

703-620-3660 (telephone)

Learning Disabilities Association of America (LDA)
4156 Library Road
Pittsburgh, PA 15234

412-341-1515 (telephone)

National Adult Literacy and Learning Disabilities Center (NALLD)
Academy for Educational Development
1875 Connecticut Ave., N.W.
Washington, DC 20009-1202

800-953-2553 (telephone)

National Attention Deficit Disorder
   Association (ADDA)
P.O. Box 488
West Newbury, MA 01985

800-487-2282 (telephone)

National Center for Learning
   Disabilities (NCLD)
99 Park Avenue, 6th Floor
New York, NY 10016

212-687-7211 (telephone)

Orton Dyslexia Society
724 York Road
Baltimore, MD 21204

800-222-3123 (telephone)

A large number of Canadian resources are listed in Lingenfelter (n.d.).

12

On Your Own

In the previous chapter, we worked with some hard situations that come up in the area of student learning difficulties. Most of the time, student needs are more routine. Nevertheless, they have their challenges, not least because there usually is something you can do. Many of the students you work with will have multiple causes for their difficulties: It is seldom the case that the only problem is poor strategies or a gross mismatch between student and teacher learning style or tendency to high anxiety, and so on. Usually, all of these—and the other factors we have looked at—are interwoven. One may be temporally the first factor, but by the time the difficulty reaches you, the other aspects may have become so tangled in that you will need to address all of them together.

In this chapter, we revisit learning strategies, student feelings, learning style mismatches, your expectations and feelings, and taking care of yourself in several ways. Although the focus of the book is not on what to do, taking considered action can be a good way of testing your hypotheses (as we saw in section 11.5.1 about addressing learning disabilities). In the cases that follow, some suggestions are made to be try out with the student. Each is based on a set of hypotheses about what is going on with the student. If a suggestion works, the underlying hypothesis receives some support. If it does not, an alternative hypothesis may be called for.

12.1 *John* Revisited

Let us review John and see how some of what we have looked at would apply to him. Here is what we know about John (taken from earlier chapters).

John is a highly successful senior executive with considerable experience in taking over and solving problem situations. He was appointed to a responsible position that required substantial language proficiency in speaking and reading. John entered his study of language with a great deal of self-confidence and motivation; he says he has never encountered a problem for which he couldn't find a practical solution. After six weeks of language training, using a mix of communicative and more structured training to help prepare him for this position, he found out that his proposed assignment had been canceled. Despite that his training has been difficult for him, he wishes to continue studying the language to go to another position where the language is spoken, so he has remained in class.

After 8 weeks of language learning, John is still not making very good progress, and his classmates have begun to complain that he is holding them back. John himself has started to express concern that he will not achieve the level of language he needs for his professional purposes. You, as his teacher for the last month, are experiencing increasing frustration with his learning.

In the course of class activities and after a short interview with John, you get some more information.

John has never learned a foreign language before. As a child he had some problems with stuttering and received considerable training and attention from specialists for it. Today, his speech shows no sign of a stutter.

The first two weeks of training, John was in a class where students had a variety of language learning abilities. From the start, it was apparent that he had considerable trouble with listening comprehension and pronunciation and was trailing his classmates. Following the second week, for logistic reasons he was moved into a class with two students younger than he. His new classmates take a more leisurely approach to their study than his previous class.

John was upset by the change and wanted to remain with his previous classmates. He believed that he should be in class along with the "best and brightest" students, as well as people in more senior

290 UNDERSTANDING SECOND LANGUAGE DIFFICULTIES

positions, so he could be stimulated and challenged as well as associate with those closer in occupation. He asked to be returned to his original class and was counseled that he would do better in a class that moved ahead at a less pressured pace, so that he could get a solid base in the language on which to build as he continued to progress. He went along with this advice and continues to work in the slower-moving class, but he socializes actively during the breaks and outside class with his previous classmates. He thinks his current classmates are overly laid back and do not take their language learning seriously.

When the curriculum follows the textbook closely, John works steadily and systematically. He readily performs the drills and exercises that fill the text. When asked to participate in more free-form activities such as storytelling or roleplays, John grumbles and stumbles. He becomes upset when too much new vocabulary is introduced in the course of an hour's activities, and he regularly mistranslates because he assumes that every English word will have a close equivalent in the new language. He takes almost no conversational risks in the target language.

Early in the introduction of John in Chapter 1, I asked some questions. How would you answer them now?

What are your guesses about what is going on with John? What is your evidence for the guesses? What are the assets you see in John that you can use to work with him? What are his weak areas? What more would you like to know about him?

John's learning style is clear—in fact it is so clear that he has been presented as an prototype of a highly sequential processor who prefers to learn things one step at a time and in a clearly established order. His low tolerance of ambiguity can be inferred from his discomfort in taking risks involved in using language he does not feel he has mastered in relatively uncontrolled situations. John much prefers a program with a clear and detailed syllabus; he prefers the teacher to adhere closely to lesson plans that build up control of each piece of language in an orderly way.

How does John come out on some of the models used in the preceding chapters? On the four-track model introduced in Chapter 6, John works largely in Tracks 3 (Hard Work) and 4 (Control). His access to Track 1 (Interpersonal) is largely through extraversion; it is helpful because it leads his teachers to want to help him. He is very weak in Track 2 (Cognitive Flexibility). He probably has neither field independence nor field sensitivity, either of which would assist with the tolerance of ambiguity that is so beneficial in second language learning and is therefore probably a Type 4 learner. A learner with this kind of profile probably prefers to spend more time on railroads and highways (section 4.2.4) than on trails and especially open country. His lack of ambiguity tolerance causes him so much trouble in open country that he avoids it.

In the affective domain, John is characteristic of a number of learners who come to language learning from successful careers in which they have been able to maximize their preferences and avoid weakness. John has had a history of building his sense of self-efficacy and hence his self-esteem on his hard work, control, and ability to make contacts. On the four-track model, we can see that these areas are where John continues to put most of his energy (Tracks 3, 4, and, to some degree, 1). Unfortunately, his usual approach is not working very well for him.

John's approach is to resort to defensive behaviors. He engages in complaining and avoidance in particular; to some degree he blames the program. He appears to put much of his energy into socializing with students whose company enhances his sense of his own worth.

John has a number of strengths. He is used to working patiently to achieve results. He is self-disciplined and willing to accept help. He usually interacts well with people (though he is rather instrumental in his motivation for mixing with them). In areas other than language learning, John has considerable self-confidence. He is old enough to have a lot of knowledge and experience, on which he can draw both for topics and for ways of solving problems. His main lack is cognitive agility of the abstract sort needed in his language class.

12.2 Helping Students: Variations on Themes

Here is a little more information about John: He is an ESTJ (Chapter 6), with clear preferences. He has thick ego boundaries (Chapter 6), both internal and external (this pattern should be no surprise to you by now). His pattern on the MLAT part scores (Chapter 9) is the one I have found to be characteristic of many Type 4 learners: Parts 1 and 5 moderate; Parts

2, 3, and 4 quite low. John is thus consistent on the learning instruments and in his learning style.

When he studies, John goes through the lesson material that has been covered that day and the assignments the teacher has given, if any. He makes heavy use of word lists, which he reads through several times. He also uses audiotapes, which he does in a highly sequential manner. John has heard that he should listen and read without knowing every word, but when he tries it with authentic material, he finds the experience so chaotic that he has decided that it is not worth his time. Every time the teacher writes a word on the board, John writes it down in his notes. He hates it when the other students ask for new words, because it means more work for him. Another thing, John gets very uncomfortable in the long hours of class time, but he thinks it is improper to do anything but sit and try to pay attention.

Suppose John were to come to you for advice.
What would you like to tell him?

There are a number of things we could do for John, and high on the list is helping him use his time more effectively. John is very much a surface learner (Chapter 8). He probably sees his homework as tasks to be gotten through quickly and efficiently. He does not find the material very interesting for its own sake, so he does not invest much of himself in it. He has solved other problems by a frontal "attack," why not this one, too? If we are to help John work smart, the first step may be to make him aware of "deep" learning strategies (Chapter 8). John probably does not have much practice at using these for verbal material, but he may have used them for some other kind of learning or problem solving in the course of his education or his career. So drawing an analogy between John's previous experience and the demands of this one is a good start.

John will probably need explicit instructions on techniques to use. Begin by giving him some that do not require a lot of simultaneous processing. Provide step-by-step directions at first. As John becomes more comfortable with this kind of study, encourage him to suggest some of his own deep processing activities and give less step-by-step instruction. Let John start on materials that are likely to be fairly easy for him. Let him slowly build up his tolerance of increasing ambiguity and increasingly realistic language use, as he finds that he can succeed at this kind of activity.

John may also need to discharge some of his kinetic energy. Encourage him to put away the first-grade teacher in his head who is telling him to sit still and pay attention. Help John find some way to move during the long class hours. In addition, work with John to find material in the language on subjects he finds interesting. Once he gets enough of a base to read and listen without snags, he can get a lot of pleasure and incidental learning by books, periodicals, films, and so forth that he uses for pleasure as well as study. (This, by the way, is advice I give to almost everyone.) Making himself responsible for "every golden word" that goes by in class is a recipe for failure. John needs help setting priorities in the words he learns and the material he studies. Help him learn to give himself "advance organizers" by previewing material and making decisions about what is most important. John can probably also use some help with evaluating his progress and the effectiveness of his study activities.

Terry is a very different kind of learner from John. As you read about her, decide what is going on with her and consider the advice you would give her to help her learn more effectively.

Terry grew up bilingual, born and raised in a country that speaks a language cognate to the one she is now studying. However, she has never learned a foreign language in an academic environment. She has been in your class for some weeks, now, and is not progressing as well as you expected she would. Despite being urged to focus more on structure and accuracy, Terry seems to think that the best way for her to learn the language is to collect the maximum amount of vocabulary and phrases. She uses every available opportunity to get new words and expressions. She has been spending considerable class and study time in putting together these word lists and making flashcards for the items, but she does not use these words in any class activity. She does not like to work on grammar exercises, drills, and functional phrases that help make conversations move along. Repetitive activities bore her, and she often interrupts them with irrelevant questions. When questioned, she has smiled and politely said that she would prefer to learn the language "her way." You are concerned that she will not achieve her goals if she does not change. On the MBTI she reports herself an ESFP.

Terry is letting us know a lot about her learning style, which appears to be very global and random. She is probably a Type 3 learner who relies primarily on the interpersonal learning track. She would be happy to spend a lot of time in open country, but the trouble is, she keeps getting lost!

Terry is also letting us know that she does not have very much flexibility in her style. This much lack of flexibility could indicate some kind of learning dysfunction (perhaps even learning disability); we would want to know a lot more about how she perceives and processes. Rather than having a preference for random learning, it is possible that Terry really has some kind of deficit in sequencing. The MBTI sensing preference suggests a preference for concrete learning over the kinds of abstractions Terry is so assiduously avoiding. Because Terry is not making use of suggestions she has already received about more effective study techniques, the issue does not seem to be simply a matter of poor study strategies.

Probably, Terry is also defending her self-esteem in a taxing situation by avoidance of activities that are very hard for her. She may feel some shame at her difficulty with sequential tasks that seem to come much more easily for her classmates. She thus disrupts class, avoids certain tasks, and politely rejects advice.

Suggestions for Terry will need to take all these possible factors into account. In any event, you and Terry can work together to find activities that Terry can do that will be more productive than simply amassing words. Because Terry is invested in the words, you might well use them as the base for the activities you design, though. For example, let Terry decide which are the most important, and then design activities around those. Or use some of the phrases she has learned as the foundation for grammar—let her try to make other phrases and sentences similar to the ones she has selected. Terry may well respond well to opportunities to learn by doing in roleplays and simulations. Your corrections in these should be directed toward errors that interfere with communication—leave emphasis on accuracy for later, when Terry is more self-confident and has a better knowledge base in the language. You can also play to her strengths by working with her on compensation and communication strategies that will make up for some of her gaps in precision.

Olivia is having yet another kind of difficulty. She is in a class that makes a lot of use of communicative methodology, with reduced emphasis on grammar. Here is what she tells you in an interview:

I've never thought of myself as much of a language learner, but I did enjoy picking up the very small amount of language I've had in my school classes. I love grammar and miss it in my course. Actually, I went and bought a grammar book and I'm using it on my own, but now I have to make up for lost time, when I couldn't understand much of what I heard. Frankly, I don't much like learning in group situations, either. I don't interact well in groups until I get to know them. Now that I've found some ways to learn by myself, it feels somewhat better. The thing is, it's humiliating not to do well, and that was especially so when the class was split and I ended up in the lower half. I've always done well in my other classes—in fact, I've never had to think much one way or the other about my grades. But in this class, I don't like to sound like an idiot, so I try to wait until I can do whatever it is well. It's really harder to learn when I don't feel good about myself. I just wish we could set it up so I could have most of my time in study on my own, and just meet with a teacher from time to time to check out what I'm learning.

Part of the problem for me is that I'm not a detail person. I like to get things top-down, big picture first. Sometimes this language learning business seems like nothing but a mass of details, and I get bogged down. The grammar book is helping some—it gives me a way to start organizing it for myself. The occasional grammar explanation we get from the teacher also helps me make sense of what's coming by, but the handouts are even better. Give me a rule and a collection of examples and let me learn the grammar systematically, one step at a time. There are still loose ends, though, and I hate that.

I do like the other students in the class, and the atmosphere is really pleasant. That makes a big difference for me. On the other hand, I sometimes hesitate to "make waves" when everyone else seems so comfortable. In truth, one of the best learning days I had was when I was home and could work right through the tapes, one-two-three.

Olivia, an INFJ, is quite explicit about her learning preferences. She is an analytic and deductive learner, probably field independent but not field sensitive (Type 2) who prefers visual input (the handouts are better than the lecture; she works well with her grammar book). Olivia is quite sequential, and her learning is disrupted by much of the random-type communicative learning in the program. The emphasis on language for communication also conflicts with the strong perfectionism frequently found among INFJ learners. Her introversion is clear in her strong preference for learning alone. Olivia is a largely reflective learner who needs time during which she can stay with a mental set (this is one reason why her time at home with the tapes was so congenial for her). My conclusion about Olivia was that her stylistic needs could be considered preferences and thus were not so rigid as to be either learning dysfunctions or learning disabilities.

Much of what is going on with Olivia has to do with her feelings. She is very protective of her self-image as someone who does things well, indeed perfectly. Making the errors that are inevitable in language learning is bad enough, but she also feels that she is looking much worse as a learner than her classmates. She may feel that in some way she is letting her teacher down, which would be hard for Olivia, because she likes her teacher.

There is indeed a learning style mismatch between Olivia's relatively analytic and low-risk approach and the communicative approach in her classroom. It is probably causing Olivia to doubt some of her competence, and thus the effect on her feelings is probably the first issue that needs attention. Olivia's teacher can indeed find ways to adapt some of the course to Olivia's needs, including providing information on what is coming in the syllabus, giving more advance organizers, and helping Olivia structure her preparation to cope with the "random" activities coming up. Even more important, though, is to help Olivia reframe her view of what is going on from seeing herself as sounding like "an idiot" and being humiliated by imperfect performance. If Olivia can be helped to see her process as quite natural in view of the style mismatch, her ongoing foundation building, and the course expectations, she may find the mismatch less disruptive.

As it turned out, Olivia was on the verge of reaching a threshold of competence beyond which the language input was less confusing. Within a few weeks, Olivia's comfort with conversational activities had gone up considerably, as a result of both teacher interventions and of her increasing linguistic competence. The teacher did make some efforts to provide extra wait time for Olivia while she processed what she had heard and what she was going to say, and she pointed out whole paradigms when portions were introduced to other students. Olivia was also provided with reading and listening material on topics of interest to her. Later in the course, when she was talking about what had happened earlier, she said, "It took me a while to realize that it's not just that I can't learn, but that I can ask for some changes."

The cases in this book are based on students of multiple ages and ethnic origins. Some of the interactions we examine are influenced by these demographic factors, but most could be high school students, university students, young adults, and learners in midcareer. They represent native English speakers learning foreign languages; they also reflect the learning patterns that show up in learners of English as a second language. The tools I have introduced to you in this book apply to all of them.

12.3 Helping Yourself

As mentioned in sections 10.3.2 and 11.5.2, you cannot save them all. (I suggest you review these sections.) Several of the cases in this book indicate the importance for you of managing your expectations of yourself. We saw that the counselor had to lower expectations for helping Sheldon (10.3) because of the realities of the learning setting. Laurie (11.3) and Melvin (11.4) presented great difficulties; Melvin especially was not about to let anyone help him. With students who have relatively severe learning disabilities, as is possibly the case for Joe (11.1), it is very helpful if you can manage your criteria for success. Just as it may be a great achievement for a beginning student to get 10% of an authentic text, it may be an equal success for you to help Joe learn enough of the new language to function effectively even if not precisely in high-frequency situations. In cases of students such as Melvin, sometimes the best you can do is offer help, cover yourself bureaucratically, and then step back and let it be up to Melvin what he does with the resources available to him. (I have sometimes called this quitting before you are behind.)

Another way to describe this point of view is to realize that all your students cannot be virtuosos, and you cannot be the ideal "parent" or mentor. Most of the time, good enough is good enough.

Teachers often identify their teaching with a certain methodology. The methodology may be one that fits well with their teaching style, or it may be the one in which they were trained. A useful shift in thinking is to see your work as student driven as much as methodology driven.

Methodologies are useful for providing conceptual frameworks within which you can rationalize your actions and for helping make teaching decisions. The trick is not to let them confine your options. Almost any methodology will work well with some of your students. If you are an adept teacher, it may work well with most of your students because you are expert at general approaches that enhance learning. No methodology, however, will work well for all students. No matter how good you are, you will have some students who have difficulty in your class. This is the time to suspend your methodology and look at what is going on from the point of view of the student. If what you are doing is not working, and a change might help, try the change, no matter what the methodology or the rulebook says.

There will be times when you are discouraged, frustrated, even angry at your students. Teaching is similar to being a parent. Even the best parents sometimes feel as if they could hate their children, and the children's behavior probably has earned that feeling. Sometimes you may feel anger and even hate for a student who gives you a hard time. This is part of being involved in relationship with another person: Conflict is natural, and conflict is often accompanied by feelings that are not wearing party clothes. The key is what you do with the feelings. Acknowledging to yourself that the student's behavior has aroused hurt or angry feelings in you is appropriate. The next step is to try to understand why the student felt the need to behave that way and use that as a way to design a different way of defining the terms of your interaction with the student. The defense mechanism construct (section 7.4.2) can help you get some insight into the student's behavior (and your reactions). I also suggest that you review the practice activities in Chapters 6, 7, and 11 to find where some of your "hot buttons" may be.

All of this advice no doubt sounds easier than it really is. None of us is a saint or famous psychotherapist. We all make mistakes, and we can get hurt. One way to help yourself is to enlist the support of another person. Trusted friends, colleagues, and supervisors can listen (in itself very helpful), provide a new perspective, make suggestions, and validate your worth no matter how frustrated you are. Another person—especially a colleague or supervisor—can take a more active role if need be, too.

A final word of advice comes from Eugene Kennedy (1977):

> Helpers who concentrate too much on the problem run the risk of missing the person who is troubled. This occurs, for example, if we perceive the problem as separate or even separable from its possessor's reactions to it.
>
> Actually, we do not have to solve problems; we only have to help other persons accept the responsibility for themselves. . . . If we get

the individual into proper focus, we will automatically get the problem into the right perspective.

It is a great relief for many counselors when they realize that they do not have to solve every problem or have the answer to every difficulty. This does not lessen the challenge of sensitively understanding people with problems, but it factors out of a counselor's life a considerable amount of unnecessary stress. (p. 13)

Helping others take responsibility for themselves is what this book is really about.

12.4 Last Words

The cases that have appeared in these chapters show a great deal of variation among learners. There are many other variations that have not been introduced here, of course, and you will meet learners who offer completely new combinations of familiar characteristics. Every learner is different, though some of the patterns we have seen recur. It is these patterns that enable us to make sense of the learners. It is the differences and surprises that keep the work challenging.

12.5 Practice

1. Go back and review the cases that were introduced in the earlier parts of this book in the same way as we have done for John. In what ways do you understand them better?

2. As suggested above, go back to the practice sections of Chapters 6, 7, and 11. Do the exercises that have you look at yourself again, in the light of the rest of this book. Has anything changed for you?

3. In Chapters 7 and 8, one of the practice exercises suggested that you write yourself up as a case. What changes would you make in that case now?

4. At the end of Chapter 1, you were urged to choose one or two students to observe. Now that you have finished this book, how have your views of the student(s) changed? What do you plan to do next in your work with them?

Appendix A
Sample Biographic Background Questionnaire

LANGUAGE BACKGROUND QUESTIONNAIRE

Date:_____ Language:_____

1. Name:_____2. School, Company, Agency[1]:_____

3. Expected position (or date of graduation):[2]_____

4. Date of Birth:_____5. Native Language:[3]_____

6. Countries lived in previously, and purpose of stay: _____

_____

7. Education:
(Circle highest level): Secondary Jr. College BA/BS MA/MS Law Doctorate Other

School	Degree	Date	Major	Minor	GPA

8. What were your favorite subjects?_____

   And your least preferred subjects?_____

9. What were your SAT or GRE scores (most recent)?_____

10. When did you last attend a class or take a course of any sort?

    from mo/yr_____to mo/yr_____

    What was the class?_____

11. Which languages do you speak and read, and how well? (If you know the ILR/ACTFL level, please use it. If an estimate, please so indicate.)

Speak:_____Read: _____

_____

12. How did you learn the languages (e.g., through college classes, work, travel, on own, tutor)? (Continue on back if necessary)

Language   How learned?   How long?   Did you enjoy it?

_____

_____

13. Were you ever in contact with other languages while growing up?
    Yes _____ No _____

If yes, please describe briefly

_____

14. Do you find learning foreign languages easy? _____

15. Is there anything that might interfere with your learning and using another language? (dyslexia, vision or hearing difficulties, etc.)

_____

16. Please add any additional comments about your past or anticipated language learning experience that might be helpful:

_____

Thank you.

Notes

1. Use whichever organizational unit is appropriate for you.
2. Use whichever information about onward plans is appropriate to the setting.
3. For adult programs and programs that have students of nontraditional age.

Appendix B

An Instrument for Sequential and Random Processing

PROBLEM INTEGRATION STRATEGY TEST

This is neither an intelligence nor an aptitude test. It is intended to help determine how you can develop your study methods. Do not attempt to read anything into the questions but give the first answer that comes to mind. Above all, be honest—*there is no grade or score for this test.*

Part I

Shown below are 20 arithmetic problems, some in addition and some in multiplication. Your task is *not* to solve these problems, but *to determine the order of solution which would please you most.* Assume that, were you actually solving the problems, there would be no time limit. Indicate next to the letters *a* through *t* in the box below the problems your order of solution by writing the numbers 1 to 20 next to the corresponding problem letters. For example, if you would do problem *f* first, then write the number 1 in the box next to *f,* and so on.

Do not change any answers!

a.   2   b.   7   c.   376   d.   22   e.   3   f.   67
     ×4   ×8   ×482   ×3   ×4   ×81

g. 8,649   h.   3   i.   20   j.   87   k.   4   l. 9,987
   ×302   ×4   ×1   ×8   ×396   ×4,463

m.   1   n.   47   o. 6,809   p.   84   q.   3   r.   87
     +1   +92   +42   +2   +6   +59

s.   87   t.   6
    946   +3
    787
   +295

a._____   f._____   k._____   p._____
b._____   g._____   l._____   q._____
c._____   h._____   m._____   r._____
d._____   i._____   n._____   s._____
e._____   j._____   o._____   t._____

Part II

Answer the following questions:

1. Which problem irritates you most?_____

2. Which problem is more irritating to you, *k* or *s*?_____

3. If you were actually solving these problems, would you check your work?

_____

(If yes, answer the following:

When would you check?_____

If you found an error, would you erase the incorrect answer or cross it out?

_____

4. Have you enjoyed taking this test? (Be honest) _____

Memorization Steps—Line Integrators

1. Familiarize: Listen to the material—for example, a dialogue from a textbook—several times.

2. Imitate: *Carefully* imitate each utterance, one at a time, in order, until you are satisfied you can repeat it perfectly. If you have difficulty with any sentence or utterance, go to step 2a.

> 2a. Analyze: Listen to the sentence on the tape. Mark the syllables that seem loudest. Between each pair of marks there is a slight pause, which may or may not be marked by a space between words or a punctuation mark. Find these pauses and mark them with a slash (/). Remember that some slashes may go right through the middle of a printed word. You have now divided the sentence into *phrases*. Now, memorize the last *phrase*. Next, memorize the *next to last* phrase. Put it together with the last phrase. Go one phrase further back, memorize it, and "assemble" it to the last two. Repeat this process until you have learned the entire sentence.

3. Anticipate: Stop the tape just before the first sentence begins and say the sentence. Then play the tape as a confirmation of your utterance. If you are right, try to say the next sentence before the tape does. If you

can't get it in the time allowed, go back and keep trying until you can. Repeat this until you can anticipate all the sentences in order.

4. Participate: Take the part of only one of the speakers in the dialogue, and use the tape as a "conversation partner." You should find this easy if you have done Steps 1 through 3 correctly.

Memorization Steps—Point Integrators

1. Familiarize: Listen to the material—for example, a dialogue from a textbook—several times.

2. Imitate: Repeat the first sentence that comes to mind or that seems easiest. Continue listening to the entire set until you can repeat all the sentences.

3. Anticipate: Still playing the entire segment of tape material, start trying to anticipate the sentences before you hear them, regardless of the order. If you have trouble with any particular one, go to step 2a above.

4. Participate: Take the part of one of the characters, and, still using the entire sequence, try to learn the part. Do not attempt to learn in order, but do "what comes naturally."

5. Associate: While or just after participating, try to associate what you are saying with something else. "Something else" may be another line of dialogue, a native-language translation, or something completely silly. It doesn't make any difference, as long as the result seems logical to *you* and results in a complete performance of the material.

SOURCE: Adaptation of material received from Allen Weinstein (1978).

Appendix C
Motivation and Strategies Questionnaire

Name: _____ Date: _____

Language: _____

Part I: Aptitude and Motivation

1. How do you rate your own ability to learn foreign languages relative to others in general?
   1. Poor
   2. Below average
   3. Average
   4. Above average
   5. Superior

2. How well do you think you will do in this language course?
   1. Poor
   2. Below average
   3. Average
   4. Above average
   5. Superior

3. How motivated are you to learn this language?
   1. Not at all motivated
   2. Not motivated
   3. Sufficiently motivated
   4. Very motivated
   5. Highly motivated

4. Why are you taking this language? _____

_____ _____

5. How much do you want to do what you described in Item 4 above?
    1. Not at all
    2. Not very much
    3. Sufficiently
    4. Very much
    5. Really looking forward to it

6. Students have indicated that they are motivated to learn languages by one or more of the following. Please check off those that apply to you now. (TL = target language, the language you are studying now.)

_____ Meeting a program requirement   _____ Language learning is fun

_____ Getting a payment for proficiency   _____ Like country where the TL is used

_____ Need it to do my job   _____ This is a real challenge

_____ Want to be top in my class   _____ Enjoy talking with TL people

_____ Hope to get an award   _____ Love to learn something new

Other motivations:_____

7. I would say my anxiety about learning this language is:
    1. None at all
    2. Not very much
    3. A fair amount
    4. A lot
    5. Really nervous about it

8. My anxiety about speaking in class (answering questions, giving reports, asking questions, etc.) is about this level:
    1. None at all
    2. Not very much
    3. A fair amount
    4. A lot
    5. Really nervous about it

MSQ Part IIa: Learning and Teaching Techniques

A variety of techniques may be used to help you learn, by you and by your teachers. How helpful do you think you will find these ways of teaching/learning? Please use the following scale to rate each item.

    1. Waste of time   3. Neither/nor   5. Nearly indispensable
    2. Not very helpful   4. Helpful

1. _____ The instructor systematically follows a textbook or syllabus.

2. _____ A written in-class exercise in which students fill in the correct form of verbs in sentences, for example:

    (walk)   Martha _____ to school every day.

3. _____ The class breaks up into smaller groups to talk.

4. _____ Students ask each other questions in pairs.

5. _____ Students interview language X speakers and report on the interviews.

6. _____ Teacher explains grammar in English, with examples and a handout.

7. _____ Teacher reads new material in the textbook aloud, followed by students reading it aloud one by one.

8. _____ Each student finds and reports on an interesting news or magazine article in language X.

9. _____ Students are given a list of words that will appear in an article they will read later. They look up the words in the dictionary and copy out the translations.

10. _____ Students select an article of interest to them to read in class, guessing the meanings of unknown words from context, without a dictionary.

11. _____ Teacher speaks in language X while explaining grammar.

12. _____ Teacher gives a sentence, to which entire group responds orally, changing the sentence in some way indicated by the teacher, for example making it negative:

    Teacher.   John walks to school.
    Class.   John doesn't walk to school.
    Teacher.   John is walking to school.
    Class.   John isn't walking to school.

1. Waste of time   3. Neither/nor   5. Nearly indispensable
2. Not very helpful   4. Helpful

13. _____ Students have a classroom discussion of some topic such as the economy or social problems. The emphasis is on exchanging personal opinions.

14. _____ Students read a number of sentences, finding and correcting the mistakes.

15. _____ The teacher calls on each student in turn to make a change in a target sentence in some specified way, for example:

Teacher.	John walks to school. Monica.
Monica.	John doesn't walk to school.
Teacher.	Good. John is walking to school. Victor.
Victor.	John isn't walking to school.

16. _____ Teacher corrects all mistakes in students' writings.

17. _____ The teacher pays attention to the ideas and feelings in students' writings.

18. _____ There are chances to get up and move around in the classroom.

19. _____ The class takes field trips to places where we can use the language outside the classroom.

20. _____ The teacher corrects all our mistakes when we speak.

21. _____ Students help design the program as it goes along.

22. _____ We learn dialogues by heart.

23. _____ The class goes away for several days or more for an "immersion" learning experience.

24. _____ Sometimes we are forced to use what we know to communicate, however little, even though it isn't exact.

25. _____ I discover grammar patterns for myself.

26. _____ We do roleplays, simulations, and skits in class.

27. _____ I listen to material that is "over my head."

28. _____ I read material that is "over my head."

1. Waste of time   3. Neither/nor   5. Nearly indispensable
2. Not very helpful   4. Helpful

29. _____ There is plenty of early pronunciation drill, so it will be perfect early.

30. _____ We master one thing before going on to more material or a new grammar point.

31. _____ Group study with classmates is part of the lesson.

32. _____ The program takes it step-by-step, so I won't be confused.

33. _____ The teacher has the main responsibility to see that I get what I need.

34. _____ I use language X at the training site as much as I can.

35. _____ I use language X outside the training site as much as I can.

36. _____ I study alone.

37. _____ I study with others outside class.

38. _____ Classroom exercises use my hands (drawing, pointing, construction, etc.)

39. _____ I use audiotapes in the language lab or at home.

40. _____ I use videotapes at school or outside.

41. _____ I use computer-assisted instruction.

MSQ Part IIb: Personal Learning Techniques

You may do various things to help yourself learn. How often do you think you are likely to do the following? Please use the following scale to rate each item.

1. Almost never	3. Sometimes	5. Most of the time
2. Rarely	4. Often	

1. _____ I usually plan out what I will cover and how I will study when I start to study.

2. _____ I need to take study breaks.

3. _____ I remember better if I have a chance to talk about something.

4. _____ I have a number of projects going on, in varying states of completion.

5. _____ Mental images help me remember.

6. _____ I like to know how the "system" works and what the rules are, then apply what I know.

7. _____ I like to work with some background music.

8. _____ I try to keep my mistakes and reverses in perspective.

9. _____ If I write things down, I can remember them better.

10. _____ I like to be able to move around when I work or study.

11. _____ I don't mind it when the teacher tells us to close our books for a lesson.

12. _____ I can trust my "gut feeling" about the answer to a question.

13. _____ I take a lot of notes in class or lectures.

14. _____ I find ways to fill in when I can't think of a word or phrase, such as pointing, using my hands, or finding a "filler" word (such as "whatchamacallit" or equivalent in the target language).

15. _____ I hear words in my mind when I read.

16. _____ I work better when it's quiet.

1. Almost never   3. Sometimes   5. Most of the time
2. Rarely   4. Often

17. _____ I look at the ending when I start a book or story.

18. _____ If I use a computer to learn, I like programs with color and movement.

19. _____ My mind wanders in class.

20. _____ Figuring out the system and the rules for myself contributes a lot to my learning.

21. _____ It's useful to talk myself through a task.

22. _____ I feel the need to check my answers to questions in my head before giving them.

23. _____ I forget things if I don't write them down quickly.

24. _____ I consider myself a "horizontal filer" (e.g., my desk has piles of papers and books all over it),

25. _____ but I can find what I need quickly. (answer only if #24 is 3, 4, or 5).

26. _____ When I need to remember something from a book, I can imagine how it looks on the page.

27. _____ I can do more than one thing at once.

28. _____ I prefer to jump right into a task without taking a lot of time for directions.

29. _____ I am comfortable using charts, graphs, maps, and the like.

30. _____ I try to be realistic about my strengths and weaknesses without dwelling on the weaknesses.

31. _____ I like to complete one task before starting another.

32. _____ I prefer to demonstrate what I've learned by doing something "real" with it rather than take a test or write a paper.

33. _____ I have trouble remembering conversational exchanges word for word.

34. _____ Hearing directions for a task is better for me than reading them.

35. _____ I like to be introduced to new material by reading about it.

SOURCE: Adapted from Ehrman and Christensen (1994).

Appendix D
Interpretations of MSQ Items

The following indicate some of the learning style dimensions that seem to be associated with items in the MSQ, based on low to moderate correlations (20s to 40s) with other instruments and experience in consultation interviews with students. Interpretations immediately follow the item summary description. Correlations are listed in parentheses.

The interpretation suggests that people with the named learning style preference are somewhat more likely than not to find this kind of activity at least comfortable and perhaps necessary. People of the opposite preference may well reject the item, perhaps even describing it as a waste of time. *These interpretations are tentative and should all be treated as hypotheses to be explored with the person who filled out the questionnaire.*

High scores on the Hartmann Boundary Questionnaire indicate thin boundaries, and low scores indicate thick boundaries. The 12 subscales address boundaries between states of wakefulness ("sleep"), between thinking and feeling ("thoughts"), among memories of earlier ages ("child"), as well as to experiences of ESP ("unusual (experiences)"), sensitivity to slights ("sensitive"), interpersonal receptivity ("interpersonal"), need for neat surroundings ("neat"), preference for sharp or fuzzy lines in visual images ("edges"), opinions about various age groups ("opinions"), lines of authority ("authority"), ethnic groups ("peoples"), and abstractions such as beauty or truth ("abstractions"). High scores on " neat and edges" indicate low need for neatness and preference for fuzzy visual lines, respectively. (See Chapter 6.)

The MBTI subscales are extraversion-introversion, sensing-intuition, thinking feeling, and judging-perceiving, as described in Chapter 6. The

MLAT subscales are Part 1 (Number Learning); Part 2 (Phonetic Script); Part 3 (Spelling Clues); Part 4 (Words in Sentences); Part 5 (Paired Associates). They are described in Chapter 9.

The abbreviation (neg.) *indicates* a negative correlation: that is, if the item tends to be high, the correlated scale will tend to be low, and vice versa.

Number of cases for correlations in parts I and II: MBTI 250, HBQ 249, MLAT 118.

Abbreviations

EOTS: End-of-training proficiency in speaking and interactive listening (oral interview)

EOTR: End-of-training proficiency in reading (interactive reading test)

HBQ: Hartmann Boundary Questionnaire (Chapter 6)

MBTI: Myers-Briggs Type Indicator (Chapter 6)

MLAT: Modern Language Aptitude Test (Chapter 9)

TOA: Tolerance of ambiguity.

Not all the items in this questionnaire have interpretations.

Item   Description.   *Interpretation*   *(Correlates)*

(i.e., usually favored by)

Part I: Self-efficacy, Motivation, Anxiety

1. [overall aptitude]: *Previous success, self-efficacy.* (MBTI intuition; HBQ thin esp. neat; EOTS, EOTR; MLAT Pts. 1, 2, 3, 4, 5, Total)

2. [how well will you do in this course?]: *Previous success, self-efficacy.* (MBTI intuition; HBQ thin esp. neat; EOTS, EOTR; MLAT Pts. 2, 3, 4, 5, Total)

3. [how much want to learn the language]: *Motivation for the language.* (MBTI thinking; HBQ thin; MLAT Pt. 2)

4. [why learning the language]: *Gives information on nature of motivation, how voluntary.*

5. [importance of reason for learning]: *Weight for student of end goal.* (HBQ thin)

6. [List of motivators]: Column 1: *extrinsic motivators; Column 2: intrinsic motivators.*

7. [anxiety about this experience]: *Overall language learning anxiety.* (MBTI feeling; HBQ thin, esp. sensitive, abstractions; EOTS (neg.), EOTR (neg.); MLAT Pt. 4, Total (both neg.))

8. [anxiety about speaking in class]: *Anxiety about oral performance, often the most threatening part of language study.* (MBTI feeling; HBQ thin, esp. sensitive, abstractions; MLAT Total (neg.))

Part IIa: Learning and Teaching Activities

1. [systematically follow syllabus]: Sequential learning, need for external structure. (MBTI thinking, judging; HBQ (all neg.) edges, interpersonal, sleep, thoughts, unusual experiences, Total; MLAT Pt. 2)

2. [fill-in exercise for verb forms in-class]: *Analytic processing.* (MBTI thinking, judging; HBQ (neg.) neat)

3. [small-group conversation]: (HBQ interpersonal, opinions about different ages, peoples)

4. [ask each other questions in pairs]: (HBQ (neg.) sleep)

5. [interview native speakers and report]: *High TOA, random, open-ended learning.*

6. [explain grammatical rule in English, with handouts]: *Need for external structure, field dependent.*(MBTI judging; HBQ (all neg.) neat, edges)

7. [teacher reads aloud; students read same material aloud one by one]: *Sequential, need for external structure.*(MBTI sensing, judging; HBQ (all neg.) neat, edges)

8. [each student finds and reports on article in target language]: *Open-ended learning.*

9. [look up words on list & copy translations]: *Low TOA, high need for external structure.* (MBTI sensing, thinking; HBQ (all neg.) neat, edge, abstractions, Total; MLAT Pt. 4 (neg.))

10. [find article, guess words without dictionary]: *Open-ended learning, high TOA, random.* (HBQ thoughts, unusual, interpersonal, sensitive, Total)

11. [explain grammar in target language]: *Field sensitive, global learning, high TOA or high level of proficiency.* (HBQ organizations, thoughts; MLAT Pt. 2, Total)

12. [choral transformation drill]: *High need for external structure.* (MBTI thinking; HBQ thoughts; MLAT Pt. 4)

13. [classroom discussion on controversial subjects, emphasis on opinions]: *High TOA, low need for external structure, random, global.* (MBTI intuition; HBQ sleep, thoughts, unusual, neat, abstractions, interpersonal, Total; EOTR.)

14. [find and correct mistakes in written sentences]: *Analytic, field independent.* (HBQ (all neg.) child, peoples, Total)

15. [transformation drill, one student at a time]: *Need for external structure.* (HBQ neat)

16. [teacher corrects all mistakes in writings]: *Perfectionism; analytic.* (MBTI thinking)

17. [teacher pays attention to student feelings]: *Rejected by analytic learners.* (MLAT Pt. 3 (neg.))

18. [chances to move around classroom]: *Kinesthetic learning.* (MBTI feeling; HBQ opinions, peoples, Total; MLAT Pt 2 (neg.))

19. [field trips]: *Open-ended learning, kinesthetic, global, low structure.* (MBTI extraversion; HBQ opinions, sensitive; MLAT Pt. 4 (neg.))

20. [correct all oral mistakes]: *Perfectionism; analytic.* (MBTI thinking; HBQ (all neg.)) neat, interpersonal, Total)

21. [students help design program]: *Open-ended, low need for external structure.* (HBQ interpersonal, opinions, peoples, thoughts, sensitive, Total; MLAT Pt. 1)

22. [memorize dialogues]: *Sequential, high need for external strucure, low TOA.* (MBTI thinking, judging)

23. [immersion]: *Open-ended, global, kinesthetic, low need for structure.* (MBTI extraversion, intuition, perceiving; HBQ neat, interpersonal, opinions, peoples, sensitive)

24. [use what one knows to communicate even if not exact]: *Open-ended, global, high TOA.* (EOTS (neg.))

25. [discover grammar patterns for self]: *Field independent, analytic, high TOA, inductive.* (MLAT Pt. 4)

26. [roleplays, simulations]: *Open-ended, low need for structure, global, big picture.*(HBQ interpersonal, opinions, sensitive, thoughts, Total; MLAT Pt. 5)

27. [over-the-head listening]: *Open-ended, global, high TOA.*(HBQ neat, organizations, sleep, Total; MLAT Pts. 3, 4, 5, Total)

28. [over-the-head reading]: *Open-ended, global, high TOA.*(HBQ neat, sleep; MLAT Pts. 1, 2, 3, 4, 5, Total)

29. [early pronunciation drill so it will be perfect]: *High need for external structure, perfectionism, low TOA (?).* (MBTI thinking)

30. [master one thing before moving on]: *Sequential, low TOA, high need for external structure.* (MBTI judging; HBQ (neg.) edges, neat, organizations; MLAT Pt. 4 (neg.))

31. [group study is part of program]: *Global, extraversion?*

32. [step-by-step program]: *Sequential, low TOA, high need for external structure.* (MBTI sensing, judging; HBQ (all neg.) edges, neat, organizations, Total; MLAT (all neg.) Pts. 1, 2, 4, Total)

33. [teacher has main responsibility to see that I get what I need]: *High need for external structure, low TOA.* (HBQ (neg.) edges, organizations, peoples; MLAT Pt. 4 (neg.))

34. [talk at training site in target language]

35. [talk outside training site in target language]

36. [study alone]: *Analytic, introversion?* (EOTR)

37. [study with others outside class]: *Extraversion.* (MBTI extraversion)

38. [use hands in classroom activities]: *Kinesthetic learning.* (MBTI extraversion; HBQ (neg.) organizations)

39. [use audiotapes]: *Auditory.* (HBQ (neg.) child)

40. [use videotapes]: (MBTI extraversion, intuition, perceiving; HBQ opinions)

41. [use computer-assisted instruction]

Part IIb: Personal Learning Techniques

1. [plan task]: *Metacognitive strategies, reflective.*

2. [frequent study breaks]: *Extraversion, kinesthetic.*

3. [remember better if talk about it]: *Auditory, (Kinesthetic?), extraversion.*

4. [multiple incomplete tasks]: *Random, multitasking (doing more than one thing at once).*

5. [visualize images]: *Visual (objects, actions).*

6. [know system, rules, then apply]: *Deductive learning.*

7. [work with background music]: *Multitasking).*

8. [keep reverses in perspective]: *Affective strategies (affective self-management).*

9. [remember better if write it down]: *Visual (text), possibly kinesthetic.*

10. [study better if can move around]: *Kinesthetic, possibly extraversion.*

11. [doesn't mind closed book]: *Auditory.*

12. [trust intuitions]: *Intuition, impulsivity, global.*

13. [take a lot of notes]: *Visual (text), possibly kinesthetic.*

14. [fill in for missing word]: *filler word may be intuition; use of hands may be kinesthetic; compensation strategies.*

15. [when reading, hear in head]: *Auditory.*

16. [quiet place]: *Low on multitasking, distractible.*

17. [look at ending in book]: *Random; most sequential learners reject this.*

18. [color and movement on computer]: *Kinesthetic.*

19. [mind wanders in class]: *Multitasker, kinesthetic.*

20. [figure out system, rules]: *Inductive learning.*

21. [talk self through tasks]: *Auditory.*

22. [check answers]: *Reflective.*

23. [write down in order not to forget]: *Visual (text), distractible.*

24. ["horizontal filer"]: *May be a random learner, perceiver.*

25. but knows where things are] (answered if # 24 is 3, 4, or 5): *Random perceiver.*

26. [visualize image of text on page]: *Visual (text).*

27. [do more than one thing at once]: *Multitasking.*

28. [start by doing]: *Kinesthetic, impulsive.*

29. [remember verbatim]: *Low-auditory.*

30. [comfortable with charts, graphs]: *Visual (schematics), possibly field independent.*

31. [complete one task before starting another]: *Sequential.*

32. [realistic view of strengths and weaknesses]: *Affective strategies, affective self-management.*

33. [demonstrate knowledge by applying it]: *Kinesthetic, random, concrete, global.*

34. [hearing directions]: *Auditory, extraversion.*

35. [start by reading about new material]: *Visual.*

Appendix E
Case Data Highlights

These snapshots are organized roughly as follows: MBTI type, ego boundary thickness, field independence type, sensory channel style, cognitive style, verbal or quantitative orientation, tested language aptitude, affective factors, learning strategies, other information. Data are not available in every category for each case.

Some of the terms used below:

> Myers-Briggs type categories: INTJ, ESFP, etc. (Chapter 6)
>
> Thick and thin ego boundaries. (Chapter 6)
>
> Verbal versus quantitative orientation (Chapter 8)
>
> Field independence types: Type 1—field independent and field sensitive; Type 2—field independent and field insensitive; Type 3—field dependent and field sensitive; Type 4—field dependent and field insensitive. (See section 5.2.)
>
> Conceptual tempo: reflective, impulsive, often combined with accurate and inaccurate; fast-accurate describes an impulsive who is also accurate. (See section 6.4.1)

Alice: ENTP, Type 1, random, exceptionally independent learner, needs an unusual amount of autonomy, high language learning self-efficacy, experienced language leaner, knows how languages work.

Angela: ENFJ, generally thin boundaries, Type 3?, overall satisfactory MLAT but with Parts 3—Spelling Clues—and 5—Paired Associates—low, extrinsic, instrumental motivation at a moderate level, angry, anxious, defense by withdrawal of emotional energy.

Bernice: ESTJ, generally thick ego boundaries, very sequential and goal oriented, foreign born with many years of classroom English, uneven MLAT profile, intrinsic motivation, endorses use of deep strategies,.

Bert: INTP, Type 2, reflective, relies on cognitive flexibility and control, anxiety—especially interpersonal, defense through avoidance/inhibition, independent learner.

Betty: ENTJ, abstract, older learner, example of adult resistance.

Beverly: ENTJ, average ego boundaries, Type 3? visual learner, sequential, concrete, deductive, strong MLAT, on which the weakest part is 5—Paired Associates, surface strategies, good previous language exposure.

Calvin: ISTJ, relies on surface strategies.

Celia: ISFJ, intense anxiety, self-sabotage, defensive acting out.

Corwin: ESFP, wants a lot of external structure, dependent learner, low self-efficacy as language learner, indirect expression of anxiety, withdrawal defenses.

David: ISTJ, Type 3, concrete, low tolerance of ambiguity.

Deborah: ISTP, describes self as "dyslexic," auditory retention difficulties.

Dennis: ISTJ, needs a lot of external structure and scaffolding, doesn't know how to learn.

Ellis: INTP, thick ego boundaries, Type 2, kinesthetic, visual, reflective, quantitative orientation, little anxiety.

Elsa: Probably N, thin ego boundaries, Type 3, strongly global, previously diagnosed as language-learning disabled, not motivated for language of study though highly motivated for another, extremely anxious, prefers open-ended learning activities.

Evan: ENTJ, average ego boundaries, kinesthetic, reflective, average tolerance of ambiguity, verbal orientation, previous in-country learning success, high educational level, high general intelligence but somewhat below average tested language aptitude, hearing loss, previous diagnosis as dysgraphic, anxious, high extrinsic motivation began with ineffective strategies, wants social learning.

George: INTJ, history of confrontational problem solving.

Holly: ISTJ, Type 4, inexperienced language learner, needs a lot of external structure and scaffolding, doesn't know how to learn.

Janet: INFP, Type 1? , random, inductive, previous successful learning experiences, resists classroom routine.

Jenny: INFP, thin ego boundaries, Type 3, verbal orientation, experiences anxiety, does not prioritize, information "mushes" together, relies on interpersonal skills.

Joe: ESTJ, very thick ego boundaries, Type 4, kinesthetic, visual, detail oriented and concrete, very low tolerance of ambiguity, quantitative/technical orientation, first-time foreign language learner, extremely low tested aptitude, highly motivated, low anxiety, good general study skills but few deep strategies, relies on repetition, history of avoiding unusual verbal demands in life.

John: ESTJ, thick ego boundaries, Type 4, sequential, concrete, low tolerance of ambiguity, almost entirely extrinsic motivation, defensive of self-esteem, indirect expression of anxiety, defense through avoidance and displacement, relies on control and hard work, surface strategies, needs external structure, childhood stutter.

Karen: ISFJ, thickish ego boundaries, Type 3?, auditory, random, average MLAT with low Part 3-Spelling Clues, needs some external structure, good previous language learning background, effective learning strategies.

Keith: ESTJ, thick ego boundaries, Type 4, sequential, concrete, low tolerance of ambiguity, little anxiety.

Kelly: INFJ, visual, form before meaning, low tolerance of ambiguity in listening, defends by withdrawal of emotional energy.

Laurie: ENTJ, tested aptitude in average range but below classmates, extreme anxiety, very high need for achievement, low language learning self-efficacy, high need for control, externalizing defenses, anxiety expressed in body symptoms, relies on social skills and social learning strategies as well as intense effort.

Linda: ISFJ, perfectionism, increasingly low self-efficacy as language learner, high need for achievement, anxious, defense by preemptive pessimism.

Logan: ESTP, independent learner, assertive in class.

Lonnie: ENTJ, thick ego boundaries, Type 4, sequential, concrete, quantitative, very weak on MLAT Part 3-Spelling Clues, anxious, needs external structure.

Mari: ESFJ, extrinsic motivation, little expectancy of long-term payoff, anxiety, influence of family's culture of origin.

Mark: ENFP, average ego boundaries, kinesthetic and auditory, sequential, previous language learning background, slightly above average tested aptitude, high extrinsic motivation, extremely anxious, low sense of self-efficacy as language learner.

Matthew: ISTP, thick ego boundaries, Type 4?, sequential, perfectionistic, low tolerance of ambiguity, good tested aptitude but with uneven MLAT profile, high need for achievement, extrinsically and instrumentally motivated, anxious, defensive fantasy, childhood stutter.

Melvin: ESFJ, adequate aptitude, frustrated and angry, high anxiety, externalizing defenses, wants external guidance and structure, help-seeking and help-rejecting

Miriam: INTP, thin ego boundaries, Type 1, visual, kinesthetic, very random, impulsive/fast-accurate, verbal orientation, some anxiety (social), very strong tested aptitude, intrinsic, assimilative motivation, high language learning self-efficacy, experienced language learner, knows how languages work.

Olivia: INFJ, Type 2, visual, sequential, deductive, reflective, perfectionistic, anxious, withdrawal defense, prefers to study alone.

Patricia: ESTP, Type 3?, very high proficiency in two languages, describes self as dyslexic, learns in context, uses global strategies.

Roger: INTJ, average ego boundaries, Type 2, deductive, quantitative orientation.

Sandy: ISFP, thin internal ego boundaries, medium to thick external ego boundaries, field independence and field sensitivity about the same, thus something similar to a Type 1 when not under stress, otherwise similar to a Type 4, strongly kinesthetic and somewhat visual, good tested language aptitude, not initially anxious but later very much so, emotional outbursts, defensive acting out, little need for external structure.

Sheldon: INTJ, Type 2?, visual, sequential, previous history of successful language learning, angry.

Shirley: INFP, thin ego boundaries, Type 3?, auditory, sequential, concrete, low tolerance of ambiguity, strong need for external structure, very self-aware, uses wide range of strategies

Simon: ENFJ, inefficient learning strategies.

Suzanne: ESTP, good language aptitude, extrinsic motivation, externalizing defenses.

Sylvia: ENFP, Type 3, abstract, externalizing defenses.

Terry: ESFP, Type 3 global style, bilingual from childhood in cognate language, first time in formal language class, defensive avoidance, ineffective strategies, uses interpersonal skills, little stylistic flexibility, possible learning dysfunction (sequencing).

Vanessa: INFP, average ego boundaries, Type 1, visual, inductive, multitasker, verbal orientation, makes use of cognitive flexibility and interpersonal approaches, extrinsic, instrumental motivation, defense through detachment, independent learner.

Victor: INTJ, average ego boundaries, probably Type 2, visual and low auditory, sequential, moderate tolerance of ambiguity, quantitative orientation, nonnative speaker of English, strong MLAT for a nonnative speaker, low anxiety.

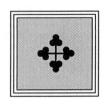

References

Allright, D. (1988). *Observation in the language classroom*. New York: Longmans.

Allright, D., & Bailey, K. (1991). *Focus on the language classroom: An introduction to language classroom research for language teachers*. New York: Cambridge.

Anastasi, A. (1988). *Psychological testing* (6th ed.). New York: Macmillan.

Bailey, K. M. (1983). Competitiveness and anxiety in adult second language learning: Looking at and through the diary studies. In H. Seliger & M. Long (Eds.), *Classroom oriented research in second language acquisition*. Rowley, MA: Newbury House.

Barbe, W. B., Swassing, R. H., & Milone, M. N. (1979). *The Swassing-Barbe Modality Index in the Zaner-Bloser Modality Kit*. Columbus, OH: Zaner-Bloser.

Barr, V. (1993, April). *Foreign language requirements and students with learning disabilities* (ERIC Digest No. ED 355 834). Washington, DC: ERIC Clearinghouse on Languages and Linguistics.

Bayne, R. (1995). *The Myers-Briggs Type Indicator: A critical review and practical guide*. New York: Chapman & Hall.

Biggs, J. B. (1992). Study process questionnaire. In J. B. Biggs (Ed.), *Why and how do Hong Kong students learn? Using the learning and study process questionnaires*. Hong Kong: Faculty of Education, University of Hong Kong.

Brown, H. D. (1991). *Breaking the language barrier*. Yarmouth, ME: Intercultural.

Brown, H. D. (1994). *Principles of language learning and teaching* (3rd ed.). Englewood Cliffs, NJ: Prentice Hall Regents.

Carroll, J. (1990). Cognitive abilities and foreign language aptitude: Then and now. In T. Parry & C. W. Stansfield (Eds.), *Language aptitude reconsidered* (pp. 11-29). Englewood Cliffs, NJ: Prentice Hall.

Carroll, J., & Sapon, S. M. (1959). *Modern Language Aptitude Test*. New York: Psychological Corporation.

Chamot, A. U., & O'Malley, J. M. (1994). *The CALLA handbook: Implementing the cognitive academic language learning approach*. New York: Addison Wesley.

Chapelle, C. (1992). Disembedding "disembbed figures in the landscape": An appraisal of Griffiths and Sheen's "reappraisal of L2 research on field dependence/dependence". *Applied Linguistics 13*, 375-384.

Chapelle, C., & Green, P. (1992). Field independence/dependence in second language acquisition research. *Language Learning, 42*, 47-83.

Cohen, A. D. (1990). *Language learning: Insights for learners, teachers, and researchers.* Boston: Heinle & Heinle.

Cohen, A. D., & Hosenfeld, (1981). Some uses of mentalistic data in second language research. *Language Learning, 31*, 285-314.

Crookes, G., & Schmidt, R. W. (1991). Motivation: Reopening the research agenda. *Language Learning, 41*, 469-512.

Curran, C. A. (1978), *Understanding: A necessary ingredient in human belonging.* Apple River, IL: Apple River.

Day, R. R. (1990). Teacher observation in second language teacher education. In J. C. Richards & D. Nunan (Eds.), *Second language teacher education* (pp. 43-61). New York: Cambridge.

Demuth, K. A., & Smith, N. B. (1987). The foreign language requirement: An alternative program. *Foreign Language Annals, 20*, 67-77.

Dornyei, Z. (1994). Motivation and motivating in the foreign language classroom. *Modern Language Journal, 78*, 23-284.

Dornyei, Z. (1995). On the teachability of communication strategies. *TESOL Quarterly, 29*, 55-85.

Downey, D. M. (1992, April). *Accommodating the foreign language learning disabled student.* Paper presented at the Foreign Language and learning Disabilities Conference, The American University, Washington, DC. (As cited in Barr, 1993)

Dunn, R., & Dunn, K. (1978). *Teaching students through their individual leaning styles.* Reston, VA: Reston.

Dunn, R., & Dunn, K., & Price, G. E. (1978). *Learning style inventory.* Lawrence, KS: Price Systems.

Dunn, R., & Dunn, K., & Price, G. E. (1979). *Productivity environmental preference survey.* Lawrence, KS: Price Systems.

Educational Testing Service (1975). *Hidden Figures Test-CF-1 (Rev.).* Princeton, NJ: Author.

Ehrman, M. E. (1989). Ants and grasshoppers, badgers and butterflies: Qualitative and quantitative investigation of adult language learning styles and strategies. *Dissertation Abstracts International, 50*(12), 5876B. (University Microfilms No. 9005257).

Ehrman, M. E. (1993). Ego boundaries revisited: Toward a model of personality and learning. In J. E. Alatis (Ed.), *Strategic interaction and language acquisition: Theory, practice, and research* (pp. 331-362). Washington, DC: Georgetown University.

Ehrman, M. E. (1994a). The Type Differentiation Indicator and language learning success. *Journal of Psychological Type, 30*, 10-29.

Ehrman, M. E. (1994b). Weakest and strongest learners in intensive language training: A study of extremes. In C. Klee (Ed.), *Faces in a crowd: Individual learners in multisection programs* (pp. 81-118). Boston: Heinle & Heinle.

Ehrman, M. E. (forthcoming). *A study of the Modern Language Aptitude Test for predicting learning success and advising students.*

Ehrman, M. E. (in press). Personality, language learning aptitude, and program structure. In James Alatis (Ed.), *Linguistics and the education of second language teachers: Ethnolinguistic, psycholinguistic, and sociolinguistic aspects.* Washington, DC: Georgetown University.

Ehrman, M. E. (in press). Psychological type and extremes of training outcomes in foreign language reading proficiency. In A. Horning & R. Sudol (Eds.), *Understanding literacy: Personality preferences in rhetorical and psycholinguistic contexts.* Cresskill, NJ: Hampton.

Ehrman, M. E., & Christensen, L. (1994). *Language learner motivation and learning strategies questionnaire.* Unpublished manuscript.

Ehrman, M. E., & Oxford, R. L. (1990a). Effects of sex differences, career category, and psychological type on adult language learning strategies. *Modern Language Journal, 73*(1), 1-13.

Ehrman, M. E., & Oxford, R. L. (1990b). Adult language learning styles and strategies in an intensive training setting. *Modern Language Journal, 74*(3), 311-327.

Ehrman, M. E., & Oxford, R. L. (1991). *Affective survey.* Upublished manuscript.

Ehrman, M. E., & Oxford, R. L. (1995). Cognition plus: Correlates of language learning success. *Modern Language Journal, 79*(1), 67-89.

Ely, C. (1989). Tolerance of ambiguity and use of second language strategies. *Foreign Language Annals, 22,* 437-446.

Fuller, G. E. (1987). *How to learn a foreign language.* Washington, DC: Storm King.

Gajar, A. H. (1987). Foreign language learning disabilities: The identification of predictive and diagnostic variables. *Journal of Learning Disabilities, 20,* 327-330.

Ganschow, L., Sparks, R., Javorsky, J., Pohlman, J., & Bishop-Marbury, A. (1991). Identifying native language difficulties among foreign language learners in college: A "foreign" language learning disability? *Journal of Learning Disabilities, 24,* 530-541.

Gardner, R. C. (1985). *Social psychology and second language learning: The role of attitudes and motivation.* London: Edward Arnold.

Gardner, R. C., & Lambert, W. E. (1972). *Attitudes and motivation in second language learning.* Rowley, MA: Newbury House.

Gardner, R. C., & Tremblay, P. F. (1994a). On motivation, research agendas, and theoretical frameworks. *Modern Language Journal, 78,* 359-368.

Gardner, R. C., & Tremblay, P. F. (1994b). On motivation: Measurement and conceptual considerations. *Modern Language Journal, 78,* 524-527.

Gregorc, A. F. (1982a). *An adult's guide to style.* Maynard, MA: Gabriel Systems.

Gregorc, A. F. (1982b). *Gregorc style delineator.* Maynard, MA: Gabriel Systems.

Griffiths, R., & Sheen, R. (1992). Disembedded figures in the landscape: A reappraisal of L2 research on field dependence/independence. *Applied Linguistics, 13,* 133-148.

Guild, P., & Garger, S. (1985). *Marching to different drummers.* Alexandria, VA: Association for Supervision and Curriculum Development.

Hartlage, L. C. (1985). Identifying and understanding the learning disabled adult. In D. P. Swierinsky (Ed.), *Testing adults: A reference guide for special psychodiagnostic assessments* (pp. 179-187). Kansas City, MO: Test Corporation of America.

Hartmann, E. (1991). *Boundaries in the mind: A new psychology of personality.* New York: Basic.

Hermann, N. (1984). *Hermann Participant Survey.* Lake Lure, NC: The Whole Brain Corporation.

Horwitz, E. K., Horwitz, M. B., & Cope, J. (1986). Foreign language classroom anxiety. *Modern Language Journal, 70,* 125-132.

Horwitz, E. K., & Young, D. J. (1991). *Language anxiety: From theory and research to classroom implications.* Englewood Cliffs, NJ: Prentice Hall.

Jackson, F. H. (1994). Books for language learners: An annotated bibliography. *Journal of Southeast Language Teaching, II*, 70-77.

Jung, C. G. (1971). *Psychological types* (H.G. Baynes Trans., Rev. R. F. Hull.) Bollingen Series 20, 6. Princeton, NJ: Princeton University. (Original work published 1921).

Kagan, J. (1965). Impulsive and reflective children. In J. Krumboltz (Ed.), *Learning and the educational process*. Chicago: Rand McNally.

Kagan, J. (1966). Reflection-impulsivity: The generality and dynamics of conceptual tempo. *Journal of Abnormal Psychology, 71*, 17-24.

Keefe, J. W., & Monk, J. S. (1986). *Learning style profile: Examiner's manual*. Reston, VA: National Association of Secondary School Principals.

Keefe, J. W., & Monk, J. S., with Letteri, C. A., Languis, M., & Dunn, R. (1989). *Learning style profile*. Reston, VA: National Association of Secondary School Principals.

Keirsey, D., & Bates, M. (1978). *Please understand me* (3rd ed.). Del Mar, CA: Prometheus Nemesis.

Kennedy, E. (1977). *On becoming a counselor: A basic guide for non-professional counselors*. New York: Continuum.

Kolb, D. (1985). *Learning styles inventory*. Boston: McBer.

Kroeger, O., & Thuesen, J. (1988). *Type talk*. New York: Delacorte.

Kummerow, J. N., & Quenk, N. L. (1992). *Interpretive guide for the MBTI expanded analysis report*. Palo Alto, CA: Consulting Psychologists.

Larsen-Freeman, D. (1991). Second language acquisition research: Staking our the territory. *TESOL Quarterly, 25*, 315-350.

Lawrence, G. (1993). *People types & tiger stripes* (3rd ed.). Gainesville, FL: Center for Applications of Psychological Type.

Leaver, B. L. (1993). *Teaching the whole class*. Salinas, CA: AGSI Press.

Lee, J. (n.d. a, retrieved 6 July 1995). *Some specific learning difficulties still remaining in adults*. Dyslexia 2000 network. [Internet site.] Available through http://www.furturenet.co.uk/charity/ado/index.html.

Lee, J. (n.d. b, retrieved 6 July 1995). *The learning styles of adults with dyslexia*. Dyslexia 2000 network. [Internet site.] Available through http://www.furturenet.co.uk/charity/ado/index.html.

Lefrancois, J., & Sibiga, T. C. (1986, May). *Use of the Modern Language Aptitude Test (MLAT) as a diagnostic tool*. Unpublished manuscript, no source indicated.

Levine, M. D. (1987). *Developmental variation and learning disorders*. Cambridge, MA: Educators Publishing Service.

Lightbown, P. (1985). Great expectations: Second language research and classroom teaching. *Applied Linguistics, 6*, 173-189.

Lightbown, P., & Spada, N. (1993). *How languages are learned*. New York: Oxford.

Lingenfelter, M. (n.d.; retrieved 6 July 1995). *Learning disabilities and the adult student of English as a second language*. Saskatchewan, Canada: ESL Centre of the SIAST Wascana Institute [Author's affiliation]. TESL-L [On-line list]. Available: LDMANUAL A and LDMANUAL B.

Lofland, J. (1971). *Analyzing social settings*. Belmont, CA: Wadsworth.

Lokerson, J. (n.d.). *What are learning disabilities?* (ERIC Digest No. E516, ED 352 779). Washington, DC: ERIC Clearinghouse on Languages and Linguistics.

MacIntyre, P. D. (1995a). How does anxiety affect second language learning? A reply to Sparks and Ganschow. *Modern Language Journal, 79*, 90-99.

MacIntyre, P. D. (1995b). On seeing the forest and the trees: A rejoinder to Sparks and Ganschow. *Modern Language Journal, 79*, 245-248.

328   UNDERSTANDING SECOND LANGUAGE DIFFICULTIES

Malamah-Thomas, A. (1987). *Classroom interaction.* New York: Oxford.

Marshall, T. (1989). *The whole world guide to language learning.* Yarmouth, ME: Intercultural.

McCarthy, B. (1987). *The 4MAT system: Teaching to learning styles with right/left mode techniques.* Barrington, IL: Excel.

McDonough, S. H. (1981). *Psychology in foreign language teaching.* London: George Allen & Unwin.

Merriam, S. B. (1988). *Case study research in education: A qualitative approach.* San Francisco: Jossey-Bass.

Myers, I. B., & Briggs, K. (1976). *The Myers-Briggs Type Indicator, Form G.* Palo Alto, CA: Consulting Psychologists.

Myers, I. B., & McCaulley, M. (1985). *Manual: A guide to the development and use of the Myers-Briggs Type Indicator.* Palo Alto, CA: Consulting Psychologists.

Myers, I. B., with Myers, P. (1980). *Gifts differing.* Palo Alto, CA: Consulting Psychologists.

Myers, K. D., & Kirby, L. K. (1994). *Introduction to type® dynamics and development: Exploring the next level of type.* Palo Alto, CA: Consulting Psychologists.

Myers, P. I., & Hammill, D. D. (1990). *Learning disabilities: Basic concepts, assessment practices, and instructional strategies* (4th ed.). Austin, TX: Pro-ed.

National Association of Secondary School Principals (1979). *Student learning styles: Diagnosing and prescribing programs.* Reston, VA: Author.

National Association of Secondary School Principals (1982). *Student learning style and brain behaviors: Programs. Instrumentation. Research.* Reston, VA: Author.

Newman, J. (1995). *Brain and personality: A review of theory and research.* Paper presented at the meeting of the Association for Psychological Type, Kansas City, MO.

Norton, R. W. (1975). Measurement of ambiguity tolerance. *Journal of Personality Assessment, 39,* 608-619.

O'Brien, L. (1990). *The learning channel preference checklist.* Rockville, MD: Specific Diagnostic Studies.

Oltman, P. K., Raskin, E., & Witkin, H. A. (1971). *Group embedded figures test.* Palo Alto, CA: Consulting Psychologists.

Oxford, R. L. (1990). *Language learning strategies: What every teacher should know.* New York: Newbury House.

Oxford, R. L. (1996). Language learning motivation in a new key. In R. L. Oxford (Ed.), *Language learning motivation: Pathways to the new century.* Honolulu: University of Hawaii.

Oxford, R. L., Ehrman, M. E., & Lavine, R. Z. (1991). "Style wars": Teacher-student style conflicts in the language classroom. In S. Magnan (Ed.), *Challenges in the 1990s for college foreign language programs* (pp. 1-25). Boston: Heinle & Heinle.

Oxford, R. L., & Shearin, J. (1994). Language learning motivation: Expanding the theoretical framework. *Modern Language Journal, 78,* 12-28.

Parrott, M. (1993). *Tasks for language teachers.* New York: Cambridge.

Parry, T. S., & Child, J. R. (1990). Preliminary investigation of the relationship between VORD, MLAT, and language proficiency. In T. Parry & C. W. Stansfield (Eds.), *Language aptitude reconsidered* (pp. 30-66). Englewood Cliffs, NJ: Prentice Hall.

Parry, T., & Stansfield, C. W. (Eds.). (1990). *Language aptitude reconsidered.* Englewood Cliffs, NJ: Prentice Hall.

Patton, M. Q. (1980). *Qualitative evaluation methods.* Beverly Hills, CA: Sage.

Petersen, C. R., & Al-Haik, A. R. (1976). The development of the Defense Language Aptitude Battery (DLAB). *Educational and psychological measurement, 6* 369-380.

Pfeiffer, J. W. and Jones, J. E. (Eds.). (1972). *The 1972 annual handbook for group facilitators.* San Diego, CA: University Associates.

Piaget, J. (1967). *Six psychological studies.* New York: Random House.

Pimsleur, P. (1966). *The Pimsleur language aptitude battery.* New York: Harcourt, Brace, Jovanovich.

Plaister, T. (1993). *ESOL case studies: The real world of L2 teaching and administration.* Englewood Cliffs, NJ: Prentice Hall Regents.

Ramírez III, M., & Castañeda, A. (1974). *Cultural democracy, bicognitive development and education.* New York: Academic.

Reid, J. (1987). The learning style preferences of ESL students. *TESOL Quarterly, 21,* 87-111.

Reid, J. (1995). *Learning styles in the ESL/EFL classroom.* Boston: Heinle & Heinle.

Reinert, H. (1976). One picture is worth a thousand words? Not necessarily! *Modern Language Journal, 60,* 160-168.

Richards, J. C., & Lockhart, C. (1994). *Reflective teaching in second language classrooms.* Cambridge University Press.

Richards, J. C., & Nunan, D. (1990). *Second language teacher education.* New York: Cambridge.

Rogers, J. (1979). *Understanding people or how to be your very own shrink.* Chicago, IL: Nelson-Hall.

Rotter, J. B. (1966). Generalized expectancies for internal versus external control of reinforcement. *Psychological Monographs, 80*(whole no. 609), 1-28.

Rubin, J., & Thompson, I. (1994). *How to be a more successful language learner: Toward learner autonomy* (2nd ed.). Boston: Heinle & Heinle.

Salzberger-Wittenberg, I., Henry, G., & Osborne, E. (1983). *The emotional experience of learning and teaching.* New York: Routledge Kegan Paul.

Sapountzis, P. S. (undated). *Defense mechanisms.* Unpublished handout. Arlington VA: Foreign Service Institute.

Saunders, D. R. (1989). *Type Differentiation Indicator manual: A scoring system for Form J of the Myers-Briggs Type Indicator.* Palo Alto, CA: Consulting Psychologists.

Schmeck, R. R. (1988). An introduction to strategies and styles of learning. In R. R. Schmeck (Ed.), *Learning strategies and learning styles.* New York: Plenum.

Schön, D. A. (1983). *The reflective practitioner: How professionals think in action.* New York: Basic Books.

Silver, L. B. (n.d.). *Attention deficit disorders (formerly called minimal brain dysfunction [MBD] or hyperkinetic syndrome): Booklet for the classroom teacher.* [Brochure]. No publication information available.

Skehan, P. (1989). *Individual differences in second language learning.* London: Edward Arnold.

Skehan, P. (1991). Individual differences in second language learning. *Studies in Second Language Acquisition, 13*(2), 275-278.

Sparks, R. L., & Ganschow, L. (1993). Searching for the cognitive locus of foreign language learning difficulties: Linking first and second language learning. *Modern Language Journal, 77:* 289-302.

Sparks, R. L., & Ganschow, L. (1995). A strong inference approach to causal factors in foreign language learning: A response to MacIntyre. *Modern Language Journal, 79,* 235-244.

Sparks, R. L., Ganschow, L., Kenneweg, S., & Miller, K. (1991). Use of an Orton-Gillingham approach to teach a foreign language to dyslexic/learning-disabled students: Explicit teaching of phonology in a second language. *Annals of Dyslexia, 41*, 96-113.

Spielberger, C. D., Gorsuch, R. L., & Lushene, R. E. (1970). *Test manual for the State-Trait Anxiety Inventory*. Palo Alto: Consulting Psychologists.

Stevick, E. W. (1980). *Teaching languages: A way and ways*. New York: Newbury House.

Stevick, E. W. (1989). *Success with foreign languages: Seven who achieved it and what worked for them*. New York: Prentice Hall International.

Stevick, E. W., (1996). Memory, meaning, and method: A view of language teaching (2nd ed.). Boston: Heinle & Heinle.

Tarone, E., & Yule, G. (1989). *Focus on the language learner: Approaches to identifying and meeting the needs of second language learners*. New York: Oxford.

Torrance, E. P., Reynolds, C. R., Riegel, T. R., & Ball, O. E. (1977). Your Style of Learning and Thinking (SOLAT), Forms A and B. *Gifted Child Quarterly 21*, 564-573.

Tremblay, P. F., & Gardner, R. C. (1995). Expanding the motivation construct in language learning. *Modern Language Journal, 79*, 505-518.

Tyacke, M. (1995). *Reading aptitudes: Case studies of six "expert" language learners introspecting as they carried out a variety of reading tasks*. Unpublished manuscript. Toronto, Canada: University of Toronto.

Tyler, L. (1965). *The psychology of human differences* (3rd ed.). New York: Appleton-Century-Crofts.

Vaillant, G. E. (1977). *Adaptation to life*. Boston: Little, Brown

Vaillant, G. E. (1993). *The wisdom of the ego*. Cambridge, MA: Harvard.

Wajnryb, R. (1992). *Classroom observation tasks: A resource book for language teachers and trainers*. New York: Cambridge.

Weinstein, A. E. (1978). *Problem Integration Strategy Test*. Unpublished manuscript.

Weinstein, C. E., Palmer, & Schulte, A. C. (1987). *LASSI: Learning and study stratetgies inventory*. Clearwater, FL: H & H.

Wenden, A., & Rubin, J. (1987). *Learner strategies in language learning*. Englewood Cliffs, NJ: Prentice Hall.

Wesche, M. B. (1981). Language aptitude measures in streaming, matching students with methods, and diagnosis of learning problems. In K. C. Diller (Ed.), *Individual differences and universals in language learning aptitude*. Rowley, MA: Newbury House.

Willing, K. (1989a). *Teaching how to learn: Learning strategies in ESL: A Teacher's Guide*. Sydney, Australia: Macquarie University National Centre for English Language Teaching and Research.

Willing, K. (1989b). *Teaching how to learn: Learning strategies in ESL: Activity Worksheets*. Sydney, Australia: Macquarie University National Centre for English Language Teaching and Research.

Winnicott, D. W. (1971). *Playing and reality*. New York: Routledge

Witkin, H. A. (1969). *Embedded Figures Test*. Palo Alto, CA: Consulting Psychologists.

Witkin, H. A., & Goodenough, D. R. (1977). Field dependence and interpersonal behavior. *Psychological Bulletin, 84*, 661-689.

Witkin, H. A., & Goodenough, D. R. (1981). *Cognitive styles: Essence and origins: Field dependence and field independence*. New York: International Universities.

Zappala, S. (1995). *Roadmap to communicating in Italy: Information for students entering Italian language training* (Unpublished handout). Arlington, VA: Foreign Service Institute.

Case Index

AUTHOR'S NOTE: Numbers refer to specific sections.

Linda: 7.3, 7.4.1, 7.4.2.
Logan: 7.6.
Lonnie: 4.5.2, 4.5.3, 8.1.1, 9.5.2.

Mari: 7.2.2, 7.4.1, 8.1.3.
Mark: 10.5, 11 (Summary), 11.3.
Matthew: 7.2.2, 7.4.1, 7.4.2, 9.6.
Melvin: 11.4, 11.5.2, 12.3, 12.7.
Miriam: 5.2, 6.3.1, 6.3.3, 6.4.1, 6.7.3, 6.9, 7.2.1, 7.4, 8.1.5, 9.1, 10.4.1.

Olivia: 12.2.

Patricia: 11.2.2, 11.2.4, 11.5.1.

Roger: 5.2, 6.2.2, 6.3.1, 6.3.3, 8.1.1.

Sandy: 2.2, 2.3, 2.3.1, 2.4, 3.1, 3.3, 3.8, 4.1, 4.2.3, 4.4, 4.5.3, 6.3.3, 7.4.1, 7.4.2, 7.6, 9.5.2, 10.2, 10.3.2.
Sheldon: 10.3, 11 (Summary), 12.3.
Shirley: 4.5.1, 4.5.3, 6.5, 6.7.1, 6.7.3, 10.4, 11 (Summary), 11.2.4.
Simon: 8.5.
Suzanne: 7.6.
Sylvia: 5.1, 5.2, 6.2.2, 6.3.3, 7.4.2.

Terry: 12.2.

Vanessa: 5.2, 6.2.2, 6.3.1, 6.3.3, 6.6, 7.2.1, 7.4.2, 8.2.2, 8.1.1.2.3.

Victor: 9.5.2.

Topic Index

312-316, 318. *See also* Ego
boundaries
HBQ. *See* Hartmann Boundary
Questionnaire
Hemispheric Mode Indicator, 74
Hemisphericity. *See* Left-right hemisphere
metaphor
Henry, 285
Hermann Participant Survey, 74
HFT.*See* Hidden Figures Test
Hidden Figures Test (HFT), 89
Highways, 55-56 (box), 127, 144, 146, 216
(box), 222. *See* Transportation
metaphor
Hoffman, xi
Horwitz, E., 156, 162
Horwitz, M., 156
Hosenfeld, 46
Hyperactivity, 61, 266
Hypotheses, 1, 2, 7, 9, 14, 16, 17, 24, 25,
31, 42, 49, 74, 90, 101, 107, 113,
115, 101, 123 (figure), 133, 146,
148, 160, 165, 188, 199, 204, 205,
207-208, 209, 213, 214, 218, 220,
222, 229, 230, 233-234, 239,
254-256, 257, 259, 260, 272, 273,
276, 281, 288, 312
Hypothesis testing, 49, 105

Impulsive (style), 67, 102, 116, 317-318,
321-322. *See also* Conceptual tempo
Independent learning. *See* Learning,
independent
Inductive (style), 8, 47, 53, 63, 72-73, 74,
75, 83, 90, 103, 192 (table), 215,
222, 244, 246, 253 (table), 316-317,
320, 322
Inference, 17-18, 19, 21, 49, 63, 68, 88,
101, 114, 150, 264
Instrumentation, xii, 7, 8, 11, 28, 44, 47,
59, 62, 67, 71, 88-89, 107, 114,
117, 121, 156, 185, 198-225, 231,
269, 292, 301, 312
Intelligence, 89, 166, 206, 208, 212, 228,
281, 301, 320
crystallized, 209, 211
fluid, 209, 211
tests, 89, 201, 211, 225

Interests, 39, 71, 139, 142, 162, 164-165,
167-168, 172, 192 (table), 250
Interpersonal relations, 58, 76, 78, 124,
125, 259, 260, 320
Interpretation (of data), 18, 31, 43, 160,
161, 230, 312
Interviewing, 7, 10, 16, 23-46, 101, 107,
198, 199, 298, 220, 221, 222, 229
technique, 45, 101
Introversion (Myers-Briggs), 53, 58, 72, 95,
98, 99 (table), 100 (figure), 103, 122,
128, 134 (n), 176, 204, 219
Intuition (Myers-Briggs), 57, 58, 68, 71, 93,
94, 96, 98, 99 (table), 100 (figure),
103-104, 106, 107, 109, 114-115,
117-118 (figure), 122, 124, 130, 134
(n), 200, 204, 210, 214-215, 216
(box), 217 (box), 221, 228, 312-317
Intuitive feeling (Myers-Briggs), 97, 101,
105, 114, 259
Intuitive judging (Myers-Briggs), 102, 106
Intuitive thinking (Myers-Briggs), 101, 105,
111, 115, 190, 241, 278
Intuitive perceiving, 101

Jackson, xi, 196
Johnson, xi
Jones, 154 (box)
Judging (Myers-Briggs), 68, 93, 96, 97, 98,
99 (table), 100 (figure), 104,
105-107, 108, 109, 119, 124, 134
(n), 216, 221, 249, 312, 314-316
Judging function, 94, 96. *See* Feeling,
Thinking
Jung, 92-96, 118

Kagan, 116
Kaplan, xi
Keefe, 62, 68, 116, 212
Keirsey, 133, 278
Kennedy, 298
Khilji, xi
Kim, xi
Kinesthetic (style), 39, 40, 47, 53, 54, 58,
59-63, 75, 78, 90, 111, 129, 178,
205 (box), 206, 219, 222, 234, 253
(table), 256, 261, 282 (box),

About the Author

Madeline Ehrman combines a background in applied linguistics and clinical psychology. She has worked at the Foreign Service Institute (FSI) of the U.S. Department of State in a variety of capacities. She has supervised instruction in nearly all the languages of East and Southeast Asia, during which time she developed textbooks in Cambodian and Indonesian as well as supplementary material in Japanese. She served as Department Chair for Asian and African Languages and is now the Director, Research Evaluation and Development for FSI's School of Language Studies, where she is heads a staff responsible for institutional research, staff and program development, language proficiency testing, and consultations for students having special learning difficulties.

Dr. Ehrman's PhD is in Clinical Psychology from the Union Institute, and her Bachelor's and Master's degrees are in Linguistics from Brown and Yale Universities. She received post-doctoral training from the Washington School of Psychiatry in psychoanalytic psychotherapy. In addition, she is an experienced administrator and trainer for the Myers-Briggs Type Indicator.

She has published a book on the semantics of the English modal auxiliaries (*The Meanings of the Modals in Present-day American English*), several textbooks in Southeast Asian languages, and multiple articles on individual differences in second language learning. She headed a task force that recently designed a minicourse for language teachers on enhancing learner independence, and she is currently working with Robert Sternberg of Yale University on a language aptitude test that examines ability to cope with the unfamiliar.